Animal Pragmatism

Edited by
Erin McKenna and
Andrew Light

Animal Pragmatism

Rethinking
Human-Nonhuman
Relationships

Indiana University Press
Bloomington • Indianapolis

This book is a publication of

Indiana University Press
601 North Morton Street
Bloomington, IN 47404-3797 USA

http://iupress.indiana.edu

Telephone orders 800-842-6796
Fax orders 812-855-7931
Orders by e-mail iuporder@indiana.edu

The paper used in this publication meets the minimum requirements of American National Standard for Information Sciences—Permanence of Paper for Printed Library Materials, ANSI Z39.48-1984.

Manufactured in the United States of America

Library of Congress Cataloging-in-Publication Data

Animal pragmatism : rethinking human-nonhuman relationships / edited by Erin McKenna and Andrew Light.
    p. cm.
Includes bibliographical references and index.
  ISBN 0-253-34422-0 — ISBN 0-253-21693-1 (pbk.)
  1. Pragmatism. 2. Human-animal relationships. 3. Human ecology—United States. I. McKenna, Erin, date
II. Light, Andrew, date
  B832.A55 2004
  179′.3—dc22
                                                 2003026470

1 2 3 4 5   09 08 07 06 05 04

To our nieces and nephews,
Alex, Bonnie, Corrine, Grace, Jennifer,
Johanna, Nathaniel, Tamara, and Quentin.

May the next generation live better
with our fellow critters.

Contents

Foreword

How we are educated by children, by animals!

—Martin Buber, *I and Thou*

Animals indeed! If anyone thinks that the lives and habitat of the animals are not existentially central to the meaning of human life, I urge them to reconsider. At times, the presence of animals is electrifying, as in my witnessing the snarled upper lip of a ferocious leopard who was displeased by my gaze. More telling is an event undergone forty years ago, and yet as sensorially present as if it were happening now. The place is Yellowstone Park and I have five young children in the car. Several grizzly bears meander down the hillside, including a mother bear and her cub. My children want to exit the car, say hello, and toss them some forbidden food. I say, no! It is very dangerous for you and it is not good for the bears. As only children can do, they grouse. Ahead of us is a car with a more pliant and foolish set of parents. They allow their children to leave the car and, incredibly, toss Hershey chocolates at the bears. Mistake! The cub picks up a Hershey bar and instantaneously, Mama Bear belts the cub and sends it flying toward Yosemite. While doing this, the mother bear lets out a roar that stripped the paint from our car and sent frozen, paralyzing chills down the spines of each of the seven of us, ne'er to be forgotten to this very day.

My parental response was simple. I told the children, now more than willing to listen, that they had come close to the inner world of the animal kingdom. Awe is appropriate, but pedagogically the better word is respect. As John Dewey is fond of saying, nature has its own affairings and for us as human naturals to ignore, trample, or exploit those ontological rhythms is to court disaster.

More often and less dramatically, our animals are around and about, providing a subtle yet pervasive sensibility as to the irreducible and ineluctable fact that we, too, are animals. Now just what sort of animals are we? Historically, the millennia-long effort to separate human animals from animals *ueberhaupt* is by rendering humans as "higher animals." Such an appellation runs the risk attendant upon any use of hierarchy as a nomenclature entailing content. The assumption here is that the higher one reaches on the ladder, ostensibly the more quality is obtained. Surely, and deleteriously, this contention does not hold if one surveys the personal histories of many popes, political and military leaders, chief executive officers, and, lamentably, parents.

I cite but two obstacles to the acceptance of hierarchy as a positive source for evaluation of worth. First, what ladder? The long-held belief that higher is better rests on the cultural residue of a discredited geocentric cosmology. High and low, up and down are but temporal constructs, having no ultimate purchase in infinite space. Second, the claim to be "higher" often blocks us from the wider recesses of experience, namely, from those affective sensibilities available only horizontally. Human animals are not "higher" than other creatures. They are, however, different, in some ways profoundly and markedly so, as witness the arts, mathematics, and a capacity for a publicly articulated history. In other ways, the difference is malodorous, as instanced in the persistent practice of violence for reasons other than survival and the pervasive intent to deny mortality. The destructive trait of self-deception is characteristic of human animals and is not found among the other creatures. On this matter, Albert Camus has it right. "Man [woman] is the only creature who refuses to be what he [she] is." That refusal has given us the Sistine Chapel, the technology of dazzling artifact, and the Holocaust. A complex, rich, and perilous message to be sure. Contrariwise, the messages of the other creatures are simpler, more direct, and always authentic.

I am an inveterate listener to "stories" and I am, after my own fashion, a storyteller. Now in my eighth decade of stories heard and told, I offer that those told by us about animals seem to be singularly free of human self-centeredness and of trickery or dissembling. Telling stories about animals brings out the best in us, for I believe that we take the animal at face value, horizontally and not from a position of superiority. Here, I tell but two stories, one a slight vignette and the other a pedagogically enriching trauma.

When my children were young, we had the pleasure of caring for a medium-sized iguana. One day, scampering about, our iguana caught its tail in the baseboard heating coils. Irritated and frustrated, the iguana pulled mightily and succeeded in freeing itself. A price was paid, for the iguana severed its tail. We took the tail and the iguana to the veterinarian. Reconstructive surgery was not possible, so the wound was cauterized and an antibiotic medicine prescribed. The iguana returned home to loving, constant care and a diet of the most favorable and nutritiously helpful food for this period of recovery. In short, we did everything necessary to assuage and save the iguana. For a short time, the skin color of the iguana turned a foreboding shade and it became listless. Soon, it was found on its back—dead. The children asked me, What happened? We did everything to heal the iguana. Why did it die? I replied that the iguana died of a broken heart. How come? Because an iguana cannot live without its tail. We too, each of us, have a "tail" without which we cannot live. The animals teach us to diagnostically search for our tail, *mutatis mutandis,* without which "life is *not* worth living." I told each of the five children to get busy and locate their personal tail.

Our second story is told on behalf of Michael Bear, an exquisitely and naturally coiffed thirty-five-pound terrier who had an extraordinary intelligence with loyalty to match. When I was a boy, I lost my first dog to distemper. I still see him writhing on the cellar floor of our home in New York City. Contemporary animal medicine could now save him as it did save Chapin, a Labrador puppy with parvovirus. I recall wetting her lips as her eyes became increasingly vacant until, and against the diagnostic grain, a veterinarian intervened and healed her, miraculously.

But Michael Bear was different. He was 15 years of age, that is, in human terms, 105 years old, far beyond his actuarial assignment. I do not detail here the rich family history enjoyed by the presence of Michael Bear, nor of the increasing sadness visited on all of us in his last years. I cut to the quick, the end, when incontinent and no longer able to stand, he looks directly at us and "says," "You promised me not a moment beyond my dignity," the telling spiritual word behind the stock phrase *quality of life*. We kept our promise, painful though it was and still is for us. His request as delivered has a haunting resonance in an American society that responds to analogous requests by dying humans with the booming industry of geriatric warehousing, cloaked by the self-deception that life goes on forever.

It is right and salutary, as some essays in this volume detail, to protest, vigorously, the scabrous treatment of animals by the food industry. Ironically, however, domesticated animals fare better than human animals when the time comes to die. Having been host over the decades to fish, small mammals, birds, tarantulas, water moccasins, a giant boa constrictor, cats, and dogs, I can say that they have taught me directly the difficult lesson of the inevitability of my own death. But the pedagogy given to us by animals is not only eschatological, it is also temporally enriching. I note a recent program to enlist life-imprisoned violent offenders to participate in the training of service dogs. The results of this match have been startling, for the animals have effected a profound personal transformation in the prisoners who, although guilt-ridden and shorn of hope, have been able to reconstitute their lives by an engendering of human qualities, loyalty, affection, care, and selflessness once barren in their persons.

This collection of essays on the contribution of American philosophical reflection to our understanding of animals is a propitious event in American thought. For the most part due to the perceptive and innovative work of the editors, Erin McKenna and Andrew Light, we are given a series of imaginative, informed, judicious, and helpful investigations that provide us with a fresh intellectual landscape on behalf of ameliorating our relationship with the animals.

The tradition known generically as classical American philosophy can be interpreted from a number of different vantages, none of them mutually exclusive. One take, characteristic of these essays, is to focus on the role of pragmatism as a hallmark of this tradition. I prefer to employ the term *pragmatic sensibility*, by which I mean the systemic alertness to the presence of consequences in all of our practices and decisions. Following C. S. Peirce, William James, and John Dewey, the mantra here is that propositional claims are hollow until their consequences are brought to bear. It is one thing for a society to eat animals. It is quite another thing to lay bare what is involved in the treatment of these animals such that they can be eaten. It is aesthetically pleasurable to wear a fur coat, but quite another experience to visit a mink "farm" set up to yield this pleasure. The philosophical grasp of consequences is no mere epistemic sleight of hand. Rather, in order for us to assess consequences, we must have an awareness of processes as they press into future experience. Put simply and directly, we have to grasp the ongoing web of relations which adhere, inhere, cohere, surround, penetrate, obviate, float, shrink, squash, deceive, render inert, cause perversion, erupt idiopathically or iatrogenically, and just lurk as a buried land mine. One thinks here of the furtive upshot slowly emerging from the use of biotechnology in the feeding of animals.

The following essays are signally free of sentimentality, ideology, and naiveté. These issues pertaining to our relationship with animals are very thorny and not amenable to jejune proclamations or self-righteous manifestos. This volume is a launching pad for serious philosophical inquiry as fed by American philosophy. Subsequent efforts could consider the deep influence of philosophical Stoicism, especially the *Meditations* of Marcus Aurelius, on this American intellectual tradition. The bequest of Aurelius is his implacable stress on the inviolable bond humans undergo with the fabric of nature and the lives of all the creatures. In so doing, taking American philosophy as a "naturalism" would enlist the thought of Jonathan Edwards, himself the precocious master of spiders; Ralph Waldo Emerson; the Transcendentalists; and, above all, Walt Whitman. Indeed, John Dewey's *Experience and Nature* can be taken as a philosophical lattice in and through which we and the animals undergo our shared affective rhythms. Within the framework of American philosophical naturalism would rest the history of animals as locally sacred, as sources of mythopoesis, and as undaunted, fabled companions over the centuries until this very day. No matter what our disagreements, philosophical or otherwise, it is, in Dewey's phrase, "accrued wisdom" that only at our collective peril do we ignore the messagings of the animals, indeed, of all "live creatures."

All who read these essays should be enlightened as to the existence of heretofore hidden perspectives, culturally rich and philosophically wise. We therefore are deeply grateful to the editors for their programmatic insight, editorial wisdom, and personal dedication in bringing these important essays to a concerned public.

John J. McDermott
Texas A&M University

Acknowledgments

We would like to thank each of our authors for their contributions to this volume. We would also like to thank those whose work was initially to be part of this volume. Because of limitations of space, we were unable to use several very interesting pieces. We would also like to express our appreciation to the Society for the Advancement of American Philosophy and to the Summer Institute in American Philosophy for providing venues where we could begin to discuss this work and generate ideas.

For specific help with computer issues (and for their patience), we would like to thank Tracy Williamson, senior administrative assistant for the Division of Humanities at Pacific Lutheran University, and Margaret Crayton, director of Academic User Support at Pacific Lutheran University. We would also like to thank Dee Mortensen, our sponsoring editor at Indiana University Press, for her unwavering support of this project, Alice Falk, our copyeditor, for many suggestions that greatly improved the text, and Chris Schlottmann at NYU for offering many valuable changes to the final manuscript. Erin would also like to thank her canine companions, Pandora and Nemesis, for putting up with some very long hours in the office.

Animal Pragmatism

Introduction: Pragmatism and the Future of Human-Nonhuman Relationships

Andrew Light and Erin McKenna

Our lives are lived with other animals. It is implausible that anyone would deny this fact. But even given the long history of philosophical reflection on human identity, relationships, and morality, it is only recently that a critical mass of attention has focused on our possible ethical obligations to other animals. Yet this recent attention, which is producing shock waves in the public realm, is substantial; indeed, it may represent the largest expansion of the domain of moral consideration in the West since the era of debates over slavery and women's suffrage. Its potential, if fully realized, could fundamentally change the terms of our day-to-day lives, as well as our social, political, and economic structures. Further, from the perspective of the discipline of philosophy, this new focus on animals may stand as one of only a few noteworthy exceptions to our self-imposed exile into the academy and consequent retreat from anything approximating a public role for our ideas.

The evidence for the expanded concern over animal welfare and rights is substantial. In a recent review of the literature on this subject, Peter Singer, whom many would call the philosophical father of the contemporary animal rights movement, cites Charles Magel's bibliographic research, which lists "only ninety-four works on the moral status of animals in the first 1970 years of the Christian Era." From 1970 to 1988 there were 240 works, and Singer estimates the "tally now would probably be in the thousands" ("Animal Liberation at 30" 23).

In the United States the debate over our moral relationships with other animals has reached new heights of popular discussion. Michael Pollan's 2002 front-page story in the *New York Times Magazine* on animal rights ("An Animal's Place") is one indicator. Critical though it was of this literature it was not wholly unsympathetic, and the attention that the article paid to such ideas demonstrated the social importance of better understanding our relationships with other animals.[1] More important was the settlement negotiated by the animal advocate Henry Spira (and later taken up by People for the Ethical Treatment of Animals—an organization now with 750,000 members) under which

McDonald's agreed to establish standards of humane treatment for slaughter-houses and egg suppliers that exceeded those required by U.S. law (a move which has reverberated throughout the fast-food industry). This decision was followed in November 2002 by the passage of a ballot initiative in Florida banning the confinement of pregnant sows in crates so narrow that they cannot turn around and nuzzle their newborns (Singer, "Animal Liberation at 30" 26). It is important to recognize, however, that even with such changes Americans are only beginning to catch up with already more ambitious ethical standards established by the European Union, which, for example, will begin phasing out battery cages for chickens in 2008.

Why all of this attention now, and what does philosophy have to do with it? In undergraduate courses in philosophy we are often asked by our students how philosophical ideas, especially debates over moral principles, ever come to have any influence. Usually, though not always, we tell a story about how these ideas take a long time to gestate—hundreds of years, at least—and then eventually filter into public debates over social issues, possibly finding a home as the foundation for new governmental institutions or laws. A handy, and we hope familiar, example is found in John Locke's theories of property ownership as a critical component of democratic governance, passed down through Thomas Jefferson to become a founding principle of the American colonial Declaration of Independence and later to be embodied in the Constitution of the United States. Similar stories could be told concerning theories of liberation and equal rights that eventually influenced movements for the emancipation and equal treatment of African slaves and women.

But for some reason things are moving substantially more quickly when it comes to arguments over animal welfare. Today's philosophical debates are having an impact on tomorrow's arguments by animal advocates. Though it is true that there were arguments put forward over animal welfare prior to the 1970s, they were different in kind than those offered now. Augustine and Kant claimed that we ought not to treat animals cruelly because to do so will numb us toward treating each other cruelly. This kind of argument, however, does not require that we grant any direct moral consideration to other animals—that we consider the scope of ethical theory and practice to be inclusive of the interests of other animals—but rather claims only that our treatment of other animals can instrumentally affect our treatment of each other. The scope of direct moral consideration in this instance is still limited to humans.

Some would argue, and there is something of a case to be made on this point, that our new, more direct consideration of the question of whether we do have moral obligations to other animals is a product of the gradual progress of morality (for a consideration of this possibility, see, for example, Jamieson). This is not necessarily to say that the scope of morality "naturally" expands so as to be more and more inclusive—a position that fairly invites incredulity. It may be only to claim that we have reached a historical stage in most of the developed world characterized by some general consensus that all persons should in principle be afforded equal minimal moral consideration—or if not, that the implications for extending equal consideration to everyone are always present as a set of ethical choices which we must consider. At the extreme, this means that everyone's "interests," however those are understood, should be given equal consideration whenever possible despite the differences between them. Of course, this does not mean that people are not in fact still treated differently based on contingent traits such as class, race, gender, and sexual orientation, as well as intellectual or physical capacities. Many would argue that sexism, racism, homophobia, and the like are still rampant and often codified in law and policy. Yet we seem to agree that equal consideration of interests is a reasonable moral question for individual behavior as well as social policy, even if we disagree about the implications of what achieving equal consideration would entail in all cases. We recognize, for example, that the recent legalization of gay marriage in Canada, together with its continued prohibition in the United States, marks a moral and not just a geopolitical boundary. Across this divide we understand that the fundamental issue at stake is an ethical one and not simply a question of personal choice or social prudence, even if we disagree at the level of policy.

If we agree that equal consideration of interests is appropriate among and between persons, then it makes sense to ask the next question: Are human interests the only ones that matter in a complete moral scheme? Further, if we reject racism and the like, what justifies what Singer has identified as "speciesism," the idea that it is permissible to "give preference to beings simply on the grounds that they are members of the species *Homo sapiens*" ("Animal Liberation at 30" 23)? How can we morally justify avoiding harms and granting benefits to humans and not doing the same (or weighing differently) the harms and benefits thought appropriate to other animals? While many arguments have been put forward to justify human exceptionalism in moral consideration—the existence of a soul, superior mental capacities, custom, and so forth—such criteria generally do not hold up to careful scrutiny (see, for example, the discussion by McMahan). And once we have admitted that we do as a matter of course grant minimal moral consideration to members of our own species—such as infants and the mentally infirm—who lack many capacities thought to warrant moral treatment in "normal" adult humans, it then becomes very difficult to claim that there is no moral issue at stake in our treatment of other animals.[2]

A clear question is raised by the notion of the "progress" of morality: Why not animals? If nonhuman animals are to be included in the various accounts given of the proper moral calculus—consequentialist, nonconsequentialist, and virtue theories—then a number of questions come up. We must question whether it is permissible to produce them for food and fiber, and if so whether we should treat them the way that we do now. We must question whether we should experiment on them for a range of purposes—some banal, like developing new cosmetics; some profound, like finding a cure for deadly diseases. We must question whether we should keep them in preserves, zoos, and even our homes, either as curiosities or as companions. And once we have settled on answers we must consider the best means to achieve those ends. Is the goal only to minimize suffering in these processes? Is it total emancipation? Or is it some kind of in-crementalism by which we seek short-term changes in treatment now to ap-proach long-term changes that would halt such practices completely?

But still, some kind of ethical account of how we should treat other animals would not explain why the philosophical reflection on this possibility has cap-tured so much popular attention. As suggested at the start, with due respect to the few exceptions, philosophers have long since ceded their place in the public sphere as commentators on important issues of the day. Philosophers are much more content these days to address only each other in the most abstract and arcane intramural language, often impenetrable to those without graduate de-grees in the subject. However, that so many commentators have argued that the rise of the contemporary animal rights movement is intimately tied to the emer-gence of this philosophical literature since the early 1970s is telling. In this case we have a very important exception to the typical relationship between philo-sophical theory and ethical practice (see, for example, Jasper and Nelkin; Finsen and Finsen). The struggle over animal welfare and animal rights is clearly only beginning, and the continued relevance of philosophy and philosophers to this debate is yet to be determined—but the stakes are extraordinarily high. For even with the proliferation of the literature in animal welfare and rights, the fact is that 10 billion birds and mammals were raised and killed for food last year in the United States without much by way of an ethical quibble or second thought by most of those benefiting from their consumption. If one implication of the expansion of the realm of moral consideration to other animals is that we should not kill and eat them—at least not in the way that we do now—then some would argue that we may be living in the midst of a process morally related to forms of human genocide (for a dramatic statement of this claim, see Coetzee). Whether one agrees or not with this sentiment, it now appears to deserve a re-sponse.

In this light, new contributions to the literature on animal welfare and rights may need little justification, though their particular merits may vary. Our aim with this volume is to bring the resources of American pragmatism, that pecu-liar brand of philosophy indigenous to the United States, to bear on the questions related to these issues as they have already been raised by other philosophers from other schools of thought. Because there is no established spokesperson from the ranks of pragmatists on moral issues involving animals, this volume will at a minimum simply add to the chorus participating in a lively set of philo-sophical debates. But because those debates are actually influencing vital public deliberations on these topics, the strain offered by pragmatism, a school of thought born in part out of the desire to make philosophical labor more relevant to public concerns, may be even more necessary. The last heyday of public phi-losophy in the United States was during the period between the Civil War and World War II, when figures such as John Dewey held sway over critical debates of the time (see Menand). Even today many of the most prominent philosophers recognized outside the academy are self-described pragmatists, such as Richard Rorty and Cornel West. In this context, the silence of pragmatists on the question of moral consideration of animals is striking and needs to be addressed. Before summarizing the contents of the volume we will try to further justify this point.

Animal Welfare, Animal Rights, and Animal Liberation

Despite the common claim that Peter Singer is the father of the animal rights movement, strictly speaking such a suggestion is false, as Singer would no doubt agree. The reason has nothing to do with his influence on this community but rather concerns the term *animal rights*. For Singer, humans, let alone other animals, do not have rights in the technical sense of this term. The language of "rights" in this context is thought by many devotees of Singer's work to have rhetorical merit only. Rather than attribute rights to nonhuman animals, Singer argues that the capacity to suffer is the basic, necessary, and sufficient reason to give equal consideration to the interests of a being.

> The capacity for suffering and enjoyment is a *prerequisite for having interests at all*, a condition that must be satisfied before we can speak of interests in a meaningful way. It would be nonsense to say that it was not in the interests of a stone to be kicked along the road by a schoolboy. A stone does not have interests because it cannot suffer. Nothing that we can do to it could possibly make any difference to its welfare. The capacity for suffering and enjoyment is, however, not only necessary, but also sufficient for us to say that a being has interests—at an absolute minimum, an interest in not suffering. A mouse, for example, does have an interest in not being kicked along the road, because it will suffer if it is. (Singer, *Animal Liberation* 7–8)

Singer then uses utilitarian moral theory to calculate the importance of the pain and pleasure involved in various practices such as factory farming and animal experimentation. He notes the lengths to which some philosophers have gone to argue that animals do not have rights, but he sees this question as irrelevant to the arguments for "animal liberation" (above and beyond older claims that we should pay attention to "animal welfare"), since the capacity to suffer is what matters. So, while there is not always consistency in how these terms are used in the philosophic or popular literature, Singer is most accurately connected to arguments concerning animal liberation or to more advanced accounts of animal welfare (which Francione dubs the "new welfarism"). Talk of "animal rights" is better reserved for theorists like Tom Regan.

Regan provides an animal rights perspective based on the idea that at least some animals have intrinsic ethical value: specifically, any being who is the "subject of a life." Rejecting utilitarian moral theory, Regan uses a nonconsequentialist deontological approach to argue that justice demands that we treat individual "subjects of a life" with respect—as an end in themselves and not merely as a means to advancing our own ends.

> The criterion the rights view proposes . . . is that of being the subject of a life, a criterion that specifies a set of psychological capacities (for example, the capacities to

desire, remember, act intentionally, and feel emotions) as jointly sufficient for such value. At least some nonhuman animals (for example, mammalian animals and birds) arguably possess these capacities; they are thus subjects of a life and, given the rights view, to be treated as ends in themselves. (Regan, "Ethical Theory" 17)

Like Singer's argument, this approach calls into question our current practices of raising animals for food or fur and using them in experiments. But Regan, unlike Singer, is squarely in the rights camp.

Regan provides an interesting discussion of the differences between various approaches to examining the human treatment of nonhuman animals: anti-cruelty, animal welfare, animal rights, and animal liberation ("What's in a Name?"). He does not believe that anti-cruelty and animal welfare approaches go far enough. They are merely reformist positions that tend to justify our continued uses of nonhuman animals as long as we address their suffering. He puts Singer in the reformist camp. Regan favors the animal rights position, which he says argues for abolition of unjust practices and systems rather than mere reform. Animal rights are, for Regan, the only real basis for animal liberation. Obviously Singer disagrees and the debates between these figures, and between their philosophical followers and the groups which they influence, continue.

The arguments between the utilitarian and deontological approaches to these questions have now gone on for decades. While we in no way intend to offer an exhaustive discussion or review of the philosophical literature concerning these matters, it is important to note that a few alternative voices have emerged as well. The utilitarian and deontological approaches, while divided on some central issues, share a common starting point: the importance of reason in discerning our proper relationship to nonhumans. Both approaches seek to provide a rational framework for moral debate and both ultimately rely on human rational capacity as fundamental in judging the interests of, and moral consideration due to, any being. While Singer relies on suffering and the protection of interests, it becomes quite clear for him that greater rational capacity makes possible greater suffering. Thus human interests often trump the interests of less rational (less intelligent) beings: "There are many matters in which the superior mental powers of normal adult humans make a difference: anticipation, more detailed memory, greater knowledge of what is happening, and so on" (Singer, *Animal Liberation* 16). And later he argues that "we could still hold . . . that it is worse to kill a normal adult human, with a capacity for self-awareness and the ability to plan for the future and have meaningful relations with others, than it is to kill a mouse" (19). For Regan, being a subject of a life requires, among other things, the ability to "have beliefs and desires; perception, memory, and a sense of the future, including their own future" (*Case for Animal Rights* 243). Though Regan allows for preferential treatment in cases of moral conflict, his rationale differs from Singer's and in some cases his conclusions differ as well. As a result, different starting points lead to different principles governing our relations with nonhuman animals. Given the history of debates over rational deliberation in Western philosophy, such an outcome is no surprise. Such disagreements are a good sign of a healthy arena of philosophical discussion, but they do not address whether the terms of this debate exhaust the questions raised. No doubt the participants in these debates would accept that there is indeed room for more voices.

One area from which challenge has come is feminist philosophy. Specifically with regard to nonhuman animals, Mary Midgley, for one, began in the 1980s to suggest that concepts of rights arise out of compassion as much as reason and that reason and intelligence arise from our living in community with all sorts of other beings. An "ethic of care," which has evolved out of the literature in general feminist ethics applied to these issues, generates an "animal defense" or "animal advocacy" perspective based on a "relational ontology" that grounds reason in the emotional and caring response elicited by particular situations (see Donovan and Adams). This view offers an alternative to the animal rights view in a way different from Singer's consequentialism. The care perspective is often linked to ecofeminist theory as well. Ecofeminism begins from a nonhierarchical ontology of connectedness and rejects dichotomies that divide reason from emotion, male from female, culture from nature, and human from nonhuman. These alternative perspectives claim to challenge the utilitarian-deontological debates by going beyond what is argued to be their reliance on classical liberalism and their focus on rational, autonomous, atomistic individuals as the primary foundation and object of moral deliberation.

There is of course much more that can be said about the various debates and positions in the current literature on animal ethics. Again, we wish in this introduction to provide not a survey of this literature but only a taste of it so as to put in context the contribution that pragmatism can make. It is important to remember, though, that because of the closer connection between philosophers and advocates on these issues than is evident even in other areas of applied philosophy, these debates involve questions of strategy and practice as well as of theory. For example, Gary Francione argues that a true animal rights position would be squarely opposed to the sort of concerns over the role of emotion in moral theory and practice raised by ecofeminists. He directs this criticism not against ecofeminists themselves but against the new welfarists, a group in which he includes Singer, who not only do not embrace a rights view but also favor a tactical position of gradualism, reformism, or incrementalism—that is, they accept that short-term improvements in animal welfare are an acceptable path to long-term equal consideration of their interests. For Francione, such a view is both morally and strategically in error. He argues instead that

> Advocates of animal rights are not interested in *regulating* animal exploitation, but in *abolishing* it. The primary concern for the rights advocate is not kindness; after all, we do not make respect for the interests of minorities or women dependent upon some "kindly" disposition toward those people. Respect is instead a question of *justice;* if animals are rightholders, then those interests that are protected by right cannot be traded away simply because their "sacrifice" will benefit humans. Animal rights advocates reject the supposed superiority of humans over animals and challenge institutionalized animal exploitation as violative of relevant animal

interests, irrespective of the "humaneness" with which the exploitation is supposedly conducted. (Francione 110; emphases in original)

The case that Francione builds against the new welfarism is theoretical, structural, and empirical. He also argues against claims that criticism within the animal welfare and rights communities is unnecessarily divisive and should be avoided (a view often repeated), as well as contentions that a strong rightist perspective is infeasible and utopian.[3]

Though we are skeptical of this view, it is evocative of the need both in general to explore alternative positions to those outlined and in particular to seek some clarification of what would be meant by a "pragmatist" alternative to the literature on animal ethics. We will address the latter issue in the next section. As for the former, while many would argue that the philosophical contributions to the animal advocacy community have already evinced a high degree of pluralism in their practicality—if they did not, their considerable influence would indeed be curious—it is clear from arguments like Francione's that in this area there is still a high degree of divisiveness, driven by philosophical arguments. Francione is critical not only of Singer but also of Spira and PETA (taking on, for example, the settlement with McDonald's cited earlier). He goes so far as to make a strong analogy between the emancipation of animals and that of African slaves, labeling our current treatment of animals as a form of slavery. Those who seek better treatment of animals on farms and in laboratories (even as a short-term strategy toward the goal of more ambitious changes in the future) are morally equivalent to those who sought more humane treatment of slaves, "such as recognizing the validity of slave marriages to prevent the hardships caused by breaking up slave families." In contrast, the true abolitionists "were opposed to such reformers and regarded the institution of slavery and any attempt to regulate or 'reform' that institution as morally iniquitous" (Francione 41). Later, Francione argues for something of a disanalogy between these two situations, suggesting that the abolition of slavery "occurred relatively quickly" in part because the American economy was "far less dependent on slavery than it presently is on animal exploitation" (111). Curiously, he fails to mention that the most devastating war ever fought on American soil was in part generated by this moral conflict. Though it is implausible that we would experience something similar arising from issues of animal rights or animal liberation, the intense moral rhetoric in this account—an intensity not altogether uncommon in the literature—calls attention to the need for more sober philosophical argument and strategic advice.

Why Pragmatism?

Could pragmatism make such a contribution? Not if one is convinced by Francione's account of it. For him, and he is not alone in his view, the term *pragmatism* designates short-term, crass, "ends-justify-the-means" thinking rather than any coherent body of thought. It represents exactly what he sees as wrong in Singer's way of thinking about incrementalism. Quoting from James Jasper and Dorothy Nelkin's 1993 sociological study of the animal rights movement, Francione defines pragmatists as "those who believe that nonhumans are entitled to moral consideration but who also believe that 'certain species deserve greater consideration than others and would allow humans to use animals when the benefits deriving from their use outweigh their suffering'" (39). Though he does identify some important confusions in this account—he points out, for example, that Jasper and Nelkin claim that those they call "fundamentalists" could also be pragmatists—he clearly views pragmatism as a bad thing. Indeed, what Jasper and Nelkin see as the useful pragmatic tactics in Henry Spira's various campaigns, Francione sees as so much consorting with and appeasement of the enemy. But pragmatism is much more than the narrow definition given above, and its possible contributions to these debates can be fully understood only if its history and current development are clarified.

Pragmatism arose as a coherent school of American philosophy in the late nineteenth and early twentieth centuries. While there is some debate about the canon, its principal founders include Charles Sanders Peirce, William James, George Herbert Mead, Josiah Royce, and especially John Dewey. What can pragmatism, more carefully considered, bring to the literature on our moral relationships with nonhumans? While the essays in this volume provide more particular answers to this question, four general points can be made from the outset. First, while there are different versions of pragmatism, on the whole it has the potential of embracing the strengths of the other positions mentioned above while adding a further important component: being grounded in an approach that is pluralistic, fallibilistic, and flexible. This means it can more readily adapt to changing circumstances and practices because it is not inalterably wedded to principles that are too often divorced from people's everyday lived experience. Most of its adherents suggest that in any inquiry we should start with where we are and with how we commonly understand the world; as we push against those intuitions, we should continually check in with the actual experiences we have had and are having on any particular ethical issue. In this way, pragmatism challenges received experience and inherited wisdom and impels people to be critical of their habits. Rather than just providing principles to guide practice, it focuses on developing a critical approach to life in which all people can engage.

Take, for example, the use to which pragmatism has been put in contemporary bioethics or medical ethics. Like the philosophical literature on the moral status of animals, academic work in medical ethics is divided into schools of thought derived from larger schools of philosophical ethics: utilitarians, deontologists, principalists of various sorts, feminists, and others. But while adhering to a strongly principled account of a life-and-death issue in medicine can serve to bring out critical conceptual issues, the same approach is not always helpful in an applied, clinical context. Jonathan Moreno even goes so far as to argue that any bioethicist must necessarily take a stance, broadly speaking, as a pragmatist or "naturalist." Thus bioethics in practice entails a kind of pragmatist methodology even without any reference to the canonical literature in pragmatism. Among Moreno's arguments is that bioethics is a social activity. It is not a field for those who wish simply to sit in their philosophical armchairs, especially if they want to engage in the most interesting and exciting work in the field. The practice of philosophy in this case occurs in settings and groups—case conferences, ethics committees, institutional review boards, the media, bedside rounds, government panels, and civic organizations. In these forums, philosophy needs to change either how it is done or how it is communicated in order to have an impact on nonphilosophers, who of course make up most of the participants in these settings.

Applying pragmatism to issues involving animal welfare may also bring out similar concerns and practices. Though it would be a stretch to claim that all applied versions of animal ethics eventually become pragmatist, especially given their current influence on animal advocates, pragmatism could at least highlight important practical questions that an ethical consideration of animals will entail. It could be especially effective in such a role when ideas on animal welfare are presented to those who have not previously considered our treatment of other animals as a moral issue, properly speaking. Some form of pragmatism may be better equipped to help those unsure about or even hostile to the idea of moral consideration of nonhumans to rethink their views by making a stronger appeal to everyday lived experience. The true test of such a method would come in actual ethical debate and practice, but the experimentalism inherent to pragmatism—its willingness to revisit positions based on what works and what does not and its focus on the moral and epistemological value of community deliberation and democratic discourse—may make it more amenable than other methods to such appeals.

Second, while pragmatism is like utilitarian and deontological approaches in challenging speciesism and the automatic privileging of human interests and suffering, it also challenges the split between metaphysics and ethics that can be found in them. Utilitarian and deontological views on animals both ask us to abandon speciesism; however, each is grounded in a philosophical view that privileges certain forms of reasoning and thus each, ironically, tends to reinforce the dichotomous and hierarchical approach that supports speciesism in the first place. Their shift in ethics is not always supported by a shift in metaphysics or epistemology. In the end, pragmatism may provide a more consistent challenge to speciesism in both theory and practice.

Third, like feminist theory, pragmatism rejects "either-or" dichotomies and instead takes a "both-and" approach. For instance, both feminism and pragmatism see reason and emotion as integrated, not opposed. As Dewey says in *Human Nature and Conduct*, "We do not act from reasoning; but reasoning puts before us objects which are not directly or sensibly present, so that we then may react directly to these objects, with aversion, attraction, indifference or attachment. . . . Joy and suffering, pain and pleasure, the agreeable and disagreeable, play their considerable role in deliberation" (139–40). Here, Dewey challenges the traditional privileging of reason as the primary source of knowledge, judgment, and action—the privileging on which most arguments for speciesism rest.

Pragmatism thus has the further advantage of having developed a method of inquiry consistent with its altered approach to metaphysics and epistemology. It is these shifts in attitude and inquiry that are explored in the essays in this volume.

Finally, as mentioned above, pragmatism, at least historically, is a philosophy not only at home with but necessarily engaged with public issues of the day. Although those calling themselves pragmatists today do not always live up to this legacy, and certainly can be as guilty as any other kind of philosopher in addressing only a like-minded audience, the history of pragmatism nonetheless serves as a standard guiding any kind of truly pragmatic inquiry. This historical standard more specifically demands that the arguments of the philosopher have public relevance to actual problems of the day. John Dewey was hailed by the *New York Times* as "America's philosopher," and though this influence is only now a memory it still weighs on those calling themselves "pragmatists" today. Therefore the example already set by figures such as Singer and Regan, addressing this issue in a more publicly engaged manner as they work out of more traditional areas of philosophy, is one that pragmatists should respect and, it is hoped, be in a position to emulate. We may at minimum be able to usefully intervene in the more strident forms of the debates between theorists as evidenced by Francione's interventions in this literature. Louis Menand argues that pragmatism arose directly from the conflict over the American Civil War, including the very debates about emancipation that Francione wishes us to consider relevant to the question of animal rights. Though this analogy and Francione's use of the term *slavery* to describe our treatment of other animals hardly prove that pragmatism may play a key role in these debates, it does lend support to the proposition that a form of philosophy that evolved out of intense moral conflict may be of some help in considering both the theoretical and strategic approaches that we should take in what may be the next great arena of moral debate.

The case for such a proposition and for the other advantages of a pragmatist approach to animal welfare remains to be made: this volume is just a start. Though the various authors in this collection differ on whether and what forms of pragmatism would best serve those concerned about animal welfare, all believe that a pragmatist perspective on our treatment of nonhuman animals should be articulated. It is a voice, hitherto missing, that may more deeply challenge our views of our place in the world and thus also more effectively serve to alter current practice. This volume provides a forum for that voice. Even if pragmatism is rejected in and of itself as applicable to any particular debate discussed in these chapters, the arguments of pragmatists on these various issues may help others to develop new insights within the context of the more established positions in this literature.

Overview of the Volume

This book could have been arranged in a variety of ways, as there are interesting links between many of the chapters. The organization we settled on is one that moves, loosely, from considerations of theory to considerations of method and finally to pragmatism's more direct application to issues. We say "loosely" because all of the essays address all three aspects; most pragmatists do not see them as easily separable. Here such distinctions indicate only the relative emphasis in each chapter. Each essay can therefore be read on its own and provide significant insight into the potential of a pragmatist influence on the discussion of the moral standing of nonhuman animals. However, the intersections among the chapters also draw them together as a whole. As a result this collection should be useful for those interested in American pragmatism as well as those interested more specifically in the moral standing of nonhuman animals.

In part 1, "Pragmatism Considering Animals," we have assembled four essays that explicitly address both what some of the central founding theorists of pragmatism have to say and what they imply about our relations with nonhuman animals. While the work of John Dewey clearly dominates this entire volume (as Dewey scholarship currently dominates the work in pragmatism in general), and is addressed by three of the four essays in this section, these authors also consider the work of several other American pragmatists and "proto-pragmatists" —Emerson, Thoreau, James, and Peirce. As a whole, these four essays present what is distinct about the pragmatic contribution to our view of ethics and to our perception of our relatedness to nonhuman animals. They lay out the history of the animal rights debates, point to the shortcomings of the traditional utilitarian and deontological perspectives in those debates, and offer a pragmatic alternative. At the same time, they indicate some of the possible shortcomings within the pragmatic tradition and seek both to strengthen it and to usefully apply it to questions regarding the moral standing of nonhuman animals.

We start the section with James Albrecht's " 'What Does Rome Know of Rat and Lizard?': Pragmatic Mandates for Considering Animals in Emerson, James, and Dewey." This chapter suggests that in addition to the traditionally cited work of Henry David Thoreau, those interested in American philosophy and environmental and animal issues can also turn to Ralph Waldo Emerson, William James, and John Dewey. From Emerson and the others, Albrecht draws out the importance of realizing that we are often blind to experiences not like our own. Because of this blindness we need to work to develop a sympathetic understanding of other beings. Albrecht then ties this argument to a Deweyan ethic grounded in a flexible process of intelligent inquiry.

Next, Steven Fesmire's "Dewey and Animal Ethics" presents further development, and critique, of a Deweyan ethic as it applies to nonhumans. After discussing some of Dewey's own prejudices with regard to nonhuman animals, Fesmire argues that Dewey's ethics can be a resource for the debates about animal ethics, offering, among other things, a radical redescription of moral theory, an acknowledgment of our kinship with nonhuman animals, a focus on amelioration, a concept of natural piety, attention to actual contexts in which our relations with nonhumans occur, and an acknowledgment of the importance of empathy in understanding those relationships.

In "Overlapping Horizons of Meaning: A Deweyan Approach to the Moral

Standing of Nonhuman Animals," Phillip McReynolds critiques what he calls the "extension" model of ethics and offers instead a basis for moral standing in community. Using the work of Beth Singer, McReynolds finds Dewey's claims about the separate status of nonhuman animals to be inconsistent with his principles expressed elsewhere. McReynolds offers his own concept of overlapping horizons of meaning as constituting a sense of community, and thus of ethics, that includes human and nonhuman animals.

With the final piece in this section we return to where pragmatism began—Charles Sanders Peirce. Douglas R. Anderson's "Peirce's Horse: A Sympathetic and Semeiotic Bond" presents Peirce's theory of phenomenological perception as a ground for sympathetic relations between humans and nonhumans. Peirce's theory of continuity (synechism) produces a worldview with no ontological breaks between species, thereby laying the groundwork for reconsidering our normative relations with nonhumans.

Part 2, "Pragmatism, the Environment, Hunting, and Farming," contains four essays that employ various pragmatic methods of inquiry to explore topics involving the moral standing of nonhuman animals. Issues of environmental ethics, of hunting, and of raising livestock are all discussed. Most of the authors discuss and employ a Deweyan method of inquiry, which relies on the "method of intelligence" and the "method of democracy." Because Dewey's corpus is large and rich, the essays are all able to draw on different aspects of his theory. While taking the method of inquiry as central, they move on to discuss his theory as a method of conflict resolution, as a way to sort out competing ethical claims, and as a way to investigate a problem.

The part begins with Ben A. Minteer's "Beyond Considerability: A Deweyan View of the Animal Rights–Environmental Ethics Debate." This chapter takes on the common perception that the projects of environmental ethicists and the projects of animal rights or animal welfare theorists are inherently and uncritically at odds with one another. Pragmatism can help to bridge this divide by challenging the idea that the attribute of moral standing and significance is the main question to be settled. A Deweyan ethics provides the method of intelligent judgment, which Minteer connects to contemporary theories of conflict resolution. Minteer then uses this notion of conflict resolution to reframe the debates between environmental and animal ethicists.

Andrew Light's chapter, "Methodological Pragmatism, Animal Welfare, and Hunting," takes a more general—or as he puts it, "methodological"—pragmatist approach. Like Moreno's description of naturalism in bioethics, Light's methodological pragmatism was originally offered as a way for philosophers of various persuasions in environmental ethics to move their work toward more practical ends rather than only advancing debates in ethical theory or meta-ethics, without requiring them to sign on to an orthodox Deweyan or otherwise historically grounded version of pragmatism. After reviewing this approach, Light first applies it to the environmental ethics–animals welfare debates discussed in the previous chapter and then, in turn, applies the results to debates involving the hunting of animals.

This essay is followed by two chapters that focus on the raising of livestock in "factory farms" or intensive, confined animal feeding operations (CAFOs). Paul B. Thompson's "Getting Pragmatic about Farm Animal Welfare" argues that pragmatism's focus on actual issues encourages a different approach to some questions than is found in the traditional literature on the subject. That focus challenges the propriety of using a set of arguments developed in one context in another. Thompson's central questions concern our production and use of farm animals. He contends that the dominant animal rights theories, developed in response to the use of nonhuman animals in research labs, were transferred to agriculture with no acknowledgment of the different relationships in these two different contexts. Economic systems, not the farmer's attitude toward animals, are what must be addressed. Thompson argues that those interested in improving animal welfare need to find ways to support and sustain the market for animal products that are humanely produced rather than demanding their outright prohibition.

Following up on Thompson's conclusion that vegetarianism is but one, and perhaps not the best, option open to pragmatists, Erin McKenna's "Pragmatism and the Production of Livestock" uses the pragmatic theory of inquiry to gain a better understanding of why we have arrived at our current intensive methods of livestock production. Asking what problems each shift in agriculture was supposed to "solve" and looking at some of the new problems that arose from these "solutions," McKenna argues that while pragmatism does not require vegetarianism it does require each of us to take a critical look at our society's current agricultural practices, take responsibility for their effects, and alter our habits intelligently.

Part 3, "Pragmatism on Animals as Cures, Companions, and Calories," collects four essays that take a pragmatic approach to some of the specific ways we relate to, use, and care for nonhuman animals. Again, while Dewey is the main focus of these essays, each draws on different aspects of his theory to address the topic at hand. Dewey's ethics, Dewey's theory of democracy, Dewey's method of intelligence, and Dewey's aesthetics are all employed to expand our understanding of our responsibilities to, and relatedness with, various nonhuman animals.

The first two chapters address issues connected with the use of nonhuman animals in scientific research. In "Is Pragmatism Chauvinistic? Dewey on Animal Experimentation," Jennifer Welchman argues that despite Dewey's apparently speciesist remarks regarding animal experimentation, his pragmatist ethics is not speciesist. Welchman contends that for Dewey, nonhuman animals are owed only the negative duty of noninterference. In contrast, we have positive duties to other humans; thus, animal experimentation is morally permissible when seen as a necessary part of carrying out this positive duty. However, such cases should be seen as tragic.

Part of what Welchman asks of pragmatists is continual oversight of animal experimentation. Todd M. Lekan develops this argument in "A Pragmatist Case for Animal Advocates on Institutional Animal Care and Use Committees."

Lekan uses Dewey's theory of democracy to make a case for the inclusion of animal advocates on such committees. Rather than blindly supporting "scientific progress," we should provide open forums for critique and communication. Such committees are currently required to have a veterinarian and one external community member: Lekan suggests that the animals' perspective needs to be included as well. Adding an animal advocate fosters the purpose of democratic inquiry.

The third chapter in this section turns from our social and moral obligations with regard to animal experimentation to address our responsibilities to the animals found in many of our homes. In "Pragmatism and Pets: Best Friends Animal Sanctuary, Maddie's Fund^{SM}, and No More Homeless Pets in Utah," Matthew Pamental takes the pragmatic method of democratic intelligence and applies it to the real-life problem of the overpopulation of pets in the United States. He looks at several specific programs and argues that they embody Dewey's five-step process of democratic inquiry. While their work is on-going, Pamental nonetheless concludes that the programs have been quite successful at creating a democratic community, employing experimental inquiry, and improving the lives of many animals.

The final chapter of this part asks how we can have the kinds of attachments to our pets described by Pamental and still eat animals as a regular part of our diet. In "Dining on Fido: Death, Identity, and the Aesthetic Dilemma of Eating Animals," Glenn Kuehn argues that we need to learn to identify more fully with the animals we eat and to see the aesthetic possibilities in the fact that we dine on flesh. Kuehn points out, as do others engaged with this subject, that while most of us want our vegetables to look like vegetables we want our meat to look like anything but a dead animal. We are embodied creatures sustained by the flesh of other embodied creatures. Although some are bothered by this relationship, Dewey's aesthetics makes us see that growth entails decay and life subsists on death.

This collection clearly covers a great deal of ground. Still, it is just a beginning. The essays here represent individual articulations of a pragmatist approach to a variety of animal-related issues. This volume does not exhaust all possible understandings of pragmatism, of the topics, or of pragmatist positions on those topics addressed. We hope, however, that it at least serves to provide an important start on which others will build.

Notes

1. It is telling that Pollan's opening line in the article squarely connects the social movement for animal rights with the philosophical literature: "The first time I opened Peter Singer's 'Animal Liberation,' I was dining alone at the Palm, trying to enjoy a rib-eye steak cooked medium-rare" ("An Animal's Place" 58). This was not Pollan's first foray into this area. His books on gardening are extremely important, and in a previous *New York Times Magazine* cover article he examined the beef industry, following a steer from ranch to feed lot to his plate (see "Power Steer").

2. This kind of consideration gets us the "argument from marginal cases." See Dombrowski for a discussion.

3. Note, however, that Francione rejects not all incrementalism but only that which he thinks actively hinders an animal rights agenda and continues to treat animals instrumentally as mere means to our ends.

Bibliography

Coetzee, J. M. *The Lives of Animals.* Princeton: Princeton University Press, 1999.

Dewey, John. *Human Nature and Conduct. The Later Works, 1925–1953,* edited by Jo Ann Boydston, vol. 1. Carbondale: Southern Illinois University Press, 1983.

Dombrowski, Daniel. *Babies and Beasts: The Argument from Marginal Cases.* Urbana: University of Illinois Press, 1997.

Donovan, Josephine, and Carol J. Adams, eds. *Beyond Animal Rights: A Feminist Caring Ethic for the Treatment of Animals.* New York: Continuum, 1996.

Finsen, Lawrence, and Susan Finsen. *The Animal Rights Movement in America: From Compassion to Respect.* New York: Twayne, 1994.

Francione, Gary L. *Rain without Thunder: The Ideology of the Animal Rights Movement.* Philadelphia: Temple University Press, 1996.

Jamieson, Dale. *Morality's Progress.* New York: Oxford University Press, 2003.

Jasper, James M., and Dorothy Nelkin. *The Animal Rights Crusade.* New York: Free Press, 1993.

Magel, Charles. *Keyguide to Information Sources in Animal Rights.* New York: McFarland, 1989.

McMahan, Jeff. "Animals." In *A Companion to Applied Ethics,* edited by R. G. Frey and Christopher Heath Wellman, 525–36. Malden, Mass.: Blackwell, 2003.

Menand, Louis. *The Metaphysical Club.* New York: Farrar, Straus and Giroux, 2002.

Midgley, Mary. *Animals and Why They Matter.* Athens: University of Georgia Press, 1983.

Moreno, Jonathan D. "Bioethics Is a Naturalism." In *Pragmatic Bioethics,* edited by Glenn McGee, 5–17. Nashville, Tenn.: Vanderbilt University Press, 1999.

Pollan, Michael. "An Animal's Place." *New York Times Magazine,* November 10, 2002, 58–64+.

———. "Power Steer." *New York Times Magazine,* March 31, 2002, 44–52+.

Regan, Tom. *The Case for Animal Rights.* Berkeley: University of California Press, 1983.

———. "Ethical Theory and Animals." In *Defending Animal Rights,* 1–27. Urbana: University of Illinois Press, 2001.

———. "What's in a Name?" In *Defending Animal Rights,* 28–38. Urbana: University of Illinois Press, 2001.

Singer, Peter. *Animal Liberation.* Rev. ed. New York: Avon Books, 1990.

———. "Animal Liberation at 30." *New York Review of Books,* May 15, 2003, 23–26.

Part One: *Pragmatism*
                    Considering Animals

1 "What Does Rome Know of Rat and Lizard?": Pragmatic Mandates for Considering Animals in Emerson, James, and Dewey

James M. Albrecht

We can be ethical only in relation to something we can see, feel, understand, love, or otherwise have faith in.

—Aldo Leopold, "The Land Ethic"

In their search for intellectual ancestors in the tradition of American transcendentalism, environmentalists have understandably focused not on Ralph Waldo Emerson but on Henry David Thoreau. As Lawrence Buell has argued, Thoreau's writings evince an emerging interest in "defining nature's structure, both spiritual and material, for its own sake," while Emerson's works, though representing a "great stride" toward a "more audaciously secularized" and naturalistic view of nature's "philosophic, or at least theologic" significance, remain committed to an anthropocentric consideration of "how nature might subserve humanity" (118, 117). Yet for those who believe that American pragmatism offers a distinctive contribution to the present debate on the moral status of animals, the line of influence between Emerson and his pragmatic descendants William James and John Dewey constitutes another important genealogy in the American environmental imagination. Specifically, though Emerson celebrates human intelligence—including our language, concepts, and technology—as a powerful extension and augmentation of nature's creative energies, he is also acutely concerned with the ways that our individual acts, and the cultural constructs that empower and focus them, blind us to aspects of the living and changing world of which we are a part. This Emersonian apprehension takes on, in the works of James, an explicitly ethical significance, an obligation to attend sympathetically to the significance of other beings' experiences, to their desires and demands. Nonhuman animals tellingly emerge as examples in both Emerson's and James's prose when they pursue this line of ethical concern, but neither thinker explicitly pursues the possible consequences for the moral status of animals. Just how this concern might support a pragmatic argument for increasing the moral consideration we grant animals becomes clearer in light of Dewey's analysis of ethics—specifically, as Dewey's analysis enables a critique of the two dominant positions shaping the animal rights debate, the utilitarian approach of Peter Singer and the rights-based approach of Tom Regan.

While pragmatism has clear affinities with the utilitarian approach, one significant difference is pragmatism's emphasis on the legitimate and indeed necessary role that emotions or sympathy play in moral reflection and choice. For Dewey, emotionally felt obligations to other beings are a fundamental, naturally occurring aspect of our associated existence as human beings; as such they are legitimate starting points in the moral dissatisfactions that trigger the process of moral reflection, action, and change. Emotional dispositions also shape and determine our ability to perceive consequences that should be included in moral reflection. Last, emotions are an unavoidable determinant in moral decisions, which, both James and Dewey argue, involve not only quantitative calculations about future consequences but also our desires and choices about the *quality* of happiness to be found, and the quality of character to be cultivated, in striving to achieve different ends. From a pragmatic perspective, extending the moral consideration we grant to animals is such a choice, and thus cannot be settled merely by rational arguments—whether of the Singer or Regan variety—about why the mental status of animals entitles them to greater consideration. Within this process of moral inquiry, a greater openness toward the diversity of experience and the diverse experience of others, such as Emerson and James urge us to cultivate, can encourage a pragmatic choice to grant animals greater moral consideration.

But why start with Emerson, since these arguments, admittedly, could be made with reference only to James and Dewey? First, if the pragmatic tradition does have something distinctive to offer to the animal rights debate, our understanding of that contribution will be stronger, richer, and more historically accurate if we appreciate its origins and development. Moreover, there is a practical political value in seeing this tradition as a developing one, for though the relevance that pragmatic concerns have for the status of animals becomes increasingly clear as one proceeds from Emerson to James to Dewey, *none* of these thinkers—including Dewey, who, for instance, argued strongly in favor of experimenting on animals (in "Ethics of Animal Experimentation")—articulated this relevance. That task remains for us; and seeing the pragmatic view of animals as an evolving one can encourage us, in good pragmatic fashion, to appropriate the ideas of the classic pragmatists and revise them to meet the demands of our social circumstances and ethical commitments. Finally, while beginning with Emerson can illuminate the evolution of a pragmatist position on animals, it can, conversely, also illuminate the status of "nature" in Emerson's thought and the significance of his contribution to American ethical and environmental thinking.

* * *

Emerson's attitudes toward nature are characterized by many of the tensions evident in other Romantic thinkers; for instance, he on the one hand views nature as a source of organic integrity that provides an antidote to the alienations and fragmentations of culture, while, on the other hand, he celebrates cultural technologies such as the steam engine or railroad as products of a human creativity that finds its roots in nature. Though Buell is correct in noting Emerson's primary stress on the human uses of nature, Emerson increasingly moved toward a naturalistic vision that decentered humankind's position. Even in his first book, *Nature* (1836), which retains clear vestiges of an idealist metaphysics, Emerson's assertion that nature finds its highest meaning in the aesthetic, ethical, and spiritual uses that humans make of it is balanced by his rejection of any intellectualization that would deny or degrade the substantial reality of nature or the emotional intimacy of our connection to it.[1] In later essays, such as "Nature" (1844) and "Fate" (1860), Emerson moves further toward a vision of the human self as wholly implicated in the physical processes of nature, as driven by natural impulses for growth and self-expression and limited by the "tyrannizing" forms of our physical embodiment ("Fate" 946). "The craft with which the world is made," he writes, the "calculated profusion" and "exaggeration" which casts a "prodigality of seeds" so that "if thousands perish," "tens may live to maturity" and reproduce, "runs also into the mind and character of men" ("Nature" 550). Emerson's resulting ethics, which urge us to pursue the limited yet sufficient opportunities for power and knowledge that exist within the "mixed instrumentalities" of nature ("Fate" 772), are frankly melioristic, and directly anticipate the melioristic ethics of both James and Dewey.[2]

Emerson's Romantic naturalism can also be seen as in significant ways a precursor of pragmatism's naturalistic view of human intelligence and of the relation between the ideal and actual aspects of experience. In *Nature*, Emerson describes human intelligence—such as our development of language and technologies—as emerging from nature, anticipating the Deweyan view that human arts constitute an extension and augmentation of experience's natural processes of growth and consummation. "Nature, in its ministry to man," Emerson writes, "is not only the material but is also the process and result," and "the useful arts are reproductions or combinations by the wit of man, of these same natural benefactors" (12), and he cites the steam engine and railroad as such technological extensions of nature:

> He no longer waits for favoring gales, but by means of steam, he realizes the fable of Æolus's bag, and carries the two and thirty winds in the boiler of his boat. To diminish friction, he paves the road with iron bars, and mounting a coach with a ship-load of men, animals, and merchandise behind him, he darts through the country, from town to town, like an eagle or a swallow through the air. By the aggregate of these aids, how is the face of the world changed, from the era of Noah to that of Napoleon! (12–13)

As this passage shows, Emerson, like the pragmatists after him, celebrates the unique power of human intelligence to reshape the environment so as to extend and secure our enjoyment of the goods of experience. Our cultural intelligence—making available the full range of human languages, tools, ideas, and artifacts—provides individuals with incredible powers: "[W]e wish for a thousand heads, a thousand bodies," Emerson notes, and "in good faith, we are multiplied by our proxies. How easily we adopt their labors! Every ship that comes to America got its chart from Columbus. Every novel is a debtor to Homer. Every carpenter who shaves with a foreplane borrows the genius of a forgotten inventor" ("Uses of Great Men" 620).

Even as Emerson affirms the power of human ideas to empower us, his writings also express an enduring anxiety that our concepts, misused, can enervate and impoverish us. While he shares James's and Dewey's view that the proper function of human ideas is to facilitate action that will enrich experience, he also anticipates their criticism that ideas too often are treated more as ends than as means to continued activity and growth. An overreliance on the ready-made ideas and tools that culture provides us, Emerson argues, can prevent us from seeking the more primary good of actively expressing and cultivating our own capacities: "What the former age has epitomized into a formula or rule for manipular convenience, [the mind] will lose all good of verifying for itself, by means of the wall of that rule. Somewhere, sometime, it will demand and find compensation for that loss by doing the work itself" ("History" 240). A second, and related, concern focuses on the ways our existing concepts may prevent us from perceiving and engaging aspects of our environment that might elicit novel experiences, activities, and results. The self depends on interaction with its environment—both cultural and natural—to elicit its potential powers: "No man can antedate his experience, or guess what faculty or feeling a new object shall unlock," Emerson observes, "any more than he can draw today the face of a person whom he shall see to-morrow for the first time" ("History" 255). Cultural objects and influences provide one powerful resource for unfolding such discovery, but Emerson is deeply concerned that the actions they motivate, and the products which result from such actions, threaten to obscure other aspects of experience. As he argues in his essay "Circles," each set of human actions, practices, and ideas that defines a new perception of reality—a new "circle," in Emerson's metaphor—becomes in turn an obstacle to further creative acts and novel perceptions.[3] The antidote, Emerson suggests, lies in a continual effort to move beyond the results, satisfactions, and certainties of each completed act by commencing new acts: "Power," he insists in a famous passage from "Self-Reliance," "ceases in the instant of repose; it resides in the moment of transition from a past to a new state, in the shooting of the gulf, in the darting to an aim" (271). This ethos of abandonment and transition can open our perception to aspects of experience that lie beyond what is already conceptualized or humanized, such perception being necessary to growth and change: "When good is near you," Emerson asserts, "it is not by any known or accustomed way; you shall not discern the foot-prints of any other; you shall not see the face of man; you shall not hear any name[.] . . . You take the way from man, not to man" ("Self-Reliance" 271).

There are not, given Emerson's interest in nature, a large number of references to animals in his writings, nor any sustained attention to the quality or value of animal experience. One tantalizing comment does appear in an 1867 lecture; reflecting on the ways modern science has undermined the anthropocentrism of traditional worldviews, Emerson voices a naturalistic assertion of the essential continuity of human and animal intelligence: "The study of animals disclosed the same intellect as in man, only initial, only working to humble ends, but, as far as it went, identical in aim with his: full of good sense, baffling him sometimes, by showing a more fertile good sense in the animal, than in the hunter; but everywhere intelligent to us, because like ours" ("Rule of Life" 378). Such direct reflection on the quality of animal experience is rare in Emerson. Yet even if he himself did not recognize it, one possible implication of the ethical concerns outlined above is a mandate to extend a more sympathetic attention to the nonhuman aspects of nature. George Kateb, for instance, has described Emersonian self-reliance as an intellectual method that strives to move beyond the constraints of any particular perspective, a method that cultivates an "indefinite receptivity" and openness to the intrinsic value of the particulars of our world; this ethos, Kateb concludes, might be enlisted in a "preservative politics" that fights to maintain the world in all its diverse particularity (33–34). These potential implications of Emerson's thought become most apparent, as I hope to show, in the larger context of a pragmatic perspective on our obligations to animals. But I would like to explore one striking instance in Emerson's writings where the issue of extending our moral consideration of animals does emerge explicitly.

This instance is the conclusion to Emerson's essay "History." The bulk of the essay explores how history—considered broadly as the entire collection of human artifacts resulting from the acts of previous individuals and societies—provides a rich record of human possibility that individuals can use to discover and unlock their own latent capacities and to interpret their present historical moments.[4] Yet the essay ultimately betrays the tension, outlined above, between this confidence in the power of culture and Emerson's contrasting fear that culture's tools will obscure our perception of the living world around us. This tension becomes clear when Emerson, having focused on the "civil and metaphysical history of man," acknowledges in the essay's final section that "another history goes daily forward,—that of the external world,—in which he is not less strictly implicated" (253–54):

> He is the compend of time; he is also the correlative of nature. His power consists in the multitude of his affinities, in the fact that his life is intertwined with the whole chain of organic and inorganic being. In old Rome the public roads beginning at the Forum proceeded north, south, east and west, to the centre of every province of the empire, making each market-town of Persia, Spain, and Britain pervious to the soldiers of the capital: so out of the human heart go, as it were, highways to the heart of every object in nature, to reduce it under the dominion of man. A man is a bundle of relations, a knot of roots, whose flower and fruitage is the world. His faculties refer to natures out of him, and predict the world he is

to inhabit, as the fins of the fish foreshow that water exists, or the wings of the eagle presuppose the air. He cannot live without a world. (254)

This passage initially appears to be a confident assertion of the power of our cultural intelligence to connect us to the natural world and bring it under human control. Yet the clash in Emerson's metaphors reveals a tension in this relationship: the organic tropes place humankind, like fish and eagles, in the natural world, describing the world as the "flower and fruitage" of human faculties, while the imperialistic trope of Rome places humankind as a foreign conqueror extending military and economic "dominion" over nature. The danger here seems clear: if humankind "cannot live without a world," if we depend on our environment to call forth the latent possibilities of our human nature, and if our power indeed "consists in the multitude of [our] affinities" to the "whole chain of organic and inorganic being," then the violence of our culturally mediated relation to nature threatens to obscure as much as it reveals. The imperial "highways" of human intelligence, paved in our headlong rush to secure certain goods, will lead us to trample on other aspects of the world we inhabit.

The tension that here is largely implicit in Emerson's metaphors becomes the explicit topic of the essay's closing paragraphs, which voice an abrupt and dramatic shift of argument:

> Is there somewhat overweening in this claim? Then I reject all that I have written, for what is the use of pretending to know what we know not? But it is the fault of our rhetoric that we cannot strongly state one fact without seeming to belie some other. I hold our actual knowledge very cheap. Hear the rats in the wall, see the lizard on the fence, the fungus under foot, the lichen on the log. What do I know, sympathetically, morally, of either of these worlds of life? As old as the Caucasian man,—perhaps older,—these creatures have kept their counsel beside him, and there is no record of any word or sign that has passed from one to the other. . . . Yet every history should be written in a wisdom which divined the range of our affinities and looked at facts as symbols. I am ashamed to see what a shallow village tale our so-called History is. How many times must we say Rome, and Paris, and Constantinople! What does Rome know of rat and lizard? What are Olympiads, and Consulates to these neighbouring systems of being? Nay, what food or experience or succour have they for the Esquimaux seal-hunter, for the Kanaka in his canoe, for the fisherman, the stevedore, the porter? (255–56)

This passage anticipates two important strands of the pragmatic logic for broadening our moral consideration of animals that I hope to trace through James and Dewey. First, when Emerson "rejects all" he has written, and faults the distortions of "our rhetoric," this is an admission—characteristic for Emerson[5]— that human truths are partial and tend to falsify the antagonistic or conflicting aspects of experience. He is not really rejecting the view expressed through most of his essay—the view, shared by the pragmatists, that human cultural intelligence *can* engage nature in powerful ways and bring new areas of nature under our perception, understanding, and control. Rather, with his question "What does Rome know of rat and lizard?" echoing and undermining his earlier im-

perial metaphor, he is acknowledging the opposing truth, that each conceptu-
alization and reshaping of nature obscures or obliterates other possibilities. Here
Emerson anticipates James's sense of the tragic aspect of our moral lives: our
efforts to realize some of our ideals inevitably "butcher" others (James, "The
Moral Philosopher" 608–609). Moreover, Emerson's references to the "Esqui-
maux," "Kanaka," and "stevedore," as well as "rats," "lizard," "fungus," and "li-
chen," anticipate as well James's insistence, best articulated in "On a Certain
Blindness in Human Beings," that other beings—both human and nonhuman—
are involved in those possibilities we butcher. Along these lines, Emerson calls
our attention to the nonhuman presence, the "neighbouring systems of being,"
that exist, literally, within or alongside our systems and institutions but are ignored by them—the rats in our walls, the lizards on our fences.

In a poem left unpublished at his death, Emerson ponders, in terms markedly
similar to this passage from "History," our ignorance of the nonhuman life
around us:[6]

> Who knows this or that?
> Hark in the wall to the rat
> Since the world was, he has gnawed;
> Of his wisdom, of his fraud
> What dost thou know
> In the wretched little beast
> Is life & heart
> Child & parent
> Not without relation
> To fruitful field & sun & moon
> What art thou? His wicked cruelty
> Is cruel to thy cruelty. (*Collected Poems* 385)

Here, more directly than in "History," Emerson asserts that animals' lives embody a purposeful and meaningful experience akin to our own: a "life and
heart" with "relation" to "Child & parent," to "fruitful field & sun & moon."
Moreover, he attributes the alien appearance of nature to a sympathetic failure
in humans: "What art thou?" Emerson challenges the reader (and himself), noting that the rat is "cruel to thy cruelty"—that is, "wicked" and cruel only when
defined as such from a narrow anthropocentric perspective.

One cannot claim that such reflections articulate an environmental vision or
advocate any direct duties to animals. Still, the eruption of a nonhuman presence into Emerson's prose at a key moment such as the conclusion to "History"
is no mere coincidence; it indicates that a pragmatic ethic of cultivating an
openness to those aspects of experience obscured by our culturally constructed
purposes may indeed push us toward a rethinking of our ethical relation to animals. In this sense, the dramatic rhetorical reversal voiced in the conclusion of
"History"—Emerson's claim to "reject all that I have written"—is a quintessen-
tially Emersonian performance with important ethical overtones, enacting his
view, outlined above, that we can cultivate a salutary openness to the otherness

of experience (and to the experience of others) by being willing to renounce previously held conclusions, truths, or certainties. It is little wonder that James approvingly cited the conclusion of this essay as an example of Emerson's refusal to "repress" dogmatically the "rank diversity" of facts,[7] and it is to James's ruminations on the "moral life" that we must turn to consider the extensions of these Emersonian attitudes.

A second line of connection between Emerson and his pragmatic descendants is indicated by the important role that sympathy plays in his analysis of the failures and possibilities of human knowledge. The emphasis on sympathy noted in the poem above is echoed in the conclusion to "History." The question posed there by Emerson, "What do I know sympathetically, morally, of either of these worlds of life," suggests that the "[b]roader and deeper" history he calls for must constitute a more emotionally generous way of knowing. The "way into nature," he concludes, is evidenced not by "the path of science and of letters" so much as by the "idiot, the Indian, the child, and unschooled farmer's boy" (256). These stereotypes for a nonrational, intuitive connection to nature express a Romantic critique of a narrow empiricism, which, as Russell Goodman has argued, constitutes a major line of influence running from Emerson to James and Dewey. It is in the works of James and, especially, Dewey, that this Emersonian call for a more sympathetic stance toward nature finds its clearest pragmatic articulation, and its clearest relevance to the moral status of animals.

* * *

These Emersonian concerns are eloquently elaborated in the writings of William James, which express an abiding fear that our individual purposes and habits, and the cultural constructs that focus them, threaten to blind us to other aspects of reality. In the chapter from his *Principles of Psychology* titled "The Stream of Thought," James argues that we humans, as finite creatures who must habitually and continually focus our attention in order to fulfill our desires, "actually *ignore* most of the things before us" (70). In addition, he stresses that language itself "works against our perception of the truth," its syntactic rhythms reinforcing our "inveterate" "habit" of obscuring the more evanescent and transitional parts of consciousness by focusing on the "substantive parts alone" (34, 38).[8] In the concluding pages of "The Stream of Thought," James raises the ethical implications of this selective attention, arguing that since ethics involve choices between competing possibilities (72), nearly all human consciousness is imbued with an ethical character: "the mind is at every stage a theatre of simultaneous possibilities," he notes, involving the "selection of some, and the repression of the rest by the reinforcing and inhibiting agency of attention" (73). Significantly, nonhuman presences from nature emerge as examples in James's prose at precisely this point, signaling his awareness that when we repress some possibilities of a given situation, we repress as well the experiences and interests of other beings. Noting that our very notion of what a "thing" is, what qualifies as a constituent part of reality, is shaped by our selective attention, he asserts that "in itself, apart from my interest, a particular dust-wreath on a windy day is just as much of an individual thing, and just as much deserves an individual name, as my own body does" (71). Similarly, noting that every creature experiences the world from its own perspective, splits the world into a "'*me*' and '*not-me*,'" as it were, James imagines that "[e]ven the trodden worm . . . contrasts his own suffering self with the whole remaining universe, . . . for him it is I who am the mere part" (72). In sum, James moves beyond a narrowly anthropocentric view to describe an ethical universe in which our perceptions, purposes, and actions coexist alongside, and in competition with, the perceptions and demands of other beings: "Other minds, other worlds from the same monotonous and inexpressive chaos! My world is but one in a million alike embedded, *alike real to those who abstract them.* How different must be the worlds in the consciousness of ant, cuttle-fish, or crab!" (73; emphasis added).

In his famous essay "On a Certain Blindness in Human Beings," James identifies this incapacity to perceive the value of other beings' experiences as an obstacle against which we are morally obliged to struggle. As "practical beings" with "limited functions" we are inevitably "absorbed" in events relating to our own satisfactions, and thus prone to "stupidity" and "injustice" as regards "the significance of alien lives" (629–30). Here again, and more deliberately than in "The Stream of Thought," James includes "*creatures and* people different from ourselves" in his ethical scope (629; emphasis added), approvingly citing the following passage from Josiah Royce that enjoins us to acknowledge throughout nature strivings akin to our own:

> Pain is pain, joy is joy, everywhere, even as in thee. In all the songs of the forest birds; in all the cries of the wounded and dying, struggling in the captor's power; in the boundless sea where the myriads of water-creatures strive and die; amid the countless hordes of savage men; . . . everywhere, from the lowest to the noblest, the same conscious, burning, willful life is found, endlessly manifold as the forms of living creatures, unquenchable as these impulses that even now throb in thine own little selfish heart. (634–35)

Though "On a Certain Blindness" does not pursue further the question of animals' moral status, the conclusions James does reach are clearly relevant to a pragmatic stance on this question. He first formulates our duty in "negative" terms: an awareness of our blindness "absolutely forbids us to be forward in pronouncing on the meaninglessness of forms of existence other than our own; and it commands us to tolerate, respect, and indulge" other beings' efforts to pursue happiness, "provided those ways do not assume to interfere by violence with ours" (644–45). As I argue below, this injunction can, within the context of James's own model of ethics, be reasonably extended to nonhuman animals. Second, in the opening paragraphs of his companion essay, "What Makes a Life Significant," he articulates our obligation in more positive terms as a duty to cultivate a sympathetic attention to other beings. Our profoundest appreciation of the significance of other beings comes, James argues, with those whom we love: an emotional concern for others literally disposes us to perceive realities we would otherwise miss. Taking the intimacy of lovers as an ideal model for our relations to others, he claims: "We ought, all of us, to realize each other" in this "intense, pathetic, and important way," arguing that despite the difficulties of such a lofty aim, there is "nothing intrinsically absurd" in striving to emulate those people who demonstrate "an enormous capacity" for "taking delight in other people's lives" (646). To cultivate a more sympathetic attention to others may never afford us a sufficient appreciation of their realities, but at least it can help us to develop an increased "sense of our own blindness" and so "make us more cautious in going over the dark places" (646). James's argument here clearly implies that we cannot grant sufficient moral weight to the interests of other beings without a sympathetic effort to appreciate their interests—an injunction that is the more urgent the more those beings, whether human or nonhuman, differ from us.

To assert that we owe other beings, including nonhuman animals, a sympathetic tolerance that will allow them to pursue their own happiness, so long as those pursuits do not unfairly infringe on our own interests, does not provide a rule or formula for determining the relative weight we ought to grant nonhuman animals when conflicts do occur—and indeed James, like Dewey after him, insists that we must seek such answers not in any rigid principles or set calculus but in an experimental and democratic process of moral inquiry and action. In "The Moral Philosopher and the Moral Life," James offers his vision of such a process in terms that clearly indicate why pragmatism is conducive to considering the interests of nonhuman animals. James offers a thoroughly naturalistic account of ethics,[9] arguing that "goodness" can consist only in the satisfaction of some concrete creature's demands, and that every such demand has moral weight:

> Take any demand, however slight, which *any creature*, however weak, may make. Ought it not, for its own sake, to be satisfied? If not, prove why not. The only possible kind of proof you could adduce would be the exhibition of another creature who should make a demand that ran the other way. The only possible reason there can be why any phenomenon ought to exist is that such a phenomenon actually is desired. Any desire is imperative to the extent of its amount. Some desires, truly enough, are small desires; they are put forward by insignificant persons, and we customarily make light of the obligations which they bring. But the fact that such personal demands as these impose small obligations does not keep the largest obligations from being personal demands. (617; emphasis added)

According to this logic, the demands of nonhuman creatures clearly carry moral weight and ought, for their own sake, to be satisfied. Yet, as James insists, morality is fundamentally a question of choice; our world is a moral world because it requires choices, because the "actually possible in this world is always vastly narrower than all that is demanded" (621), and the realization of one good inevitably comes at the cost of precluding the realization of others. As James puts it in a famous phrase that captures the tragic sensibility in pragmatism, "Some part of the ideal must be butchered, and [the ethical philosopher] needs to know which part. It is a tragic situation, and no mere speculative conundrum, with which he has to deal" (622).

Given this conflict between various beings' valid demands, the "guiding principle" of ethics, James concludes, must "simply be to satisfy at all times *as many
demands as we can*," to strive for the "best," most "inclusive" "whole"—that
situation which allows the most ideals to be realized, and "awaken[s] the least
sum of dissatisfactions" (623). This is to be achieved, James insists, only through
a process of experimentation and negotiation:

> On the whole, then, we must conclude that no philosophy of ethics is possible in
> the old-fashioned absolute sense of the term. Everywhere the ethical philosopher
> must wait on facts. . . . [T]he question as to which of two conflicting ideals will
> give the best universe then and there, can be answered by him only through the aid
> and experience of other men. . . . There is but one unconditional commandment,
> which is that we should seek incessantly, with fear and trembling, so to vote and to
> act as to bring about the very largest total universe of good which we can see. Ab-
> stract rules can indeed help; but they help the less in proportion as our intuitions
> are more piercing, and our vocation is the stronger for the moral life. For every real
> dilemma is in literal strictness a unique situation; and the exact combination of
> ideals realized and ideals disappointed which each decision creates is always a uni-
> verse without a precedent, and for which no adequate previous rule exists. . . . [The
> philosopher] knows he must vote always for the richer universe[.] . . . But which
> particular universe this is he cannot know for certain in advance; he only knows
> that if he makes a bad mistake, the cries of the wounded will soon inform him of
> the fact. In all this the philosopher is just like the rest of us non-philosophers, so
> far as we are just and sympathetic instinctively, and so far as we are open to the
> voice of complaint. (625–26)

This passage summarizes, perhaps as well as anything in James or Dewey, the
pragmatic view of ethics as an experimental and democratic *process*. Three aspects of James's approach are particularly relevant to the question of how pragmatism would weigh the interests of nonhuman animals. First, there is a pronounced democratic or egalitarian commitment in pragmatism, as is evidenced
both in James's choice of inclusiveness as a guiding ethical standard and in his
corollary insistence that the success of any endeavor must be judged by communal consensus, so that we must listen for the "cries of the wounded"—must
acknowledge where a newly achieved social compromise impinges on particular
groups or beings. There is nothing logically mandated about such a commitment; as Regan notes, there are ethical schools, such as perfectionism, which do
not have such egalitarian presuppositions or aims (233–35). One can see here
pragmatism's affinity to the egalitarian thrust of utilitarianism, which Singer
has deployed as such a powerful argument for animal liberation:[10] given James's
assertion that the demand of *any creature* has a legitimate claim to satisfaction,
there is no logical reason why the interests of nonhuman animals should be excluded from our attempts to create a more inclusive whole. Moreover, James also
insists that we must remain "sympathetic" and "open" to the "voice of complaint" if we are to consider sufficiently the interests of other beings—an injunction that is particularly urgent in regard to animals, who are voiceless in our
human councils (as it is in the case of human moral patients, such as infants,

who cannot speak for their interests). This is one way in which an Emersonian or Jamesian mandate to cultivate a more sympathetic perception of the world around us plays a crucial role in moral reflection on the status of animals.

Second, James insists that the purpose of moral inquiry is to diagnose problems that have arisen in a specific set of conditions and to remedy them by working to create new conditions in which more demands will be satisfied, more ideals realized. "Abstract rules can indeed help," but they must be treated as tools for intelligently engaging with and transforming specific circumstances. Here again we see pragmatism's affinities with utilitarianism, and see as well why pragmatism would reject the Kantian approach to animals that Regan takes, which insists that morality lies in following the dictates of a principle, regardless of specific consequences. Third, it is crucial to note that the appeal to facts and consequences does not eliminate contingency and choice from ethics: while we must predict as best we can the probable consequences of our moral choices, we cannot know in advance how successful the actual outcomes of our efforts will be. Moral decisions are always an experiment or a gamble. Though utilitarians would no doubt admit as much, pragmatism here departs in a significant fashion from utilitarianism by insisting on the legitimate and substantial role that our desires and emotions play in these moral choices. While not explicitly expressed in the passage above, this is the argument James makes in essays such as "The Will to Believe" and "The Sentiment of Rationality": namely, that moral questions, by definition about "what is good, or would be good if it did exist," cannot be settled by "pure intellect" but must be referred to "our heart" ("Will to Believe" 729–30), especially because moral questions often involve competing hypotheses whose ultimate validity or verification may literally depend on our belief and the actions it inspires—as, for instance, a belief that "life is worth living" may motivate acts whose consequences will in fact make life worthwhile ("Sentiment of Rationality" 339–40). Accordingly, pragmatism suggests that the question of what moral weight we ought to give to animals' interests will never be settled once and for all by a rational argument. It will instead be a matter of choosing to grant animals greater moral consideration, and of reshaping existing social conditions to make this possible, in the hope that such a choice will produce results that we will approve as more inclusively and richly satisfying the demands of the beings, human and nonhuman, with whom we share the planet. Here, too, Emerson's and James's ethos of cultivating a more sympathetic openness has a solidly practical benefit: it encourages us that such a moral choice on behalf of animals is worth the gamble.

James's description of ethics as a process of inquiry indicates, in broad strokes, the main features of a pragmatic approach to the moral status of animals, as well as how that approach reaches back to its Emersonian roots. John Dewey's more systematic analysis of ethics further extends and illuminates many of these Jamesian themes, while also clarifying how pragmatism might offer an alternative to the opposition between Regan's rights-based approach and the utilitarian stance of Singer that has dominated recent efforts to articulate our moral obligations to animals.

Peter Singer's *Animal Liberation* (1975; rev. ed., 2002) and Tom Regan's *The Case for Animal Rights* (1983) are both highly nuanced works, yet the fundamental conflict between their approaches can be stated succinctly. Singer has located in utilitarianism a powerful rationale for critiquing our "speciesist" bias toward animals, specifically in utilitarianism's egalitarian axiom that in our attempts to maximize the satisfaction of interests, we must give equal consideration to the interests of all sentient beings (those with the capacity for suffering and enjoyment) (*Animal Liberation* 5–9). While equal consideration does not require equal treatment, especially between different types of beings with different interests (*Animal Liberation* 3), it would, Singer argues, prohibit any practice in which relatively trivial human interests—such as eating meat when a nutritional and tasty vegetarian diet is easily available to us, or harming animals in scientific experiments whose ends are dubious and whose results may not be capable of extrapolation to humans—are satisfied through immense sacrifice and suffering imposed on animals (*Animal Liberation* 18–19). In contrast, Regan argues that our treatment of animals must be determined by rights animals possess in virtue of their status as individual beings with "inherent value," a status Regan ascribes to beings who are "subjects of a life"—that is, beings that have memory; beliefs, desires, and preferences; the capacity for intentional action; sentience and emotions; a sense of the future; a "psychophysical identity over time"; and an individual welfare (264). Individuals with inherent value, Regan argues, have the right to treatment that respects that value, which precludes treating them merely as "receptacles of value," as he claims utilitarianism does when it justifies harming an individual in order to maximize the aggregate good for a larger community (248–49). Individuals who are subjects of a life—whether human or nonhuman—must be treated with requisite respect, *regardless* of the consequences. In effect, Regan extends to animals a Kantian-style argument that individuals must be treated as ends-in-themselves, never as mere objects or means to an end. Thus, aside from a few exceptional cases,[11] he concludes we are never justified in eating or killing animals who are subjects of a life, nor are we justified in harming them for scientific studies that may benefit humans.

While both thinkers thus agree that there is a clear logical argument against treating animals, in Singer's words, "as research tools" or "mere lumps of palatable living flesh" (Regan and Singer, "Dog in the Lifeboat" 57), they disagree vehemently over the relative merits and implications of their opposing logics. Regan argues that utilitarianism is far too weak a moral theory. Because it must define morality solely in terms of consequences, he claims, utilitarianism cannot unequivocally condemn even the most egregious injustice—such as slavery (Regan and Singer, "Dog in the Lifeboat" 56); and since it must consider the interests of all beings even indirectly affected by a decision, it can never sufficiently muster the empirical data to prove its case conclusively (Regan 222–23). In short, since it cannot logically preclude harming individual animals in the name of a collective good, utilitarianism fails to respect the inherent value of animals. Singer, in contrast, argues that Regan's approach is unnecessary and inflexible. Singer agrees that animals who are subjects of a life have inherent value, but he argues that the principle of equal consideration of interests sufficiently respects this value ("Animal Liberation or Animal Rights?" 10–11). The real disagreement between a utilitarian and Kantian approach, he argues, is about what constitutes just acknowledgment of inherent value: utilitarians "prefer to maximize benefits to individuals, rather than to restrict such benefits by a requirement that no individual may be harmed" (11). Equal consideration of interests, Singer insists, is a sufficient tool for condemning practices that *unjustly* sacrifice the interest of some beings to satisfy the interests of others. Singer acknowledges that a utilitarian approach cannot categorically claim it is unjust to harm some individuals (human or nonhuman) to produce consequences that contribute to the common welfare; in so doing, however, utilitarianism avoids, he argues, the far more glaring inconsistencies and rigidities that follow from a Kantian disregard for consequences (Regan and Singer, "Dog in the Lifeboat" 57).[12]

This brief sketch will be sufficient to suggest how a Deweyan pragmatist might intervene in this debate. An overview of the analysis of ethics that Dewey offers in the 1932 edition of his *Ethics,* coauthored with James Hayden Tufts,[13] indicates key characteristics of a pragmatic approach. First, Dewey views ethics fundamentally as a *process* of intelligent inquiry and action that, like other types of inquiry, originates in response to some troublesome aspect of a present situation, analyzes existing conditions to determine the causes of the trouble, projects hypotheses of how conditions might be reshaped to remedy it, and embarks on a provisional course of action that will be open to revision based on its actual consequences. Moral theories are simply extensions of this process of reflection (*Ethics* 163–64), summaries or reminders of important ethical considerations: a "moral principle" is not an absolute "command" but a "*tool for analyzing a special situation*" (280). Principles can "render choice more intelligent, but they cannot replace choice" (165): we can apply a principle intelligently only by attending to the conditions of a particular situation and the possible specific consequences of a proposed action; moreover, as I will discuss below, even when we have done our best to rationally predict possible consequences, choice—and the desires and preferences that shape choice—play an inescapable role in morality.

Second, pragmatism insists that any theory that either ignores consequences (as Kantian ethics purport to) or focuses too exclusively on consequences (as hedonistic utilitarianism does) distorts the actual connection in experience between motive and consequences. Because of the contingency that exists between our intentions and the outcomes of our acts, we must judge the morality of an action, Dewey argues, on its *tendency* to produce beneficial consequences. If a surgeon with the best of intentions performs an operation in which the patient dies, Dewey notes in one example, we do not pronounce his action immoral on the basis of its results (*Ethics* 173). Conversely, if an ill-intended act unwittingly results in a good outcome, we do not praise the act as moral.

Last, because it views moral theories as emerging from experience, as describing different aspects of our practices of moral inquiry, pragmatism does not attempt to articulate one, overarching principle of ethics—such as utilitarianism's equal considerations of interests, or a Kantian notion of categorical duty. Instead, Dewey outlines three interrelated but distinct approaches to ethics, describing fundamental areas of ethical concern that overlap without any being reducible to any other (*Ethics*, chaps. 12–14). One approach, focusing on ends, views ethics as the question of how best to fulfill human desires, with the primary task of intelligently discriminating good ends from false ones. For Dewey, this means choosing the most "enduring" and "inclusive" ends, those that "unify in a harmonious way" an individual's "whole system of desires" (*Ethics* 185, 197). Another approach, focusing on duties and rights, views ethics as the question of how to subordinate human desires to a sense of obligation, with the primary task of identifying an authority or principle sufficient to define such obligation. Dewey argues that our duty to others, our obligation to strive for the common good, arises naturally from the fact of our associated existence, but he insists that the formulation of *any particular* duty must be open to question and revision (227). A third approach focuses on the pervasive role that social approbation plays in morality, and concludes that the primary task of ethics is to move beyond its merely customary force by adopting an impartial, rational standard for approbation. Dewey stresses the crucial role of individual character in applying any such standard (241–42); indeed, he argues that cultivating individual character—a responsibility, he insists, that falls to communities as well as to individuals[14]—is essential to all the main goals of ethics: society must help individuals to cultivate both the habits of "good practical judgment" necessary to discriminate enduring and inclusive ends and a strong "sense of duty" to the common good (233).

Dewey's approach to these three interrelated aspects of ethics provides a framework for analyzing the Singer-Regan debate, and for outlining a pragmatic perspective on increasing the moral consideration we grant to animals. Consider the question of duties and rights. Regan's attempt to imbue animals who are subjects of a life with individual rights can be placed within a broader liberal tradition, tracing back to Locke, that views rights as an inherent property of the individual considered in isolation from society—an unreal model of individuality, Dewey argues, that is utterly false to our experience as social beings (*Ethics* 323; *Reconstruction* 190–93). He thus approaches the issue of rights from a radically different perspective, describing our duties to others as communal in origin, as a fundamental aspect of our associated existence: "the exercise of claims is as natural as anything else in a world in which persons are not isolated from one another but live in constant association and interaction. . . . Because of inherent relationships persons sustain to one another, they are exposed to the expectations of others and to the demands in which these expectations are made manifest" (*Ethics* 218). Obligations are not, as liberal theory would have it, some "artificial" (if regrettably necessary) social restraint imposed on the "natural" liberty of individuals (*Ethics* 333; *Reconstruction* 190). While particu-

lar obligations may indeed be judged "despotic" or onerous, the fact of obligation itself is felt by an individual as "expressio[n] of a whole to which he himself
belongs," and "even when the demand runs contrary to his uppermost desire he
still responds to it as to something not wholly alien" (*Ethics* 218).

Accordingly, right or duty is not, as a Kantian view would have it, a transcendent principle independent of consequences; rather rights are best understood
as principles—that is, as tools—that express the consequences of our associated
behavior and help us to cope with them: "Right expresses the way in which the
good of a number of persons, held together by intrinsic ties, becomes effica-
cious in the regulation of the members of a community" (*Ethics* 228). Thus, in
analyzing Kant's argument for the universality of our duty to treat individuals as ends-in-themselves—precisely the kind of respect Regan claims animals
deserve—Dewey argues that the validity of Kant's test, "to ask ourselves if the
motive of that act can be made universal without falling into self-contradiction"
(*Ethics* 222), lies not in a transcendence of consequences but precisely in its being an injunction to consider consequences as broadly and impartially as possible: "It says: Consider as widely as possible the consequences of acting in this
way; imagine the results if you and others always acted upon such a purpose as
you are tempted to make your end, and see whether you would then be willing
to stand by it" (223).

This Deweyan view of duties suggests that our obligations to animals should
be understood as a consequence of our interdependence with them. While
Dewey's discussions of the duties that arise from "association" is clearly focused on human community, his analysis, when extended to a broader notion
of interdependence, can encompass and illuminate our relations with nonhuman
animals.[15] If, as Dewey argues, duties express the fact that our social interdependence exposes us to the demands and expectations of other humans, there
clearly are similar ways in which we acknowledge the demands and expectations
of animals. Anyone who has adopted a pet into his or her home and family
knows how an intimate relationship of expectations and demands becomes established: our pets expect (and demand) that we feed them, provide them affection, and play with them; in return they provide affection and company to
us, and learn to obey rules and meet expectations we place on them. Even those
who raise livestock with the ultimate intention of slaughtering the animals can,
under the right conditions, develop a deep sense of obligation to tend to the
needs of their animals, an obligation that cannot be reduced to mere expediency, as it expresses as well an emotional acknowledgment of interdependence.
Indeed, one powerful argument against factory farming methods is that they
preclude the types of interactions with animals that can foster such a sense
of relatedness and obligation, allowing producers to conceptualize and treat
animals as little more than "inputs" in a production machine. Beyond such relations with domesticated animals, we extend a sense of obligation to wild animals when we develop an environmental or ecological ethic. While they cannot express demands directly to us as domesticated animals do, wild animals,
and the environment itself, can be described as responding to our actions in

a way that apprises us of their needs and demands, making us aware of our interdependence with them—as, for instance, when declining numbers of wading birds apprise us of how our actions are reducing the wetland habitat that we also depend on for the purity of our water supply. In this sense, Dewey's view of duties is compatible with Aldo Leopold's claim that we must develop a "land ethic" in which we extend our sense of communal interdependence to include the environment—a compatibility that, I would argue, constitutes a clear advantage over Regan's individualistic rights view, which he admits may be irreconcilable with environmentalism's holistic approach (Regan 361–63).

It is important to stress that our sense of duty to others, on Dewey's view, expresses more than mere expediency. There is a practical necessity, Dewey acknowledges, to include the reactions of other beings among the predicted consequences of our actions. Other humans, for instance, express approval or disapproval of our acts through the "promise" or "withdrawal" of "aid and support" or the "infliction of penalty" (*Ethics* 218). Yet our sense of duty cannot be reduced to "servile" calculations of expediency: "if the ultimate 'reason' for observance of law and respect for duty lies in the hope of reward and fear of penalty, then the 'right' is nothing but a round-about means to the hedonistic end of private satisfaction" (*Ethics* 226). A sense of duty, Dewey insists, expresses a much more fundamental and intimate feeling that we belong to a larger whole, that our lives are intertwined with those of other beings. As noted above, we do not experience the demands that other beings make on us as "wholly alien" to ourselves. Thus, though there certainly are issues of expediency involved in developing an environmental ethic—for example, if we do not attend to the way the nonhuman environment responds to our actions, we run the risk of exterminating ourselves—our sense of obligation to nature and to wild animals expresses a more fundamental and emotional sense of interdependence. Here, too, a Deweyan model of duty supports Leopold, who insists that the development of an environmental ethic will depend on our ability to cultivate an emotional sense of our connection to the entire "biotic community": "We can be ethical only in relation to something we can see, feel, understand, love, or otherwise have faith in" (214).

A pragmatic view of duties provides not only a framework for understanding the obligations we accept in relation to animals but also a mandate for rethinking and revising them. While pragmatism can locate, in the fact of our interdependence, a basis for acknowledging our obligations to animals, it could never justify elevating such an acknowledgment, as Regan does, into a categorical right that individual animals have to be treated as ends-in-themselves, regardless of consequences. Such rigid formulations of duty, Dewey insists, are "dangerous" and obscure the "proper function of a general sense of duty," which is to "make us sensitive to the relations and claims involved in particular situations" (*Ethics* 232). However, it is precisely *because* pragmatism sees our duties not as absolute but as means for regulating the consequences of our interdependent existence—and because it subsequently insists there is no hard-and-fast line between the moral and the nonmoral, as a broader sense of the consequences of our actions may lead us to attribute moral significance where formerly we admitted none (*Ethics* 169–70)—that a Deweyan view of duties invites us, indeed requires us, to reflect intelligently on and regulate the consequences of our interdependence with animals. On the basis of a pragmatic process of moral reflection, we may choose to redraw the specific moral obligations we accept in regard to animals.

What might it mean, within such a pragmatic process of moral reflection, to acknowledge our duties to animals? If we extend Dewey's argument, discussed above, that a Kantian principle of duty is best understood as an injunction to consider the consequences of our actions as broadly and impartially as possible, it follows that our primary obligation to animals would be to include just such a broad and impartial consideration of their interests in our reflections on the consequences of our actions. In other words, a pragmatic formulation of our obligation to animals might result in something like the utilitarian principle of equal consideration of interests that Singer champions. Yet unlike Singer, Dewey emphasizes the central role that sympathy plays in such obligatory consideration. The broad and impartial consideration of consequences that is our duty toward others may be facilitated by principles, but these are only reminders or guides to direct a habitual and sympathetic sense of obligation: "A generalized sense of right and obligation," such as is summarized in a principle of duty, "is a great protection; it makes the general habit consciously available." But such a principle "grows out of occasions . . . actuated by direct affection," and "[a] sense of duty is a weak staff when it is not the outcome of a habit formed in whole-hearted recognition of the value of ties involved in concrete cases" (*Ethics* 233).

This question of the role emotions play in morality raises perhaps the most significant difference between Dewey's and Singer's approaches, a difference that is evident in Dewey's critique of hedonistic utilitarianism and his subsequent stress on the role of character. Dewey raises two main objections to hedonistic utilitarianism's claim that the morality of an act can be determined by its future consequences measured as the aggregate quantity of pleasure and pain. First, Dewey claims that such a view is false to human psychology and conduct, inverting the proper relationship between a present activity and its end-in-view. We do not, when we choose a moral path, enjoy the future pleasures we predict will result from it; rather, we find happiness in the quality of our present activity, which takes on an enriched meaning through its purposeful relation to that end-in-view (*Ethics* 194–95). Second, a judgment about which future consequences would be desirable cannot be reduced to a calculation of the quantity of pleasure; as James also insisted, it inevitably involves our human desires, preferences, and choices about the relative quality of different pleasures (196–97). Bringing these two ideas together, Dewey argues that moral choices determine "what one will be, instead of merely what one will have" (274): they are not just about what future to create, but more primarily about what kind of person to become in the present, what kind of meaning or satisfaction to find in striving toward a chosen end.[16] Each decision to pursue a particular end-in-view, and the satisfaction experienced in pursuing it, strengthens one's disposition to find pleasure in the pursuit of this quality of end. Each choice reinforces or remakes our character, which Dewey defines as the "interpenetration" of the various habits and dispositions that constitute the self (*Human Nature* 29; *Ethics* 171). Or, as Emerson puts it: "The force of character is cumulative. All the foregone days of virtue work their health into this" ("Self-Reliance" 266).

For Dewey, character, considered as this dynamic process, describes one of the primary tasks of ethics: that of choosing enduring and inclusive ends that will harmonize and unify our competing desires—for example, by finding personal satisfaction in pursuing ends that also satisfy our fundamental sense of duty to others. The practical path to such harmony, Dewey argues, lies in the deliberate cultivation of character:[17]

> Many an individual solves the problem. He does so not by any theoretical demonstration that what gives others happiness will also make him happy, but by voluntary choice of those objects which do bring good to others. He gets a personal satisfaction or happiness because his desire is fulfilled, but his desire has first been made after a definite pattern. . . . He has achieved a happiness which has *approved* itself to him, and this quality of being an approved happiness may render it invaluable, not to be compared with others. By personal choice among the ends suggested by desire of objects which are in agreement with the needs of social relations, an individual achieves a *kind* of happiness which is harmonious with the happiness of others. (*Ethics* 248)

I want to stress here both the element of choice and the role that sympathy and emotions can play in it. In judging that one end is higher or nobler than another because it is consistent with the common good of other beings, we choose to be the kind of person who works toward that particular end. In the process, we literally remake ourselves, creating or strengthening our disposition to find satisfaction in pursuing nobler ends: our ethical choices become intimate parts of who we are, of our dispositional and emotional makeup. For pragmatism, there is nothing absolute about this. There is no guarantee that one end is truly nobler than another, or that the consequences of pursuing it will indeed provide us a higher satisfaction. But pragmatism *does* empower us to see moral choices as true choices, and invites us to work toward our chosen ends in the belief that such striving, and perhaps realization, will provide a higher type of satisfaction. However, we must, as James puts it, "wait on facts": what validates a choice, ultimately, is the type of consequences it tends to produce, but pragmatism insists that sympathy plays a legitimate role *both* in an initial choice and in our eventual estimation of its consequences. If our sympathy toward other beings, including animals, encourages us to judge one type of pleasure as higher than another—as, for instance, to enjoy a vegetarian diet more than one that includes meat—pragmatism would allow that sympathy as a legitimate constituent of that moral choice and of the intelligent judgment of its consequences.

Some types of utilitarianism can embrace these pragmatic attitudes; indeed, in his *Ethics*, Dewey cites John Stuart Mill as articulating the crucial need to replace a hedonistic focus on pleasure with an emphasis on character (241–45). But Singer's arguments in favor of animal liberation have tended to dismiss the role of emotions and insist that our obligations to animals can and should be based on purely rational grounds. In part, this reflects Singer's understandable tactical choice, when *Animal Liberation* first appeared in 1975, to avoid the charges of sentimentalism aimed, perhaps justly, at animal activists (Singer, "Feminism and Vegetarianism" 36–37). When pushed, Singer has acknowledged a positive role for emotions—for instance, in moving those who have been convinced by rational arguments to take action—but he still asserts it is both desirable and possible to determine our moral obligations to animals "in a completely impartial and truly disinterested manner" ("Feminism and Vegetarianism" 37). It is hard to find a more tireless advocate than Dewey for the necessity of intelligent, even "scientific," method in morals, yet Dewey departs significantly from Singer in arguing, as James does, that sympathy, emotions, and desires play a crucial role at various stages in the process of moral reflection and choice. They signal dissatisfaction with present circumstances, and thus spur inquiry into the causes of that dissatisfaction. They support such inquiry by enabling us to perceive consequences more impartially and broadly: a person with the cultivated habit of compassion will literally perceive how his or her acts impact others in a way that a callous person will tend to miss (*Ethics* 242). Last, in the ways outlined above, one's sympathies, desires, and emotions, as embodied in one's character, help one choose what ends are worth pursuing and judge the consequences of those choices.

Such critiques of Regan and Singer suggest, in broad outline, a pragmatic stance on the question of expanding the moral consideration we grant animals. Perhaps the neatest summary is to say that for pragmatism, the question must remain *open* for intelligent and sympathetic reflection and choice. For those, like Regan, who seek an ironclad injunction against harming animals in the name of larger goods, such a pragmatic conclusion will seem pallid. But for others, who resist the absolutism of the rights approach, such pragmatic openness will be an energizing invitation to advocacy and experimentation. Pragmatism invites us, for example, to make the case, and test it by experiment, that to become an individual who does not eat meat (or to become a society that does not employ factory farming methods or harm animals in scientific research) will result in a richer and more inclusive way of life. It provides a framework for asserting that we have obligations to animals as a natural consequence of our interdependent existence on earth. It insists that this principle of obligation must be employed flexibly as a tool for intelligently analyzing and reconstructing existing social conditions, that it is best understood as an injunction to consider consequences broadly and impartially enough to include the interests of animals. It encourages us to turn away from theoretical attempts to establish, once and for all, the moral status of animals, and to concentrate our efforts instead on intelligently analyzing and reconstructing current social practices that harm animals. It emphasizes the importance of cultivating character—not merely as an individual responsibility, but as a social necessity—and so directs our attention to current practices that prevent us from cultivating a sympathetic sense of our interdependence with animals, such as factory farming methods that alienate farmers from their livestock, or marketing practices that alienate consumers from the animals whose flesh and by-products they consume.

Finally, pragmatism legitimizes the role our emotions play in informing each step in such processes of reflection and choice. It is in the context of this pragmatic mandate to explore and remake the moral consideration we grant animals that Emerson's and James's calls to cultivate a more sympathetic attention to alien aspects of experience find their fullest meaning for our treatment of animals.

Notes

1. See the "Idealism" and "Spirit" chapters of *Nature* (esp. 38–41), in which Emerson argues *for* an idealism that asserts the power of human thought to reshape matter, but rejects as "ungrateful" any idealism that questions the substantial value of nature or our physical and emotional connections to it:

> if it only deny the existence of matter, it does not satisfy the demands of the spirit. It leaves God out of me. It leaves me in the splendid labyrinth of my perceptions, to wander without end. . . . Nature is so pervaded with human life, that there is something of humanity in all, and in every particular. But this theory makes nature foreign to me, and does not account for that consanguinity which we acknowledge to it. (41)

2. For a brief discussion of how Emerson's essay "Fate" anticipates James's meliorism, see Albrecht, "The Sun Were Insipid" 144–48.

3. "For it is the inert effort of each thought, having formed itself into a circular wave of circumstance,—as, for instance, an empire, rules of an art, a local usage, a religious rite,—to heap itself on that ridge, and to solidify and hem in the life" (Emerson, "Circles" 404).

4. Emerson's analysis is primarily hortatory: he pragmatically asserts that the meaning of past events must lie in the use to which we can put them in our present, encouraging readers to adopt a healthy, if not audacious, confidence in appropriating the records and artifacts of past events as interpretive tools and symbols. For a cogent analysis of Emerson's hortatory purpose in "History," as well as of some of the paradoxes implicit in his appropriative or possessive theory of meaning, see Larson.

5. See, for example, the opening of "Fate," where Emerson says of the opposing facts of liberty and determination: "This is true, and that other is true. But our geometry cannot span these extreme points, and reconcile them" (943). Instead of arguing that the antagonistic truths of experience can be resolved in some new logical synthesis or generalization, Emerson advocates adopting an intellectual method that articulates and explores each partial perspective in turn: "By obeying each thought frankly, by harping, or, if you will, pounding on each string, we learn at last its power. By the same obedience to other thoughts, we learn theirs, and then comes some reasonable hope of harmonizing them" (943).

6. I am indebted to my colleague Joseph M. Thomas for calling my attention to this poem.

7. See James's letter of September 2, 1909, to W. C. Brownell, quoted in Perry 1:144. For a discussion of this letter in the context of James's overall assessment of Emerson's thought, see Albrecht, "What's the Use" 416–18.

8. For an excellent discussion of how James, in such passages, extends Emersonian attitudes, see Poirier 14–18, 47–48.

9. James argues that "ethics have as genuine and real a foothold in a universe where the highest consciousness is human, as in a universe where there is a God as well. 'The religion of humanity' affords a basis for ethics as well as theism does" ("Moral Philosopher" 619). However, in the essay James ultimately hedges on this naturalistic stance, arguing that a belief in God may be necessary to elicit the "strenuous mood"—to inspire the devoted action necessary to realize moral ends (627–29). Here James differs from Dewey, who contends in *A Common Faith* that the purely human significance of our strivings imbues them with a sufficiently ideal or "religious" character to inspire our most devoted efforts. From this Deweyan perspective, James's argument for the continuing necessity of a theological element in ethics appears as a form of tender-minded backsliding from a truly naturalistic pragmatism.

10. A brief summary of Singer's position is included in the final section of this essay. I do not mean to imply that James articulates anything as specific as the principle of equal consideration Singer advocates: that "the interests of every being affected by an action are to be taken into account and given the same weight as the like interests of any other being" (*Animal Liberation* 6).

11. For Regan's discussion of exceptional cases in which an animal's prima facie right not to be harmed is overridden by other interests, see 286–312.

12. For instance, Singer notes the bizarre implications of Regan's view that consequences must be barred from moral considerations, regardless of the magnitude of suffering or number of individuals involved. This leads Regan, in one of his exceptional cases where he acknowledges it is justified to sacrifice an animal life to preserve a human life—that of throwing a dog overboard from a lifeboat to save a human passenger—to conclude that it would be equally just to sacrifice a million dogs' lives to save that one human life. Singer notes the contradiction between this claim and Regan's insistence that it is categorically wrong to sacrifice "even one dog . . . in a lethal but painless experiment to save one or more human beings" ("Ten Years of Animal Liberation" 50).

13. Though *Ethics* was coauthored by Dewey and Tufts, in their preface they indicate their separate authorship of the different sections of the book. Dewey wrote part II, "Theory of the Moral Life," from which the material discussed above is taken (*Ethics* 7).

14. See note 17 below.

15. Phillip McReynold's essay in this volume offers a cogent analysis of how Dewey's concept of community—and hence moral standing—might be expanded beyond an exclusively human model of association enabled by linguistically shared meanings, to embrace a broader sense of "overlapping horizons of meaning that are founded in a nonlinguistic intercorporeality" (p. 63).

16. In "The Stream of Thought," James similarly emphasizes the centrality of character in ethical decisions: "in these critical ethical moments, what consciously *seems* to be in question is the complexion of the character itself. The problem with the man is less what act he shall now choose to do, than what being he shall now resolve to become" (73).

17. It is important to stress that when Dewey emphasizes the importance of indi-

vidual character, he is not arguing that morality is merely a matter of individual choice and transformation. Quite the opposite: he insists that cultivating individuality is a social concern that can only be achieved by social means. As Dewey argues in *Reconstruction in Philosophy,* "Individuality in a social and moral sense is something to be wrought out," and "social arrangements, laws, institutions" are not means of catering to the needs of already formed individuals, but are primarily "means of *creating* individuals" (191). To contend, as Dewey does, that because moral judgments are made by individuals, our "only guarantee" of ethical conduct is to cultivate "personal character" (*Ethics* 222), is not merely to demand individual initiative but also to assert that a community has a fundamental interest in cultivating the habits of ethical reflection and action in its individual members. Thus, Dewey's emphasis on character requires us to examine social conditions that either foster—or hinder—the habits of intelligent and sympathetic ethical reflection.

Bibliography

Albrecht, James. "'The Sun Were Insipid, If the Universe Were Not Opaque': The Ethics of Action, Power, and Belief in Emerson, Nietzsche, and James." *ESQ* 43 (1997): 113–58.

———. "What's the Use of Reading Emerson Pragmatically? The Example of William James." *Nineteenth-Century Prose* 30, nos. 1–2 (Spring–Fall 2003): 388–432.

Buell, Lawrence. *The Environmental Imagination: Thoreau, Nature Writing, and the Formation of American Culture.* Cambridge, Mass.: Harvard University Press, 1995.

Dewey, John. *A Common Faith. The Later Works,* vol. 9, *1933–1934,* 1–58.

———. "The Ethics of Animal Experimentation." In *The Later Works,* vol. 2, *1925–1927,* 98–103.

———. *Human Nature and Conduct. The Middle Works, 1899–1924,* edited by Jo Ann Boydston, vol. 14, *1922.* Carbondale: Southern Illinois University Press, 1988.

———. *The Later Works, 1925–1953.* Edited by Jo Ann Boydston. 17 vols. Carbondale: Southern Illinois University Press, 1981–90.

———. *Reconstruction in Philosophy. The Middle Works, 1899–1924,* edited by Jo Ann Boydston, vol. 12, *1920,* 77–201. 1982. Reprint, Carbondale: Southern Illinois University Press, 1988.

Dewey, John, and James Hayden Tufts. *Ethics. The Later Works,* vol. 7, *1932.*

Emerson, Ralph Waldo. "Circles." In *Essays and Lectures,* 401–14.

———. *Collected Poems and Translations.* New York: Library of America, 1994.

———. *Essays and Lectures.* New York: Library of America, 1983.

———. "Fate." In *Essays and Lectures,* 941–68.

———. "History." In *Essays and Lectures,* 235–56.

———. *Nature.* In *Essays and Lectures,* 5–49.

———. "Nature." In *Essays and Lectures,* 539–55.

———. "The Rule of Life." In *The Later Lectures of Ralph Waldo Emerson, 1843–1871,* edited by Ronald A. Bosco and Joel Myerson, 2:376–88. 2 vols. Athens: University of Georgia Press, 2001.

———. "Self-Reliance." In *Essays and Lectures,* 259–82.

———. "The Uses of Great Men." In *Essays and Lectures,* 615–32.

Goodman, Russell. *American Philosophy and the Romantic Tradition.* Cambridge: Cambridge University Press, 1990.

James, William. *The Letters of William James.* Edited by Henry James III. 2 vols. 1926. Reprint: New York: Kraus Reprint, 1969.

———. "The Moral Philosopher and the Moral Life." In *The Writings of William James,* 610–29.

———. "On a Certain Blindness in Human Beings." In *The Writings of William James,* 629–45.

———. "The Sentiment of Rationality." In *The Writings of William James,* 317–45.

———. "The Stream of Thought." In *The Writings of William James,* 21–74.

———. "What Makes a Life Significant." In *The Writings of William James,* 645–60.

———. "The Will to Believe." In *The Writings of William James,* 717–35.

———. *The Writings of William James: A Comprehensive Edition, Including an Annotated Bibliography Updated through 1977.* Edited by John J. McDermott. Chicago: University of Chicago Press, 1977.

Kateb, George. *Emerson and Self-Reliance.* Thousand Oaks, Calif.: Sage, 1995.

Larson, Kerry. "Individualism and the Place of Understanding in Emerson's Essays." *ELH* 68, no. 4 (Winter 2001): 991–1021.

Leopold, Aldo. "The Land Ethic." In *A Sand County Almanac, and Sketches Here and There,* 201–26. 1949. Reprint, New York: Oxford University Press, 1989.

Perry, Ralph Barton. *The Thought and Character of William James.* 2 vols. Boston: Little, Brown, 1936.

Poirier, Richard. *The Renewal of Literature: Emersonian Reflections.* New York: Random House, 1987.

Regan, Tom. *The Case for Animals Rights.* Berkeley: University of California Press, 1983.

Regan, Tom, and Peter Singer. "The Dog in the Lifeboat: An Exchange." *New York Review of Books,* April 25, 1985, 56–57.

Singer, Peter. *Animal Liberation: A New Ethic for Our Treatment of Animals.* New York: Avon Books, 1975.

———. "Animal Liberation or Animal Rights?" *The Monist* 70, no. 1 (January 1987): 3–14.

———. "Feminism and Vegetarianism: A Response." *Philosophy in the Contemporary World* 1, no. 3 (Fall 1994): 36–38.

———. "Ten Years of Animal Liberation." *New York Review of Books,* January 17, 1985, 46–52.

2   Dewey and Animal Ethics

Steven Fesmire

The Silence of Pragmatism

Animal ethics, which investigates the appropriate ethical relationship between humans and nonhuman animals, emerged in the 1970s as a response to the powerful impact of human practices on other species. As is true of environmental ethics more generally, this investigation has a significant bearing on how we understand ourselves and on what policies we will endorse. The field is dizzying in scope, encompassing topics as varied as animal experimentation, zoos, hunting, bushmeat, livestock agriculture, landscape sustainability, biodiversity, ecosystem management, ecological restoration, companion animals, diet, sabotage, the moral status of animals, animal suffering, animal mentality, biotechnology, and animal rights.

It is also a field ignored by most contemporary philosophers working in the classical pragmatist tradition. There are several reasons for this neglect. The pragmatist tradition, despite its empirical naturalism, has historically tended toward anthropocentrism both in its valuations and in its descriptions of the generic traits of existence (see appendixes 2-1 and 2-2). At the same time, because the analytic philosophers who dominate animal ethics draw from a tradition more explicitly concerned with discursive form than specific substantive content, they are at greater liberty to widen the sphere of moral considerability. Moreover, animal ethics has been dominated by utilitarians and Kantians, who hold monistic positions that strike classical pragmatists as flat. Quite simply, one who sidesteps a confrontation over the relative merits of the utilitarian maxim or practical imperative as supreme moral principles is not likely to quibble over anthropocentric versus sentientist variations of these principles. An unfortunate, though understandable, result is that pragmatism has been silent in one of the most conceptually rich and practically significant fields of contemporary ethics.

Pragmatism and Animal Ethics

From a pragmatic standpoint, particularly as inspired by John Dewey, ethics is the art of helping people to live richer, more responsive, and more emotionally engaged lives.[1] This art is a branch of pragmatic philosophy, understood as the interpretation, evaluation, criticism, and redirection of culture. Such an understanding is closer to Aristotle than to Kant, who approached ethics primarily as the rational justification of an inherited moral system. While advocating the guidance of principles, rules, moral images, and the like as a means to perceptive and responsible moral behavior, pragmatist ethics does not assume, prior to inquiry, that there is one "right thing to do" in moral situations. Nor does it provide a univocal principle or supreme concept to "correctly" resolve all ethical quandaries about right and wrong or to solve conflicts over values.

The word *theory* is derived from the Greek *theōrein*, "to behold," and a good theory enlarges and stimulates observations about how experience hangs together. All theories highlight and hide relevant moral factors, so they cannot finally resolve conundrums. Conundrums are resolved, at least at the level of practical policy, by the cooperation of individuals.[2] Nonetheless, resolutions are more trustworthy when those individuals approach conflicts over values with a toolbox of carefully honed theories, even in the absence of a "right" standpoint from which these theories can be seen as fully commensurable. Like Dewey's notoriously misunderstood educational theory, pragmatist ethics mediates between polarities of closed systems of ready-made principles, on the one hand, and offhanded recklessness, on the other hand. In pursuit of coordinated thinking, experimental intelligence, and imaginative forethought, the pragmatist in ethics steers between the Scylla of haphazard drifting and the Charybdis of pat solutions.

The central dogma of ethical theory is that it identifies a moral bedrock that tells us the right way to organize moral reflection. Moral skeptics accept this dogma, plausibly reject the possibility of discovering or erecting such a foundation, and hear the bell toll for ethics. Many self-described normative ethicists hear no such bell. They argue, or uncritically assume, that the fundamental fact of morality is our capacity to set aside our patchwork of customary beliefs in favor of moral laws, rules, or value rankings derived from one or more foundational principles or concepts. This is indeed an ineliminable assumption of ethics, moral skeptics rejoin, but sadly we all lack such a capacity.

A siren lure compels the hyperrationalist's quest for the grand theory or meta-ethical principle that will systematically unify, without sacrificing robustness, competing and seemingly incommensurable ethical theories. Yet in contemporary philosophical ethics there is a growing demand to reject unidimensional theories in favor of multiple considerations, a demand stemming in part from the past century's rejection of ahistorical matrices for values. But the plea by pluralists for multiple considerations arises primarily from honest attention to the complex textures and hues of moral life.[3] The apparent trajectory toward pluralism in ethics is far less visible in animal ethics, however.

On this meta-ethical quest for a nexus of commensurability, animal ethicists concur with some of their holistic critics in environmental ethics—for example, J. Baird Callicott, who regards animal ethics of the 1970s and 1980s as an ancestral form of nonanthropocentrism predating the ascendancy of a communal land ethic ("Introduction"). Callicott adopts a meta-ethical variation of one-size-fits-all monism, grounded in "the community concept." Monism, he argues, is the only alternative to the "intellectual equivalent of a multiple personality disorder": pluralism (*Beyond the Land Ethic* 175). The pluralist adopts an incoherent set of foundational ideas by "facilely becoming a utilitarian for this purpose, a deontologist for that, an Aristotelian for another, and so on" (172). I argue in this section that Callicott's description of pluralism is itself facile.

In "Three Independent Factors in Morals," Dewey presents a pragmatic pluralism that can ameliorate current debates. He argues that ethical theorists should cease asking which principle *or* concept is the ultimate and unifying one and should attempt instead to reconcile the inherent conflicts between irreducible factors that characterize all situations of moral uncertainty. He identifies three such factors that need to be coordinated: individual ends (the origin of consequentialist ethics), the demands of communal life (the origin of theories of duty and justice in deontological ethics), and social approbation (the principal factor in virtue theories).

The preference for three primary factors may be an aesthetic one for Dewey, and he knowingly exaggerates differences among the three ("Appendix 5: Three Independent Factors" 503). What is more interesting is his idea that moral philosophers have abstracted one or another factor of moral life—say, the community concept in the case of Callicott; amelioration of suffering, for Peter Singer (*Animal Liberation*); and inviolate subjectivity, for Tom Regan (*Defending Animal Rights*)—as central and then treated it as the foundation to which *all* moral justification is reducible. This tendency to reify moral factors explains why ethical theories are categorized according to their chosen bottom line.

Two theories have dominated the past twenty years of ethical reflection on animals. Peter Singer offers a utilitarian grounding for the principle of equality and then compellingly argues that to be rational and consistent, we must give equal consideration to relevantly similar interests of all sentient beings. Tom Regan objects that Singer misses the fundamental wrong, which is that we violate the rights of any subject of a life whenever we treat the being as a mere means to an end. Meanwhile, many environmental ethicists claim that both miss the forest for the trees, because both limit moral considerability to individuals and relegate the integrity and stability of ecosystems to a secondary, supporting role.

Each of these theories serves to streamline moral reflection. Our relationship with nonhuman animals is inherently ambiguous and conflict-ridden, so we need all the help we can get to make judgment more reasonable, less biased by what Dewey calls "the twisting, exaggerating and slighting tendency of passion and habit" (*Human Nature* 169). The practical imperative or utilitarian maxim, like Callicott's broader communitarian concept, serves moral life. In Dewey's words, such a conceptual tool provides a way of

> looking at and examining a particular question that comes up. It holds before him certain possible aspects of the act; it warns him against taking a short or partial view of the act. It economizes his thinking by supplying him with the main heads

by reference to which to consider the bearings of his desires and purposes; it guides him in his thinking by suggesting to him the important considerations for which he should be on the lookout. (Dewey and Tufts, *Ethics* [1932] 280)

For example, Tom Regan's neo-Kantian notion of animal rights—that it is disrespectful to treat any subject of a life simply as an instrument for others' satisfactions—has been taken by some as an inescapable indictment of anthropocentrism. Regan argues, "The fundamental wrong is the system that allows us to view animals as our resources, here for us, to be eaten, or surgically manipulated, or put in our cross hairs for sport or money" ("Case for Animal Rights" 14). Certainly the practical imperative summarizes a great deal of moral wisdom. Taken as a guiding hypothesis, it is a tool for perceiving the vagaries of moral situations. Although the tool was honed by Kant for use on human issues, our current scientific understanding of animal mentality renders obsolete the suggestion that there is nothing worth respecting in the interior lives of at least some other animals. Still, the pragmatist ethicist refuses to play the winner-take-all game. The practical imperative is a trusty tool but no more than a tool: it is valued and evaluated by the work it does and thus is subject to reworking.

For a taxonomy of some current approaches, consider the ethics of hunting. Because most ethical theories reduce all but one of the following questions to secondary status, they cannot *on their own* do justice to the ambiguity and complexity of situations. The ecocentrist helpfully asks, Is therapeutic culling of "management species" (especially ungulates such as deer or elk) ecologically obligatory, regardless of whether anyone desires to pull the trigger?[4] The biocentrist inquires, Is nonsubsistence hunting compatible with respecting an animal as a fellow "teleological center of life" pursuing its own evolved good? The virtue theorist wonders, What traits of character are cultivated by sport and trophy hunting, and do these contribute to the best shared life? Do humans have predatory instincts that are most healthily expressed through hunting? Is hunting essential to a healthy relationship with the land, as Aldo Leopold believed? The deontological rights theorist inquires, Do other animals have rights; that is, might their interests as we perceive them override any direct benefits they might offer humans as prey?[5] The feminist ethicist of care asks, Does hunting affect our ability to care for animals; indeed, are we genuinely capable of caring about beings with whom we have no sustained relationship? The utilitarian questions, Should all sentient animals' preferences or interests as we perceive them, including our own, have equal weight when we evaluate consequences? Can human preferences for hunting, if nonbasic, justifiably trump basic animal interests in life, liberty, and bodily integrity?

To spotlight only one of these pressing questions risks bringing ethical deliberation to a premature close. The moment when deliberation culminates in a resolutely formed plan of action always provides strong subjective reinforcement, which supplies a psychological motive to find a unifying ethical theory to do the job. But no practical ethicist wishes merely to taste the subjective satisfaction of theoretical tinkering. The aim is, or ought to be, to mediate objective difficulties in the lifeworld, not simply to "resolve" an ethical quandary in inner mental space. To achieve that aim requires a greater tolerance for suspense than monism typically affords. The pragmatic pluralist cultivates habits of swimming against a psychological current that propels us toward easy answers and quick solutions to complex problems.

This psychology of suspense and belief is captured by William James in his watershed essay "The Sentiment of Rationality." James argues that the whole point of rationality is the restoration of manageability to doubtful circumstances. Because this restoration culminates an uneasy process, it is marked by "a strong feeling of ease, peace, rest" (317). He dubs this state of resolution the rational sentiment, a telltale sign that fluid interaction has been restored. But this seemingly oxymoronic "rational sentiment" is not to be equated with truth. For *classical* pragmatism, to discern the *truth* (in its older sense of "trustworthiness") of a proposed course of action requires investigating what follows from acting on it. How will the world answer back? At the same time, the rational sentiment is felt *whenever* doubt is replaced with substantive belief.

In *How We Think,* Dewey takes this a step further. He argues that deliberation is "a kind of dramatic rehearsal. Were there only one suggestion popping up, we should undoubtedly adopt it at once." But when alternatives contend with one another as we forecast their probable outcomes, the ensuing tension sustains inquiry (200). Monistic ethical theory is too impatient to sustain the tension needed; it sacrifices nuanced perception in favor of theoretic clarity. Reliable moral knowledge, as Martha Nussbaum explains, entails "seeing a complex, concrete reality in a highly lucid and richly responsive way; it is taking in what is there, with imagination and feeling" (152). This is why pragmatic pluralism, which employs univocal ethical theories as directive hypotheses, marks a path toward *responsibility.* Responding to a situation's multiple factors is not analogous to a personality disorder; failing to do so because of an obsession with theoretical reductions should, however, give a psychologist pause.

To return to the issue of hunting: what is at issue is not exclusively a matter of establishing who has rights or of equally weighing human and animal preferences or of valuing the overall biotic community. Tunneled perception can inhibit deliberation at least as much as it helpfully focuses it. On the view that there are *plural* primary factors in situations, the role of moral philosophy shifts. It functions not to provide a bedrock but to clarify, interpret, evaluate, and redirect our natural and social interactions. Some may find these pluralistic conclusions, or their implications, unsatisfying. But the principal aim of ethics is the amelioration of perplexing situations, even at the cost of the ease, peace, and rest we feel when we sort out an internally consistent theory.

Pragmatism and Paleopragmatism

Our sense of who we are, how we understand other species, the way we relate to nonhuman nature, and what we see as possible policies depends significantly on our moral images of nature. Hilary Putnam implies that ethics is better served by exploring such tethering centers than by constrictive argumentation that is insensitive to what James calls the world's "relational mosaic" (Putnam 51). For example, it *matters* for deliberation if we conceive animals anthropocentrically: as resources (for human consumption or use), as property (commodities to be owned and sold), or as God's dominion (given to humans to subdue and rule over, or to steward wisely). It also matters if we conceive animals nonanthropocentrically, either as individuals with their own needs, feelings, and unique ways or as inseparable parts of ecosystemic wholes. Alternatives available under one model of animals or nature may not be available under another.[6]

This observation highlights a central difficulty in disjunctively framing the individualism-holism debate in environmental ethics: we cannot respond to what we do not perceive. "We grieve only for what we know," Leopold observes (52). We starve deliberation of the relations it needs when we exclude at the outset parts *or* wholes, individuals *or* systems—the "independent factors" of organic interaction—from our moral purview. These insights provide the ingredients for a Deweyan animal ethics, though the phrase appears oxymoronic, given Dewey's characterization of animals (see appendixes 2-1 and 2-2).[7]

After more than 3 billion years of organic evolution on Earth, creatures with extraordinary mental capacity emerged, sized things up, and projected their own mentality onto the cosmos as its necessary source, sustainer, and culmination. Having committed this hubris, they interpreted nonhuman animal nature as lacking the mentality that they had elevated to a godlike trait. Dewey takes us beyond the former conceit, but not the latter. Larry Hickman argues that for Dewey, "the principal difference between human beings and the rest of nature is not that there is no communication elsewhere than within human communities, but that human beings are unique in their ability to exercise control over their own habit-formation and therefore to alter in deliberate ways both the course of their own evolution and the evolution of their environing conditions" (51). This distinction is plausible and defensible. But contrary to Hickman's claim, Dewey *does* deny communication and all related capacities to other animals.[8]

On Dewey's "ground-map of the province of criticism" (*Experience and Nature* 309), sometimes referred to as his metaphysics, humans live alone on a third plateau (208), a field of interaction that includes all mental life and all individuating factors. Appendixes 2-1 and 2-2, which present Dewey's thoughts on animal mentality and on the three plateaus, reveal residual traces of philosophies Dewey elsewhere discredits, such as an echo of the hierarchical great chain of being (absent Aristotle's teleological anthropocentrism), as well as a vestige of Cartesianism in which animals are mindless automatons. The mind is embodied, but only human bodies have minds. Moreover, when demarcating the "human plane," Dewey's picture surprisingly recalls planes of freedom and necessity in Kant's metaphysics of morals. With regard to animals, it is difficult to distinguish Dewey's view from a philosophical orthodoxy that may be empirically as obsolete as Ptolemaic astronomy or Aristotelian biology, insofar as his is a Darwinian landscape with Cartesian blotches on the horizon. The irony of all of this from the pen of the most anti-Cartesian and radically empirical of philosophers is itself a powerful reminder of the inescapably cultural and historical nature of inquiry.

A focus on imagination is perhaps the best way to reveal what is redemptive in Dewey's model. He is calling us to actualize our humanity, to establish social and material conditions that liberate our energies from enslavement to mechanized habits toward a life of critical inquiry, social responsiveness, emotional engagement, and artful consummations. By repeatedly casting animals in the role of unintelligent and unemotional brutes ruled by the inertia of habit, he attempts to throw into relief the human potential: Aristotle's rational animal becomes Dewey's imaginative animal.

Dewey scholars have yet to look out of the corner of their eyes to scrutinize this part of Dewey's horizon. Yet to keep the vitality of pragmatism from ossifying into paleopragmatism, it is essential to disclose passively accepted beliefs that inhabit and shape the roots and edges of American philosophy. There is a pressing need to supplement and correct pragmatism's uncritical perpetuation of prejudices and to confront complex issues of how best to comport ourselves toward other species. To pretend that our second-order desires simply outrank their first-order needs is prejudice premised on a metaphysical or ethical caste system, not ethical reflection. The beauty of Dewey's naturalistic empiricism is that his own perspectives must be run through its threshing machine: "Only chaff goes, though perhaps the chaff had once been treasured. An empirical method which remains true to nature does not 'save'; it is not an insurance device nor a mechanical antiseptic. But it inspires the mind with courage and vitality to create new ideals and values in the face of the perplexities of a new world" (*Experience and Nature* 4).

Pragmatism and Vegetarianism

How might we interpret the behavior of the girl in figure 2.1? willful public ignorance of the source of our food? a child's innocence of our appropriate role in the cycle of life and death? humane sympathy prior to the emotional hardening of enculturation?

Some very general remarks about vegetarianism may give a better sense of the tone and texture of a pragmatic pluralist approach to animal ethics. As situational and contextual, pragmatist ethics is responsive to social, political, and environmental contexts of eating, including the redemptive value of some traditional practices. Pragmatism does not fall prey to possible biases in utilitarian and rights theories that, according to Kathryn Paxton George, take dietary access and requirements of middle-class males as physiological and cultural prototypes and regulate to a "moral underclass" infants and children, pregnant and lactating women, some elderly people, and members of nonindustrialized societies.

Figure 2.1. *National Geographic* 57, no. 3 (March 1930): 347. Photo by R. R. Sallows.

Robert Newton Peck explores the tensions thoughtful people feel about slaughtering animals in his widely read children's book *A Day No Pigs Would Die*. In this fictional coming-of-age story set in rural Vermont, a child (much like the little girl in figure 2.1) grapples with the fate of his pet pig being raised for slaughter. In doing what is to be done, he eventually leaves his childlike innocence behind and joins an adult world in which felt preferences do not always square with the daily demands of living. Upon reading the book, a dairy farmer in upstate New York said approvingly: "A boy grows up when he sees there's things in the world he's got to do, not just do the things he wants to do" (Lovenheim 136).

It is simply not possible to survive, even as a vegan or vegetarian, without killing sentient beings. A belief in such a possibility could be held only by someone who had never tilled and tended a garden. Moreover, one who regards sustainable living as a virtue should concede the organic agriculturalist's point that free-range livestock agriculture (fed on grass and by-products) can be part of, and in a cold climate like Vermont's may even be essential to, a sustainable landscape. A diet, more or less like my own semi-vegetarian one, that depends in part on hundreds of calories of fossil fuel to transport a few calories of soy product across the country is at least not the *only* way to go. Real problems like these admit of more than one responsible moral resolution.

"Sure, I understand the pain the pigs must go through when their tails get chopped off," a student recently wrote in response to reading a chapter from

Peter Singer's *Animal Liberation.* "And I understand the pain the chickens must go through when they are debeaked. However they weren't born for fun and games and to have a painless life. They were only born to feed millions of Americans. And if some pain is necessary for this then that is fine with me. Why should the pigs, cows, and chickens have space to roam and be comfortable? They were simply born to die for us."

Many would find this bald statement troubling, including most of the 96 percent of Americans who, according to a 2002 Time/CNN Poll, do not consider themselves to be vegetarians (Corliss). This uneasy response by meat eaters provides an emotional opening seized on by animal rights advocates, who correctly point out that modern industrial animal agriculture—now involving the slaughter of more than 10 billion animals each year in the United States—is premised on precisely this reduction of other animals to market commodities. They are conceived for and consumed by us.

Vegetarianism is one way to coherently express regard for nonhuman animals, but it is myopic to suppose this is the only way. To anyone not already caught in the orbit of ethical theorizing, what immediately stands out about the aforementioned student's remark is not its violation of an expanded practical imperative but its callous tone. His unquestioning subordination of other animals to human interests is ethically relevant, but secondary. The Talmudic story of Rabbi Judah makes the point:

> One day, the story goes, Rabbi Judah was sitting at a café in a small town when a wagon came by carrying a calf to the slaughterhouse. The calf cried out to Rabbi Judah for mercy, but the rabbi replied, "Go, for this you were created." For his callousness, God punished Rabbi Judah with a painful illness lasting seventeen years. Then one day, seeing his housekeeper about to sweep a weasel from the house, Rabbi Judah told the woman to treat the animal gently, and his illness ended. (Lovenheim 236)

The moral of the story, according to Talmudic scholars, is not that Rabbi Judah failed to save the calf but that the calf's fate should have elicited compassion rather than cold disregard (Lovenheim 236). The student's statement might be similarly interpreted.

This story indicates that it may be neither incoherent nor hypocritical to eat a turkey dinner or steak while responding with sincere moral concern when others exhibit callous attitudes toward livestock animals. But there *are* difficulties here, perhaps best disclosed by analytic argumentation. At least two hidden premises deserve mention:

1. A mature (dutiful, virtuous, beneficial, caring, respectful, or the like, depending on one's dominant ethical paradigm) ethical relationship between humans, other animals, and the rest of nonhuman nature *requires* (strong version) or *permits* (weak version) a system of production in which we breed, kill, and eat some of them.
2. Granting that callousness toward animal welfare is ethically problematic, emotional responsiveness toward animals can be *fully* exhibited

within customary consumption habits (i.e., while fully participating as a consumer in the commodification of animals—and workers—in industrial agribusiness).

Premise 2 seems sufficiently suspect to place the burden of ethical proof on the consumer, so I limit my brief remarks to premise 1.

Teleological anthropocentrism should be measured in half-lives, given its obstinacy as a habit of mind persisting through more scientific paradigm shifts than can be enumerated. It has, however, long disappeared from intellectually respectable circles, destroying forever any basis for an existential hierarchy of perfection and value. At least among most academics, Aristotle's remarks in the *Politics* (in the context of his justification of human slavery) now ring hollow: "Now if nature makes nothing incomplete, and nothing in vain, the inference must be that she has made all animals for the sake of man" (1256b).

At the same time, remnants of the medieval great chain of being pervade our intellectual habits and behaviors. As Dewey observed, moral progress has not kept pace with scientific advance. This is apparent in our treatment of other animals. When an evangelical Christian lobbyist in August 2001 urged President George W. Bush not to "reduce all human life to laboratory rats" by supporting stem cell research, he could safely assume that the moral considerability of rats was not at issue. In the House debate on therapeutic cloning that was front-page news prior to September 11, 2001, the conservative Representative Tom DeLay argued that therapeutic cloning "crosses a bright-line ethical boundary that should give all of us pause. This technique would reduce some human beings to the level of an industrial commodity" (DeLay). That is, it would place humans in the same category as animals, whose fluctuating worth is measured by prices fetched on economic markets. This should indeed give us pause, but unfortunately, DeLay's listeners are not likely to wonder whether his logic extends to other animals already so treated. That this hierarchy requires reasoned justification is obvious. It is equally obvious that such justification is seldom demanded, even among the millions who would regard Aristotle's comment quoted above as quaint.

Once crude forms of anthropocentrism are abandoned, at least two potentially defensible arguments for premise 1 are left. First, an ecocentric argument: As animals in trophic systems, we participate, whether or not we are vegetarians, in food chain cycles of life and death. We should not pretend to be "above nature." Thus, consuming other animals is at least permissible, and indeed conscious participation in this cycle may help us to cultivate an appropriately tragic sense of life. Proponents of this argument must, however, probe more deeply than an implicit appeal to entrenched customary views of what is "natural" for humans: The vegetarian gorilla participates in trophic systems no less than the omnivorous chimpanzee, and we do not suggest that the gorilla is above nature. Second, a popular organic agriculturalist argument: If we value a sustainable, working landscape that renews rather than depletes the soil, and if we seek a viable local food-source alternative to the environmental and social disaster of much industrial agribusiness, grass-fed livestock agriculture can, or must, play an integral part. However, given the limited availability and greater expense of such meat, the consistent organic agriculturalist may practice a mostly vegetarian diet. On both arguments, it is tragic that animals will die for us, but consuming them does not logically entail cold disregard.

Dewey-Inspired Resources for Animal Ethics

I have underscored Dewey-inspired pragmatism's virtue as a pluralistic yet nonrelativistic framework within which to *listen* to and incorporate the insights of divergent theoretical perspectives. There is no univocal "pragmatic stance on animal ethics," nor does Dewey offer much in the way of specific guidelines for deliberation in cases in which conflicting goods of humans, animals, and ecosystems must be prioritized. He would have left such conflicts to democratic colloquy. Nonetheless, pragmatism has several additional resources to offer animal ethics.

1. Dewey carries out a radical redescription of moral inquiry that lays bare underappreciated deliberative capacities, chief among which is imagination. And he makes a compelling case for an artistic-aesthetic ideal of moral perceptiveness and responsiveness.[9]
2. Like contemporary biocentrists, the classical pragmatists took our shared ancestry with nonhumans seriously. *Human,* after Darwin, is an adjective for our specific animal nature, not the pinnacle of a hierarchy of final causes or something sui generis.
3. Dewey's "democratic ideal" is a resource to further develop what Bryan Norton and Andrew Light have articulated as a pragmatic method of policy convergence (see Light and Katz). When interests conflict, the democratic way of life elicits differences and gives them a hearing instead of sacrificing them on the altar of preconceived biases. This approach taps into our imaginative capacity to stretch perception beyond the environment we immediately sense. A democratic imagination opens up an expansive field of contact with which to flexibly interact so that goods are enjoyed rather than repressed and so that difficulties can be treated comprehensively instead of in isolation. This "greater diversity of stimuli" (Dewey, *Democracy and Education* 93) opened by imagination expands the sense of exigencies struggling for recognition. Integrative values may emerge to reconstruct and harmonize conflicting desires and appraisals. A democratic imagination— which may also operate as an *ecological* imagination—enables policy decisions to be made in richly responsible colloquy among advocates for competing values.[10]

Pragmatism values democratic colloquy over soliloquy. In contrast, in Singer's engaging and aptly titled *Ethics into Action,* the theorist discerns the ethical thing to do, then urges activists to turn up the rhetoric to get it done. The problem is that one may "do the right thing" at the price of ignoring what does not fit one's preestablished trajectory. Democratic inquiry is the best check on this suspect assumption of epistemic privilege. Thus pragmatism engenders a democratic method of policy convergence that sidesteps theoretical debates of the winner-take-all variety and strives for amelioration rather than definitive solutions.

4. Dewey's concept of "natural piety," set forth in *A Common Faith*, can be reconstructed as a virtue exhibited by those who realize that parts of nonhuman nature are looking back at them with awareness and emotion. Unreconstructed, Dewey's virtue falls short of a "full percep-tual realization" (*Art as Experience* 182) of the lifeworld in which we are part. An incomplete piety would suffer, in John McDermott's words, from "relation deprivation." Without a deep perception of the kinship and differences between ourselves and other animals, reverence toward nature is severely limited. What ensues may be a pseudo-piety in which the ways of other species are uncritically subordinated to our own along pathways set by conventional morality.

   Reconstructed, natural piety is a trait of character that contributes to the best lifeworld. It is not quite identical to Albert Schweitzer's biocentric reverence-for-life (though the two concepts share a certain vagueness) since it extends beyond living organisms to the greater "imaginative totality we call the Universe" (*Common Faith* 14). Deweyan natural piety does not idealize nature à la Rousseau, overly romanticize, or otherwise fail to extricate itself from assumptions of a providential natural order.

5. The starting point is the *problem*. The pragmatist in ethics does not simply deduce, on the basis of prior conclusions, how to respond to an issue at hand. Toolbox of principles in hand, the pragmatic pluralist attends to situational factors overlooked by theorists of other orienta-tions.

6. In mainstream environmental and animal ethics, the starting point is to determine who or what has *moral standing*. This approach aids prioritization when values conflict, but it ironically conceives the domain of the "moral" too *narrowly*. As Mary Midgley explores in *Animals and Why They Matter*, empathy develops with use. As a trait of character, empathy diminishes when switched on and off as each candidate's credentials for moral status is scrutinized. If a certain type of biological organism does not have "feelings of well-being" or is not a "subject of a life," then according to Singer or Regan it is not a candi-date for moral consideration or cross-species empathy. This stance res-cues theories of animal liberation or animal rights from the absurdity of extending rights ad infinitum, and it focuses attention on beings whose interests have hitherto been thought irrelevant. But it also places blinders on moral perception. Squashing an insect is an act with *some*

moral bearing. On a related note, democratic inquiry is best served by giving a pink slip to some environmental ethicists who are attempting to detail *precisely* how to prioritize competing goods among humans, animals, and ecosystems.

Many additional resources of pragmatic pluralism could likewise be explored. It is committed to a self-correcting fallibilism; it acknowledges the genuineness of moral conflicts, dilemmas, and tragedy; it eschews "mysterious" notions of "inherent value," rightly criticized by Mary Anne Warren; and it recognizes the aesthetic as a nonsubjective factor in moral choice.

Anthropocentric Conclusion

Some environmental and animal ethicists dismiss all anthropocentrism with casual disdain, despite their awareness of how rarely moral life embraces humanity. These ethicists risk trading in one form of obtuseness for another. To the degree that we are morally educable, the ancients rightly perceived that we must cultivate traits of character that contribute to our flourishing as social beings. An environmental or animal ethic that marginalizes our social environment is irresponsible. Still, the teleology of the ancients is no longer tenable, and it served to subjugate slaves to masters, women to men, and of course nonhuman nature to humans. The persistent attempt in ethics to exclude nonhumans from moral consideration has lost its credibility.

We cannot logically exclude any form of cruelty or needless subjugation from our moral framework. This is no less true if our primary commitment is to ameliorate our own plight. If our treatment of those who are vulnerable and dependent may be taken as a test for our values, then there is, to paraphrase John Steinbeck, a failure that topples all our success exhibited by our treatment of disadvantaged humans *and* animals.

Building on Dewey's pragmatic pluralism, animal ethicists need not drive a wedge between anthropocentrism and nonanthropocentrism. The arch-anthropocentrist Kant, in his way, was right to observe that our treatment of other animals has a bearing on our treatment of each other. Kant thought we only had duties "regarding" animals, none directly "to" animals. But if it became commonplace in moral education to (nonanthropocentrically) expand our sphere of care to include direct concern for other animals and nonhuman nature, this expansion would (anthropocentrically) supplement, reinforce, and render more rationally coherent our exertions to deal with the atrocities we commit against each other. It would also make us better planetary stewards for future generations, enrich our lives, fuel our sympathetic capacities, and cultivate a much-needed humility to replace our sadly entrenched vanity.

Appendix 2-1. Dewey on Animal Mentality

1. *Consciousness.* The most comprehensive ethological critique of the categorical claim that nonhuman animals are "passive reflex devices" is Donald Griffin's *Animal Minds.* Griffin helpfully distinguishes "perceptual" from "reflective consciousness." The former includes all awareness (such as memory, anticipation, choice, means-end thinking, etc.), while the latter is a subset in which "the content is conscious experience itself" (8). According to Dewey, both (not only the latter, as may be justified) are restricted to humans. Humans have "goods," which are conditioned by thought, while all other animals have "pleasures," which are accidental (*Human Nature* 146). In all nonhumans, responses are simply released by environmental conditions.

2. *Social Communication, Language, Thought.* Dewey believed only humans to be capable of social communication. Communication is possible because of language/speech, and it is a prerequisite for both thought and imagination. In Dewey's words, "If we had not talked with others and they with us, we should never talk to and with ourselves": "Through speech a person dramatically identifies himself with potential acts and deeds" (*Experience and Nature* 135). "Thought," Mead adds, "is but an inner conversation" ("The Social Self" 146). The upshot for animals of defining language narrowly as verbal speech is wittily captured in Dewey's quip: To claim that "lower animals, animals without language" are thinking beings is analogous to claiming a forked branch is a plow (*Experience and Nature* 215). Work on apes and aquatic mammals suggests a need to reinterpret this rich human-centered model of communication (e.g., see Fouts and Mills, or Cavalieri and Singer).

3. *Culture.* "[W]ith human beings, cultural conditions replace strictly physical ones" (*Freedom and Culture* 78). In *Freedom and Culture,* Dewey helpfully identifies at least six chief factors of culture (79): (1) law and politics, (2) industry and commerce, (3) science and technology, (4) the arts of expression and communication, (5) "morals, or the values men prize and the ways in which they evaluate them," and (6) social philosophy, "the system of general ideas used by men to justify and to criticize the fundamental conditions under which they live." In *The Evolution of Culture in Animals,* John Bonner offers a more inclusive definition now used in ethological studies, such as widely publicized work on chimpanzees and orangutans: "Certain kinds of information can only be transmitted by behavioral means. If the transmission of this kind of information is adaptive, then there would be a strong selection pressure for culture" (183). For a sustained criticism of the claim "that survival tactics [in nonhumans] must be hard-wired and instinctive" (19) rather than cultural, see Frans de Waal. On chimpanzee culture, see Gretchen Vogel; on orangutan culture, Carel van Schaik et al.

4. *Emotion.* Dewey contrasts "emotion" with blind discharges of "animal passion" (*Middle Works [MW]* 10:282, "Fiat Justitia, Ruat Coelum"; cf. *Art as Experience* 68). Emotion enables humans to experience pain as more than "blind, formless" (*Early Works [EW]* 5:361, review of H. M. Stanley's *Studies in the Evolutionary Psychology of Feeling;* cf. 362–67). Lacking emotions, animals do not anticipate the future or remember the past. Because their experience is not situated in an ongoing narrative, the animal parallel of human pain involves "simply a shock of interrupted activity" (*EW* 4:179; cf. 183–85, "The Theory of Emotion"). Ahead of the curve of a priorist scientific dogma for the century to come, in the 1890s Dewey derided as "unduly anthropomorphic" any attempt to claim an analogy between animal stimulus-response and human emotional experi-

ence. Animals *act* afraid, angry, and the like, but they lack the imaginative perception of past and future requisite to calling their experience emotional. It is instead inflexibly habitual (*EW* 5:364, review of Stanley; *Art as Experience* 276). (A historical parallel is Descartes's famous thought experiment, in the *Discourse on Method,* about a machine that mimics human behaviors.) Animals therefore are exempt from any sort of aesthetic experience, which for Dewey requires a unifying emotional quality from tensive beginning through consummation (*Art as Experience* 42–43; cf. *MW* 10:321–24, "Introduction to *Essays in Experimental Logic*"). For a contemporary discussion of animal emotions, see Masson and McCarthy.

5. *Imagination, Deliberation, Dramatic Rehearsal.* Animal pleasures and pains are accidental, for Dewey, caused by chance evolutionary hardwiring. Natural selection has geared animals for immediately satisfied instinct, "very much like a machine" (*Later Works [LW]* 17:258, "Periods of Growth"). Dewey is here observing chickens, but he goes on to generalize about all nonhuman animals. Animal pain gives rise to "blind, formless movements" useful by evolutionary chance, not choice. Implicitly echoing Descartes's praise of the providential order of animal "clockwork," Dewey asserts that an animal's sheer organizational mechanisms are perfected to deal with crises without "the additional problem of pain to wrestle with" (*EW* 5:361, review of Stanley). Animal action is immediate and overt, in contrast with what is found in humans: indirect imaginative forethought and experimental probing sparked by the tension of disrupted habits. Thus, for instance, there is nothing "on the animal plane" analogous to love. Nonhumans pursue the "physiologically normal end" of sex without any sort of redirection of impulses—such as in humans results in poetry—into other channels (*Art as Experience* 83).

Only with humans are "means-consequences tried out in advance [in imagination] without the organism getting irretrievably involved in physical consequences." Animal actions are "fully geared to extero-ceptor and muscular activities" and hence immediately translate into overt rather than indirect behavior (*Experience and Nature* 221). In 1939, Dewey wrote of "distinctively human behavior, that, namely, which is influenced by emotion and desire in the framing of means and ends; for desire, having ends-in-view, and hence involving valuations, is the characteristic that marks off human from nonhuman behavior" (*Theory of Valuation* 250; cf. *LW* 17:256–58, "Periods of Growth"; *Experience and Nature* 221; *MW* 10:282, "Fiat Justitia, Ruat Coelum"). On this model, other animals appear to be utterly outside the realm of moral agents *or* patients. This view played a role in Dewey's unqualified confidence that "scientific men are under definite obligation to experiment upon animals" (*LW* 2:98, "Ethics of Animal Experimentation"; cf. *LW* 13:333, "Unity of the Human Being").

Appendix 2-2. Dewey's Three Plateaus

All three "planes" or "plateaus" below involve the "interaction of a living being with an environment" (*Art as Experience* 276). Because "the human animal is a *human* animal" (Dewey and Tufts, *Ethics* [1908] 335), operations of the higher include the lower, but not vice versa. Here, as with Peirce's doctrine of synechism, there are no ontological barriers to continuity between human and other forms of life, though of course developmental constraints in the other direction exist. For Dewey, these are descriptive categories for "fields of interaction"; unlike Aristotle's parallel categories, they do *not* support a fundamental ontology, hierarchy of final causes, or fixed teleology of any sort. Thus he fully understands that this categorization is fallible and revisable in light of new evidence (such as that available today). He says of the categories: "They stick to empirical facts noting and denoting characteristic qualities and consequences peculiar to various levels of interaction" (*Experience and Nature* 208).

III. The Human Plane (Aristotle: Thinking)

The "third plateau" (*Experience and Nature* 208) is the "highest" field of interaction, of art, science, morality, and religious life. It is the object of social sciences.

Mind is "the body of organized meanings by means of which events of the present have significance for us" (*Art as Experience* 276). This property is added to *and* incorporates the animal plane.

The primary relationship of the human plane is *means-consequence,* "responding to things in their meanings" (*Experience and Nature* 278). Experience does not merely end; it is consummated and fulfilled, perhaps superficially and hastily, but better artfully and perceptively. Only humans are "conscious of meanings" or have ideas.

Human goods are conditioned by thought. Unless we are subsisting on an animal plane (e.g., attacking someone as a reflex response), human goods are deliberate. Our instincts are directed through foresight of consequences.

The human capacity for learning, growth, stems from sociocultural interdependence and the fact that meanings enter "that are derived from prior experiences" (*Art as Experience* 276). Growth is a social, not physical, gift (*Democracy and Education* 48).

The human field of interaction includes conscious experience; freedom, culture; education (vs. mere mechanical "training"—see *LW* 2:359, *The Public and Its Problems; Ethics* [1908] 190; *How We Think* 130); desire, effort, hope; valuation; creative intelligence (reason), memory, deliberation; reflective imagination; emotion; artistic-aesthetic experience; "objects, or things-with-meanings" (*Experience and Nature* 278); planning, constructing, means-end relationship, ends-in-view, purposes; variation, progress; language, communication; sympathy; individuality; temporality (narrative perception of past-present-future).

II. The Animal Plane (Aristotle: Appetitive/Sensitive)

The second plateau is a "lower" physical field of interaction. This plateau of brute animal nature may be dubbed "psycho-physical, but not 'mental,' that is, not aware of meanings" (*Experience and Nature* 198). It is literally the "state of nature": an object of the physical sciences (*Theory of Valuation* 229).

The primary relationship of the animal plane is *cause-effect.* Animal bodies, driven by necessity, are pushed appetitively to "a mere end, a last and closing term of arrest"

(*Experience and Nature* 278). There is no perception of past and future, thus no control of means, no intelligence.

This is the level of sense and brute feeling, but not of emotion. Other animals *have* feelings, "but they do not know they have them" (*Experience and Nature* 198). Consciousness is a prerequisite for emotional life, and animals are not conscious. Lacking mind, animal behaviors that we take to be pain or grief or loving attachment are reflex responses. These reflexes are well suited to survival, but they are blind.

Behavior on the animal plane is determined by instinct pushed by unthinking appetite. Driven by the inertia of habit and impulse, nonhuman animal life is marked by mechanical recurrence and uniformity.

Nonetheless, the appropriate ethical relationship toward this plane is *not* simply to view it as a means to human ends. Such narrow anthropocentrism would entail impiety toward nature. The virtue of "natural piety" rests "on a just sense of nature as the whole of which we are parts, while it also recognizes that we are parts that are marked by intelligence and purpose" (*Common Faith* 18).

I. The Vegetative Plane (Aristotle: Nutritive)

The vegetative plane is a strictly physical field of interaction. It encompasses life, but no feeling. See *Experience and Nature* 198, 200.

Notes

I am grateful to students in my spring 2003 "Animal Ethics" course at Green Mountain College for their sincere intellectual engagement with these perplexing issues. I am also grateful to Indiana University Press for permission to use, in substantially revised form, some material from my book, *John Dewey and Moral Imagination: Pragmatism in Ethics* (Bloomington: Indiana University Press, 2003).

1. The pragmatist conception of ethics is discussed in my *John Dewey and Moral Imagination*. For a helpful overview of Dewey's ethics that takes stock of recent scholarship, see Pappas.

2. Callicott, in *Beyond the Land Ethic*, takes an opposing view.

3. On pluralism and animal ethics, see, for example, Sorabji.

4. Varner provides a noteworthy treatment of obligatory management of ungulates.

5. See Wise's case for limited legal rights for some animals, based on levels of cognitive autonomy.

6. See Lakoff's analysis of liberal and conservative metaphors for nature in *Moral Politics*.

7. Given that one can be a "Nietzschean feminist," perhaps the idea of a Deweyan animal ethicist will not stretch credulity.

8. Moreover, Dewey's approach to defining key concepts of mentality may be too narrow. As the primatologist Frans de Waal observes, we historically have defined terms such as *communication* and *culture* in an anthropocentric way that excludes other beings in advance of empirical scrutiny. Analogously, if we derive the meaning of *flying* from a songbird's flight, then chickens cannot fly. Yet chickens do take wing and, to the annoyance of farmers, end up perched in tree limbs.

9. My *John Dewey and Moral Imagination* explores these themes.

10. The most comprehensive study of Dewey's democratic credo is Westbrook's acclaimed biography, *John Dewey and American Democracy.* Also see Eldridge, with a response by Westbrook, "Democratic Faith." For an upbeat study of the potential for Deweyan democracy in a multicultural setting, see Green.

Bibliography

Aristotle. *The Politics.* Edited by Stephen Everson. Cambridge: Cambridge University Press, 1988.

Bonner, John. *The Evolution of Culture in Animals.* Princeton: Princeton University Press, 1980.

Callicott, J. Baird. *Beyond the Land Ethic.* Albany: State University of New York Press, 1999.

———. Introduction to *Environmental Philosophy,* edited by Michael Zimmerman et al., 7–16. 3rd ed. Upper Saddle River, N.J.: Prentice Hall, 2001.

Cavalieri, Paola, and Peter Singer, eds. *The Great Ape Project.* New York: St. Martin's Press, 1993.

Corliss, Richard. "Should We All Be Vegetarians?" *Time,* July 15, 2002, 56.

Delay, Tom. "Majority Whip DeLay Floor Statement Opposing Cloning." http://tomdelay.com/html/prelease.cfm?release_id=150 (accessed October 2003).

Dewey, John. "Appendix 5: Three Independent Factors in Morals." In *The Later Works,* vol. 5, *1929–1930,* 496–503.

———. *Art as Experience. The Later Works,* vol. 10, *1934.*

———. *A Common Faith.* In *The Later Works,* vol. 9, *1933–1934,* 1–58.

———. *Democracy and Education. The Middle Works,* vol. 9, *1916.*

———. *The Early Works, 1882–1898.* Edited by Jo Ann Boydston. 5 vols. Carbondale: Southern Illinois University Press, 1967–72.

———. *Experience and Nature. The Later Works,* vol. 1, *1925.*

———. *Freedom and Culture.* In *The Later Works,* vol. 13, *1938–1939,* 63–188.

———. *How We Think. The Later Works,* vol. 8, *1933.*

———. *Human Nature and Conduct. The Middle Works,* vol. 14, *1922.*

———. *The Later Works, 1925–1953.* Edited by Jo Ann Boydston. 17 vols. Carbondale: Southern Illinois University Press, 1981–90.

———. *The Middle Works, 1899–1924.* Edited by Jo Ann Boydston. 15 vols. Carbondale: Southern Illinois University Press, 1976–83.

———. *Theory of Valuation.* In *The Later Works,* vol. 13, *1938–1939,* 189–251.

———. "Three Independent Factors in Morals." In *The Later Works,* vol. 5, *1929–1930,* 279–88.

Dewey, John, and James Hayden Tufts. *Ethics* [1908]. *The Middle Works,* vol. 5, *Ethics, 1908.*

———. *Ethics* [1932]. *The Later Works, 1925–1953,* vol. 7, *1932.*

Eldridge, Michael. "Dewey's Faith in Democracy as Shared Experience." *Transactions of the Charles S. Peirce Society* 32, no. 1 (1996): 11–30.

Fesmire, Steven. *John Dewey and Moral Imagination: Pragmatism in Ethics.* Bloomington: Indiana University Press, 2003.

Fouts, Roger, and Stephen Tukel Mills. *Next of Kin: My Conversations with Chimpanzees.* New York: Avon Books, 1997.

George, Kathryn Paxton. *Animal, Vegetable, or Woman? A Feminist Critique of Ethical Vegetarianism.* Albany: State University of New York Press, 2000.

Green, Judith. *Deep Democracy: Community, Diversity, and Transformation.* Lanham, Md.: Rowman and Littlefield, 1999.

Griffin, Donald. *Animal Minds.* Chicago: University of Chicago Press, 2000.

Hickman, Larry. "Nature as Culture." In *Environmental Pragmatism*, edited by Andrew Light and Eric Katz, 50–72. London: Routledge, 1996.

James, William. "The Sentiment of Rationality." In *The Writings of William James: A Comprehensive Edition, Including an Annotated Bibliography Updated through 1977*, edited by John J. McDermott, 317–45. Chicago: University of Chicago Press, 1977.

Johnson, Mark. *The Body in the Mind.* Chicago: University of Chicago Press, 1987.

———. *Moral Imagination.* Chicago: University of Chicago Press, 1993.

Lakoff, George. *Moral Politics.* Chicago: University of Chicago Press, 1996.

Leopold, Aldo. *A Sand County Almanac, with Essays on Conservation from Round River.* 1949. Reprint, San Francisco: Sierra Club; New York: Ballantine Books, 1970.

Light, Andrew, and Eric Katz, eds. *Environmental Pragmatism.* London: Routledge, 1996.

Lovenheim, Peter. *Portrait of a Burger as a Young Calf.* New York: Harmony Books, 2002.

Masson, Jeffrey Moussaieff, and Susan McCarthy. *When Elephants Weep: The Emotional Lives of Animals.* New York: Dell, 1995.

Mead, George Herbert. "The Social Self." In *Selected Writings*, edited by Andrew Reck, 142–49. Chicago: University of Chicago Press, 1964.

Midgley, Mary. *Animals and Why They Matter.* Athens: University of Georgia Press, 1984.

Nussbaum, Martha. *Love's Knowledge.* Oxford: Oxford University Press, 1990.

Pappas, Gregory F. "Dewey's Ethics: Morality as Experience." In *Reading Dewey*, edited by Larry Hickman, 100–123. Bloomington: Indiana University Press, 1998.

Peck, Robert Newton. *A Day No Pigs Would Die.* New York: Random House, 1994.

Putnam, Hilary. *The Many Faces of Realism.* Chicago: Open Court, 1987.

Regan, Tom. "The Case for Animal Rights." In *In Defense of Animals*, edited by Peter Singer, 13–26. New York: Perennial Library, 1986.

———. *Defending Animal Rights.* Urbana: University of Illinois Press, 2001.

Singer, Peter. *Animal Liberation.* Rev. ed. New York: Avon Books, 1990.

———. *Ethics into Action.* Lanham, Md.: Rowman and Littlefield, 1998.

Sorabji, Richard. *Animal Minds and Human Morals.* Ithaca, N.Y.: Cornell University Press, 1993.

Van Schaik, Carel P., Marc Ancrenaz, Gwendolyn Borgen, Birute Galdikas, Cheryl D. Knott, Ian Singleton, Akira Suzuki, Sri Suci Utami, and Michelle Merrill. "Orangutan Cultures and the Evolution of Material Culture." *Science* 299 (2003): 102–105.

Varner, Gary. "Can Animal Rights Activists Be Environmentalists?" In *In Nature's Interests? Interests, Animal Rights, and Environmental Ethics*, 98–120. Oxford: Oxford University Press, 1998.

Vogel, Gretchen. "Chimps in the Wild Show Stirrings of Culture." *Science* 284 (1999): 2070–73.

Waal, Frans de. *The Ape and the Sushi Master.* New York: Basic Books, 2001.

Warren, Mary Anne. "A Critique of Regan's Animal Rights Theory." In *Environmental Ethics*, edited by Louis Pojman, 46–51. Mountain View, Calif.: Mayfield Publishing, 2000.

Westbrook, Robert. "Democratic Faith: A Response to Michael Eldridge." *Transactions of the Charles S. Peirce Society* 32, no. 1 (1996): 31–40.

———. *John Dewey and American Democracy.* Ithaca, N.Y.: Cornell University Press, 1991.
Wise, Steven. *Drawing the Line: Science and the Case for Animal Rights.* Cambridge, Mass.: Perseus Books, 2002.

3 Overlapping Horizons of Meaning: A Deweyan Approach to the Moral Standing of Nonhuman Animals

Phillip McReynolds

In this essay I examine the question of the moral standing of nonhuman animals from a pragmatic point of view. Rather than assuming that there is some abstract trait that confers moral standing, as do most approaches, I examine the context in which moral concepts are used and locate their basis in some form of community. I explore John Dewey's insight that community, communication, and commonality are related but find, with Beth Singer, that Dewey's understanding of these concepts is too limited and colored by his normative stance. Specifically, Dewey's notion of communication and inference are overly linguistic, and his analysis of community does not do justice to the presence of conflict in sociality. I propose, starting from a pragmatic account of habit and action, that sociality, and therefore moral standing, is based on overlapping horizons of meaning that are founded in a nonlinguistic intercorporeality. Finally, I argue that when overlapping horizons of meaning are present, sociality is possible. Sociality becomes actual as we negotiate with other beings in the context of forming, maintaining, and modifying webs of common and mutual dependencies. Moral standing is implicit in such social negotiations. Moreover, in light of our mutual and common dependencies, we would do best to explicitly acknowledge the moral standing of nonhuman animals and take more care with our relations to them than we currently do.

* * *

Modern approaches to the question of the moral standing of nonhuman animals have generally relied on what I call *the extension model of moral standing*. An extension model begins with the assumption that there is some essential trait, feature, or characteristic that a being must have in order to have moral standing. For example, such a model might begin by accepting the Kantian claim that one must be a rational being in order to have moral standing. The task then is to sort beings as subject to moral claims or not by identifying in them the presence or absence of this distinctively moral trait. Thus, at least part of the interest in studying animal intelligence derives from the quest to determine whether nonhuman animals have a sufficient amount of reason to count as moral agents or patients, assuming in this case that reason is *the* distinctively moral trait.[1] Under the extension model, the identity of the distinctively moral trait remains controversial. In addition to reason, the ability to feel pain and the ability to be "the subject of a life" have been suggested as likely candidates (by Peter Singer and Tom Regan, respectively).[2] Thus, what I am calling the extension model begins with the following schema: trait T is the essential trait for moral standing. If being B possesses T (in sufficient amounts or degrees), B has moral standing. If being B lacks T, B lacks moral standing.

This approach to moral standing exhibits a peculiar pattern of historical development. No matter which morally relevant trait is chosen, this trait is first observed as a quality not of all human beings as such, but of only a particular subset of human beings. Genuine rationality was initially attributed not to all human beings but only to human beings of a particular sort: for example, Greek, male citizens of a particular social status and breeding. Moral standing is understood as applying to this group, allegedly in virtue of their unique possession of the morally relevant trait. Later, as more people gain political power and are able to demand that they be treated as moral agents and patients, the procedure of testing them for trait T is applied and (typically) members of the new group are found to have the trait and therefore are justified in being attributed moral standing. In this way, women, non-Europeans, and children, though first denied moral standing because they were thought to lack the morally relevant trait, had moral standing *extended* to them once the trait had been identified in sufficient numbers of individuals.

Given this pattern of development, one might wonder whether the morally relevant trait test might not be an act of misdirection—that is, whether the point of the "test" is really to deny moral standing to a group to whom it would be inconvenient to grant it. In this situation, the test would serve merely as a casuistic exercise to lend philosophical respectability to what is a political fait accompli. The role of the trait-based sorting procedure would be merely to provide cover initially for denying and later extending moral standing, when convenient, to particular groups.

We need not resort to a conspiracy theory to observe that this historical pattern points to a significant structural feature of the extension model. Under the extension model, moral standing is generally attributed first to the people doing moral philosophy, is referred to characteristics among them that they prize and see as distinctive in themselves, and is later, only reluctantly, extended to others who appear sufficiently similar to the initial group, based on that similarity.[3] Thus, the structural feature: whenever moral standing is *extended to* a new group, it is granted to the new group *to the extent of and on the basis of their similarity to* members of the old group.

There are two problems with formulating moral standing in terms of similarity to the initial group. First, it is unclear that the initial group has any special claim to morality, and thus the selection of the ideal group and the essential trait of that group, which is conceived of as necessary for moral standing is, if not arbitrary, highly prejudicial. That any given trait is taken as distinctive of a group and prized by them is no evidence of its connection with moral standing. Rationality, intelligence, and subjectivity have all been highly valued by "Western Man," who has been considered (by "Western Man") as the paradigm of morality, but these traits may not have anything at all to do with morality as such.

Second, because our abilities develop in order that we may be better adapted to particular and different forms of life, abstract qualities such as rationality, intelligence, and even subjectivity are extremely difficult to compare. Mary Midgley makes this point with reference to intelligence: "Artists and scientists, farmers, grandmothers, children, engineers, civil servants, Eskimos, and explorers constantly overlook the evidence of one another's intelligence because they are looking for it in the wrong places. . . . Does every intelligent creature have to do things of which we can see the point and show its intelligence in ways which we can recognize?" (157). The question applies with equal force to the other traits that have been regarded as essential for moral standing. While the selection of the morally relevant trait (by us) says a lot about what we tend to value, it does not necessarily tell us anything about value in general; nor does it constitute a proper test for moral standing, because difference is almost inevitably conceived as a failure to measure up. Thus the new groups to whom moral standing has been extended tend to participate in an inferior or "honorary" way in moral life.[4]

* * *

But if the search for essential traits that are necessary and sufficient to have moral standing is ruled out on these grounds, with what are we left to decide cases in which moral standing is in question? The pragmatic approach to problems is to begin with experience. Real problems do not arise out of the blue. They are always situated within a context that provides the frame for the problem, and the clues to its solution (Dewey, *Logic* 110–12). Thus, a pragmatist approaches the problem by asking the question, "What do we know about the moral life from its practice, from our lived experience of it?"

It might be objected that "beginning with experience," which is necessarily "our" experience, is no better than the extension model, which begins with "our" prized characteristics and then attempts to find them in others. It appears that pragmatism, in beginning with "our experience," assumes a "we" (and hence a community) that is no less privileged than that of the extension model. The situation might be slightly improved by its owning up to its biases more explicitly, but pragmatism would still seem to be subject to the same charges (e.g., sexism, Eurocentrism, anthropocentrism) as the extension model.

While this line of criticism raises important questions about the constitution of community, and while pragmatists have sometimes passed too lightly over the question of whose experience counts and the systematic omission of the experience of some classes of persons as a starting point of inquiry, the fact is that we must begin with where we are, from our limited, interested, and biased positions in the world.[5] As dependent creatures of limited intelligence, we have no other choice. This is one of the fundamental insights of pragmatism. Another fundamental insight of pragmatism is that our situatedness is not an obstacle to achieving knowledge but is the very condition of its possibility. We are not disembodied Cartesian cogitos—wholly detached minds—that must find a way out of our epistemological and normative solipsisms. We are not separated from the world by our bodies and interests. Rather, our bodies and interests constitute our connection to the world. This response is necessarily abstract and tentative, but I will have more to say about this question later, in the context of developing the notion of overlapping horizons of meaning. For now, it is sufficient to note that for pragmatists, because problems emerge in the contexts of lived situations, it is to those lived situations that we must look for the solution to the problems. In the context of the moral life, that lived situation is one of associated living.

If we want to learn anything about moral standing, we must characterize the situations in which morality appears. If we understand morality as a natural development in the history of culture, we must ask the following questions: How has morality evolved? What can we learn about the nature of morality by examining its emergence in the context of cultural development? What forms of life are present when we encounter distinctively moral concepts and behaviors?

What we find when we ask these questions is that *ethics is at the same time a product of and condition for communal life.* Ethics and communities have co-evolved because it is not possible to have one without the other. No search for timeless, essential traits will help us to determine who has moral standing, because we are never in a position simply to define, identify, and apply moral categories in the abstract. Moral standing, like community membership, is always a product of negotiation and is never solved once and for all.[6] *Moral standing* is a philosophical term of art for referring to the constantly shifting answers that we give to such practical questions as, How should I treat this person with whom I must deal in order to survive and flourish? What is their relation to me? What interests do we have in common? What demands is this person (or others) likely to make upon me? How do others treat or regard this person? What roles do we play in one another's lives, not only in getting along but in making those lives meaningful?[7]

In short, *moral* is an adjective that refers to a dimension of highly complex communal relations within which we always already find ourselves. I do not mean to suggest by this that we are never confronted by situations in which the moral standing of another being is in doubt. Such a question is, after all, the topic of this essay. I am arguing, however, that philosophers have tended to address this problem in the wrong way. Rather than beginning with moral experience in which community is always implicit and constitutive,[8] they have tended to find or define some property of individuals that is distinctively moral completely divorced from the only context that could give meanings to moral categories. The task is then to figure out how to "build up" a community and "social morality" from these atomic constituents.[9]

By contrast, pragmatist approaches to ethics do not begin with the extension model of moral standing and its associated search for an abstract set of characteristics that can be established independently and that would allegedly guarantee moral standing. Pragmatic ethical inquiry starts rather with the recognition of the fact that we live together in common. *Moral standing is possible and has meaning only in the context of a community.* One has moral standing in virtue of being a member of a community.[10]

*　*　*

To approach ethics and therefore questions involving moral standing pragmatically is to begin with community. But, as already observed, *community* is not, itself, a philosophically unproblematic concept. What does it mean to be in community, and what sorts of communal relations are required to give meaning and force to moral concepts, claims, and standing?

The pragmatist philosopher John Dewey observed that the meaning of *community* is tightly bound up with that of *communication* and *commonality*: "There is more than a verbal tie between the words common, community, and communication. Men [*sic*] live in a community in virtue of the things which they have in common; and communication is the way in which they come to possess things in common. What they must have in common in order to form a community or society are aims, beliefs, aspirations, knowledge—a common understanding—like-mindedness as the sociologists say" (*Democracy and Education* 7).

Dewey contrasts communication and communal relations to the "purely mechanical" coordination of, for example, machine parts or, according to Dewey, organic but nonhuman collective behavior. This nonmechanical coordination defines community in terms of the meanings of mutual and conjoint activities. Such associated behavior involves the recognition or discovery of (1) the connection between one's own actions and certain specific consequences (foresight or intelligence), (2) the implications of one's actions for the ends of others and vice versa, and (3) the mutual adjustment of actions in view of desired consequences.

Thus, for Dewey, common interest is the defining feature of community in both its descriptive and normative senses. Yet interests and therefore community membership are not fixed and pregiven. It is not sufficient merely to have similar interests. To have a community, our interests must be *made common*, and to discover and create common interests is the function of communication. Recognizing, unifying, relating, and communicating common interest is identified by Dewey as the ongoing task of community. Discovering our mutual interests and making them mutual through communication—in short, ethics— is the telos of community.

In contrast with approaches to ethics that are construed as reasoning about and a search for a transcendent good, ethics in a pragmatic vein is simply inquiry that aims at constructing the common good. This notion of constructing the good might seem paradoxical if one assumes, first, that the objects of knowledge exist independently of the activity of knowing and, second, that our ability to measure them necessarily depends on some guide outside, above, or beyond our practices. Pragmatists tend to deny both propositions and in this way have reached conclusions similar to those of Spinoza, on the one hand, and recent empirical inquiries in science studies, on the other.[11]

Inquiry is very much an activity, a practice; as such, its objects are not pre-existent but must be brought into being as objects of knowledge by inquirers. All sorts of objects of knowledge—scientific, technical, political, and ethical—are literally made by inquirers, according to Dewey. However, the fact that scientific and moral facts are *made* by humans does not imply that they are "made up."[12] In the search for common interests, we must (re)weave a natural-social reality, a process that involves ascertaining present natural and social conditions —our present interests and habits and their conditions and consequences—and, based on and in the process of this determination, deciding how best to adjust, modify, and strengthen the various relationships among interests to achieve harmony, stability, and fecundity. In this way, inquiry into the common good is an act of both discovery and creativity. It is an act of discovery because the possibility of being in a community with one another requires that our interests share some common conditions of fulfillment. In other words, there must be some discoverable networks of relations in order for interests to be constructed in the first place.[13] It is an act of creativity because inquiry is a process in which our initial interests, the networks of relations in which we find ourselves embedded "at the outset," are transformed through mutual acts of understanding and thereby made common, which is not the same thing as identical.[14] A community is not a fixed thing. It is a process more than it is a product; and, against the transcendence view, the questions of "What is the good?" and "Who constitutes the community?" can never be decided once and for all, because they amount to different ways of putting the same question.[15]

This pragmatic approach to ethics effects a much-needed reorientation of ethics and moral standing. Ethics is no longer grounded in transcendence nor viewed as a separate realm of meaning. It is, rather, construed as the business of defining and achieving common goods.[16] It is a question of investigation, communication, and negotiation. Moral standing is a matter of being relatable by, to, and in this process.

Yet such statements are all too abstract. As important as this pragmatic reorientation of ethics from the "up there" of transcendence and the "in there" of abstract properties is, we have not yet answered the crucial questions. Whose interests must be taken into account in this process of ethical inquiry, and how are they to count? If moral standing is a question of membership in some form of community, we must determine what it takes to count as a community member.

Though he maintained that *community* is an evolving concept and an ongoing project, Dewey had some very definite opinions about the starting point of the project. According to Dewey, only human beings count as members of the moral community, because only human beings are capable of having goods in common in the sense outlined above. Because communication is the key to community, and because he thought that human beings and only human beings can engage in genuine communication, Dewey believed that only they were capable of participating in genuinely social relations. Thus, for Dewey, only human beings have moral standing.

Dewey's account of communication involves a strong distinction between merely organic behavior and linguistic behavior, the latter being the essence of communication (*Logic* 49–51). Moreover, for Dewey linguistic behavior involves a sort of immanent transcendence that is a question of *judging*, or being able to understand the meaning of a situation—a form of behavior that he thought animals incapable of. "Merely organic" behavior is a function of the particular relationship obtaining between an individual organism and its immediate environment. In *Knowing and the Known* he refers to this coordination as "signing behavior." When a dog sees a rabbit's ear, the ear is the *sign* of the rabbit in the sense that the seeing of the rabbit's ear is involved in an ongoing organism-environmental coordination that ends up with the dog chasing the rabbit (Dewey with Bentley 139–40). The dog does not see the rabbit ear and *judge* "rabbit." Rather, the rabbit ear acts as a sign for the dog because this is how dogs, rabbit ears, and their common environment are set up.

By contrast, according to Dewey, when Robinson Crusoe sees the footprint on the island, what results is not merely *signing* but *linguistic* behavior. It involves more than seeing the footprint and responding according to a previously established organism-environment-habit complex. It is a case of seeing the footprint *as* the presence of someone else. Crusoe transcends the temporality of his specific situation in the act of *judging* the presence of a possibly dangerous stranger:

> Organic behavior is a strictly temporal affair. But when behavior is intellectually formulated, in respect both to general ways of behavior and the special environing conditions in which they operate, propositions result and the terms of a proposition do not sustain a temporal relation to one another. It was a temporal event when someone landed on Robinson Crusoe's island. It was a temporal event when Crusoe found the footprint on the sands. It was a temporal event when Crusoe inferred the presence of a possibly dangerous stranger. But while the proposition was about something temporal, the relation of the observed fact as evidential to the inference drawn from it is non-temporal. The same holds of every logical relation in and of propositions. (*Logic* 50–51)

This nontemporal transcendence is not the importation of some mysterious, extra-organic phenomena. It is merely the ability to bring to presence something that is not currently present.[17] In calling judgment linguistic, Dewey does not mean that Crusoe is talking to himself (or anyone else). Because "language" for Dewey covers any behavior that makes something that is absent present, it includes talking, toolmaking, and inferencing (*Logic* 51–52). In this way, Dewey deploys an account of language that does not involve the importation of occult entities to explain a gap between mind and world. The unique core of language is not mental but the ability to relate entities that are remote from one another in space, time, or both, an ability that enables us to function more effectively in the world. This embodied intellectual behavior is for Dewey the mark that distinguishes communication from mechanical coordination.

According to Dewey, linguistic behavior is the basis for all culture and human sociality—that is, the possibility of community: "For man is social in another sense than the bee and ant, since his activities are encompassed in an environment that is culturally transmitted, so that what man does and how he acts, is determined not by organic structure and physical heredity alone but by the influence of cultural heredity, embedded in traditions, institutions, customs and the purposes and beliefs they both carry and inspire" (*Logic* 49). It is this claim—human beings possess culture and animals do not—that leads Dewey to conclude that nonhuman animals are not part of the moral community and that, for example, it is acceptable (in fact obligatory) to experiment on them. Whereas both nonhuman animals and humans experience physical pain, only human beings can signify to themselves something that is absent—that is, can understand the *meaning* of a situation. Thus, because only human beings are capable of experiencing socially mediated pain, "Instead of being the question of animal physical pain against human physical pain, it is the question of a certain amount of physical suffering to animals . . . against the bonds and relations which hold people together in society, against the conditions of social vigor and vitality, against the deepest of shocks and interferences to human love and service" ("Ethics of Animal Experimentation" 100). For Dewey, humans and nonhuman animals do not have the same moral standing because the latter are incapable of having common interests, in the relevant way. Nonhuman animals aren't members of our community nor do they even inhabit communities of their own, because they cannot communicate, they cannot judge situations, and they are therefore incapable of seeing their interests *as* common.

* * *

What is the status of these claims about the relative abilities of animals and humans? As already pointed out, judging the presence, absence, or quality of some abstract characteristic such as intelligence or the ability to make judgments is notoriously difficult, even among humans. Surely Dewey had good reasons for drawing such strong distinctions between the human and the nonhuman regarding the question of community. It turns out that he did: but when we examine those reasons we will find that they tell us more about Dewey's views about what is right and wrong with human society than about the moral standing of nonhuman animals. To understand and evaluate Dewey's remarks we must approach the task of interpretation pragmatically, that is, by attending to his dominant metaphors and their relation to the context of his remarks.

First, it is important to note that when Dewey remarks on distinctively human abilities and actions he nearly always contrasts them with superficially similar but "mechanical" ways of doing things. Moreover, the "mechanical" is associated with the animal, either animals themselves or the "animal side" of human nature.[18] Second, we must attend to what Dewey does not say: he does not claim that human relations are always or even often genuinely social in the sense of involving active (not routine) judgments about common goods. That human relations and conduct are far too often merely mechanical and "brutish" is one of Dewey's most frequent refrains. In fact, generally when Dewey distinguishes community from other forms of sociality, intelligence from routine, and the human from the merely mechanical or animal, he is keen to emphasize the need for better (more creative, interesting, genuinely communicative) relations among human beings, especially in the context of living and working conditions in a newly industrialized world. The point here is that he was interested in drawing the distinction not so much in order to say anything about the specific abilities or qualities of machines or animals as to point out a deficiency in the realization of human capacities under current social arrangements. Thus, the mechanical and the animal serve as oppositional metaphors in Dewey's work, not necessarily signifying purely by themselves but providing a handy contrast to what he viewed as more ideal conditions of human association. When understood in this context, Dewey's ambiguity in distinguishing normative (honorific) and descriptive senses of community, communication, intelligence, and judgment becomes evident, resulting in definitions of these concepts that are far too narrow to account for the forms they take in human life.

In "Dewey's Concept of Community: A Critique," Beth Singer argues that Dewey conflated the descriptive and honorific senses of community, reduced the former to the latter, and "allowed his metaphysical position to be excessively influenced by his normative stance"; she states that "the same bias colors some of his empirical judgments," including those he makes regarding nonhuman animals.[19] Specifically, Singer claims that two of Dewey's conditions for community, the having of common interests and the direct coordination of actions in view of the meanings of the actions of others, are absent in many forms of human association that we, nonetheless, must call communal or social. For example, Singer points out that rather than having a common aim, people competing for the same job have mutually exclusive aims and yet their relations are clearly social and they form a sort of community. Similarly, combatants in warfare clearly coordinate their behavior in view of shared meanings and constitute a sort of community insofar as they are in conflict with one another (B. Singer 560–61).

Like kinship and marriage relations, traditional warfare is an activity of reciprocal coordination that, despite its obvious physical component, functions almost exclusively on a symbolic level. It is hard to find a field of human endeavor that is more symbolically mediated—from the honor accorded one's enemy, countless songs of war, the pride of the nation, and lines of armies on the field to the very serious games of war practiced by Native Americans who in many cases intended not to kill or even to wound anything more than the pride of the opponent (see Stannard). Even in the case of contemporary "total war," the killing of soldiers or civilians is neither sufficient nor intended to bring about victory by "sheer force." Rather, the goal is *to communicate* to the other side the futility of resistance and to demonstrate one's (or one's nation's) material and moral superiority.[20] Thus, even in this most bellicose form of reciprocal coordination, communication and a degree of commonality are essential to the very meaning of the enterprise.

Dewey defines commonality and the achievement of shared meanings as distinctively human in order to praise them and to point out the lack of humanity in present social conditions. Despite his pragmatic commitments to continuity, Dewey uses the language of division between the human and the nonhuman (e.g., human and animal; human and mechanical) to call attention to a promise inherent in Enlightenment humanism that is in danger of being betrayed.[21] Thus, the animal and the mechanical (as perhaps the "primitive" or "savage") function as points of contrast that Dewey uses to criticize contemporary society. In this way, Dewey is well within the tradition of humanism that begins with Renaissance thinkers like Giovanni Pico della Mirandola, who felt it necessary to lower the status of nonhuman animals and inanimate things in order to proclaim and elevate the dignity of humanity.[22]

Beth Singer also argues that Dewey has an impoverished, specifically overly linguistic, conception of judgment—an observation worth developing, as it points the way to more genuinely pragmatic conceptions of interests, commonality, and meaning that can help us to understand just in what way we and other animals are related. Singer calls attention to the overly linguistic character of Dewey's concepts of communication and judgment by noting that many of our putatively nonlinguistic actions involve a mutual coordination in view of meanings. For example, when two people dance, the body of each calls forth an active response from the other. Although she does not use this term, Singer appears to be indicating the dialogical character of many of our interactions, not only with one another but with the world. A situation calls out to me and demands a response. Like the dancer's constant adjustment, my reply is not mechanical—it is not a function of stimulus and response. Rather, I must interpret the situation and respond accordingly. Moreover, even though this active response is not linguistic, it is an instance of signing behavior. The situation constitutes a sign and my action constitutes the meaning of that sign.[23] On this view, the actions of even nonhuman animals are not mere mechanical reflexes but are interpretive responses to their situation, reflecting a form of judgment requiring appraisal.

In order to capture the precise nature of shared and active response that is the basis of communication, Singer introduces the notion of a *perspectival community,* which she defines as "a sphere of potential communication." By perspective, she intends not a "subjective viewpoint," "mental attitude," or "intellectual outlook." Rather, she defines it as "a framework of behaviors, dispositions, habits, attitudes, values, ideas, or understandings (or any combination of these) with which one approaches a given situation or situations of a given sort" (B. Singer 568). She writes that all human activity (including judgment) presupposes and reflects a perspective.

In Singer's use of the term, entities share perspectives to the extent that they share, among other things, "behaviors, dispositions, or habits" (B. Singer 568). A perspective is not, according to Singer's usage, a subjective attitude or an intellectual stand or orientation. Instead, consistent with the pragmatic challenge to subject/object dualisms, a perspective can be understood as an organic response in light of the relationship between an organism and its environment. She observes that entities "who are affected in similar ways by comparable factors in their lives come to share perspectives" (568).

Singer also notes that the individual organisms that constitute a perspectival community need not be in direct or even indirect contact with one another, because their sharing of perspectives is a function of how they tend to interpret the meaning of a situation; such interpretation is in turn a function of their mode of life rather than of an ability to communicate about that situation. Such perspectival communities must be possible in the absence of direct or indirect communication because perspectival community is what makes communication possible and is the basic form of sociality.

One major advantage of Singer's notion of a perspectival community is that it clears up an ambiguity in Dewey's thought. Whereas Dewey supposed that communication is a necessary condition for community, Singer argues that the reverse is true: communication presupposes a perspectival community of some sort. In order to share meanings and signs, one must first share a common framework within which to judge jointly (B. Singer 568). According to Dewey, community and communication mutually implicate one another, and, if anything, communication is necessary for the achievement of community; according to Singer, a perspectival community is the condition for communication, which is required to achieve community in the more honorific sense of that term—that is, a social group that is organized around a unity of purpose and welfare. Singer's concept of a perspectival community is intended to explain just what sort of community renders communication possible and to distinguish this from community in its honorific sense, which can only be the product of certain forms of communication. We share a perspectival community by virtue of not common interests but of common habits, which enable (in fact require) us to interpret situations in similar ways.

As helpful as Singer's analysis is, her concept of perspectival community suffers from several difficulties; they present themselves with particular clarity when we try to use the concept to gain insight on the question of moral standing, both in general and particularly as it pertains to nonhuman animals. First, although her notion avoids the more honorific senses of community that are problematic in Dewey's account, it is unclear how a perspectival community is a community in our ordinary understandings of the word. At least one of its ordinary meanings—that associated with a small town—shows that the perspectival community is clearly too narrow, since strangers and foreigners have moral standing, even as strangers and foreigners (in fact, we may have special obligations to them because of their status). Moreover, despite her attempts to use the term in a novel way, *community* still seems to imply more or less direct interaction (though possibly mediated by distance) rather than possession of similar sets of habits.

Second, while Singer's account is an improvement over Dewey's in that it leaves more room for conflict, it does not adequately take account of the social as a field of negotiation. Being involved with others socially is not merely a question of mutual coordinations of behavior. Social relations involve enlisting others in one's projects, being enlisted, and attempting to keep one another in line. Moral standing is a general concept for one's position that is at the same time constantly being modified by these shifting arrangements. Moral standing is not something that is merely assigned. Rather, as a general form of social status, *it is negotiated,* and *negotiation is part of its very meaning.* It is a general term of basic social status that is constantly being negotiated with, by, and on behalf of others. This is simply another way of saying that moral standing occurs within networks of social relations that are fluid, not static. Although we often speak of negotiation in relation to all sorts of heterogeneous objects (we negotiate with our boss for a raise, but we might also negotiate a curve in the road), social negotiations occur only among certain types of entities—those that have common habits.

As Dewey pointed out, the having of a habit is a function not merely of an organism but of a relation between the organism and its environment. A network of habits constitutes a field of action, mutually implicating the organism and its surroundings. An environment is not simply a place. It is that set of features of the world (including other organisms) that responds to and provides the meaning for the capacities of the organism. For reasons I will explain in a moment, we might think of this habit-environment relation that determines the meaning of situations as a *horizon of meaning.* Entities that have similar habits and that consequently respond to the world in similar ways can be thought of as having *overlapping horizons of meaning.* Thus, to return to the previous discussion regarding sociality and negotiation, my claim is that *social negotiations occur only among entities that have overlapping horizons of meaning.* Sharing a horizon of meaning is required for an association to be social at the most basic level of sociality.

Recalling Beth Singer's argument, we must not interpret "meaning" in an overly intellectualistic, linguistic, or subjectivistic sense. If we view actions as "active judgments," following Justus Buchler, "an act is not a mechanical reflex but an appraisive or interpretive response to the circumstance that elicits it" (B. Singer 566). In other words, as the product of selective emphasis, a situation constitutes a sign; the active response *elicited* in an organism by that situation constitutes the meaning of that sign.[24] What meaning a situation has for an organism is a function of its habits, behaviors, or dispositions. Insofar as two entities share habits, behaviors, or dispositions, they will interpret a situation similarly.[25] The situation will have the same meaning for them and the entities can be said to inhabit the same horizon of meaning.[26]

In my view, the concept of a horizon of meaning is an improvement over that of a perspectival community in at least three respects. First of all, despite the best intentions, Singer runs into the same problem that Dewey encountered in his attempts to reform the language by using ordinary terms in extraordinary ways. A perspectival community is so far from being a community in our ordinary use of the word that perhaps another term could avoid continued confusion. Second, despite Singer's attempts to de-emphasize the intellectual and subjectivistic connotations of the term, *perspective* means "point of view"; thus, our commonality is a question of our subjective take on the world rather than our common integrative responses to similar states of affairs. Part of the problem stems from the explicit visual metaphor that operates in the term. Admittedly, *horizon* is also visual, but here I intend its phenomenological sense; that is, the boundary of a field of action that surrounds us. A horizon is that which bounds our sense of space, and what it encompasses is a function of where we stand. Whereas in order to share a perspective we have to be standing in the same place and looking in the same direction, we can share overlapping horizons if the horizons that surround and encompass each of us happen to include the same territory. Practically, this means that we have overlapping horizons of meaning not because of any sort of identity that we experience but because we have some of the same habits, which call forth similar interpretations of specific situations.

A third advantage of horizon over perspective is that the concept of a horizon always indicates a "more." Whereas a perspective suggests that the landscape is dominated completely by the gaze, a horizon calls attention to that which is beyond our view. We might move our horizons (by changing our habits), but we can never transcend them. Though the same territory may be bounded by our overlapping horizons, my attention to my horizon as a boundary indicates that there is always a beyond that will never be subordinated to my gaze. In the field of social relations, what lies beyond my horizon is the other. But rather than being necessarily separated or alienated by our horizons, we are joined by them to the extent that they overlap.

Sharing a horizon of meaning is the barest condition for sociality because it constitutes the basis for understanding. We need not agree with one another or share one another's goals, but our interpretations of a situation must be minimally commensurate for our relationship to be social. This relationship is not yet communication, nor do we constitute a community in the fullest sense of that term; but having overlapping horizons of meaning is the condition of communication, which is the condition of community in its normative sense. Entities that share a horizon of meaning can and typically do treat each other differently than entities that do not share a horizon of meaning. You may be more or less indifferent to me, we may be in conflict with one another, or one of us may be actively seeking to manipulate the other as a resource, but if I suspect that a situation has the same or similar meanings for you as it has for me, that commonality becomes the basis for social negotiation. In fact, I must take into account the meaning that a situation has for you if I am to act effectively in the world. This necessity arises for two reasons. First, "force" just as much as "reason" is a negotiation strategy that relies on meaning for its effectiveness. Second, if we do share a horizon of meaning, we are both embedded in the same networks of dependencies, and effective action in the world occurs not in the agent as a result of the agent's "motive force" but as a function of negotiating one's network of dependencies.[27] I use the term *negotiation* because neither of us is in the position to simply decide what the situation or our relationship amounts to *tout court*. I use the term *social* because our relationship is mediated, or rather constituted, by shared meanings.

Once entities enter into social negotiations with one another, moral standing enters the field of play. To use traditional philosophical language, I no longer treat you as a "mere object" but relate to you in terms of your "subjectivity." This language is highly problematic, though, which is why I have articulated a behavioral notion of horizon of meanings. Other language that I might have used, but is also very misleading because of its ambiguity, is that of "interests." In one sense, treating other beings as having interests is to acknowledge their moral standing. However, something can be in my interests without my realizing it, and we then must deal with the problem of the recognition of interest, which also returns us to the infertile soil of subject/object language, a field that has been so scarred by philosophical battle that it is best to look for new ground.[28]

Taking account of the common territory bounded by our horizons of meaning —that is, acknowledging the moral standing of another individual—is a mode of behavior; it is a stance in social negotiations. This acknowledgment may be explicit or implicit. Consider the case of slavery. Although deplorable, and by no means a model for social conduct, the relationship between master and slave is nevertheless a social relationship. Nearly every interaction between master and slave is conducted on the level of meanings, based on a shared horizon of meaning, even those that appear to be the most "physical." If the threat of deprivation of food and water is used to motivate labor, it is because both master and slave share an understanding of the meaning of food and water, owing to a shared repertoire of behaviors. To negotiate with one another on the basis of shared meanings is to accord one another moral standing, at least implicitly. To be sure, the slave is explicitly denied anything but the most basic social status, but negotiations occur on the assumption of a basic moral standing and, often, in hopes of improving one's social situation.[29]

Organisms share horizons of meaning to the extent that they share behaviors. All animals share a number of basic behaviors (e.g., respiration, locomotion, excretion, secretion), and mammals in particular share a large number of behaviors. Although we seldom attend to it, we rely on this shared repertoire and the associated common horizon of meaning when we interact with other animals, and they with us. When training a dog, a person can use food to get the dog to behave in certain ways rather than others, not because of some internal motive force of the food but because of the meaning of food for the dog, a meaning that we share. By the same token, it is because we inhabit the same horizon of meaning that the dog will beg for food in hopes of receiving it. In both cases, though we may deny it explicitly, we take the moral standing of the other for granted implicitly in our appeals to one another as fellow interpreters. I chose food as an example, because despite its being the most "physical" of things, it still operates on the level of meaning between organisms that share common behaviors.[30] I might as easily have referred to the role that shame and other more abstract concepts play in animal training, or to the use of the highly abstract concept of *enemy* in social negotiations with attack dogs. Moreover, such implicit moral standing is not confined to animals with which we share explicit and acknowledged social relations. The hunter relies on the interpretation that his or her prey will make of whatever bait is offered in order to practice hunting more effectively.

* * *

The question remains, if my analysis of the meaning and import of moral standing is correct, concerning what, if anything, it compels us or prevents us from doing to and with our fellow perspectival community members. Can we eat nonhuman animals? Can we experiment on them? Must we seek their permission before we use them as pets or enlist their aid in agriculture? While my account does not offer any definitive answers to these questions, it does suggest a transformation of our relationships that might ensue if we were to take it seriously.

We share horizons of meaning with all sorts of other beings. This commonality exists in virtue of common behaviors being embedded in common chains of dependencies. Although we implicitly accord moral standing to many nonhuman animals, we do not always take seriously the implications of that standing and the demand for communication that it entails. If we wish to be true to our own interests, interests that are irrevocably linked with those of our fellow creatures, it behooves us to learn to communicate better with them, and not only on human terms. A nonanthropocentric model of moral standing that is based in networks of social negotiations and that takes account of conflict is a necessary first step toward communicating with our fellow inhabits of our planet. Although a common horizon of meaning is the condition of realizing that goal, and points to the efficacy of making better attempts to communicate, it is not sufficient to bring about such communication.

Communication among human beings is difficult enough across differences of race, class, and language. How much more difficult might interspecies communication be? It would be absurd to hold that just because we do not presently communicate with other beings that we ought not to attend to their moral standing and try to communicate with them. Genuine communication is always a challenge. Projection is as much of a problem as indifference. We can never inhabit the perspective of the other; and to think that one has done so, no matter how good one's intentions, is often an obstacle to communication. We can, however, come to better understand one another by better taking account of our position. To inhabit a horizon of meaning is to be embedded in a specific set of dependencies with other entities. We can understand others by noting how we are related in these networks of dependencies. To inhabit a horizon of meaning is also to have a specific set of habits. Horizons are not fixed; though we cannot transcend them, they move with us. Our horizons are mobile. That our horizons do not currently overlap with those of certain other entities does not mean that they never will. We move our horizons by taking up different habits. Communicating with others involves expanding our horizons.

Since communication involves the identification of common interests, it means starting where we are to determine what interests we and other nonhuman animals might share (this is the subject matter of ecology and related fields). But it also involves learning to listen. The trouble with the extension model is that it defines moral standing as essentially human from the outset. Morality is from the outset understood *in human terms*. To communicate genuinely means to open oneself to the other. One cannot communicate genuinely while insisting that the transaction occur solely on one's own terms. Much work on animal intelligence has been geared toward recognizing specifically human intelligence and forms in animals. Animals get to be a member of the club by being *like* us. A pragmatic approach based on overlapping horizons of meaning avoids this anthropocentrism by insisting on the plurality of interests and attending to the conditions of genuine communication. Just like any other relationship, learning to communicate genuinely with other members of the natural community requires a venture on our part.

In short, my claim is that moral standing is a natural feature of our social relations with others. Where there is a basic level of sociality, which is determined by inhabiting the same horizon of meaning, there is, at least implicitly, an acknowledgment of moral standing. Although we do not explicitly acknowledge the moral standing of others, we make use of it in the context of social negotiations. This relational notion of moral standing that is based in the concept of social negotiations has two benefits over other accounts that rely on an extension model. First, it is truer to our actual practices. Moral standing refers not to a single, immutable concept but to a range of social positions from which negotiations occur. If this were not the case, the fact of liberatory struggles for various groups throughout history would be utterly incomprehensible. Second, this account avoids the tendency of accounts based on an extension model to define moral standing in terms of an initial group and then to apply it to other groups using similarity as the criterion of judgment. Such a practice arbitrarily privileges the first group and, more often than not, sets up a requirement that other groups can never fully meet, since they are never exactly the same as the privileged group.

In "The Will to Believe," William James argues that it is rational to have religious faith despite a lack of conclusive evidence of the divine, on the grounds that such openness to the possibility of the divine is a necessary condition of its manifestation. Similarly, even lacking conclusive evidence of animal intelligence we are justified in making this venture, in taking this attitude of openness toward communicating with nonhuman animals in a collective moral enterprise. There is always the danger that we will project our own interests onto others, but we are much better off than with the extension model, which starts out with this projection.[31] I realize that such faith in the possibility of communicating with other animals lays one open to the charge of blind sentimentalism. However, it should be clear that the pragmatic principles of continuity, pluralism, and a naturalistic approach to ethics grounded in interests, coupled with some hard-nosed empirical evidence regarding animal behavior, suggest that we have more in common with our nonhuman kindred than we have previously thought. Moreover, despite our inability to know in advance whether a wider moral enterprise will succeed, we will never know if we do not make a venture. For, as James wrote, "In truths dependent on our personal action, then, faith based on desire is certainly a lawful and possibly an indispensable thing" (239).

Notes

The editors would like to note that a version of this paper won the Ila and John Mellow Prize for the best paper advancing the American philosophic tradition at the 30th Annual Meeting of the Society for the Advancement of American Philosophy.

1. Strictly speaking, those who investigate animal intelligence generally do not search for the specifically Kantian idea of rationality, the ability to act according to a maxim. Nonetheless, many view the connection between (at least certain forms of empirically demonstrable) intelligence, reason, and moral standing as beyond question.

2. Peter Singer's claim that we should take more care with beings that can feel pain is admirable, and his work in practical ethics has over the years caused many to seriously evaluate the consequences of their actions for other beings. One problem with Singer's approach is that it seems to reduce our interactions with other creatures to the lowest common denominator. Avoiding the causing of pain to other animals (or other human beings), while possibly an adequate minimum standard of ethicality, does not begin to do justice to the variety and complexity of social relations. Most people with pets (though assuredly not all) would react with horror or amusement to the suggestion that the fundamental basis of their relationship, morally speaking, is not causing pain to their pet, or vice versa. Another difficulty with Singer's position is that it radically divorces the moral standard from the moral motive. Finally, his conception of morality is based firmly within the extension model and thus, as I argue in this essay, is not firmly rooted in the nature of moral experience. Regan, for his part, adopts a Kantian position that preserves Kant's notion of a being that is an end in itself—what Regan refers to as having "inherent value"—while substituting "being the subject of a life" for the Kantian rationality criterion. The main difficulty with this sort of account is that it is probably the clearest example of the inherently problematic extension model. Another issue is that Regan's notion of "inherent value" seems rather more mystificatory than useful. Whereas the notion of "being an end in oneself" has clear cognitive content, it derives this content from being firmly attached to Kant's notions of rationality and the moral law. In his concept of "inherent value," Regan has tried to preserve this Kantian placeholder for morality, but in attaching it to subjectivity rather than rationality he has removed it from the context that gave it rational support and meaning. Moreover, Regan treats subjectivity as if it were an unproblematic, ahistorical concept while ignoring the ways in which this concept's givenness has been questioned by modern social theorists (see, for example, Foucault). "One of the central and most common theses of the institutional analyses provided by modern social theory is that subjectivity is not pre-given and original but at least to some degree formed in the field of social forces" (Hardt and Negri 195). Though not without problems itself, the existence of such work suggests that Regan takes insufficient care in using subjectivity as an unquestioned ground for moral theory.

3. We should note that the extension model need not rely on any *single* trait. Lawrence

Kohlberg fashioned a hierarchical scale of moral development based on a number of indicators. At least one of the virtues of this set of indicators is that they were more amenable to empirical testing than is a single trait such as rationality. Testing conducted by Kohlberg based on these indicators, which tend to favor abstract, universal, and impartial moral principles, has been purported to show that women *to this day* exhibit less moral development. This strikes me as fairly good evidence that the extension model and theories of moral standing that fall under it tell us more about the people doing moral philosophy (and psychology) than about morality itself. For a very brief summary of Kohlberg's research and the response of Carol Gilligan, initially one of Kohlberg's research associates, see Regan 56–57.

4. In discussing the concepts of "higher" and "lower" on an "evolutionary ladder," Midgley writes: "If man wants to set up a contest in resembling himself and award himself the prize, no one will quarrel with him. But what does it mean? All he can do by these roundabout methods is perhaps to assert a value-judgement about what matters most in *human* life" (167). I argue that we do a similar thing when we utilize the extension model in testing for moral standing, differentiating among various groups of humans (where "Western Man" is considered to be at the pinnacle) as well as between human and nonhuman animals.

5. Additionally, pragmatists are getting better at raising these questions. The development of pragmatist feminism and pragmatically informed critical race theory, for example, has done a great deal to improve the situation.

6. The reference to negotiation need not imply a Hobbesian state of nature from which we must be rescued. The idea is simply that moral standing is not that different from the social standing that gives rise to differential forms of etiquette. How we ought to treat one another varies from occasion to occasion, depending on who is involved in the negotiation, what they are negotiating for, their relations to one another and to others in the community, and a variety of other factors. If this sounds complicated, that's because it is. If it sounds too complicated to actually be the case, we must remember that much of the negotiation is implicit or has taken place in advance and is encoded in habits, principles, and customs. Even so, this approach should not be taken as apologia for the status quo. Noting the actual contexts in which moral standing and moral judgments appear does not render them uncriticizable for that reason; in fact, it makes them more criticizable because they cease to be obscured by superficial "analytical clarity."

7. Of course, moral standing is also the hook on which, by long-standing tradition, many have hung claims for justice in the context of political struggle. We will return to this use of the term shortly.

8. Community is the context that makes the content. Precisely what sense of community is required is the topic of the rest of the essay.

9. Contemporary theories of "evolutionary ethics" which attempt to derive morality from the calculations of individuals acting in their rational self-interest suffer from the same difficulty.

10. See, for example, *Early Works [EW]* 3:346–47 (*Outlines of a Critical Theory of Ethics*), where Dewey speaks of being born into a moral world. I realize that I am departing from Dewey's formal conception of moral agency here, as articulated, for example, at 242 and *Middle Works [MW]* 8:38–39 ("The Logic of Judgments of Practice"). In these passages, Dewey, characteristically, associates moral activity with "the method of intelligence." Moral agency, according to Dewey, requires having an "end-in-view" and exercising intellectual faculties to criticize that end. I have two responses to this definition. First, as I argue later in this essay, Dewey had an overly narrow notion of meaning and

communication, and his understanding of what it means to have an end-in-view is tied up with this narrow conception. Second, as in his definition of community, Dewey often conflates an honorific sense of *intelligence* with its descriptive sense. The fact is that rather than merely describing moral agency or defining it philosophically, Dewey meant to praise intelligence because he saw far too many of our actions as unintelligent. If Dewey means intelligence in a descriptive sense, it is not clear that it is limited to human activity. If he means it in its honorific sense, which seems to be his most typical usage, it is too narrow to apply to all moral agency and is, in fact, uncharacteristic of most human activity. Thus, my arguments with respect to *community* apply equally well to Dewey's ambiguous use of the word *intelligence*. For another pragmatic approach that locates the meaning and force of moral concepts in community, see Smiley.

11. In modern philosophy, Spinoza goes farthest in developing an ontology, an epistemology, and an ethico-political theology that is based on immanence. For developments in science studies, see, for example, Latour; Haraway.

12. "To be 'made' is not to be 'made up' " (Haraway 99). " 'Facts are facts,' said Bachelard. But, constructed by man, are they false for all that?" (Latour, *Nous n'avons jamais été modernes* 29–30; my translation). Dewey, in emphasizing the constructive nature of inquiry—the fact that knowledge is made—while at the same time denying that it is thereby "subjective," any more than the fact that a house is constructed by humans renders it mere fancy, has much in common with contemporary analysts of science such as Bruno Latour and Donna Haraway. By calling attention to the labor that is involved in the construction of facts so as to make them usable more widely and generically, Dewey and these scholars consistently show how the world of scientific objects is both constructed and very real. See Latour, *Science in Action* and *Pandora's Hope;* Haraway.

13. Bruno Latour describes the construction of knowledge as the building of networks of allies, both human and nonhuman. In order to be able to make a knowledge claim that will come to have the status of "fact," one must convince various sorts of entities to participate in the project; see *Science and Action* (Latour there deals with scientific and technical inquiry, for the most part, but there is no reason why this analysis cannot be applied to ethical inquiry as well). My point regarding the discovery aspect of inquiry into common interests is that the various agencies that we wish to enlist in our networks must be relatable. As I argue in this essay, *relatability* is the condition of inhabiting a common horizon of meaning.

14. As we discover common interests, they are transformed through the process of discovery. When we conceive of the activity of discovery in terms of the building of networks, gathering resources, and enlisting allies, we see that the initial materials with which we started are transformed by the various stages of negotiations and translations through which we must pass in order to build the network. It is in this way that inquiry in general (even scientific and technical) is a "making common" in terms of making common knowledge. This is what I take to be Peirce's point about knowledge being that which the community of inquiry will decide upon in the long run. As Latour points out again and again (though I am here altering his terminology somewhat), making scientific and technical knowledge claims common involves appealing to common interests. But as those in science studies warn, we must not asymmetrically explain "nature" or "science" by appealing to "society," since the "nature of society" is open to question as much as anything else is (Latour, *Science in Action* 258). Thus we must also make interests common through the same processes of subscription and enlistment, and this project is what we refer to as "ethics." There are, of course, many differences between science and ethics, including (but not limited to) the specific types of things that are brought together in

networks, the density of the networks, and the kind of literature that is produced in each type of inquiry. However, there is not a fundamental difference of type between scientific and ethical inquiry. This point is still a matter of much confusion, not least in many interpretations of the work of Dewey, which largely focuses on this very claim. See my "John Dewey's Science of Ethics."

15. Compare this with Latour's and Haraway's remarks that scientific facts are never settled once and for all. They are in fact quite fragile outside of the networks within which they are developed, and these networks require constant care and maintenance in order to persist.

16. Dewey writes,

> What, then, is moral theory? It is all one with moral insight, and moral insight is the recognition of the relationships in hand. This is a very tame and prosaic conception. It makes moral insight, and therefore moral theory, consist simply in the every-day workings of the same ordinary intelligence that measures drygoods, drives nails, sells wheat, and invents the telephone. There is no more halo about the insight that determines what I should do in this catastrophe of life when the foundations are upheaving and my bent for eternity lies waiting to be fixed, than in that which determines whether commercial conditions favor heavy or light purchases. There is nothing more divine or transcendental in resolving how to save my degraded neighbor than in the resolving of a problem in algebra, or in the mastery of Mill's theory of induction. (*EW* 3:94–95, "Moral Theory and Practice")

17. This nontemporal transcendence is not transcendence in the sense discussed in the previous section—that is, an appeal to extranatural categories to ground the good or to a transcendent nature to ground knowledge. Rather, it means being able to link a current situation to possibly distant events and circumstances. Knowledge is "transcendent" just in the sense that it is the product of travel and facilitates travel across networks (see Latour's discussion of knowledge as *re-connaisance* in *Science and Action*). The sort of transcendence Dewey has in mind might be better conceptualized as the ability of one's knowledge and one's judgments to travel.

18. This contrast between human and mechanical occurs in many passages: see, for example, *EW* 2:14–15 (*Psychology*); *MW* 1:179 (*The School and Society*); *MW* 1:185 ("Principles of Mental Development as Illustrated in Early Infancy"); *MW* 6:289 (*How We Think*); *MW* 6:451 ("Contributions to a Cyclopedia of Education"); *MW* 7:235, 282 ("Contributions to a Cyclopedia of Education"); *MW* 7:401 (a report of Dewey's address titled "The Psychology of Social Behavior"); *MW* 8:68–69 ("The Logic of Judgments of Practice"); *MW* 10:199 ("American Education and Culture"); *MW* 12:119–20, 169–71 (*Reconstruction in Philosophy*); and *MW* 15:262–63 ("Syllabus: Social Institutions and the Study of Morals").

19. I am grateful to Vincent Colapietro for calling my attention to this article.

20. It should be noted that the label *total war,* used in contrast with anything less than total, is relatively recent. Ancient warfare was often total and involved not only the killing of soldiers but also the raping of women, the taking of children, and the burning of fields. The distinction between combatants and noncombatants appears to be wholly modern. Again, even (or perhaps even especially) when warfare involves such methods, the practice of warfare appears to function on symbolic terrain.

21. For example, "The more human mankind becomes, the more civilized it is, the less is there some behavior which is purely physical and some other purely mental. So

true is this statement that we may use the amount of distance which separates them in our society as a test of the lack of human development in that community. There exists in present society, especially in industry, a large amount of activity that is almost exclusively mechanical; it is carried on with a minimum of thought and of accompanying emotion" (*LW* 3:29, "Body and Mind").

22. Unlike Dewey, the Renaissance humanists propagated the elevated images of man in order to oppose transcendentalism; Dewey typically opposed the dehumanizing forces of capitalist production. We will return to this theme shortly in order to assess the promise of the rights-based approaches to liberation projects that emerge from the related but distinct humanism of the Enlightenment.

23. Beth Singer develops Justus Buchler's concept of "active judgments."

24. Compare Merleau-Ponty on the dialogical character of perception in *The Phenomenology of Perception*.

25. For Dewey, a habit is not simply something an organism does. Habits are a function of the organism-environment complex. In fact, organisms share an environment just to the extent that they have the same habits (see *MW* 15:14, *Human Nature and Conduct*). A very similar account of the organism-environment relation can be found in the work of the biologist Richard Lewontin.

26. No two individuals inhabit the same horizon of meaning. Rather, based on their habits, behaviors, and dispositions, two individuals may be said to have overlapping horizons of meaning.

27. I take this to be the point that Dewey makes when he argues both that habits enable effective action in the world as much as they constrain it and that they are as much a function of the environment as they are of the organism (see *MW* 15:14–16, *Human Nature and Conduct*).

28. Pragmatists in general have been quick to acknowledge the difficulties raised by the term *subjectivity*. Apart from issues of dualism and the interminable debates of the epistemology industry, contemporary social theory, which focuses on the production of subjectivities, also renders this concept problematic. See the discussion of Regan in note 2, above.

29. Much of the interaction between master and slave, at least in the context of slavery in the American South in the nineteenth century, simultaneously assumes and denies moral standing. Much of the means of establishing the *difference* between master and slave is the use of systematic humiliation, a practice that makes no sense whatsoever if the slave has no moral standing and if master and slave do not both inhabit very similar horizons of meaning. See Willett's discussion (12) of Toni Morrison's *Beloved* (I am grateful to Shannon Sullivan for this reference).

30. The abuse of animals is utterly unintelligible absent the recognition that the abuser and the abused share a horizon of meaning constituted by a shared understanding not only of physical pain but also of humiliation and emotional suffering. Although I hasten to add that animal abuse is never really understandable, it is completely incomprehensible except on the assumption that animals have moral standing that is constituted in terms of a shared horizon of social meanings.

31. Under the extension model, moral standing is always interpreted in strictly anthropocentric terms, as it is graciously extended (perhaps on an honorary basis) to other beings. It is not possible to realize the fruits of community by beginning in this way. Biocentrism is no better. Because we are not capable of starting out from the nonhuman perspective but must discover it in communication, biocentrism necessarily involves the same sorts of projection as anthropocentrism.

Anthropomorphism and anthropocentrism are two polar extremes. To the objection that I am anthropomorphizing animals by attributing to them the possibility of communication, I respond that although such projection is always possible, attentiveness to a thoroughly transactional model of communications mitigates its danger.

Bibliography

Dewey, John. *Democracy and Education. The Middle Works,* vol. 9, *1916.*

——. *The Early Works, 1882–1898.* Edited by Jo Ann Boydston. 5 vols. Carbondale: Southern Illinois University Press, 1967–72.

——. "The Ethics of Animal Experimentation." In *The Later Works,* vol. 2, *1925–1927,* 98–103.

——. *The Later Works, 1925–1953.* Edited by Jo Ann Boydston. 17 vols. Carbondale: Southern Illinois University Press, 1981–90.

——. *Logic: The Theory of Inquiry. The Later Works,* vol. 12, *1938.*

——. *The Middle Works, 1899–1924.* Edited by Jo Ann Boydston. 15 vols. Carbondale: Southern Illinois University Press, 1976–83.

Dewey, John, with Arthur F. Bentley. *Knowing and the Known.* In *The Later Works,* vol. 16, *1948–1952,* 1–294.

Foucault, Michel. *The History of Sexuality.* Vol. 1, *An Introduction.* Translated by Robert Hurley. New York: Random House, 1978.

Haraway, Donna. *Modest—Witness@ Second—Millennium. FemaleMan©_Meets_ OncoMouse™.* New York: Routledge, 1997.

Hardt, Michael, and Antonio Negri. *Empire.* Cambridge, Mass.: Harvard University Press, 2000.

James, William. "The Will to Believe." In *Pragmatism and Classical American Philosophy: Essential Readings and Interpretive Essays,* edited by John J. Stuhr, 230–40. 2nd ed. New York: Oxford University Press, 1989.

Latour, Bruno. *Nous n'avons jamais été modernes: Essai d'anthropologie symétrique.* Paris: La Découverte, 1991.

——. *Pandora's Hope: Essays on the Reality of Science Studies.* Cambridge, Mass.: Harvard University Press, 1999.

——. *Science in Action: How to Follow Scientists and Engineers through Society.* Cambridge, Mass.: Harvard University Press, 1987.

Lewontin, Richard. *The Triple Helix: Gene, Organism, and Environment.* Cambridge, Mass.: Harvard University Press, 2000.

McReynolds, Phillip. "John Dewey's Science of Ethics." Ph.D. diss., Vanderbilt University, 2000.

Merleau-Ponty, Maurice. *The Phenomenology of Perception.* Translated by Colin Smith. 1962. Reprint, London: Routledge, 1989.

Midgley, Mary. *Beast and Man: The Roots of Human Nature.* London: Routledge, 1995.

Pico della Mirandola, Giovanni. *Oration on the Dignity of Man.* Translated by A. Robert Caponigri. Chicago: Gateway Editions, 1956.

Potter, Elisabeth. "Gender and Epistemic Negotiation." In *Feminist Epistemologies,* edited by Linda Alcoff and Elizabeth Potter, 161–86. New York: Routledge, 1993.

Regan, Tom. *Defending Animal Rights.* Urbana: University of Illinois Press, 2001.

Singer, Beth. "Dewey's Concept of Community: A Critique." *Journal of the History of Philosophy* 23, no. 4 (October 1985): 555–69.

Singer, Peter. *Unsanctifying Human Life: Essays on Ethics.* Edited by Helga Kuhse. Oxford: Blackwell, 2002.

Smiley, Marion. *Moral Responsibility and the Boundaries of Community: Power and Accountability from a Pragmatic Point of View.* Chicago: University of Chicago Press, 1992.

Stannard, David E. *American Holocaust: Columbus and the Conquest of the New World.* New York: Oxford University Press, 1992.

Willett, Cynthia. *The Soul of Justice: Social Bonds and Racial Hubris.* Ithaca, N.Y.: Cornell University Press, 2001.

4 Peirce's Horse: A Sympathetic and Semeiotic Bond

Douglas R. Anderson

The systematic philosophy of Charles Sanders Peirce is not the first place one might turn to in looking for a description of the relationship between human persons and other animals. The writings of Henry David Thoreau or John Muir might at first blush seem more likely homes for such a story. But Peirce's work, by his own admission, retains some features of transcendentalism; and one of these, the belief in the perceptibility or sensibility of meaning, provides a reasonable basis for developing just the sort of story that Thoreau and Muir do tell us. The difference is that Peirce's story is not so much a discourse on nature as a pragmatic outcome of his synechism, or theory of continuity, and his realistic idea of perception that underwrites his theory of inquiry.

In Lecture IV of his 1903 lectures on pragmatism, Peirce worked to describe the practice of phenomenology as the basis for all inquiry. Phenomenology, for Peirce, involves a practical attentiveness to the world—what we might call an aesthetically motivated perception. Another way in which he puts this point is that we perceive or feel meanings. As Richard Bernstein argues, Peirce was sensitive to the "dimension of felt immediacy and argued that an adequate theory of perception must give it its proper due" (177). Thus, in Peirce's own words: "all reasoning . . . turns upon perception of generality and continuity at every step" (*Essential Peirce [EP]* 191). This theory of phenomenological perception, which is akin to William James's "radical empiricism," is tied closely to Peirce's realism and synechism; taken together, they suggest "that Thirdness [generality, continuity] is operative in Nature" (*Collected Papers [CP]* 5:93).[1] That is, natural laws, relations, habits, and meanings are real and knowable. My aim here is to build from this basis an account of how we might understand our relations to animals from a Peircean perspective. We will not be able to discern a specific recipe for dealing with animals, but we should be able to establish several general suggestive claims that open up the possibilities for human-animal relationships in a Peircean world.

In Lecture IV and elsewhere, Peirce insisted that feelings have semeiotic power—that is, that they can function as signs.[2] "A mere presentment," he said, "may be a sign" (*CP* 1:313; see also *EP* 161). Thus, feelings or presentments can bear meaning and can function interpretively. It is in this sense that we can feel or perceive meaning. In an often-cited example, Peirce suggests that a blind person might maintain that the color red resembles "the blare of a trumpet" (*CP* 1:314). Finding himself understanding the blind person's meaning, Peirce considers the import of this experience:

> He [the blind person] had collected that notion from hearing ordinary people converse together about the colors, and since I was not born to be one of those whom he had heard converse, the fact that I can see a certain analogy, shows me not only that my feeling of redness is something like the feelings of the persons whom he had heard talk, but also his feeling of a trumpet's blare was very much like mine. (*CP* 1:314)

Thus, not only can we feel meanings and analogies, but we are able to share such feelings.

Let us turn aside from Peirce's pragmatism lectures for a moment to consider a relevant consequence of his synechism. In a nominalistic world constituted of discrete individual entities, the borders between species would be clearly demarcated, and there would be definite ontological breaks between species. In a synechistic world, however, all borders are continuous and consequently are inherently vague. Thus, when we consider species of similar genera, we can think of their being as continuous with one another. On such a view, there is no ontological obstacle to the possibility of communication across species and, perhaps, even across genera. At the very least, there would be borderline beings whose species home it is difficult to discern; and it would be reasonable to suppose that such borderland creatures *could* communicate with each other and with those on either side of the border. With no theoretical obstacle, Peirce is led by experience to the belief that we in fact do so communicate. He claims that animals have an instinct for communication: "for some kind of language there is among nearly all animals. Not only do animals of the same species convey their assertions, but different classes of animals do so, as when a snake hypnotizes a bird. Two particularly important varieties of this Species of study will relate to Cries and Songs (among mammals and birds chiefly) and to facial expression among mammals" (*CP* 7:379; see Sebeok).[3] In short, Peirce's synechism makes possible the experiences we have of animals from different species acting in communication, and makes sense of Peirce's suggestion that we can study the semeiotic, or sign-using, habits of all animals.

Now, if we return to Peirce's description of perception and feeling, we can see that for him there is no barrier in principle or in experience to communication or semeiosis between humans and other animals. Moreover, although some other animals may engage us with fully articulate signs, such as facial expressions and whimpers, even such forms of communication are made possible by the shared feeling of differential perceivers (as noted in the case of the blind person's association of redness and trumpet blares). That is, we humans can sympathize or feel with other animals. Peirce took this to be a commonplace of his own experience:

> I know very well that my dog's musical feelings are quite similar to mine though they agitate him more than they do me. He has the same emotions of affection as I, though they are far more moving in his case. You would never persuade me that my horse and I do not sympathize, or that the canary bird that takes such delight in joking with me does not feel with me and I with him; and this instinctive confidence of mine that it is so, is to my mind evidence that it really is so. (CP 1:314)

Most persons who have spent a good deal of time around animals will share Peirce's "instinctive confidence" in the meaning of such experiences. What is important to note, however, is that Peirce's synechistic ontology and theory of perception make sense of this instinctive confidence in ways that many nominalistic, scientistic ontologies and rationalistic epistemologies cannot.

As Peirce sees it, the semeiotic interaction between persons and animals is relatively rich. We can discern the moods of animals through body language, for example: "I can tell by the expression of face the state of mind of my horse just as unmistakably as I can that of my dog or my wife" (CP 7:379 n. 17). Peirce shares humor with his canary. He shares responses to music with his dog. Moreover, with his dog, Peirce argues, through signs of association he can establish a modest form of dialogue. When the dog "obeys" him, the dog is acting with a kind of directed purpose:

> I speak to the dog. I mention the book. I do these things together. The dog fetches the book. He does it as in consequence of what I did. That is not the whole story. I not only simultaneously spoke to the dog and mentioned the book to the dog; that is, I caused him to think of the book and to bring it. . . . The dog's relation to the book was more prominently dualistic; yet the whole significance and intention of his fetching it was to obey me. (CP 2:86)

Until studies of primates, dolphins, and whales were undertaken in the latter half of the twentieth century, it was often asked whether animals genuinely communicated with each other and whether humans could communicate with animals.[4] This question arose in part because communication was thought to hinge essentially on the use of conventional signs or what Peirce called "symbols." Thus, if one did not use words or their equivalent, one was not using language and therefore was not genuinely communicating.

But within the framework of Peirce's semeiotic system, conventional signs, symbols, or words are only one small feature of semeiosis. Strictly speaking, the use of such symbols is actually a very limited, though certainly powerful, form of communication. In Peirce's scheme of things, the universe is shot through with sign activity—he would have been surprised only if animals and persons could *not* communicate effectively. For the daily lives of both humans and animals, Peirce believed, are pervaded by "associational determinations of belief" in which we arrive at beliefs without "the exercise of our conscious intellect": "In riding a horse, I understand him and he understands me; but how we understand one another I know hardly better than he" (CP 7:456).

So far, I have only established a descriptive Peircean account of animal life and of human-animal relations. That is, animals carry on their own communication and deal with meanings—they are, ontologically speaking, beings who engage in semeiosis. Furthermore, because our lives are continuous with the lives of other animals, there is a basis for understanding our ability to sympathize and communicate with them. And finally, although this communication may ultimately reach the level of dialogue and symbolic discourse, the wider range of our communicative activity is perceptual or sympathetic. That is, we perceive or share each other's felt meanings. If this is the case, what can we say in a normative way about the Peircean relations of persons and animals?

An initial question to ask in this direction might be, What status do non-human animals have in a Peircean world? We know that they are sign users and that, at various levels, they can communicate with humans. These abilities suggest that many animals have—or, better, constitute—what Peirce called in his 1892 essay "The Law of Mind" "personality." The basis of personality is the presence of feeling. Working with the findings of the day, Peirce asserted that "a gob of protoplasm . . . an amoeba or a slime-mould . . . does not differ in any radical way from the contents of a nerve-cell." And if it is thus analogous to a nerve cell, then there "is no doubt that the slime-mould, or this amoeba, or at any rate some similar mass of protoplasm, feels" (CP 6:133; see also 255). However, for Peirce, while the protoplasm exhibits feeling, it fails to exhibit personality.

Ideas, according to Peirce, are not primordial mental atoms; rather, they grow out of a continuity of feeling: "Three elements go to make up an idea." The first of these elements is that ideas have "intrinsic qualities as a feeling." The second two elements involve the continuity of feeling and the relations of ideas. An idea also has an "energy" with which it affects other ideas and a tendency "to bring along other ideas with it" (CP 6:135). Thus, general ideas are "living feelings" that affect each other. From this mutual effect develops what we might call a local history of ideas which establishes habits and inferences, and the complex of habits and ideas provides the grounds for the reality of mind and personality.

As odd as Peirce's language may sound, his aim is to discover what makes semeiosis and communication possible. As Peirce sees it, traditional scientistic views of ideas, which see them as discrete events or entities, fail to account for real generality and the spread of ideas. We find, Peirce argues, "that when we regard ideas from a nominalistic, individualistic, sensualistic way, the simplest facts of mind become utterly meaningless" (CP 6:150). Communication is one of these simple facts of mind. The upshot for our purposes is that not only do horses, dogs, and canaries reveal a continuity of feeling (as does protoplasm), but they reveal an association of ideas in their abilities to communicate and interpret.

Peirce maintains that "personality is some kind of coordination or connection of ideas." A personality is not a concrete thing but a general idea, a "living feeling," that reveals itself through a kind of "immediate self-consciousness" (CP 6:155). Moreover, a personality involves directionality and growth. By these criteria, Peirce's horse and dog certainly seem to *be* personalities. They exhibit self-awareness, an awareness with which we can sympathize and which we can come to understand through semeiotic work: "In riding a horse, rider and ridden understand one another" (*CP* 7:447). The experiential truth of this must, within Peirce's philosophical architectonic, lead us to believe that the horse is a personality. In Peirce's synechistic world, personality may attend a variety of species in richer or thinner ways. Mammals, because of their links to humans, are a natural place to look for personality. But in Peirce's world personality puts in an appearance wherever an incipient association of ideas exists; reptiles, amphibians, birds, fish, and so on might all display some level of personality. Moreover, within any species, some individuals may display more or less personality. Thus, Peirce indirectly calls into question the natural privilege of being human. He makes all of this even more explicit in describing his dog as analogous to himself, though relying on different perceptual abilities. At first, he says, his dog's senses seemed unlike his own:

> But when I reflect to how small a degree he thinks of visual images, and of how *smells* play a part in his thoughts and imaginations analogous to the part played by *sights* in mine, I cease to be surprised that the perfume of roses or orange flowers does not attract his attention at all and that effluvia that interest him so much, when at all perceptible to me, are simply unpleasant. He does not think of smells as sources of pleasure and disgust but as sources of information, just as I do not think of blue as a nauseating color, nor of red as a maddening one. (*CP* 1:314)

Again, that animals do "think," "imagine," and interpret may not seem a radical claim to us, but it is fair to say that Peirce's outlook on this score was not common in the late-nineteenth-century world that still, for the most part, insisted on the radical separation between humans and other animals. Indeed, Jane Goodall found science still opposed to the attribution of personality to animals in the mid–twentieth century: "In those days, thirty years ago," she noted in 1992, "it wasn't very fashionable to talk about animal personality, but fortunately I did not know that" (4). Where most saw separation, Peirce and Goodall saw continuity.

Bringing Peirce's horse into the arena of personality provides a basis from which to consider our normative relations with other animals. We should, in short, treat his horse as we would other personalities. We stand in community with other animals by virtue of our communication with them. Apart from the fondness Peirce seems to display for his own animals, however, we have little to go on regarding what he believed explicitly about this community. Nevertheless, within Peirce's developing philosophical system two doors are left open that might allow us to make an abductive guess about what he might have suggested had he thought further on the issue: the door of inquiry and the door of agape.

As is well known, Peirce insisted that inquiry take root wherever doubt appeared. His own experience with and ways of thinking about other animals help to generate for us a doubt concerning whether our conventional ways of interacting with animals are appropriate. Conventionally in the West, humans have been held to be radically other in kind than animals. Peirce did not share this view. Conventionally, elaborate semeiotic processes among animals were doubted—for Peirce, they made perfect sense and their absence would have caused him surprise. Peirce's outlook must clearly include some nonhuman animals as personalities with the potential for purpose and growth, despite conventional science's routine rejection of this possibility. This outlook leads us to reconsider both the methods and content of such science—we are led, with Peirce, to doubt the efficacy of a science rooted in nominalism rather than synechism. When such doubts arise, inquiry must follow.

Inquiry into the normativity of our relationships with other animals depends in part on our knowing them better than we do at present. Learning more about other animals' lives is a scientific inquiry. And the theory of such an inquiry is at the very heart of logic, which, together with aesthetics and ethics, is a normative science. The first normative issue in our dealings with animals therefore occurs when we ask how we should study them. That is, there are appropriate and inappropriate ways to pursue inquiry and thus to pursue knowledge of animals. At this point, then, we must recall the opening discussion and keep in mind Peirce's phenomenological and realistic conception of scientific practice. Whatever behavioral and physiological studies we perform to learn about animals (or persons, for that matter) should be initiated by a phenomenological examination of their lives. This, as we recall, requires attentive perception and a sympathetic apprehension of animal life.

Peirce's synechism intrudes again as we decide how this initial inquiry should be undertaken. Persons constitute a spectrum or continuum of natural aptitudes, interests, and potentiality for development. He routinely distinguishes artists, activists, and scientists according to his categories of firstness (feeling), secondness (doing), and thirdness (thinking). Among persons, therefore, artists tend to be the best perceivers. "And let me tell the scientific men," Peirce said, "that the artists are much finer and more accurate observers than they are" (*EP* 193). In looking for inquirers into animal life, then, we ought to look for those who have an ability, by nature or training, to "feel with" animals as Peirce did with his horse. This is a matter not of romantic attachment—though that might ensue—but of actual semeiotic compatibility. Some folks communicate better with animals than do others. This is not a surprise to us experientially, and it certainly makes sense within Peirce's outlook. In her book *Primate Visions*, Donna Haraway examines the work of women in primatology and suggests ways in which, for historical reasons linked to gender, some women may be well suited to rethink the "scientific" study of primates (279–303). My guess is that this Peircean requirement of finding the most competent inquirers is probably met in practice by a kind of self-selection. That is, many who *do* study animal life were initially lured to that study by their attunement to the animals. No doubt some enter the field for more instrumental reasons, but they no longer appear to be a majority. The upshot is that the kind of study carried out by Jane Goodall in her lifelong interactions with the chimpanzees of Gombe, which was initially ridiculed by conventional scientists, makes good sense within Peirce's understanding of inquiry. In the same way that ethnologists failed miserably by watching Eskimo from outside the windows of their homes, primatologists prior to Goodall failed by not being willing or able to communicate with primates. Goodall's approach, which begins with sympathetic apprehension and finding ways to communicate, is good Peircean science.

Despite some continued criticism of her methods, there is little doubt at this point that studies such as Goodall's have proved effective and have provided us with a more intimate understanding of the animal world than has traditional nominalistic science. However, such knowledge has not entirely set the course for an ideal relationship between persons and animals. To put it bluntly, we might use such knowledge to hunt animals more efficiently as well as to befriend them more easily. Peirce offered no direct advice on this question—narrow moral recipes were not for him the function of scientific inquiry or philosophy. Nevertheless, he believed in making the world more "reasonable" through what he called an agapistic, or loving, attentiveness to the world's own possibilities for growth. It suggests one direction in which we might take a Peircean line of reasoning concerning our relationships with animals.

Peirce was not, to my knowledge, a vegetarian. But that vegetarianism might be an eventual outcome of our encounters with other animal life was certainly within the framework of his notion of development and growth in the cosmos. He might easily agree with Thoreau "that it is a part of the destiny of the human race, in its gradual improvement, to leave off eating animals" (462). Peirce very clearly asserted that human community would thrive best when driven by agape or cherishing love. That is, the growth of other persons toward their own best possibilities is effected not by a "gospel of greed," in which we each persistently pursue our own interests, but by a "gospel of love," in which you are willing to "Sacrifice your own perfection to the perfectionment of your neighbor" (*CP* 6:288). For Peirce, love's efficacy "comes from every individual merging his individuality in sympathy with his neighbor" (*CP* 6:294). If we consider that Peirce's outlook clearly acknowledges the personality of other animals, it is a short step to envisioning them as part of a larger community whose health likewise depends on the "gospel of love." If we include the work done by Goodall and others that heightens and deepens our sense that nonhuman animals exhibit personality, it becomes much clearer that we should orient our relationships with other animals toward the development of an agapistic community— a community in which we find ways to permit the growth of individual animals toward their own "perfectionments." It was to just this consideration that Roger Fouts awoke in his ongoing work in studying and teaching sign language to chimpanzees. He gradually came to see that "no one ever seemed to consider the chimpanzee's point of view" (203). In a variety of ways our culture at large has been undergoing similar, though perhaps not so radical, awakenings in recent years; what Peirce does is provide a philosophical setting in which such awakenings and the actions they engender may be construed as both scientifically and morally responsible.

Taken in this direction, Peirce's philosophy might be used to underwrite a host of revisions in how we interact with other animals—revisions such as have already begun to take shape in some practices concerning agriculture, environmental protection, and animal use. These would include maintaining habitat for some species, improved treatment of some animals in captivity, and attention to reducing animal pain in some livestock practices. Even where such measures are a result of utility, they often develop from a phenomenological account of the status of nonhuman animals. For some this is but a paltry beginning. Nevertheless, it is a beginning—and one that can appropriate Peirce's conception of inquiry into animal life. It is important to remember, however, that Peirce's outlook is not merely romantic or sentimental. Sentiment and feeling play a role in inquiry in allowing us access to communication with animals. But they are not the final word; rather, they are the proper origin of a fully scientific or experimental inquiry. Our relations with animals constitute an ongoing experiment that needs to be informed by a full understanding of animal life. Peirce is not blind to the viciousness of animals or humans; on the contrary, he is well aware of animal fallibility. Furthermore, he understands that community requires reciprocal relations. It's not just that we must be nice to animals: animals too must come to join in the community's well-being to the extent they can. If this at first seems a stiff requirement, we need only think of the roles pets play in family life to see the possibilities for reciprocity. In Peirce's world, natural laws—including the habitual behaviors of all animals—are malleable. This is the core meaning of a synechistic, evolutionary philosophy. Thus, from Peirce's perspective, the semeiotic sympathy and affinity that developed a community between him and his horse might not have been an aberration. Indeed, it may be the appropriate model for the relations among all persons and animals; it may be the ground from which an animal-human community could be more fully explored and developed.

Notes

1. Peirce's *Collected Papers* are cited by volume and paragraph number.
2. I use the spelling *semeiotic* instead of *semiotic* because it was what Peirce preferred in reference to his own work.
3. For an overview of the debate on the issue of animal-human communication, see Sebeok and Umiker-Sebeok.
4. Some still argue this case regarding language. Peirce's notion of communication hinges on the rich semeiotic structure that he developed, and for him, it is no longer a live question. That is, unless one narrows the meaning of *communication* to exclude even such events as the success of Roger Fouts (among others) in teaching sign language to chimpanzees, one has no grounds for doubting such communication.

Bibliography

Bernstein, Richard. "Peirce's Theory of Perception." In *Studies in the Philosophy of Charles Sanders Peirce: Second Series,* edited by Edward C. Moore and Richard S. Robin, 165–89. Amherst: University of Massachusetts Press, 1964.

Fouts, Roger. *Next of Kin: My Conversations with Chimpanzees.* New York: Avon Books, 1997.

Goodall, Jane. *The Chimpanzee: The Living Link between "Man" and "Beast."* Edinburgh: Alexander Ritchie and Son, 1992.

Haraway, Donna. *Primate Visions: Gender, Race, and Nature in the World of Modern Science.* New York: Routledge, 1989.

Peirce, Charles. *Collected Papers of Charles Sanders Peirce.* Edited by Charles Hartshorne, Paul Weiss, and A. W. Burks. 8 vols. Cambridge, Mass.: Harvard University Press, 1931–61.

———. *The Essential Peirce: Selected Philosophical Writings.* Vol. 2, *1893–1913.* Edited by the Peirce Edition Project. Bloomington: Indiana University Press, 1998.

Sebeok, Thomas. "Between Animal and Animal." *Times Literary Supplement,* October 5, 1973, 1187–89.

Sebeok, Thomas, and Jean Umiker-Sebeok, eds. *Speaking of Apes: A Critical Anthology of Two-Way Communication with Man.* New York: Plenum Press, 1979.

Thoreau, Henry. *Walden.* In *The Portable Thoreau,* edited by Carl Bode, 258–572. 1947. Reprint, New York: Penguin, 1982.

Part Two: *Pragmatism,*
the Environment,
Hunting, and Farming

5 Beyond Considerability: A Deweyan View of the Animal Rights–Environmental Ethics Debate

Ben A. Minteer

In environmental ethics, philosophers have made much hay from the deep gulf dividing the moral foundations of animal rights/welfare approaches and the ecologically oriented ethical stances that constitute the mainstream of the field's discourse.[1] Indeed, it is a common practice, especially when introducing students to the main positions and debates in the field, to dwell on this division and its import both for philosophical argument and for environmental practices and policies. The consensus view still appears to be that the two projects are in most important respects mutually exclusive, though as we will see below, an increasing number of essays challenging this conclusion in one way or another are perhaps the beginnings of an interesting shift in the discussion. Yet I think it is still safe to say that most environmental ethicists believe that there are at the very least serious tensions between the two bodies of theory, tensions that, especially in the founding years of the debate, were ratcheted up by the exchange of some overheated rhetoric on both sides.

In this chapter, I wish to examine how an explicit pragmatic perspective on the animal rights–environmental ethics debate—specifically, a Deweyan model of moral inquiry—might offer a new way of framing the general philosophical question over the "moral considerability" and comparative moral significance of animals and ecological wholes (i.e., natural systems and processes). In fact, I will argue that this approach implies a distinct movement *away* from the presumption that the debate is best resolved on these grounds; that is, through the articulation and defense of any particular claim based on an attribution of moral standing and significance. As I see it, part of the pragmatic legacy (and John Dewey's work in particular) is the attempt to wean us from these theoretical and methodological predilections in the search for authoritative moral standards, rules, and principles. Yet it seems that most environmental ethicists and animal welfare/rights philosophers continue to insist on the primary significance of these questions of moral considerability and the duties they impose in adjudicating environment-animal conflicts, despite the philosophical train wreck this approach seems to have caused between the two projects.

Instead, I will suggest in this chapter that we should recognize the virtues of an environmental ethical approach that moves beyond attributions of considerability, one that focuses more of its attention on the experimental method of moral inquiry and dispute resolution that figures prominently in Dewey's work. I will claim not only that this pragmatic reframing of the animal rights–environmental ethics debate is more philosophically sound, but also that it opens up a number of new and significant possibilities for intelligent problem solving in specific animal-environment conflicts. Indeed, I believe this Deweyan approach makes good on the early promise of "environmental pragmatism" as an especially useful and effective style of practical ethical reasoning, offering a number of advantages over its main rivals in environmental ethics (see Light and Katz).

I will first examine how the question of moral considerability in the animal rights–environmental ethics debate has been featured in the work of philosophers such as Peter Singer, Tom Regan, J. Baird Callicott, and Holmes Rolston III, finding that this historical emphasis on moral standing leads to irresolvable questions that would best be avoided in a pragmatism-oriented environmental ethics. In the following section, I will consider a few notable and more recent attempts at reconciling environmental ethics and animal rights that have focused on bringing the two positions together at the level of moral principle. While these efforts are significant in their attempt to establish normative compatibility between the two sets of positions, I do not believe that they pay sufficient attention to the role of experimental moral inquiry and problem-oriented thinking in specific conflicts. Accordingly, I will discuss, in the next section, how a Deweyan reconstruction of the debate—moving from general defenses of moral considerability to a recognition of the ethical weight of specific "problematic situations" involving practical contests between animal rights positions and environmental commitments—is a better way to conceptualize and address the contests between them. In the fourth section, I will make a suggestive case for the similarities shared by this Deweyan approach to ethics and some of the better-known projects appearing in the contemporary dispute resolution literature. I will conclude by arguing that a pragmatic recasting of environmental ethics as an applied process of dispute resolution can bring the field into a more useful relationship with the problems of environmental practice, including the conflicts between considerations of animal liberation/rights and environmental ethics.[2]

Reconsidering Moral Considerability: The Animal Rights–Environmental Ethics Debate

The major animal and environmental ethical approaches are familiar in the field of environmental ethics and perhaps applied philosophy more generally, but it is useful to briefly review their salient features here in order to understand why the debate has proven to be so intractable and divisive over the years. Although there are a diverse number of approaches in "animal ethics," the key distinction is commonly made between consequentialist (i.e., utilitarian) approaches, such as that championed by Peter Singer, and nonconsequentialist (i.e., rights-based) views of the kind defended by Tom Regan.[3] In environmental ethics, the historically dominant positions reflect a general philosophical view that we may refer to as "nonanthropocentric holism," in which collectives such as species, ecosystems, and natural processes are seen as directly morally considerable (i.e., possessing intrinsic value). Two exemplars of nonanthropocentric holism in environmental ethics are J. Baird Callicott and Holmes Rolston, both of whom have contributed to the debate between animal rights/welfare theorists and environmental ethicists, as we will see below.

Animal Ethics and Moral Individualism

Peter Singer's ethic of animal liberation is primarily concerned with eliminating, or at least considerably reducing, the human infliction of suffering on those individual animals able to experience states of pleasure and pain, creatures that Singer refers to as being "sentient." Singer argues that we need to recognize that sentient animals have interests that must be considered when we form judgments or render decisions that will affect them positively or negatively. While he does not make any attempt to argue that animals must in all cases be treated as literal equals to humans, Singer does claim that their interests (as beings who can be harmed or benefited) deserve equal consideration by moral agents. In doing so, Singer extends a classical hedonistic version of utilitarianism to the community of sentient nonhumans: in cases in which our actions may affect the welfare of sensate animals, we must select the alternative that has the best possible consequences for the interests of the animal in question. As Singer suggests in his landmark and widely read 1975 book, *Animal Liberation*, this extensionist utilitarian effort finds a textual warrant in Bentham's provocation regarding the criteria for granting moral status to animals. In his later and more overtly philosophical work, however (see *Practical Ethics*), Singer articulates a more sophisticated version of preference utilitarianism to account for the cognitive abilities of higher mammals and, presumably, to respond to counterintuitive readings of the implications of his early hedonistic version of the theory. While Singer's animal welfarism, as a paradigmatic consequentialist project, does not rule out the use of animals in medical research or the ultimate sacrifice of animal lives in cases in which such experimentation or deaths are expected to produce the greatest net benefits for all individuals affected by the proposed action, his approach clearly places a heavy burden on human moral agents to demonstrate that said benefits will in fact result from the action under consideration, and that they will also outweigh the harms suffered by the animal(s).

Tom Regan's approach to animal ethics, unlike Singer's utilitarian model, is properly referred to as a true "animal rights" position, even though that desig-nation commonly refers to any and all ethical arguments calling for the fair treatment and protection of animals. Whereas Singer, at least in his earlier writ-ing, locates the threshold for the moral consideration of an entity at sentience, Regan attempts to place the bar of moral consideration appreciably higher. For Regan, those animals that possess sufficient cognitive capacity such that they are able to have complex beliefs and desires are morally considerable and we have *direct* duties toward them—namely, to avoid causing them unnecessary harm. According to Regan, these beings able to have beliefs and desires (that is, those that are self-conscious) are "experiencing subjects of a life" and are there-fore "ends-in-themselves" that should not be treated as mere resources for hu-man satisfaction. This class of beings, according to Regan, includes all mentally normal adult mammals—a more restricted group than Singer's fairly inclusive set of sentient creatures. Not surprisingly, given these premises, Regan is cate-gorically against sport hunting and trapping, animal agriculture, and the use of animals in all manner of scientific and commercial experimentation. In this sense, and on its face, his position is much more abolitionist than Singer's, since it will not permit utility maximization to trump individual rights, even if great aggregate benefit may result from subordinating such rights to the greater good in a given situation. According to Regan's neo-Kantian perspective, such activi-ties will always fail to respect individual animals as ends-in-themselves.

It is not my purpose here to challenge either Singer's or Regan's criteria for moral considerability; I am simply outlining what are commonly understood to be their main identifying marks in discussions within the field of environmen-tal ethics. But I also want to make note of a shared feature of both approaches. Despite their different moral foundations (in utilitarianism and in neo-Kantian ethics/rights theory, respectively) Singer's and Regan's positions have a common structural form: both are ethically individualistic, in that each view attempts to defend the moral status of nonhuman animals, counted singly. For Singer, the positive experiences of each individual sentient animal have intrinsic value, and an individual animal's pleasure is to be maximized to the extent possible in de-cisions facing (human) moral agents that have the potential to affect the ani-mal's welfare. Similarly, for Regan, each individual mammalian "subject of a life" has a special dignity that demands respect from moral agents. Neither theory, in other words, is able to countenance the direct moral consideration of biological and natural collectives (e.g., species, natural or evolutionary pro-cesses, ecosystems, etc.). They are both morally individualistic in their extension of conventional Western ethical concepts originally intended to apply to the class of human persons.

Environmental Ethics and Moral Holism

Environmental ethicists, unlike their animal ethicist counterparts, have traditionally set up normative shop in the realm of nonhuman collectives, especially at the level of ecological systems. That is, the field has in general been ethically holistic, viewing moral considerability in terms of the value or worth of ecosystems and their natural processes. More often than not, this holism has taken on an overt and pronounced metaphysical cast. For example, J. Baird Callicott, the leading expositor and most ardent defender of Aldo Leopold's land ethic, argues for a nonanthropocentric theory of intrinsic natural value—one that humans ascribe to ecological wholes as a result of what Callicott claims is an evolutionarily fixed faculty of emotional sympathy with our surrounding community. Spurred by ecologists' tearing down of the illusory barriers separating humans and their encompassing environmental systems, Callicott expands the notion of community to encompass the biotic community of nature as well as the human social community (see *In Defense of the Land Ethic* and *Beyond the Land Ethic*). Callicott's commitment to this "weak" nonanthropocentric holism—weak in that it does not posit objective value in nature but rather defends the subjective projection of intrinsic value by a human valuer—led him to fire one of the first shots in the battle between environmental and animal ethicists in his now notorious 1980 essay, "Animal Liberation: A Triangular Affair." There, Callicott wrote of the philosophical incompatibilities between a sentience-based concern for animal welfare (such as that voiced by Singer) and a true nonanthropocentric holism (such as his own), and argued that animal liberation views and "ecocentric" views necessarily entailed divergent management and policy goals in practice. Callicott's remarks in this early paper provoked the wrath of Tom Regan, who memorably referred to Callicott's strident nonanthropocentric holism as an especially pernicious kind of "ecofascism."

Holmes Rolston, another prominent nonanthropocentric holist, goes a good deal further than Callicott with respect to the disposition of intrinsic value in the environment. For Rolston, intrinsic value is a metaphysically real and objective part of the fabric of the natural world. That is, unlike Callicott's approach, Rolston's theory of environmental value does not rely on the consciousness or the valuational activity or capacity of human valuers: intrinsic value would exist in nature even if humans had never arrived on the evolutionary scene. This objectivist ontology of natural value establishes Rolston as professing what we may refer to as a "strong" nonanthropocentric holism in environmental ethics ("strong" relative to Callicott's weaker subjectivist nonanthropocentrism). The centerpiece of Rolston's position is his notion of systemic value, or the productive and creative processes of ecosystems over time (see *Environmental Ethics*). As he puts it, "Duties arise in encounter with the system that projects and protects [its member components] in biotic community" (*Conserving Natural Value* 177). According to Rolston, it subsequently follows from this premise that the "individual members" of the biotic community (e.g., nonhuman animals), while possessing "intrinsic value" in that they defend their own good, nevertheless have little moral importance in comparison with the systemic value that resides within ecosystemic wholes. Indeed, Rolston believes animal ethicists such as Singer and Regan have put the cart before the horse: "Valuing the products but not the system able to produce these products is like finding a goose that lays golden eggs and valuing the eggs but not the goose" (*Conserving Natural Value* 177).[4]

Like Callicott, in his work Rolston has directly squared off against animal ethics approaches that adopt a more individualistic view toward moral considerability. In his contribution to a recent critical anthology of papers devoted to the work of Peter Singer, for example, Rolston gave an unvarnished assessment of the moral inadequacy of Singer's project:

> The trouble [with Singer's argument] is that this is not a *systemic view* of what is going on on the valuable Earth we now experience, before we experienced it. We need an account of the generation of value and valuers, not just some value that now is located in the psychology of the experiencers. Finding that value will generate an Earth Ethics, with a global sense of obligation to this whole inhabited planet. The evolution of rocks into dirt and dirt into fauna and flora is one of the great surprises of natural history, one of the rarest events in the astronomical universe. . . . At this scale of vision, if we ask what is principally to be valued, the value of life arising as a creative process on Earth seems a better description and a more comprehensive category than the pains and pleasures of a fractional percentage of its inhabitants. ("Respect for Life" 266–67)

Rolston clearly thinks that Singer's preoccupation with the welfare of individual animals falls far short of providing an effective moral argument for the large-scale ecological processes that Rolston believes to be the source of all value in nature.[5]

Responding to Rolston's criticisms in the same volume, Singer denied that his position was unable to take account of the value of nonsentient parts of the environment, disagreeing in particular with Rolston's interpretation that his focus on the experiences of sentient beings precludes him from expressing any concern about the condition of natural elements like plants and trees, biological collectives like species, and macrolevel processes like atmospheric regulation. On the contrary, Singer argued that he is able to morally consider these nonsentient parts of the environment by assessing the degree to which their loss leads to the harm of those pleasure- and pain-experiencing animals that depend on them ("A Response"). In other words, since the destruction of a forest ecosystem for economic development clearly harms those sentient animals that rely on this system for food and shelter, Singer could still claim that the development of the forest is ethically wrong, even if he is unable to directly consider the nonsentient parts and processes of the environment that Rolston holds in such high regard. Yet the upshot is that Singer and Rolston clearly disagree about what entities are morally considerable and subsequently about what entities or natural processes should "matter" in our moral deliberations over particular decisions, actions, and policies. The debate, which hinges on the seemingly divergent foundations of moral individualism and moral holism, would appear to be irresolvable, not the least because it is difficult to imagine just what sort of evidence could be brought to bear by either side that would convince the other that it had somehow erroneously conferred moral standing on its animal or environmental subject.

A Few Rapprochements

Despite these sharp lines drawn in the sand by environmental ethicists, there have been several notable attempts within the field to reconcile with animal liberation/rights approaches. In fact, in later work, Callicott himself backpedaled on his earlier and aggressive condemnation of animal ethics in "Animal Liberation." Specifically, in his 1988 article "Animal Liberation and Environmental Ethics: Back Together Again," Callicott wrote that animal rights approaches and ecocentric projects need not be mutually exclusive, since a communitarian ethical theory—one that recognizes a series of duties and obligations to other members of our "mixed" (i.e., human and biotic/nonhuman) communities—could accommodate *both* animal ethicists' concern for the moral considerability of individual nonhuman animals *and* holistic nonanthropocentrists' regard for ecological systems and processes. Callicott's "corrective" to his original position has been joined by a host of sympathetic accommodationist projects in environmental ethics that attempt to mend fences with various animal ethics positions. Dale Jamieson, for example, has argued that animal liberationists can subscribe to many of the same "normative views" as environmental ethicists because both are responding to the same kinds of threats to animals, humans, and ecological systems. Moreover, using an argument similar to Singer's recounted above, Jamieson suggests that animal liberationists can value nature as habitat for sentient beings: the environment possesses a "derivative value" in the sense that it plays a significant (i.e., valuable) role in the lives of sentient animals. On another front, Rick O'Neil has argued that we need not view the two camps as being in direct conflict with one another, since animal ethicists attempt to establish the *moral standing* of sentient creatures, while environmental ethicists are actually performing a philosophically separate (and not necessarily incompatible) task of defending the *intrinsic value* of nonsentient elements of nature. O'Neil's argument, which relies on some semantic hairsplitting between these two notions, is essentially an effort to create a kind of meta-ethical "zoning" that would confine both camps to their appropriate moral spheres.

Most significantly, Gary Varner has offered an intriguing argument for the normative convergence of animal liberation/rights and environmentalist commitments in the case of "therapeutic hunting" of irruptive wildlife species (such as white-tailed deer) that have a tendency to overshoot the carrying capacity of their range (these are what Varner refers to as "obligatory management species"). After working through the main elements of Singer's utilitarian animal liberation position and Regan's more stringent animal rights position, Varner concludes that someone consistently adhering to either principle would be compelled to side with environmentalists concerned with collective species viability and ecological health when faced with wildlife population control. As Varner writes, "an individual genuinely concerned with animal welfare, and even one who attributes moral rights to nonhuman animals, can support the only kind of hunting environmentalists feel compelled to support, namely therapeutic hunting of obligatory management species" (191). Varner deftly shows how "thinning the herd" in such cases actually comports with animal liberationists' concern for pain and suffering, since the skilled killing of animals that reduces their numbers to an environmentally sustainable level will avoid greater potential painful suffering and death due to sickness and starvation. He also demonstrates how therapeutic hunting is in keeping with animal rights proponents' desire to minimize the transgression of individual rights when harm to animals is inevitable. In this case, it would appear that some animals must be culled to avoid an even worse situation, one that would result in starvation and agonizing deaths for a greater number of animals over time as their habitat becomes steadily degraded.

The Contribution of Pragmatism: From Moral Considerability to Problematic Situation

While these efforts at reconciling animal and environmental ethics are conceptually significant and well-motivated, we should note that their emphasis has been mostly on achieving philosophical compatibility at the level of moral standing or moral principle. That is, these attempts at rapprochement between environmental ethics and animal liberation/rights have sought to resolve the conflict as if it were primarily, and most significantly, a general philosophical debate over the moral status of nonhuman animals and nature, rather than a series of *practical* conflicts requiring the evaluation of competing goods and deliberation over alternative proposals and claims in specific cases requiring intelligent judgment. Even Varner's project, which does engage one particular class of contexts in which the animal-environment dispute occurs in practice (the case of therapeutic hunting), is concerned mainly with questions relating to moral standing and with supporting normative principles in animal ethics in its attempt to justify an "environmental" judgment (i.e., to cull populations of certain irruptive species in order to protect ecosystem health) through a nuanced reading of the commitments of Singer's and Regan's philosophical systems.

This focus on general normative principles and broad, conceptual issues of moral standing and moral significance is not surprising, since over the course of its short academic life environmental ethics has been fairly consumed with these classic philosophical questions of moral considerability and ontology. And of course this theoretical orientation is not found only in the compatibilist approaches in environmental ethics offered by Callicott, Jamieson, and Varner; it remains the dominant form in the field, and is also embraced by those environmental ethicists who remain critical of the insufficient "moral coverage" of animal ethics (as we can clearly see in Rolston's criticism of Singer in the previous section). On all of these fronts, environmental ethicists are simply following the traditional approach to ethical theory more generally: namely, the investigation into the grounds for moral standing and the accompanying search for rules, standards, and principles by which to govern the relationship between moral agents (and in this case also between agents and moral "patients").

And, as should be clear from the above discussion, this concern with matters of moral considerability and the substantive content of moral principles in environmental ethics also characterizes much of the paradigmatic work in animal ethics. For example, the programs of Singer and Regan may be seen as seeking to extend conventional ethical concepts (respectively, utility and rights) to the previously excluded class of nonhuman animals, and both Singer and Regan devote a good deal of attention to the question of moral standing. In parallel fashion, environmental ethicists, especially nonanthropocentrists, often employ the language of intrinsic value as a kind of proxy for a moral rights–type claim about the standing of nonhuman nature, with supporting arguments and defenses of exactly what parts of nature "count" in a moral sense (for nonanthropocentric holists, those parts include entire ecological systems and processes).

Though animal and environmental ethics seem to be united in their shared recognition of the fundamental importance of questions of moral considerability and the critical role of general moral principles in delineating and justifying the corollary duties we have vis-à-vis animals and environmental systems, we may nevertheless still ask whether this kind of approach is the best way to conceptualize the ethical enterprise. In particular, we may question whether the traditional emphasis on matters of moral standing and the search for and defense of an authoritative (and usually small) set of normative principles in environmental and animal ethics provides an adequate and complete model for the kind of reflective moral inquiry required by the complex problematic situations that arise in human experience in the natural world. I do not believe it does.

The demands of plural and competing goods and claims in the moral life, together with the multilayered and textured normative and empirical contexts of practical problem-solving efforts in actual cases of animal-environment conflict, would seem to require something more than global and unidimensional attributions of moral considerability and the invocation of one or a few general principles.[6] At the very least, I would say that this standard approach is certainly not the *only* way to conceptualize the purpose and practice of environmental and animal ethics, just as it is not the only way to view moral reasoning and theorizing more generally. Here, the aforementioned pragmatic turn in environmental ethics promises to be of some help. Indeed, the developing pragmatic critique in the field has opened the door for a number of alternative models serious about linking ethical theory and environmental practice, including new methodological and normative projects either inspired by or directly adapted from the work of the classic American pragmatists.[7] While it encompasses a good deal of philosophical diversity, this pragmatic alternative in environmental ethics generally accepts, if not celebrates, value pluralism; embraces an experimental approach to ethical claims about the natural world; and focuses much more seriously on the empirical and normative contexts of moral experience than did previous theoretical efforts in the field.

Of all the pragmatist insights, John Dewey's understanding of ethics, especially his view of moral reasoning as an experimental activity carried out in the context of specific "problematic situations," is, I believe, one of the more valuable intellectual bequests for a contemporary pragmatic environmental ethics. Dewey's reconstruction of ethics (and philosophy more generally), to focus more on the methods of inquiry, deliberation, and problem solving than on broad notions of moral considerability and the a priori authority of fixed principles, provides us with a way of conceptualizing the moral enterprise that engages rather than dismisses the multifaceted nature of moral problems, including the irreducible multiplicity of goods that constitute specific practical conflicts.

Dewey famously argued, early and late, that philosophers' traditional approach to the quandaries of moral experience—applying general ethical claims articulated prior to reflection and investigation into the facts of and values already extant in specific problematic situations—was misguided. This method, in his view, did not recognize the novel demands and circumstances of each situation, nor did it adopt an appropriately provisional and fallibilist attitude toward moral principles and theories espoused before inquiry into specific contexts. Instead, Dewey suggested that the thorny difficulties and conflicts of human experience required an experimental method of inquiry similar to that employed in the natural and technical sciences. As he wrote in his 1920 landmark work, *Reconstruction in Philosophy*:

> A moral situation is one in which judgment and choice are required antecedently to overt action. The practical meaning of the situation—that is to say the action needed to satisfy it—is not self-evident. It has to be searched for. There are conflicting desires and alternative apparent goods. What is needed is to find the right course of action, the right good. Hence inquiry is exacted: observation of the detailed makeup of the situation; analysis into its diverse factors; clarification of what is obscure; discounting of the more insistent and vivid traits; tracing the consequences of the various modes of action that suggest themselves; regarding the decision as hypothetical and tentative until the anticipated or supposed consequences which led to its adoption have been squared with actual consequences. This inquiry is intelligence. (173)

For Dewey, the role of intelligence in ethics was defined by an individual's (and a community's) ability to examine the needs of an uncertain and disrupted (i.e., "problematic") situation and to "overhaul" the moral resources accumulated in previous experience for use in appraising and guiding present and future ethical analysis. This "unified method of inquiry," which Dewey argued could be profitably applied to both facts *and* values, was most fully described in *Logic: The Theory of Inquiry* (1938). In order to tackle the troubling situations that emerge in experience (including those identified as predominantly moral), according to Dewey, we must first begin by recognizing that a situation as experienced is, indeed, "problematic," and therefore acknowledging that inquiry is required because of the real deficiencies of the *situation*—not just the subjective doubts or uncertainties of the individual. The next stage in this process involved the analysis of the problem context and the creative generation of hypothetical solutions that might work to resolve the unsettled situation. This was then followed by the appraisal, in the imagination (the "dramatic rehearsal"), of each proposed solution's ability to resolve, effectively and efficiently, the troubled situation at hand. The final stage of inquiry was the act of judgment: selecting a course of action from among a set of alternatives and then carrying it out in practice (including subsequent reflection on and monitoring of performance).

This basic pattern of inquiry, derived from the logic of problem solving in the natural and technical sciences, was also linked, in Dewey's view, to the moral and epistemic virtues of democratic politics:

> The alternative method [to moral dogmatism and falling back on fixed principles] may be called experimental. It implies that reflective morality demands observation of particular situations, rather than fixed adherence to a priori principles; that free inquiry and freedom of publication and discussion must be encouraged and not merely grudgingly tolerated. . . . It is, in short, the method of democracy, of a positive toleration which amounts to sympathetic regard for the intelligence and personality of others, even if they hold views opposed to ours, and of scientific inquiry into facts and testing of ideas. (Dewey and Tufts 329)

Dewey's accounting of the role of inquiry in addressing moral problems and his description of the normative character of such inquiry (i.e., a method marked by toleration, sympathy, etc.) suggests a more *processual* view of ethics, one in which values, principles, and moral standards emerge through the method of experimentation and situational analysis rather than simply being taken off the shelf and imposed on specific moral problems and conflicts. This dynamic reconstruction of ethics thus redefines the business of normative reflection as a particular kind of practical problem solving, making it more akin to contemporary methods of dispute resolution than to traditional ethical theorizing (I will have more to say about this correspondence in the final section).

In keeping with its robust experimental framework, Dewey's ethical system also emphasized the traditionally discounted significance of discovery and creativity in any effective moral inquiry. "Inquiry, discovery take the same place in morals that they have come to occupy in sciences of nature. Validation, demonstration become experimental, a matter of consequences" (*Reconstruction* 179). This understanding of the open-ended nature of moral experience embraced the time-tested truth of value pluralism, and introduced the prospect of weighing numerous and often competing goods in practical deliberations over right actions and judgments. Dewey's view on this matter did not signal a flat-out rejection of held moral principles and their encompassing theories so much as it endorsed a more holistic model of moral reasoning, one in which the multiple values and empirical circumstances of each problematic situation were directly engaged by moral inquiry rather than dispelled by the philosophical appeal to abstract, universal principles:

> A moral philosophy which should frankly recognize that each human being has to make the best adjustment he can among forces which are genuinely disparate, would throw light upon actual predicaments of conduct and help individuals in making a juster estimate of the force of each competing factor. All that would be lost would be the idea that theoretically there is in advance a single theoretically correct solution for every difficulty with which each and every individual is confronted. Personally I think the surrender of this idea would be a gain instead of a loss. In taking attention away from rigid rules and standards it would lead men to attend more fully to the concrete elements entering into the situations in which they have to act. ("Three Independent Factors" 288)

Since moral situations, in this reading, were sufficiently complex and different from one another to challenge the uncritical reliance on any single and unmodifiable moral claim as governing inquiry into potential alternative courses of action, the search for a monolithic, universal philosophical foundation for ethical experience was doomed to failure. "A genuinely reflective morals," Dewey wrote, "will look upon all the [moral] codes as possible *data*. . . . It will neither insist dogmatically upon some of them, nor idly throw them all away as of no significance. It will treat them as a storehouse of information and possible indications of what is now right and good" (Dewey and Tufts 179). As he recognized, each problematic situation, no matter how closely it may seem to resemble previously experienced dilemmas and disruptions, always presents us with something novel and unexpected. As a consequence, according to Dewey, we should not try to constrain any particular moral discussion to the language of a single principle or set of principles prior to reflective inquiry if we wish to respond intelligently and effectively to the varying dilemmas of human experience. Dewey's view clearly suggests an image of morality as an adaptive, organic process:

> In fact, situations into which change and the unexpected enter are a challenge to intelligence to create new principles. Morals must be a growing science if it is to be a science at all, not merely because all truth has not yet been appropriated by the mind of man, but because life is a moving affair in which old moral truth ceases to apply. Principles are methods of inquiry and forecast which require verification by the event; and the time honored effort to assimilate morals to mathematics is only a way of bolstering up an old dogmatic authority, or putting a new one upon the throne of the old. But the experimental character of moral judgments does not mean complete uncertainty and fluidity. Principles exist as hypotheses with which to experiment. (*Human Nature* 164–65)

In Dewey's hands, moral principles thus play an important, though appropriately moderated, role in the process of thoughtful and reflective inquiry into specific problematic situations. While they often possess a certain force in deliberations over the right policy or action (a force owed primarily to their previous success in helping us to address earlier difficulties), they can, at best, capture only a particular and partial aspect of the larger problematic situation in which we find ourselves entangled. Again, since past experience shows that these unsettled and unbalanced contexts often find individuals struggling to harmonize disparate rights, duties, goods, and virtues—each of which competes for attention and influence in our moral judgments—the selection of any one of these for special emphasis *before* investigation into their ability to contribute to the resolution of a specific problematic situation thwarts the method of intelligent inquiry. For Dewey, the continual refinement of the method of inquiry, and the critical social learning that inquiry affords its participants, thus replaces the traditional philosophical loyalty to preexperimental general moral principles:

> No past decision nor old principle can ever be wholly relied upon to justify a course of action. No amount of pains taken in forming a purpose in a definite case is final; the consequences of its adoption must be carefully noted, and a purpose held only as a working hypothesis until results confirm its rightness. Mistakes are no longer either mere unavoidable accidents to be mourned or moral sins to be expiated and forgiven. They are lessons in wrong methods of using intelligence and instructions as to a better course in the future. They are indications of the need of revision, development, readjustment. Ends grow, standards of judgment are improved. . . . Moral life is protected from falling into formalism and rigid repetition. It is rendered flexible, vital, growing. (*Reconstruction* 179–80)

Ethical theories are, in this understanding, critical tools for analyzing and interpreting particular social problems and conflicts, not fixed ends or positions to which we must accord privileged philosophical status or, worse, which determine our behavior. In making this move, Dewey significantly shifted discussions of moral theory and argument away from a preoccupation with the ontological status of general moral principles, moving them toward the refinement of the process of intelligent inquiry and the development of better and more effective methods of cooperative problem solving. In effect, ethics here becomes an explicit form of conflict resolution. It is a process of reducing disagreement among disputants through the method of "social intelligence," which for Dewey was driven by the logic of experimental inquiry and which achieved its ends by transforming problematic situations into more "consummated" and stable organic arrangements.

Reframing the Debate: Environmental Ethics as Dispute Resolution

So what exactly does the Deweyan approach to ethics have to contribute to the debate over environmental ethics and animal rights? I believe that this pragmatic articulation of ethics as a process of experimental inquiry, unlike the historically dominant approaches within both camps (if not applied ethics as a whole), suggests that we should address ethical conflicts such as that between environmental and animal ethics as *practical disputes* requiring cooperative investigation and a deliberate method of problem solving, rather than as abstract philosophical debates over questions of considerability and comparative moral significance. That is, I think Dewey's work instructs us that we would do better if we turned our attention to refining specific methods of observation, moral analysis, and empirical evaluation, adopting a more experimental and case-based approach to ethics, than we would elaborating and defending metaphysical and moral arguments for the intrinsic value of ecosystems or the interests and rights of nonhuman animals. The pragmatic alternative, endorsing ethical pluralism as well as the provisional and instrumental nature of moral principles, thus frames ethical inquiry as a more creative and dynamic process, one in which discovery and invention play an important part in our moral deliberations over alternative claims and proposals. These commitments certainly suggest a very different orientation to philosophical disputes than has been taken by ethicists in the past.

Indeed, in many respects Dewey's reconstruction of ethics as briefly outlined above issues a view of moral life as an explicit process of cooperative dispute resolution, especially in those public conflicts (like most on-the-ground disputes over animals and the environment) that involve multiple and competing stakeholders and seemingly entrenched disagreements about alternative values, interests, and scientific and technical issues. It is therefore instructive to consider the relationship between Dewey's approach and the burgeoning dispute resolution literature that has made significant inroads in many policy and planning fields. In particular, general alternative dispute resolution (ADR) frameworks, such as those characterized as "consensus-based" or "negotiated agreement" approaches, have gained both intellectual support and administrative credibility in the past two decades as alternatives to litigation and conventional forms of adjudication between contesting parties. Common attributes of these ADR frameworks include: (1) voluntary participation in the negotiation by parties in the dispute; (2) direct, active, face-to-face participation of the disputants or, in some cases, their representatives; and (3) collective agreement by the participating parties on the process of the negotiation as well as consensus on its outcome (see Wondolleck and Yaffee). More specifically, environmental dispute resolution (EDR) techniques and processes have been employed in a variety of sociopolitical contexts, including policy-level conflicts such as environmental rule making and policy dialogues in the U.S. Environmental Protection Agency, and site-level disputes such as conflicts over the use and management of natural resources, the siting of industrial facilities, and public disputes over various land use and pollution control issues (see O'Leary et al.).

What explains the appeal of these approaches? For starters, EDR methods offer parties to an environmental dispute the hope that they can achieve their goals without having to resort to highly adversarial, risky, and expensive litigation. In addition, EDR supporters praise the method's attention to building healthy and enduring relationships among disputants, its general versatility and ability to respond to increasingly complex cross-sector and transboundary environmental problems, and its decentralized structure and efficiency compared with traditional bureaucratic approaches. While the literature on ADR and EDR methods is voluminous and expanding daily, for present purposes we can briefly consider two influential and complementary models, projects that I believe also display an intriguing Deweyan influence. One is the "principled negotiation" approach developed by Roger Fisher and William Ury in their best-selling book *Getting to Yes.* The other is the negotiated agreement framework for resolving public disputes put forth by Lawrence Susskind and Jeffrey Cruikshank in *Breaking the Impasse.*[8] It is worth outlining the core components of both models, if only in bare-bones fashion here, since I want to suggest that they offer interesting practical articulations of a Deweyan model of social inquiry that can prove useful in resolving problematic situations, including disputes between environmental ethical and animal rights claims.

The method of principled negotiation as set forth in *Getting to Yes* comprises four main activities designed to facilitate consensus in any situation marked by prima facie disagreement. These include (1) separating the people from the problem, (2) focusing on stakeholders' underlying interests rather than their stated bargaining positions, (3) searching for and inventing options to promote mutual gain and fulfill shared interests, and (4) employing in the negotiation fair standards and principles chosen through a process of collective inquiry and debate. A notable feature of Fisher and Ury's approach to dispute resolution, and one that evokes Dewey's understanding of inquiry discussed above, is its attention to the creative possibilities of collaborative negotiation strategies, in which novel solutions and tactics may arise through a process of collective deliberation and specific brainstorming efforts. Likewise, their emphasis on the role of communication in identifying underlying shared interests in situations of outward conflict over held positions indirectly evokes Dewey's commitment to cooperative inquiry and his focus on harmonizing and integrating competing interests in situations of conflict. And, as the fourth point listed above suggests, Fisher and Ury's process of negotiation places great importance on the collective search by the disputants for principles that can serve as critical standards for choosing among competing solutions to the problem at hand. This aspect also echoes Dewey's view of general principles as analytical and discursive tools for resolving practical disputes.

Susskind and Cruikshank's approach in *Breaking the Impasse* shares many similarities with the negotiation process described in *Getting to Yes,* including the importance of identifying options for mutual gain and the necessity of meaningful cooperation among disputants; yet they present a somewhat more elaborated discussion of the public negotiation process, and in doing so provide a fuller view of many of its underlying epistemological foundations. In their book, Susskind and Cruikshank describe "good outcomes" of negotiated settlements as those agreements that are (1) perceived as fair by all participants (a perception which hinges on the process being open to continual revision by the parties), (2) efficient, (3) wise (in the sense that disputants should have experience with their own community and its problems so that they can anticipate and work through them), and (4) stable (agreements must endure and include provisions for future renegotiations). One of the most interesting concepts presented in *Impasse* is what they refer to as "prospective hindsight," or the valuable problem-solving wisdom that accrues from a community's having addressed similar challenges in the past. This notion, along with Susskind and Cruikshank's emphasis on continual revision in the negotiation process and the idea that joint fact-finding can significantly reduce error in the proceedings, gives the epistemological commitments of *Impasse* an unmistakable Deweyan, pragmatic drift.

While this highly abbreviated treatment obviously cannot take the full measure of these methods as practical philosophical frameworks or policy tools, it should be sufficient to demonstrate some of their striking similarities to Dewey's project, especially to the contours of his universal pattern of inquiry. I believe this resemblance may be seen in a number of places, including, as mentioned above, both programs' rejection of the unexamined authority of a priori principles and all manner of fixed positions, as well as their emphasis on continual revision and adjustment of the negotiation process itself. Indeed, like Dewey's understanding of the ethical process, these methods require one to take a provisional and experimental view toward normative claims—including, for example, those focused on the moral status of individuals, collectives, or both. In addition, in emphasizing creative ways to engage and integrate seemingly incompatible values, goals, and objectives through careful methods of reasoning, fact-finding, and open deliberation, both dispute resolution projects clearly mirror Dewey's logic of social inquiry. Moreover, Dewey's recognition and defense of value pluralism and his accompanying arguments for tolerating different views of the good, not to mention his commitment to cooperative inquiry and the self-correcting nature of democratic discussion, suggest further harmonies between his project and these leading contributions in the dispute resolution literature. Last, these methods demonstrate a Deweyan faith in the self-regulating character of experience, in which standards and decisions arise from an iterative process of deliberation and hypothesis testing to meet inquirers' (disputants') needs and interests within the circumstances of a problematic situation.

These sympathies are also becoming more noticed and reflected on by Dewey scholars. William Caspary, for example, in his recent book on Dewey's ethics and politics, has made a compelling case that the theme of conflict resolution resounds in much of the philosopher's work. I believe Caspary is correct in emphasizing this thread in Dewey's thought, especially as it figures in his approach to ethics and his theory of public reasoning. I would suggest, in fact, that contemporary methods of cooperative dispute resolution such as those set forth in *Getting to Yes* and *Breaking the Impasse* not only revive many Deweyan themes but actually offer practical methodological frameworks that can give us a sharper and more concrete operationalization of Dewey's fairly abstract philosophy of inquiry in specific problematic situations. For these two ADR projects are good manifestations of social intelligence as Dewey understood it: the controlled, cooperative, and experimental approach to social problems, shored up by a commitment to the norms of free and open inquiry yet always aware of the limitations presented by human fallibility and the inevitable appearance of the novel and unexpected. And their value as potential ethical resources, albeit within a reconstructed, processual view of ethics, is just now being discovered.

Conclusion: Toward a Pragmatic Holism in Environmental Ethics

I can now summarize the main claims of this chapter. I have suggested that the historical intractability of the environmental ethics–animal rights debate is largely due to its being construed, even by those seeking to make philosophical amends, as a contest between general and competing claims of moral considerability. I have argued that we would be better off approaching the dispute instead as a class of problematic situations in the Deweyan sense: as concrete problems that require the application of intelligent methods of inquiry such as those found in certain consensual dispute resolution frameworks. That is to say, I have proposed that the focus in this debate should be on specific problematic cases involving environmental and animal conflicts that require cooperative inquiry and creative problem solving, rather than on the (purely) philosophical question of the comparative moral status of animals and the environment and on the deduction of general principles marking off our purported moral duties toward them. This does not mean that the intellectual task of defending animal interests and rights or the intrinsic value of ecosystems is no longer necessary or important, for it surely is. But I do not think that this task alone gets us very far in our efforts to resolve real environment-animal conflicts.

Consider the case of the "deer problem" in western Massachusetts as discussed by the sociologist Jan Dizard in his fascinating analysis of the dispute between hunters and animal rights proponents on the Quabbin Reservoir. As Dizard's account demonstrates, if we are interested in getting a grip on this particular incarnation of the animal rights–environmental ethics debate, we need not only to know how the exploding deer population in the region threatens the ecological health of the forest (which will entail learning about the history of the area's land use); we must also understand the interplay among the many competing interests and values of participants in the contentious debate over "hunting the forest back into health." This diverse group of stakeholders includes not only hunters, animal rights advocates, and environmentalists but also wildlife managers, area residents, and tourists, among others. Furthermore, we must take into consideration and evaluate specific forest management practices and the merits and consequences of the various techniques available for deer population control, not to mention the impact of deer eradication (or, alternatively, their protection) on other wildlife species, such as beavers and moose. As I see it, the Quabbin deer problem captured by Dizard is the sort of case that requires intelligent inquiry in the Deweyan sense—a flexible and open approach able to build common ground among disputants and achieve a scientifically informed, publicly constructed solution that is fair, efficient, and durable over time. I do not think, however, that such cases will be well-served by repeated general affirmations of the moral standing of deer or the forest alone.

The reconstruction of the animal rights–environmental ethics debate as a series of practical disputes, defined by unique combinations of empirical and value conflicts in specific problematic situations rooted in time and space, moves the field of environmental ethics more squarely into the realm of environmental and social practices—in particular, the sphere of public decision making and community problem solving. In doing so, it begins to advance the well-known but often hard-to-accomplish mission of pragmatism as a praxis-oriented approach that engages the real dilemmas of human experience. Here, Dewey's thorough recasting of the traditional philosophical enterprise, as he rejects all forms of indulgent speculation and theorizing disconnected from the trials and tribulations of daily life, helps us to position environmental ethics on the front lines of environmental conflict, where it may yet make some useful contributions to resolving policy disagreements and specific site-level disputes, including those hinging on the frequent tensions between animal rights and environmental health.

Again, the pragmatic approach I am advocating by no means dismisses traditional questions of moral considerability and the search for normative principles to guide human relationships with animals and the natural environment. But it does insist on viewing these commitments as tools for problem solving and dispute resolution (embodiments of "prospective hindsight"), rather than as fixed rules or directives that must be followed without question. In practice, the emphasis on fixed positions—for example, preexperiential foundations for moral standing or value—can obscure underlying shared interests and can turn disputants away from the kinds of compromise, concessions, and creative integrative solutions prized by Dewey and present-day conflict resolution theorists. Instead, I have argued in the preceding pages for greater focus on methods of cooperative inquiry and negotiated agreements, in which a variety of moral claims regarding nonhuman animals and the environment may be advanced as reasons for adopting a particular proposal or policy or for choosing a particular course of action.

What I have proposed here is not just a new tack in the animal rights–environmental ethics debate but also an alternative approach to environmental ethics more generally, one that might be called "pragmatic" or "anthropocentric" holism. It is pragmatic in its emphasis on experimental methods of inquiry and conflict resolution; its rejection of a priori, preexperiential "first principles"; and its endorsement of value pluralism and dynamism. It is holistic in its focus on the *entire* problematic situation (a situation which will most certainly include both identifiably discrete elements—i.e., individuals—*and* larger eco-physical processes and contexts), as well as in its accounting of the multiple goods and relevant empirical circumstances that define a particular conflict between opposing claims in specific environmental disputes (including those between advocates of environmental health and of animal rights and welfare). And it is anthropocentric in one sense: it insists that all values expressed in public deliberations are human values, expressed and experienced by humans. That is, all values are understood in public negotiations not as human-independent (i.e., strongly nonanthropocentric) values, but rather as ways that people do indeed value animals and nature and that may act as good reasons to select specific courses of action or policies.[9] While this approach can accommodate claims such as those declaring the intrinsic value of nature and the rights of nonhuman animals (as it can instrumental valuations), it insists on subjecting these claims to the critical test of public discussion and inquiry oriented toward the goal of securing wise, efficient, and enduring agreements among stakeholders.

I close this chapter with a simple plea. I think it is time for environmental ethics to move beyond its historically dominant emphasis on the formulation and defense of general and universal arguments for why nonhuman nature (both parts and wholes) matters. Although we can always benefit from additional work in this area, and I would not want any line of productive inquiry shut down simply because it was probing the philosophical foundations of natural value, I believe that we already are flush with a wealth of principles and theories articulating the value of nature and its nonhuman inhabitants. Instead, what we really need at this point in the field's historical development are clear and effective frameworks for dispute resolution and problem solving that can inform and improve public negotiation and debate over the problematic situations that arise in the environmental context. This does not mean the wholesale replacement of normative environmental ethics with descriptive ethics; I am not advocating that the field become an environmental application of moral sociology. But it does mean working to make environmental ethics more responsive and relevant to the concrete affairs of human environmental experience, as well as insisting that its animating philosophical debates—such as the protracted dispute with animal rights philosophies—always be joined on solid ground.

Notes

1. See, for example, Callicott, "Animal Liberation"; Sagoff; Katz; and Hargrove.

2. My approach in this chapter may therefore be seen as complementary to the "methodological environmental pragmatism" developed by Andrew Light (see his contribution to this volume). I take a much more explicit Deweyan line than Light on the animal rights–environmental ethics debate, however.

3. While "the animals rights–environmental ethics debate" is the conventional way of referring to a set of specific and recognized philosophical disagreements between animal and environmental ethicists, it should be noted that "animal rights" in this usage also include non-rights-based positions such as Singer's (utilitarian) animal welfarism.

To be more accurate, in this chapter I will employ the designation "animal ethics" when I am discussing Regan's and Singer's positions outside the "debate." When I refer to the animal-environment debate as it has been discussed historically in the field of environmental ethics, however, I will retain the "animal rights" label (referring to both Regan's and Singer's positions) for the sake of consistency.

4. It is also interesting to note that unlike Rolston, whose work has been occupied primarily with the "wilder" ends of the biophysical spectrum, Singer and Regan have to date been much more concerned with the treatment of animals in domestic or laboratory contexts, rather than as parts of comparatively more natural ecosystemic wholes. Among other things, this difference in focus leads one to wonder if some of the philosophical friction between the two sides might be unnecessary, since Singer and Regan could be viewed as simply addressing a different set of questions and concerns in these human-dominated contexts than those engaged by Rolston in more autonomous ecological systems.

5. Of course, Rolston does not only reject the nonanthropocentric individualism of animal ethicists such as Singer in favor of his strong version of nonanthropocentric holism. Like many in environmental ethics, he is also deeply—perhaps most deeply—suspicious of *anthropocentric* individualism: i.e., those philosophical projects that grant moral standing solely to individual human beings. Yet I believe that the full-scale assault on these human-oriented commitments by Rolston and others in the field has produced a number of troubling ethical and political implications, consequences I have suggested sink many nonanthropocentric claims (see Minteer, "No Experience Necessary?"). While I think the anthropocentric or "pragmatic holism" I advocate at the end of the present chapter avoids these problems, the task of filling out this approach in environmental ethics and examining more thoroughly its relationship to anthropocentric individualistic theories remains for another occasion.

6. Here it should be noted that Mary Anne Warren is one of the few philosophers who have developed a multicriterial conception of moral considerability in the literature, one importantly able to account for individuals as well as systems/wholes. See her book *Moral Status*.

7. For some examples of emerging pragmatist-inspired work in environmental ethics, see Light and Katz; Norton; and Minteer, "Intrinsic Value for Pragmatists?"

8. The books are the centerpieces of the Harvard Negotiation Project (Fisher and Ury) and the MIT-Harvard Public Disputes Program (Susskind and Cruikshank).

9. For a fuller discussion of this model of public valuation, see Norton and Minteer.

Bibliography

Callicott, J. Baird. "Animal Liberation: A Triangular Affair." *Environmental Ethics* 2 (1980): 311–38.

———. "Animal Liberation and Environmental Ethics: Back Together Again." *Between the Species* 4, no. 3 (1988): 163–69.

———. *Beyond the Land Ethic.* Albany: State University of New York Press, 1999.

———. *In Defense of the Land Ethic.* Albany: State University of New York Press, 1989.

Caspary, William R. *Dewey on Democracy.* Ithaca, N.Y.: Cornell University Press, 2000.

Dewey, John. *Human Nature and Conduct. The Middle Works, 1899–1924,* edited by Jo Ann Boydston, vol. 14, *1922.* Carbondale: Southern Illinois University Press, 1988.

———. *The Later Works, 1925–1953.* Edited by Jo Ann Boydston. 17 vols. Carbondale: Southern Illinois University Press, 1981–90.

———. *Logic: The Theory of Inquiry. The Later Works,* vol. 12, *1938.*

———. *Reconstruction in Philosophy.* In *The Middle Works, 1899–1924,* edited by Jo Ann Boydston, vol. 12, *1920,* 77–201. Carbondale: Southern Illinois University Press, 1982.

———. "Three Independent Factors in Morals." In *The Later Works,* vol. 5, *1929–1930,* 279–88.

Dewey, John, and James Hayden Tufts. *Ethics. The Later Works,* vol. 7, *1932.*

Dizard, Jan E. *Going Wild: Hunting, Animal Rights, and the Contested Meaning of Nature.* Rev. ed. Amherst: University of Massachusetts Press, 1999.

Fisher, Roger, and William Ury. *Getting to Yes.* New York: Penguin Books, 1983.

Hargrove, Eugene, ed. *The Animal Rights/Environmental Ethics Debate.* Albany: State University of New York Press, 1992.

Jamieson, Dale. "Animal Liberation Is an Environmental Ethic." *Environmental Values* 7 (1998): 41–57.

Katz, Eric. "Defending the Use of Animals by Business: Animal Liberation and Environmental Ethics." In *Business, Ethics, and the Environment: The Public Policy Debate,* edited by W. Michael Hoffman, Robert Frederick, and Edward S. Petry, Jr., 223–32. New York: Quorum Books, 1990.

Light, Andrew, and Eric Katz, eds. *Environmental Pragmatism.* London: Routledge, 1996.

Minteer, Ben A. "Intrinsic Value for Pragmatists?" *Environmental Ethics* 22 (2001): 57–75.

———. "No Experience Necessary? Foundationalism and the Retreat from Culture in Environmental Ethics." *Environmental Values* 7 (1998): 333–48.

Norton, Bryan. "Pragmatism, Adaptive Management, and Sustainability." *Environmental Values* 8 (1999): 451–66.

Norton, Bryan, and Ben A. Minteer. "From Environmental Ethics to Environmental Public Philosophy: Ethicists and Economists, 1973–Future." In *International Yearbook of Environmental and Resource Economics, 2002/2003,* edited by Tom Tietenberg and Henk Folmer, 373–407. Cheltenham: Edward Elgar, 2002.

O'Leary, Rosemary, Robert F. Durant, Daniel J. Fiorino, and Paul S. Weiland. *Managing for the Environment.* San Francisco: Jossey-Bass Publishers, 1998.

O'Neil, Rick. "Animal Liberation versus Environmentalism." *Environmental Ethics* 22 (2000): 183–90.

Regan, Tom. *The Case for Animal Rights.* Berkeley: University of California Press, 1983.

Rolston, Holmes, III. *Conserving Natural Value.* New York: Columbia University Press, 1994.

———. *Environmental Ethics.* Philadelphia: Temple University Press, 1988.

———. "Respect for Life: Counting What Singer Finds of No Account." In *Singer and His Critics,* edited by Dale Jamieson, 247–68. Oxford: Blackwell, 1999.

Sagoff, Mark. "Animal Liberation and Environmental Ethics: Bad Marriage, Quick Divorce." *Osgoode Hall Law Journal* 22 (1984): 297–307.

Singer, Peter. *Animal Liberation: A New Ethic for Our Treatment of Animals.* New York: Avon Books, 1975.

———. *Practical Ethics.* 2nd ed. Cambridge: Cambridge University Press, 1993.

———. "A Response." In *Singer and His Critics,* edited by Dale Jamieson, 327–32. Oxford: Blackwell, 1999.

Susskind, Lawrence, and Jeffrey Cruikshank. *Breaking the Impasse.* New York: Basic Books, 1987.

Varner, Gary E. "Can Animal Rights Activists Be Environmentalists?" In *Environmental Ethics and Environmental Activism,* edited by Donald Marietta and Lester Embree, 169–201. Lanham, Md.: Rowman and Littlefield, 1995.

Warren, Mary Ann. *Moral Status: Obligations to Persons and Other Living Things.* Oxford: Clarendon Press, 1997.

Wondolleck, Julia, and Steven Yaffee. *Making Collaboration Work.* Washington, D.C.: Island Press, 2000.

Methodological Pragmatism,
Animal Welfare, and Hunting

Andrew Light

In 1996 Eric Katz and I published an edited book titled *Environmental Pragmatism*. We had two aims in mind: first, to bring together a representative sampling of the growing contributions by pragmatists to the field of environmental ethics, and second, to try to push environmental ethicists away from the various meta-ethical debates in which they had become stuck toward a more pluralist methodology which could improve their ability to contribute to the formulation of better environmental policies.

The second of our aims in *Environmental Pragmatism* was to my mind the more important of the two because, as a field of applied philosophy, environmental ethics ought to be able to make some kind of contribution to resolving environmental problems at the level of law or policy. If it can't, I'm not sure why we would do this kind of philosophy in the first place. Many, however, do not share this view. J. Baird Callicott argues that environmental ethics fulfills its promise as a field of philosophy and environmental activity if it concentrates on the project either of offering an alternative human worldview toward the environment or of refining theories of why nature (either ecosystems, species, or nature writ large) has some kind of noninstrumental or intrinsic value that warrants moral recognition or obligation (see "Environmental Philosophy"). But while figures like Callicott can point to examples of how environmental ethicists have used such work to influence activist environmental organizations or the public policy process, there are ample reasons to believe either that this approach to environmental ethics is too limited or that the results are largely inconsequential for the work of environmental advocates (see Light and de-Shalit). For the fact remains that most work in environmental ethics focuses on intramural debates between and among environmental ethicists over issues such as the moral foundations for a nonanthropocentric intrinsic value of nature. Precious little in this literature is of any direct use to those who are actually trying to form laws or policies, given that the social realm of law and policy must of necessity make appeals to human, anthropocentric interests, which are usually not considered in such debates. The success of *Environmental Pragmatism* in achieving this second aim is at best mixed, because its message is still largely resisted by influential figures in the field. Callicott continues his attack on the relevance of policy to the work of environmental ethicists ("Pragmatic Power"), and the editor of the principal journal in the field, *Environmental Ethics*, has recently argued against the importance of environmental ethicists being able to communicate anything to those outside of the field (Hargrove).

I cannot complain too much about such results, though. More dire in academic circles is to have one's ideas not discussed at all rather than continually challenged. More important, the number of scholars in the field calling themselves "pragmatists" has grown sharply, and the reception of figures like Bryan Norton, one of the most distinguished senior figures writing in this circle, continues to expand. Several new introductory textbooks in the field now include sections on environmental pragmatism as one important minority view. We seem to be doing at least as well in this respect as ecofeminists and are attracting more critical attention in philosophical circles these days than are deep ecologists.

But my concerns about the successes of *Environmental Pragmatism* are more acutely raised by another issue—namely, that perhaps the two original aims of that volume were incompatible to begin with. If, as I believe, the more important goal was to push environmental ethics away from its intramural fixations, then does it actually do any good to add another dimension to the meta-ethical debates in the field by championing a voice which appears to be founded in classical American philosophy? In other words, by collecting the work of those committed to the pantheon of American philosophy—John Dewey, William James, C. S. Peirce, and so on—as they have applied the developed insights of those figures to environmental problems and the ongoing debates in environmental ethics, and giving it the proper name "environmental pragmatism," did I in essence not help to open a new front in the theoretical battles among environmental ethicists? Now, instead of simply filling the pages of *Environmental Ethics* with arguments between those influenced by Callicott, Holmes Rolston, and the like, to those same debates we can add, and indeed have added, even more pages—but by Deweyans, Jamesians, and Peirceans. Moreover, given that most philosophers educated in the Anglo-American and European Continental traditions are taught that pragmatism is a historical relic that should be rejected, if their curriculum says anything about it at all (see, e.g., Callicott, "Fallacious Fallacies" 133), isn't the side that is being offered to environmental ethicists under the name *pragmatism* one that can be quite easily ignored? If, for example, a view rejecting claims to the intrinsic value of nature is grounded in some Deweyan perspective, then can't reasonable philosophers reject it out of hand since they don't accept, don't understand, or don't take seriously Dewey's views on anything else?

One answer to such concerns is that if taking seriously an orthodox pragmatist position on environmental ethics requires taking seriously larger pragmatist themes, then so much the worse for those not trained in this literature. They will just have to learn more about pragmatism to adequately answer these arguments—and in the end, that forced education will be good for them. Another answer is that pragmatists will have to amend how they do environmental ethics if they are going to make a contribution to the field similar to those they have made in other areas of applied ethics. Given the general hostility to pragmatism in the larger philosophical world, pragmatists can't afford to come off like Thomists, simply citing chapter and verse of Dewey or someone else and then assuming that the appeal to authority will carry some weight. But there is a third answer that I vaguely and inadequately tried to float in my contributions to *Environmental Pragmatism:* that there is another use for the term *environmental pragmatism,* namely one that tries to offer a methodology that will enable environmental ethicists to set aside some of the debates that occupy most of their time and instead focus more closely on a kind of philosophical work which could be more relevant to environmental advocates on the ground. This version of environmental pragmatism doesn't have much to do with what I would call a "historical pragmatism," applying Dewey, James, Peirce, or any other figure to specific environmental problems at hand, even though there is some family resemblance between it and that approach. More critically, such a position wouldn't require those embracing this view either to become pragmatists themselves or to appeal directly to larger pragmatist themes.

Originally, I gave this kind of environmental pragmatism the highly inelegant name *metaphilosophical environmental pragmatism;* I have since switched to calling it *methodological environmental pragmatism.* I will explain in more detail below what I mean by this term. I do not know whether this idea is having much impact on the community of environmental ethicists, to whom it is directed, and no doubt it is my own fault if they find it irrelevant. My original descriptions of the approach were awkward at best, and I haven't done enough to clarify the idea in a way that could make it more easily accessible. But it has garnered the attention of several pragmatists in environmental ethics who have attacked it for not being pragmatist enough to warrant the name *pragmatism* (see Minteer). Possibly so. Yet for now, I am content to use this term and have argued that it has several advantages over more historically oriented versions of environmental pragmatism, such as that offered by Larry Hickman. My methodological pragmatism also has the benefit of being able to avoid the more troublesome hurdles presented by an orthodox application of American philosophy to environmental problems (see Light, "A Modest Proposal").

I will leave to another time both the full elucidation of this approach and a defense of it against the relevant skeptics. My aim here is to make a brief case for methodological environmental pragmatism, clarify what I take to be its virtues, and then explore its relevance to debates between environmental ethicists and animal welfare and rights views. Finally, I will show how the methodological pragmatist might approach a particular issue in the literature on animal welfare: controversies over the permissibility of hunting.

Methodological Pragmatism in Environmental Ethics

As Ben Minteer ably demonstrates in his contribution to this volume, environmental ethicists have long distinguished their work from that of their colleagues in the animal welfare and rights traditions (which I will sometimes refer to jointly under the name "animal liberationists"). Environmental ethicists focus on questions of "holistic" or ecosystemic value, as opposed to the moral obligations we may have to individual nonhumans. I will turn to this divide later in this chapter, since it presents some significant hurdles to my argument that a methodological pragmatism can be useful for issues concerning animal welfare. First, however, we need to take a step back to look at other divisions in environmental ethics in order to better understand the breach into which a methodological pragmatism can step.

There are many ways to parse the various meta-ethical and metaphysical schools of thought that have shaped the growth of this field. My preference is to track its development in terms of a series of debates, with the first and most important one involving the rejection of anthropocentrism. Tim Hayward defines ethical anthropocentrism as the view that prioritizes those attitudes, values, or practices which give "exclusive or arbitrarily preferential consideration to human interests as opposed to the interests of other beings" or the environment (51). Many early environmental ethicists were adamant that if environmental ethics was going to be a distinctive field of ethics, it must necessarily involve a rejection of anthropocentrism. If they used Hayward's definition, this amounted to a rejection of the claim that ethics should be restricted only to the allocation of obligations, duties, and the like among and between humans, thereby prioritizing in moral terms all human interests over whatever could arguably be determined as the interests of nonhumans, whether individuals, species, or ecosystems.

Among the first papers published by professional philosophers in the field (e.g., landmark papers in the early 1970s by Arne Naess, Holmes Rolston III, Richard Routley [later, Sylvan], and Peter Singer), some version of anthropocentrism was often the target even if it was not explicitly labeled as such. Regardless of the terminology, these thinkers largely took the position that axiologically anthropocentric views are antithetical to the agenda of environmentalists and to the development of environmental ethics. So pervasive was this assumption that it was often not adequately defended, and it has become one of what Gary Varner calls the "two dogmas of environmental ethics" (142). This position is still generally accepted by most environmental ethicists today. Furthermore, the notion of what anthropocentrism meant, and consequently what overcoming anthropocentrism entailed, often relied on very narrow, straw man definitions. Anthropocentrism was equated with forms of valuation which easily, or even necessarily, led to nature's destruction (little account was taken of anthropocentric values, such as aesthetic values, which might count as reasons to preserve nature).

Thus the first divide among environmental ethicists is between those who accept the rejection of anthropocentrism as a necessary prerequisite for establishing a unique field of environmental ethics and those who do not, arguing that "weaker" forms of anthropocentrism (for example, those which ascribe to nature humanly based values other than as a mere resource) are sufficient to generate an adequate ethic of the environment (see Norton, "Environmental Ethics"). But if environmental ethics is to start with a rejection of anthropocentrism, then the next step is to come up with a description of the value of nonhumans, or the nonhuman natural world, in nonanthropocentric terms. As I noted above, this has generally been as some form of intrinsic value, or at least noninstrumental value, which nonhumans or ecosystems are thought to possess in and of themselves.

Many problems with nonanthropocentric environmental ethics could be mentioned, but I find that they are arguably more practical than philosophical, or that their resolution in more practical terms is more important (at least at the present) than their resolution in philosophical terms. Regardless of the debate within the field, the more important consideration here is that those working in the world of natural resource management take a predominantly anthropocentric approach to assessing natural value, as do most other humans. As I suggested above, this is the main reason why environmental ethics appears to have little impact on debates over actual policy issues.

What would a methodological form of environmental pragmatism offer to resolve this problem? I have made a start on this question by reminding environmental ethicists that in addition to being part of a philosophical community, they are also part of the environmental community. While this connection has never been clear, the field continues to be at least part of an ongoing conversation about environmental issues, if not an outright intentional community of environmentalists. The drive to create a more pragmatic environmental ethics is motivated by a desire not only to actively participate in the resolution of environmental problems but also to hold up our philosophical end, as it were, among the community of environmentalists.

But how could environmental ethicists better serve the environmental community? The answer for the methodological pragmatist, consistent with the answer that a more historically oriented pragmatist would offer, begins in a recognition that if philosophy is to serve a larger community then it must allow the interests of the community to help to determine the philosophical problems which the theorist addresses. This does not mean that the pragmatic philosopher necessarily finds all the problems that a given community is concerned with as the problems for her own work. Nor does it mean that she assumes her conclusions before analyzing a problem, like a hired legal counsel who doesn't inquire as to the guilt or innocence of her client. It only means that a fair description of the work of pragmatic philosophers is to investigate the problems of interest to their community (as a community of inquirers) and then articulate the policy recommendations concerning these problems to those outside of their community, that is, to the public at large. The articulation of these recommendations from a more limited community to a broader public, in terms closer to the moral intuitions of the broader public, is a form of what I call "moral translation." We can think of it as the public task of a methodologically pragmatist environmental ethics.

A public and pragmatic environmental ethics would not rest with a mere description of or series of debates on the value of nature (even a description that justified something as strong as a claim for the rights of nature). A public environmental ethics would further question whether the nonanthropocentric description of the value of nature it provided could possibly cause human agents to change their moral attitudes about nature, taking into account the overwhelming ethical anthropocentrism of most humans (amply demonstrated by studies like Kempton, Boster, and Hartley's, which shows that most people view obligations to future generations as the most compelling reason to protect the environment). A public environmental ethics would therefore have to either embrace a weak or enlightened anthropocentrism about natural value (for example, arguing that nature had value either for aesthetic reasons or as a way of fulfilling our obligations to future generations) or endorse a pluralism which admitted the possibility, indeed the necessity, of sometimes describing natural value in human-centered terms rather than always nonanthropocentrically in order to win support for a more morally responsible environmental policy.

This approach is motivated by the empirically demonstrable prevalence of anthropocentric views on environmental issues rather than by an antecedent commitment to any particular theory of value. It thus does not require environmental ethicists to give up their various philosophical debates over the existence of nonanthropocentric natural value, or their position on these debates. Such more purely philosophical tasks can continue. But ethicists following this methodology must accept the public task as well, which requires that they be willing to translate their philosophical views about the value of nature, when necessary, into terms more likely to morally motivate policy makers and the general public even when they themselves have relied on nonanthropocentrism to come to their views about the value of nature. Elsewhere I have sketched in more detail how such a "two task" approach would work (see "Taking Environmental Ethics Public"). Here I merely note that this strategy, asking that ethicists sometimes translate their views into a language more resonant with the public, is required only where convergence has been reached. That is, when views among environmentalists of various camps, as well as among environmental ethicists themselves, have largely converged on the same policy end, then the public task of the philosopher is to articulate the arguments most effective in morally motivating nonenvironmentalists to accept that end. For many issues, this will involve making weak anthropocentric arguments (which also have the virtue of often being less philosophically contentious), but one can imagine that in some cases nonanthropocentric claims would be more appealing. What kind of argument works best is an empirical question. Where convergence has not been achieved, however, this public task of translation is not warranted. Under those circumstances we must continue with the more traditional philosophical task of environmental ethicists, our version of an environmental "first philosophy," attempting to hammer out the most plausible and defensible ethical views on a topic. There are many other details to fill in regarding this approach, which must wait for its full defense and explication elsewhere.

My reliance on the convergence of views among environmentalists as the warrant for engaging in this public task of environmental ethics, which is pragmatist without making explicit reference to pragmatism, owes much to Bryan Norton's "convergence hypothesis" as explicated in his book *Toward Unity among Environmentalists*. Following a study of the empirical tendency of environmental groups with different ethical foundations to focus on similar policies, Norton summarizes the view this way: "Provided anthropocentrists consider the full breadth of human values as they unfold into the indefinite future, and provided nonanthropocentrists endorse a consistent and coherent version of the view that nature has intrinsic value, all sides may be able to endorse a common policy direction" ("Convergence and Contextualism" 87). Where such convergence exists, environmental ethicists can afford to see their public role as trying to offer the largest toolbox of different moral arguments that will appeal to different human interests for some desired end rather than only wrangling over which particular argument is the right one.

Methodological Pragmatism for Animal Welfare

A survey of most environmental ethics journals reveals that such convergence is found not just among environmental organizations; most environmental ethicists tend to converge on the same ends as well, regardless of their initial philosophical starting points. This tendency has been demonstrated again and again, even in what appear at times to be the most intractable debates in the field. Most noteworthy in this respect is the gap between "holist" environmental ethicists and those who work on animal welfare and animal rights. The primary worry by holist environmental ethicists is that an animal liberation approach, such as that championed by Peter Singer, will always be insufficient to provide moral reasons for protecting the environment writ large—especially species and ecosystems, or those entities which are thought to be the proper subject of a holistic environmental science. Animal liberationists can offer us reasons to take into account the welfare or possible rights of individual animals, but they seem to provide no direct reasons for granting moral recognition to those nonsentient entities which cannot be described as having "interests" in any way similar to the interests that we attribute to humans (and that often provide the basis of the ethical reasons for why humans should be treated with moral respect). Further, given that the science of the environment focuses on the welfare of ecosystems and species and not on individual animals, won't the ethically considered goals of ecology run afoul of the moral demands of a fully realized account of animal liberation? Management of ecosystems will often require actions which will harm individual animals—especially exotic species that may threaten native flora or fauna, or those animals that have grown in such numbers as to threaten the integrity or health of a particular ecosystem. Animal liberationists, so some would have us believe, will be left in the peculiar position of having to defend the protection of individual animals at the expense of the welfare of ecosystems. Pointing to such tensions early on, Mark Sagoff's account of the original unity and later split of these two camps appeared under the humorous title "Animal Liberation and Environmental Ethics: Bad Marriage, Quick Divorce."

But even from some of these debates a pattern emerges. Often those philosophers working on environmental and animal issues are at great pains to prove to each other that their respective approaches, though different from those of their colleagues, nonetheless get to the same environmental ends. For example, in a debate on the merits of animal liberation versus environmental ethics, Dale Jamieson takes on the claim that an ethical approach focusing on the welfare of animals is insufficient for an environmental ethic because it offers no reason to directly value ecosystems or endangered species. Jamieson's strategy is to prove that there is a scheme of value whereby animal liberationists can value ecosystems intrinsically even though they are only derivatively valuable (rather than bearers of "primary value," such as humans and other sentient animals who have a perspective from which their lives get better or worse). Jamieson then tries to show that because such traditional subjects of a holist environmental ethic can be valued by an animal liberationist, they ought to be valued by such a theorist and hence the theory does not entail the ecosystemic contradictions that are cited by environmental ethicists.

Callicott ("Back Together Again"), in his reply to Jamieson, argues that there are cases of ecosystemic value which elude liberationists—examples of things in nature that we might intuitively feel as environmentalists that we should preserve but would not be of sufficiently strong derivative value to warrant the ascription of moral protection entailed by Jamieson's approach. In this exchange Callicott makes the same claim against weak anthropocentrists as well, and weak anthropocentrists in the field have likewise long tried to get their projects off the ground by proving that their methods of valuing nature capture the same ends as various forms of nonanthropocentrism (see, e.g., Norton, *Toward Unity*). At the end of this debate, though, there is little reason to conclude that an animal liberationist could not offer compelling moral reasons for protection of the entities Callicott cites as the exceptions, only that the reasons that they would give would not attribute direct moral value to these entities.

In another overview of the place of animals in environmental philosophy, Singer, after running through a series of supposed disputes in which animal liberationists and environmental ethicists wind up converging, settles on the classic case of the introduction of exotic European rabbits in Australia as an instance of the incommensurability of their competing meta-ethical positions. Introduced into the country in the nineteenth century as a food source, these rabbits have now become a major pest and pose a serious threat to the survival of native vegetation, as well as contributing to soil erosion. "Australian farmers and environmentalists are therefore united in attempting to reduce the number of rabbits in Australia. From the point of view of an ethic of concern for all sentient beings, however, rabbits are beings with interests of their own, capable of feeling pain and suffering" (Singer, "Animals" 423).

After carefully summarizing the flaws in various plans to remove the rabbits from the point of view of an animal liberationist position, Singer nonetheless seeks to find a compromise solution—a solution which would preserve the rare plants and ecosystems without necessarily doing damage to the rabbits. Importantly, Singer does not attempt to justify saving the rabbits at the expense of the ecosystem. Even though he does not grant ecosystems or native plants direct moral consideration, he does not rest with a claim that the value he does find in protecting the welfare of the rabbits trumps the need to protect the plants and ecosystem. We can assume that his reasons for continuing to seek a compromise solution are prudential, but they are nonetheless driven by something else— perhaps an unwillingness to fly in the face of conventional ecological science. Assuming that no compromise solution is available, Singer suggests that we endorse a precautionary principle that extends protection to the rare plants by virtue of the fact that they could be valuable someday to satisfy the interests of some future humans or nonhumans ("Animals" 424). The only caveat is that removal of the rabbits should be done as humanely as possible.

What environmental ethicist would disagree with this conclusion as a practical outcome? It would be an odd holist who would argue that the rabbits should be treated inhumanely for the good of the overall ecosystem. If the rabbit case is supposed to represent an instance of incommensurability between animal liberationists and holist environmental ethicists, it is thus quite weak. After all, couldn't Singer's final compromise solution, in which he claims possible harm to future moral subjects from the loss of this ecosystem as a reason for humanely removing the rabbits, be used generically in almost any case to justify protection of almost any part of nature? The drive toward convergence is strong, especially when we assert the importance of the thing we are considering and assume its value in ecological terms. One is left wondering what all the fuss is about.

No doubt someone could accuse me at this point of picking my examples too carefully. Surely there are cases in which environmental ethicists and animal liberationists disagree over the ends of environmental policy or animal welfare and will find it difficult to make compromises over competing moral claims. Consider the welfare of farm animals, historically one of the most pressing and important issues for animal liberationists. Some environmental ethicists have argued that farm animals actually are not part of nature, that their history of domestication has instead made them fleshy bits of human technology. Presumably such intuitions are strengthened as human use of genetic modification in this industry increases. We therefore do not have the same kinds of obligations to preserve farm animals as a species (one reason being that they will most likely never become extinct) that we may have regarding wild and endangered species. As a consequence, the moral arguments for vegetarianism and the like will not appear to be as relevant to the holist environmental ethicist, since farm animals are not part of "nature" and therefore do not warrant the same kind of moral protection as naturally evolved species.

But such a view, even if true (and I doubt that it is), would clearly not provide a reason for environmental ethicists to blithely eat fast-food hamburgers with a good conscience. The environmental consequences of factory farming are too well documented to be ignored. Anyone holding a view that we have moral reasons to protect ecosystems, endangered species, or the environment as a whole would find obvious fault with participation in a system which so seriously threatens those entities. This is not even to mention the huge drain on natural resources, and mitigation of efforts to achieve long-term environmental sustainability, that result from industrial agriculture. Though I will not go into the details of the position here, I think that there is something intellectually suspicious, if not completely dishonest, about the wholesale rejection of animal welfare positions by many environmental ethicists under the guise of holism. Even if one does hold the view that ecosystems have intrinsic value, such an argument does not disprove claims that we should reject speciesism, whether such rejection takes the form of arguing that other animals have interests that should be respected in a moral sense or arguing that they should be granted rights. It is even more bizarre for environmental ethicists to dismiss such positions without argument (as Varner suggests that they do), given that they start with the premise that the realm of moral consideration does not stop at the boundaries of the human community. If humans and ecosystems are things that we suppose ought to be given moral status, then surely all claims to moral respect for nonhuman components of ecosystems should be given careful consideration. Perhaps only a severe moral monist who claimed that only collective entities—species and ecosystems—had direct moral value could safely reject all claims to individual animal welfare without contradiction. But such a view would most likely also need to reject claims to the moral value of individual humans, since they too do not possess ecosystemic value in and of themselves— a rejection that would be morally suspicious if not outright repugnant on its face. If one believes that we owe moral obligations to individual humans and to ecosystems, then claims about the welfare or possible rights of animals cannot simply be skipped over.

Let us assume then that the divide between environmental ethicists and animal liberationists is not nearly as wide as has been suggested. (This point is certainly not an original one; Jamieson and several others have made the same claim.) How then does methodological pragmatism help us through these debates? Consider three issues. First, methodological pragmatism gives us a way to set aside the differences evidenced in examples such as the Jamieson-Callicott debate cited above. Where there is convergence on ends (such as a rejection of factory farming—an issue that the two authors agree on) then we need not worry about who has the most direct reason for morally grounding those ends. Methodological pragmatism requires us to consider a different criterion for argumentative efficacy, one often cited and misunderstood in the historical legacy of pragmatism: which argument is actually going to work? That is, which argument can offer appeals for stronger and better policies and laws to promote the welfare of animals and ecosystems, a goal on which these two communities converge, which will be intuitively appealing for those who do not count themselves as either environmentalists or animal advocates? Which arguments will actually morally motivate those who hear it to chip away at the vast edifice of cultural, political, social, and economic justifications propping up some of the most morally suspicious practices which now govern the bulk of our interaction with the nonhuman natural world? This certainly does not mean that any motivating argument goes for the pragmatist. There are other moral objections that could be raised against fascist defenses of vegetarianism and the like. But outside of these constraints, we arguably have more important work to do now than to spend all our time disagreeing over the reasons for taking a course of action on which we agree. I'm not suggesting that those reasons are unimportant; instead, I'm saying that it is more important at the moment to articulate as many possible reasons for the same ends (within reasonable constraints) which we think are both valid and possibly morally motivating to the public and which could be positively received within the traditions of thought which govern our current legal and political structures.

Such a position requires not that we endorse those views with which we disagree, but simply that we don't stand in the way of reasonable moral appeals to broader communities of people different from ourselves. For example, in a recent popular overview of the literature on animal welfare, liberation, and rights, Singer approvingly cites Matthew Scully's conservative Christian case for animal welfare, *Dominion: The Power of Man, the Suffering of Animals, and the Call to Mercy*. Though he certainly finds it curious that Scully, a former speechwriter to President George W. Bush, relies on the same foundations used for arguments to condemn homosexuality and physician-assisted suicide to make a case for animal welfare, Singer nonetheless sees value in making an appeal for ends on which he would agree to a community that he would most likely have little access to: "The result [of *Dominion*] is a work that, although not philosophically rigorous, has had a remarkable amount of sympathetic publicity in the conservative press, which usually sneers at animal advocates" ("Animal Liberation at 30" 25). This is not to say that Scully is being a methodological pragmatist here and Singer approves of and recognizes that approach. It is to say, though, that Singer recognizes the practical reasons for making this kind of appeal to a particular community and that such a modified endorsement does not necessarily entail acceptance of the moral framework which gave birth to it. A more committed methodological pragmatist might go one step further and actually formulate moral arguments for these ends which would appeal to Christian communities, or to others with whom they do not usually see themselves connected. I do not mean by this that if a church group asked a pragmatist to give a talk on factory farming they could begin by saying "Jesus sent me here today to tell you about our sins toward other animals." But the methodological pragmatist would be remiss not to do their homework, understand the moral framework within which this community operated, and then try to make an appeal within that framework without necessarily endorsing its other ends. And if pressed, the pragmatist certainly would have to be honest about their own moral framework for thinking about such issues if it was different from that of the community being addressed.

Second, and following from this point, methodological pragmatism also helps us to set aside another potential problem: whether it matters if people do what we think are the right things for the right reasons. Singer wants me to give up eating meat. I agree that I should. But I don't accept wholesale the larger utilitarian framework which grounds Singer's vegetarianism. I don't think this matters to either of us. Should it? What if the reason I give up eating meat is that I lived through a severe food contagion scare, such as an outbreak of mad cow disease. From that point on I decide that in the interests of avoiding unknown risks of disease I will eat lower on the food chain; moreover, whenever possible I will eat organic food, since I'm also uncertain about how widely used industrial pesticides, such as atrazine, may contribute to my long-term risks of contracting cancer. Purely from the perspective of a risk assessment of my personal health, such a position may be grounded in an overly active sense of precaution. Yet it is something that I decide to do. There is, after all, nothing morally wrong with my choosing this course of action even if it is not perfectly rational.

No doubt Singer will agree with the ends of these changes to my personal behavior and also find my decision morally underdeveloped. He will not worry too much in this case that my reasons are not grounded in a utilitarian calculus (especially since his original case against speciesism was grounded in a broader moral context); his criticism is more likely to be that I seem to be ignoring a larger moral framework in which I could be making these decisions. If I were considering that larger framework, then I would be more likely to agree with other conclusions drawn from his general position, such as rejections of vivisectionism, the wearing of fur, the testing of cosmetics on animals, and the like. Still, my reasoning would have an outcome friendly to an important part of his views on this subject. As a consequentialist, Singer would certainly more easily see this outcome as a good one. But even if he were a deontologist, seeing my actions through the lens of methodological pragmatism would help to demonstrate that my position was worthwhile despite its prudential rather than moral content. And there is another element of such a situation which any animal liberationist ought to find promising: in deciding not to eat meat for whatever reason, I create an opening for encouraging me to think about the larger moral framework of such issues. For example, once I have decided that atrazine is something I should be worried about, then I could be persuaded that this pesticide is a threat not only to my own health but also to that of other species which in the end may likely be implicated in my own welfare. Or I may come to consider the direct welfare of other animals or of ecosystems. Recent studies indicate that atrazine may be the cause of the higher rates of sexual abnormalities observed in frogs (see Lee), a trend which I should also find both indirectly and directly important. The methodological pragmatist could make an appeal to me based either on an interest in the welfare of frogs or on their role in the integrity of ecosystems, assuming there is convergence on the importance of this problem. Even if my decision is not as morally robust or complete as it could be, it still plays an important role in building a broader consensus on these issues.

Finally, even if these arguments are rejected and a rapprochement between environmental ethics and animal liberation is considered fundamentally un-workable, a form of methodological pragmatism could be of some use within the animal liberation community. The elaboration of this third point should be fairly clear by now. Because animal liberationists often converge on a wide variety of positions—despite some important points of disagreement, especially on tactics—as broad a moral appeal as possible is needed to get people to think about our relationships with other animals to effect the kinds of changes that will improve the moral content of these relationships. Philosophers do a service to the animal welfare and rights communities when they give these communities a plurality of argumentative tools rather than only a series of ethical debates on which tools are the right ones. No doubt some, like Gary Francione, would disagree with such a position. But for reasons similar to those discussed by me and Erin McKenna in the introduction to this volume, a position like his, which rejects all incremental improvements in animal welfare as so much immoral compromise, has no place in a philosophical approach that hopes to have any impact on actual policy debates. Still, it may be the case that debates among animal liberationists are not as distracting as they are among environmental ethicists. I will return to this point at the end of this essay. For now, let's consider a final test case to demonstrate both the virtues and limitations of using methodological pragmatism in ethical accounts of animal welfare: hunting.

Convergence on Hunting

Little can be easily said about the morality of hunting, whether considered from the perspective of environmental ethics or from an animal liberationist position. What can be said, though, and what is not said often enough, is that the simple dichotomy that hunting is permissible for environmental ethicists and impermissible for animal liberationists is false. The two camps demonstrate considerable initial convergence on important issues; for example, they both object to the hunting of endangered species for reasons involving the value of individual animals, the survival of species, and the sustainability of ecosystems. But even beyond this level of agreement, much more convergence is possible on a number of other issues. Few have done more than Gary Varner to demonstrate that potential at the level of policy. In chapter 5 of *In Nature's Interests?* Varner makes this compelling case for a variety of issues, but especially the "therapeutic" hunting of "obligatory management species."

Varner begins by distinguishing between "therapeutic," "subsistence," and "sport" hunting. Subsistence hunting is intended to procure food for humans; sport hunting is "aimed at maintaining religious or cultural traditions, and reenacting national or evolutionary history, at practicing certain skills, or just at securing a trophy" (101). His focus, however, is on the therapeutic variety, defined as hunting "motivated by and designed to secure the aggregate welfare of the target species, the integrity of its ecosystems or both" (100). His central claim is that animal rights and welfare advocates both can and should endorse therapeutic hunting as morally permissible and even required, especially for what he calls *obligatory management species*—any species that has a "fairly regular tendency to overshoot the carrying capacity of its range, to the detriment of its own future generations and those of other species" (101). Varner has in mind here especially those ungulates, such as white-tailed deer, elk, and bison, which have a strong propensity to overpopulate their habitat and as a result often die horrible deaths from starvation or from collisions with automobiles when they wander in search of food. Under such conditions, and especially when nonlethal means are unavailable or impractical, the only way to manage such species in a morally responsible way is to cull them.

The case that environmentalists should support such therapeutic hunting is largely noncontroversial. Hunting is a way of effectively protecting the welfare of larger ecosystems. But as Varner reminds us, the "received interpretation of the animal rights–environmental ethics split is that animal rights activists must oppose hunting even when it is biologically necessary" (103). He demurs, finding that despite the popular slogans of animal rights groups, they need not oppose sound hunting practices such as the culling of white-tailed deer populations. While I do not have the space here to fully explicate his argument, Varner's account is solid. Working first from Singer's consequentialism, Varner argues that both hedonic and preference utilitarians would have sufficient reasons to endorse therapeutic hunting of obligatory management species (and perhaps even permissible management species such as quail) living under highly stressed conditions, in order to decrease the pain of individual animals or to increase the quality of life of most other members of the species. He makes a similarly strong case starting from Tom Regan's rights-based view by exploiting Regan's "miniride" position, which allows for trade-offs in welfare when we have conflicts that involve saving morally equivalent beings from death. And even though Varner's definition of therapeutic hunting involves particular intentions—to secure the aggregate welfare of species and ecosystems—it so happens that the goals of sport hunting, responsibly managed to ensure maximum sustainable yields (even trophies), overlap considerably with the ends of therapeutic hunting. The methodological pragmatist can take this conclusion, together with my argument above concerning the question of whether doing the right thing for the right reasons matters, to encourage responsible sport hunting of obligatory management species as a way of achieving the goals of therapeutic hunting. It will not be necessary to convince hunters of the importance of considering the moral welfare of animals or ecosystems to get them to further a morally important end, even though it would be better if they did come to realize the relevance of those issues.

Assuming that Varner's case is correct (and I can only assert that here, not demonstrate it), the methodological environmental pragmatist will find much that is useful in Varner's account. More fundamentally, if this argument is right, then one of the principal reasons given for the incompatibility of environmental ethicists and animal liberationists is either entirely wrong or, at the very least, not necessarily a source of tension. The idea of direct moral consideration of other animals simply cannot be rejected wholesale whether we start from the viewpoint of the managerial holism of ecological science or of the ethical holism of most environmental ethicists. In addition, Varner argues that this resolution of the hunting issue suggests that further rapprochement can be reached between these camps on a host of other issues—possible obligations of humans to prevent natural predation, to remove exotic species to preserve biodiversity, and the breeding of endangered species in captivity. If Varner is correct in this assessment, then an even larger-scale convergence is possible between these two camps on policy ends, opening the door for the work of the methodological pragmatist to expand the community of support for those ends.

But my brief overview of the procedural warrants for methodological pragmatism raises a clear problem for this happy conclusion. Even if Varner is right about the convergence of philosophical arguments on these issues, the situation (as he admits) is trickier when it comes to the convergence of the larger environmentalist and animal liberationist communities. Many animal welfare groups will not make the distinction between different forms of hunting and will simply reject all hunting practices as unethical and impermissible. Many more will reject the moral trade-offs that are required to take such actions as eliminating exotic species in order to preserve or restore native plants, animals, or ecosystems, and they will argue that our direct moral obligations toward other animals trump the moral or prudential reasons we may have to preserve biodiversity in such ways. Recall that as I laid out the position above, the pluralist public philosophy of the methodological pragmatist is warranted only when there is convergence in the larger environmental community, in which we may include environmental ethicists. If the boundaries of the environmental community are to be expanded so as to include animal advocates, then convergence on hunting may be practically impossible.

For this reason the warrant for methodological pragmatism must occur on at least two different levels in order that its full potential as a guide to more relevant philosophical activity can be reached. First, it is a methodology which we can use, as I have argued, to make available to an expanded environmental community numerous tools so that when convergence occurs (such as in the case of the worst excesses of factory farming), more successful arguments promoting more morally responsible environmental laws and policies can be fashioned. Second, assuming for the moment that we will at least try to expand the activist environmental community to include animal advocates, then when environmental ethicists and animal activists can converge on the same policy ends (as Varner insists that they can), the work of the methodological pragmatist will be occupied in trying to persuade the expanded environmental–animal activist community to overcome their divergence on these issues. And here again methodological pragmatists will use as many arguments at their disposal as they can produce. This raises the question of who counts in each community (for example, who is an ethicist and who isn't)—something that I will have to address in more detail at some later time—but a rough outline of the distinctions between these communities should be sufficient to warrant individuals to change the priorities of their philosophical labor accordingly.

Clearly, however, hunting and other issues will often give rise to divergences between the environmentalist and animal liberationist communities, between environmental ethicists and animal liberationist philosophers, and within these advocacy groups and the ethicists working on these topics. As I noted before, in all of these instances, absent a plausible case for some kind of convergence, methodological pragmatists must go back to a philosophical square one. Their work, if they choose to consider such topics, is a form of "first philosophy," starting from pragmatist premises or whatever other ethical framework they prefer. One such vexed issue was the 1999 hunt of California gray whales by a tribe of Native Americans, the Makah. Here the methodological pragmatists have no agreed-on ends of policy on which they can justify their pluralist impulses. Nor am I certain that a historical pragmatist would have much to offer to this issue with which I, at least, would agree regarding this case.

The Makah were the first Native tribe to be granted a cultural exception to the prohibition on whaling currently enforced by the International Whaling Commission (IWC). Although the IWC prohibits all whaling except for subsistence by Arctic peoples and for scientific purposes (a rider that has been notoriously abused by the Japanese and Norwegians), it granted a unique exception (some would say through backdoor manipulation by the U.S. government) to the Makah tribe of Neah Bay in the northwest corner of Washington's Olympic Peninsula. The Makah had claimed both that they had a clear treaty right to whale—originating in an 1855 agreement with the federal government which ceded the bulk of their tribal lands in exchange for the perpetual right to whale, hunt, and fish—and that if they were forbidden these practices, especially whaling, their culture would become extinct. Their community, like that of most tribes in the United States, had been severely degraded by high rates of unemployment, drug addiction, and alcoholism on the reservation. Their ancestors had ceded their land in exchange for the right to fish and whale because these practices were the bedrock of their cultural and religious beliefs. Since the United States signed on to the IWC and had stopped whaling, they were forced to cease as well. But only the resumption of whaling, so the Makah claimed, could revive and save their culture; and because their traditional prey, the California gray whale, had been taken off the endangered species list, they should be allowed to whale.

From an ecological standpoint, there are no grounds to bar whaling by the Makah. The Makah were allowed to take only five whales a year, a number not added to the subsistence amount already allotted to indigenous peoples in the Arctic north but instead transferred to the Makah from that allotment. Thus granting permission to the Makah did not increase the maximum number of grays hunted each year by Native peoples. Though many would disagree, from a cultural standpoint the decision also seems sound, given that the Makah declared that they would use traditional whaling techniques (canoes and hand-thrown harpoons) rather than modern commercial methods. "Spiritual preparation" was as important to the training of the Makah whalers as physical practice. Even those concerned about animal welfare would have to concede that the Makah hunt could have been far worse. Accompanying the whaling canoe used for the hunt was a support boat that held another tribal member with an elephant gun to kill the whale as quickly and painlessly as possible once it had been harpooned by hand. Though whaling by the traditional method was deemed necessary to fulfill the cultural goal of the Makah, its inhumane consequence (the possibility that whales might bleed to death) was not.

Despite these considerations, environmental and animal rights groups regarded the Makah hunt with divided feelings, and it was the subject of much protest (for an extremely good and sympathetic account of the hunt and the controversies surrounding it, see Sullivan). Some environmental groups, such as the Sierra Club, either supported it or did not oppose it; Paul Watson's Sea Shepherds were adamantly opposed and helped to organize a flotilla of animal rights groups to attempt to interfere with the hunt. Ethicists who have looked at the issue also disagree.

Seeing this lack of agreement, the methodological pragmatist must retreat to a more traditional form of philosophical activity or else try to find grounds on which a convergence of views can be achieved. After having surveyed much of the literature on the Makah hunt, and after having met several members of the tribe, I see little hope for convergence, mainly because I think that in this case the Makah also count in the relevant community in which convergence would need to be achieved. I see little chance that the Makah could ever be persuaded not to hunt or that the animal rights groups would ever condone their whaling. Although some members of the Makah community opposed the hunt, it appears that the majority of the Makah, as well as of Native American tribal organizations, supported it. Given that the history of Native Americans has been characterized by oppression and violation of treaty rights by the U.S. government, most tribal organizations viewed the Makah hunt primarily as a victory for those asserting cultural rights, who often based such assertions on claims that their cultures also have intrinsic value. Moreover, the Makah see themselves both as environmentalists (and certainly in their tribal lands such a case is plausible) and as fully connected to the animals they are hunting. When the Makah finally killed their first whale, many in the community saw some details of the hunt as signs that the whale was "surrendering to the crew, and that [it] somehow considered the crew worthy" (Sullivan 256). The roots of such anthropomorphism go deep. This is not simply a neo-hippie assertion that one is "close to the earth" because one goes to Rainbow Gatherings, but comes out of a much deeper strain of conviction. No convergence is possible if we include the Makah in our relevant community, and it is highly unlikely even if we do not.

Though I do not know of any historically oriented environmental pragmatist who has looked at this particular case, I can well imagine a plausible position favoring the Makah. Because historical pragmatists by and large refuse to endorse environmental ethics' wholesale rejection of anthropocentrism—given that the conventional pragmatist position does not ascribe value without a human valuer—they are in a good position to help to temper the extreme non-anthropocentrism or even misanthropy of much contemporary environmentalism and environmental ethics. Environmental issues will never be resolved if we focus solely on the noninstrumental value of individual animals, species, or ecosystems; they will always include important trade-offs involving other priorities in human communities, particularly rights and obligations that we owe to each other. The claim of the Makah to a right to have their treaty with the United States respected may be sufficient for the historical pragmatist to endorse the hunt, especially since its scope and size are limited. If the Makah hunt does not start the larger Native community down a slippery slope to large-scale whaling, which would once again threaten the viability of this population, then the historical pragmatist may have no reason to reject it.

But as a methodological pragmatist unable to find convergence on this issue I am unconvinced. Try as I might, I can't be persuaded that the gray whale killed by the Makah in 1999 accepted its fate. That their interpretation of its response is informed by a long cosmological tradition does not make it correct. Such anthropomorphic claims represent a metaphysical view which I find no more convincing than the traditional spiritual metaphysics produced by my own culture. And while I do find the argument for the cultural rights of the Makah plausible and important, I find the case for the moral worth of cetaceans equally important. They are highly evolved mammals; indeed, it would be difficult to find a better example (short of one of the great apes) of a being that has robust interests, a sense of itself, and a sense of what it means to be harmed and for members of its kin to be harmed, and that meets other criteria which animal liberationists have argued are the basis for a rejection of speciesism.

At this point many would insist on a protracted debate over the competing claims of the two positions. Will whaling really save the Makah culture? Are cultures intrinsically valuable? Are grays as intelligent as other whales and thus deserving of moral status approximately equal to that of humans? But I do not find much utility in trying to answer these questions, given their highly speculative nature, and I don't think that I need to answer them. For even if I grant maximal moral significance to the claims of those supporting the hunt and those opposing it, I still cannot see the hunt as morally permissible. On the one hand, let us assume that the Makah are correct in claiming their right to whale and in assessing the consequences of whaling. Whaling, if allowed, will preserve and maintain their culture into the future, not only protecting its value in and of itself but also mitigating their sometimes dire problems by substantially contributing to a more cohesive social environment. On the other hand, let us assume that the whale that was killed was a being fully worthy of our moral consideration and protection, that it even had a right to exist. Then, if we fully accept the rejection of speciesism, we should be prepared to offer a substitution case to test the veracity of these assessments of maximal moral significance. If a Native tribe requested permission to kill five humans from another tribe each year in order to maintain its cultural integrity and alleviate its social problems, would we find that action permissible? Even with the possible good consequences, I can't imagine that we would. I am left with an abiding feeling of discomfort over this hunt.

This leaves the question of whether I have an obligation to protest what I find to be morally objectionable. Of this I am not certain. Perhaps the actions of the Makah occur so far outside my own moral community that they present a case akin to that of female circumcision in northern Africa. I object to this practice but can do nothing to stop it beyond giving money to organizations opposed to it that are active where it occurs. Perhaps I can only do the same with the Makah, supporting those in their community who oppose the hunt. Perhaps I must be content with encouraging them to be as humane as possible in their treatment of their prey. Animal liberationists in general seem to find themselves in the same position. Singer spends much of his review of the current state of the literature ("Animal Liberation at 30") endorsing the improvements that have been made, especially in Europe, in the treatment of farm animals; yet though the usual conditions in the United States may be worse, the animals' ultimate fate in Europe is the same. Morality is clearly not a zero-sum game. I don't have any clear conclusions here yet, only an uneasy suspicion that the acceptance of trade-offs in the ethics of our treatment of animals is made palatable by our differences from them.

It is beyond the scope of this chapter to develop this objection to the Makah hunt any further. I use the example only to illustrate that not all questions of environmental ethics or animal welfare can be pushed into the bottle of my methodological pragmatism. But from that perspective, can't a skeptical reader claim that this volume runs the same risk I mentioned at the start in connection with my earlier book *Environmental Pragmatism*? Given the divergence on moral issues between and among environmental ethicists and animal liberationists, will producing a critical mass of literature on historical pragmatism and animal welfare simply create another side to—and thus add to the intractability of—philosophical debates? Maybe. But I am encouraged by signs that the literature on animal welfare and animal rights has instead helped to productively shape public debates about our treatment of and relationship with other animals. Singer suggests that the literature on animal welfare actually serves as a good counterexample to the general lack of success in applying ethical theories to real public controversies ("Animal Liberation at 30" 25). His claim might be dismissed as self-serving, but, as was argued in the introduction to this volume, those within the animal liberationist movement have amply documented how philosophers have served important roles as midwives and caretakers of its development (see Jasper and Nelkin).

The literatures on environmental ethics and animal welfare and rights have developed very differently from each other. And for a variety of reasons, the latter has been much more productive in supporting the positions of animal advocates. That productivity leads me to think that even the elaboration of a historical pragmatist position on these issues could be helpful. My hope, though, is to see a broader role for a methodological pragmatism in these debates.

Bibliography

Callicott, J. Baird. "'Back Together Again' Again." *Environmental Values* 7 (1998): 461–65.
———. "Environmental Philosophy Is Environmental Activism: The Most Radical and Effective Kind." In *Environmental Philosophy and Environmental Activism*, edited by Don E. Marietta, Jr., and Lester Embree, 19–36. Lanham, Md.: Rowman and Littlefield, 1995.
———. "Fallacious Fallacies and Nonsolutions: Comment on Kristin Shrader-Frechette's 'Ecological Risk Assessment and Ecosystem Health: Fallacies and Solutions.'" *Ecosystem Health* 3 (1997): 133–35.
———. "The Pragmatic Power and Promise of Theoretical Environmental Ethics." *Environmental Values* 11 (2002): 3–26.
Francione, Gary L. *Rain without Thunder: The Ideology of the Animal Rights Movement.* Philadelphia: Temple University Press, 1996.
Hargrove, Eugene. "What's Wrong? Who's to Blame?" *Environmental Ethics* 25 (2003): 3–4.
Hayward, Tim. "Anthropocentrism: A Misunderstood Problem." *Environmental Values* 6 (1997): 49–63.
Hickman, Larry. "Green Pragmatism: Reals without Realism, Ideals without Idealism." *Research in Philosophy and Technology* 18 (1999): 39–56.
Jamieson, Dale. "Animal Liberation Is an Environmental Ethic." *Environmental Values* 7 (1998): 41–57.
Jasper, Jasper M., and Dorothy Nelkin. *The Animal Rights Crusade: The Growth of a Moral Protest.* New York: Free Press, 1992.
Kempton, Willett, James S. Boster, and Jennifer A. Hartley. *Environmental Values in American Culture.* Cambridge, Mass.: MIT Press, 1997.
Lee, Jennifer. "Popular Pesticide Faulted for Frogs' Sexual Abnormalities." *New York Times,* June 19, 2003, A20.
Light, Andrew. "A Modest Proposal: Methodological Pragmatism for Bioethics." In *Pragmatist Ethics for a Technological Culture*, edited by Jozef Keulartz, Michiel Korthals, Maartje Schermer, and Tsjalling Swierstra, 79–97. Dordrecht: Kluwer Academic Publishers, 2002.
———. "Taking Environmental Ethics Public." In *Environmental Ethics: What Really Matters? What Really Works?* edited by David Schmidtz and Elizabeth Willott, 556–66. Oxford: Oxford University Press, 2002.
Light, Andrew, and Avner de-Shalit. "Environmental Ethics: Whose Philosophy? Which Practice?" In *Moral and Political Reasoning in Environmental Practice*, edited by Light and de-Shalit, 1–27. Cambridge, Mass.: MIT Press, 2003.
Light, Andrew, and Eric Katz, eds. *Environmental Pragmatism.* London: Routledge, 1996.
Minteer, Ben A. "Deweyan Democracy and Environmental Ethics." In *Democracy and the Claims of Nature*, edited by Minteer and Bob Pepperman Taylor, 33–48. Lanham, Md.: Rowman and Littlefield, 2002.
Norton, Bryan G. "Convergence and Contextualism." *Environmental Ethics* 19 (1997): 87–100.

——. "Environmental Ethics and Weak Anthropocentrism." *Environmental Ethics* 6 (1984): 131–48.

——. *Toward Unity among Environmentalists.* Oxford: Oxford University Press, 1991.

Sagoff, Mark. "Animal Liberation and Environmental Ethics: Bad Marriage, Quick Divorce." *Osgood Hall Law Journal* 22 (1984): 297–307.

Scully, Matthew. *Dominion: The Power of Man, the Suffering of Animals, and the Call to Mercy.* New York: St. Martin's Press, 2002.

Singer, Peter. "Animal Liberation at 30." *New York Review of Books,* May 15, 2003, 23–26.

——. 2001. "Animals." In *A Companion to Environmental Philosophy,* edited by Dale Jamieson, 416–25. Malden, Mass.: Blackwell Publishers, 2001.

Sullivan, Robert. *A Whale Hunt.* New York: Scribner, 2000.

Varner, Gary E. *In Nature's Interests? Interests, Animal Rights, and Environmental Ethics.* New York: Oxford University Press, 1998.

7 Getting Pragmatic about Farm Animal Welfare

Paul B. Thompson

Philosophical pragmatism presents itself as an alternative to those philosophical schools of thought that descended from the empiricist-rationalist and materialist-idealist debates of the seventeenth, eighteenth, and nineteenth centuries. These schools share a commitment to "foundational" strategies that seek to establish (if only by assumption) a small set of basic methodological and metaphysical propositions, then to build the edifice of knowledge and human practice upon them. In ethics, the most likely foundational strategies have been utilitarianism, on the one hand, or some form of rights theory, on the other. Utilitarianism has a fairly coherent history in the writings of Jeremy Bentham, John Stuart Mill, and Henry Sidgwick, each of whom saw ethics as a project of choosing the course of action that results in an optimal distribution of well-being (pleasure or pain, satisfaction or suffering) for all affected parties. Rights theory has a more complex line of descent that includes natural rights theorists such as Hugo Grotius and John Locke as well as Immanuel Kant's analysis of duty and autonomy. Here the philosophical task is to identify constraints that must not be violated when framing one's morally permissible choices.

Animal ethics—the philosophical study of human duties to and responsibility for nonhuman animals—has a long history, but few would deny that it took a dramatic turn in the 1970s and 1980s largely as a result of work that extends the foundational strategies of utilitarianism and of neo-Kantian rights theory. Peter Singer has become recognized as the prototypical example of the former approach, and Tom Regan of the latter. In what sense is there a pragmatic response to Singer and Regan? While all the chapters in this volume represent different ways of answering this question, my strategy will be to draw on pragmatism's unrelenting attentiveness to real problems. The result is not so much an alternative to specific doctrines that utilitarians or rights theorists might propose as it is an alternative way of understanding the philosophical agenda for animal ethics.

Two Kinds of Animal Ethics

In his 1998 David Wood-Gush Memorial Lecture, David Fraser describes two kinds of animal ethics, arguing that one is helpful for his research, while the other is not. Fraser is a Canadian animal researcher who has long con-ducted behavioral studies on livestock species (primarily pigs) in an effort to determine how they fare in various agricultural production settings. The aim of his work is to find a basis for understanding some of the elements of animal welfare that have proved most resistant to measurement. Basic veterinary and physiological indicators of animal health have been available for many years. These include not only rates of morbidity and mortality of animals but also nutritionally oriented criteria such as growth rates, reproductive success rates, and body mass measurements. Optimizing such measures contributed signifi-cantly to the development of intensive, confined animal feeding operations (CAFOs) during the past three decades. Such facilities allowed farmers greater control over the feed and environmental conditions in which their animals live, and have made record keeping and administration of veterinary care more cost-effective. While these changes have (mostly) led to improvements in the sur-vival of farm animals—clearly an indicator relevant to their welfare—the CAFO offers livestock significantly altered opportunities for movement, socialization, and the performance of typical behaviors (such as nesting), as well as signifi-cantly different sensory stimulation, when compared to traditional extensive animal production environments (i.e., barnyards and pasture and range set-tings). Fraser has been attempting to understand the significance of these dif-ferences for animal welfare.

Fraser's task is a blend of science and ethics. The science part consists in de-veloping methods of observation, measurement, and controlled experiment that make possible comparisons between production systems with respect to specific aspects of animal behavior. Thus Fraser's work enables one to document aversive behaviors (such as fear) to determine how much effort an animal will expend in order to attain or avoid a given state, or to find out which environ-ment animals will tend to prefer when given the opportunity to select from two or more options. The ethics part comes first in deciding which aspects of animal behavior to measure. Attributing evaluative significance to these observations requires, for example, the judgment that aversive behavior is a bad thing. Sec-ond, some method must be found of weighing the value that is associated with isolated experiences of fear or stress in an overall assessment of animal welfare, an assessment that should also reflect more standard veterinary and physiologi-cal indicators. The difficulty of this cannot be overstressed, since we find it no easy task to achieve an overall picture of the welfare of creatures who are very much like us and can talk to us (i.e., other human beings).

The ethics part of Fraser's work gets still more difficult, however, for the point of his work is to provide a basis for making decisions about the accept-ability of given production systems for animal agriculture. These decisions may be made by farmers, by equipment firms, or by government regulators. Decision makers must weigh the cost of production, food safety, and the environment, as well as animal welfare. Thus a third dimension of animal ethics for Fraser occurs in the weighting or significance given to animal welfare in relation to the other normative goals of livestock production (e.g., providing food and income for people). Here, "ethics" may have more to do with ensuring that all the respective interests are reflected in the decision than with requiring a cost-benefit-style weighing of these factors. Fraser's work has been critical to the effort to include the full range of animal interests when such decisions are made.

Fraser and others who do similar work are quite sensitive to the role of ethics in understanding and promoting animal welfare. His lecture examines how academic philosophers have contributed to the ethical dimensions of what he does. For Fraser, the two best-known philosophers working on animal ethics, Peter Singer and Tom Regan, have not made contributions that speak to the problems he encounters in using his scientific work to specify norms for livestock production and to offer normative advice for decision makers. This is not, as one might initially think, because Singer and Regan are advocates who are sharply critical of current animal production methods. The Singer and Regan style of philosophizing that Fraser simply calls Type I animal ethics is also associated with philosophers such as Raymond Frey, who holds the opposite position. Fraser roughly sketches distinctions between this type of philosophy and the Type II animal ethics philosophy (done by a number of less well-known individuals) that he finds most helpful.

Type I animal ethics has three characteristics that tend to make it less applicable to the kind of problems that decision makers within the livestock industry face. First, as Fraser describes it, it tends to focus on individuals and is thus relatively insensitive to species-level needs and concerns. Second, these philosophers are focused exclusively on the question of whether nonhuman animals deserve moral consideration, and this is, as Fraser sees it, a point that has already been conceded by people in the livestock industry. Third, these philosophers display no understanding of or interest in agriculture, and therefore do not consider the issues in animal ethics that speak to agricultural situations and imperatives. Type II animal ethics is simply philosophy that takes the opposite perspective on each of these points, though what the opposite perspective is must await a bit more clarification.

Fraser's discussion of animal ethics deserves particular attention from philosophers who think of themselves as pragmatists. If there is a seminal philosophical work in pragmatism, surely it must be Charles Sanders Peirce's "The Fixation of Belief," published originally in 1877. Here, Peirce holds (against Descartes and the entire modern tradition that follows) that inquiry undertaken in response to genuine doubt differs in important respects from inquiry undertaken to address sham or hypothetical doubt. Descartes had proposed to doubt the entire framework of belief, but someone facing genuine doubt is puzzled or troubled by a particular aspect of a problematic situation. The particularity and focus of their puzzlement contains (often in nascent or implicit form) criteria for the resolution of that doubt, and generally suggests a line of inquiry. Such situations never call for the wholesale suspension of one's belief system portrayed in Descartes's *Meditations,* and pragmatists argue that such a suspension is, in fact, impossible.

Peirce thus holds that philosophy (and, for that matter, science) is a form of inquiry not different at its roots from ordinary problem solving, and he advises a skeptical view of "first philosophy" that promises more than any inquiry can hope to deliver. Not only is it appropriate for philosophers to apply themselves to the problems of people like David Fraser, but such problems are actually more appropriate for philosophical attention than are the ongoing debates spawned by the modernist attempt to ground all knowledge claims on secure foundations. This theme was, of course, followed up and expanded by John Dewey, who delivers his critique of the modern program in *The Quest for Certainty* and offers his suggestion for a reorientation of the work of academic philosophers in *Reconstruction in Philosophy*. On this ground, I submit that attention to the sort of problem raised by Fraser in Type I and Type II animal ethics provides a more revealing test for contemporary pragmatist animal ethics than does searching the texts of Peirce, James, Dewey, and other pragmatists for their thoughts on animals.

Getting Pragmatic in Theory: Examining Fraser's Distinction

One question that may be of more interest to philosophers than to Fraser himself concerns the matter of whether he has parsed anything philosophically noteworthy in making the Type I–Type II distinction. I will argue that he has, and that his Type I theorists are foundationalists, whereas Type II theorists are more likely to be pragmatists. While remaining faithful to the criteria that Fraser advances in the 1999 published version of his lecture, I will gradually substitute this more standard philosophical terminology for Fraser's. Before proceeding I must warn readers that the criteria on which Fraser relies need some additional elaboration, and that the resulting transition to a distinction between foundational and pragmatic ethics is a bit bumpy.

The first element of Fraser's distinction, the individualism of Type I theory, is particularly in need of clarification. Fraser's discussion of this point appeals to the work of Bernard Rollin, who seems comfortable enough with the pragmatist designation. Through a series of publications (see *Unheeded Cry* and *Frankenstein Syndrome*), Rollin has developed the idea of animal telos. Far from the Aristotelian notion of telos yet inspired by it, animal telos is intended to reflect the biological and functional needs that would be characteristic of a given species. Thus, if pregnant sows experience a drive for nesting behavior, this will be characteristic of the pig telos. This idea is helpful to Fraser because it allows him to attribute normative significance to felt needs that are species-specific, and that are likely to be identified by the type of scientific studies that he conducts.

However, the idea that animal ethics splits into two opposed camps over the moral status of species is not unique to Fraser, nor has Rollin's notion of telos typically been the focus of this split. It has been the basis of a long-standing critique of Singer- and Regan-style animal ethics launched by environmental philosophers such as J. Baird Callicott and Mark Sagoff. Their argument is that environmental ethics is concerned with the preservation of endangered species and with the proper functioning of ecosystems. At a practical level, this puts environmental ethics into conflict with moral norms that place the welfare or interests of individual animals above these goals. Philosophically, it suggests that environmental ethics is committed to a "holism" that bestows value on species and ecosystems rather than to an individualism that derives value from the suffering or satisfaction of individual organisms.

Gary Varner's 1998 book, *In Nature's Interests?*, provides a detailed response to the debate between individual-oriented animal rights philosophies and the environmental ethics positions taken by Callicott and Sagoff. Varner defends a form of individualism, arguing not only that a biologically informed animal rights view is capable of supporting the kind of environmental policy initiatives usually associated with holism, but also that it does so in a philosophically more coherent and consistent manner than does holism. Varner's position is relevant here because it is arguably quite well-suited to taking on the kind of problems that Fraser faces, and as such should qualify as a Type II form of animal ethics. Of particular relevance is his attentiveness to the capacities and biological needs of animals (and for that matter, plants) that are specific to the species in question. Varner is able to make his argument because he pays careful attention to how a given species' evolutionary history has produced instincts, cognitive capacities, and functional drives that collectively form the basis for both biological and desire-based interests.

Furthermore, Varner argues explicitly that the moral significance of a nonhuman organism's interests does *not* derive from an analogy to human beings. Peter Singer's *principle of equal consideration of interests,* with its stress on the importance of such analogies in animal ethics, has been extremely influential. Famously, Singer argues that the interests of human and nonhuman animals should be given equal consideration. This has led some critics to overstate Singer's position, and David DeGrazia has offered an important and detailed clarification of the principle. Insofar as human interests and experiences—such as the experience of physical pain—are comparable to those of nonhumans, they should be given equal consideration. This clarification allows DeGrazia to acknowledge at least some species differences: humans clearly have more cognitively complex, more socially extended, and temporally more far-reaching interests than do most nonhumans. But certainly some nonhuman animals (notably the great apes) have more cognitively complex, more socially extended, and temporally more far-reaching interests than do others. DeGrazia therefore understands the principle of equal consideration of interests to entail different levels of moral consideration for different species of animal, based on the extent to which their capacities are analogous to those of human beings.

In this respect, DeGrazia's clarification of the principle of equal consideration addresses Fraser's second complaint with Type I animal ethics: its tendency to treat all nonhuman animals as a uniform class. Fraser notes that the primary goal of Singer and Regan has simply been to establish the moral considerability of nonhumans, and that this focus has led them to emphasize criteria (such as sentience) in which all vertebrates are similar to humans. Fraser claims that livestock producers have not doubted that animals have feelings, and have therefore thought the animals in their care deserving of moral consideration. Thus the producers have already conceded the main claim argued by Singer and Regan. Since their method of establishing this claim has emphasized the similarities between humans and nonhumans and ignored the differences, Type I animal ethics has promoted criteria that treat all animals (including humans) as a uniform class. This has made the first generation of foundational theorists relatively insensitive to the species-specific elements of telos that are critical to the needs of livestock. DeGrazia's clarification of the principle of equal consideration partially remediates this problem, for it does allow for differential treatment of humans on the ground that humans have morally important characteristics that other animals lack. DeGrazia's clarification is quite consistent with arguments put forward by Singer himself in *Practical Ethics*.

However, read literally, DeGrazia's statement of the principle of equal consideration still does not provide a basis for attributing any moral significance to animal capacities and drives that are not also shared by the human species. Thus, since pregnant women do not experience a drive to build a nest, there would be no reason to view a pregnant sow's need to build a nest as morally significant. Perhaps the pregnant sow experiences distress or frustration that is in some way comparable to that of a human; but the drive to perform nesting behavior can be observed, while the pig's experience of psychological distress (and its similarity to distress felt by humans) is speculative. It is therefore much more straightforward to simply invest the species-specific biological interests and desires of animals with moral significance and to say that, all things considered, the satisfaction of these interests and desires "counts," irrespective of their similarity to interests and desires experienced by human beings. But this is Varner's position, not that of Singer or DeGrazia.

Though Varner's position is very much like Rollin's in this respect, Varner describes himself as a "biocentric individualist," meaning that although nonhuman interests have moral significance, these interests attach to individual organisms rather than to species or ecosystems. Rollin himself does not speak to the argument of Callicott and Sagoff, and it is reasonable to think that he might be inclined to agree with Varner on this point. But all this suggests that Fraser is not quite correct in his diagnosis of where the trouble with Type I (or foundational) ethics lies. In fact, Varner's analysis probably is a better guide than Rollin's notion of telos to the kind of problems that Fraser must address. It is possible that livestock who have been subjected to certain stimuli in their early lives may develop a conditioned response; they may be extraordinarily fearful of sudden movements or loud noises, for example. A good livestock handler will be sensitive to these needs and will handle these animals accordingly. In saying that this is a characteristic of good animal care, we are making an ethical evaluation. These conditioned responses "count for something." As conditioned responses, however, they are not part of the animal's telos; yet there may be no ready analogy to them in human beings. Varner's analysis is capable of articulating why needs that may be felt by certain individual animals have ethical significance, even if they are not characteristic of the species as a whole. In sum, what differentiates these two types of ethics is not their orientation to individual or to species but the presence or absence of an ability to take the biological needs and desires of individual animals seriously, without regard to whether they are analogous to anything experienced by humans.

Yet the thrust of the discussion thus far hardly supports the claim that Type II animal ethics is a form of pragmatism. Varner, at least, is no willing pragmatist. He is trying to build a foundational biocentric account of interests, and he characterizes his position as a development of Singer's and Regan's. In fact the pragmatism here relates to the role of problems in establishing the criteria for successful philosophy. Fraser is quite right to point out how Singer's and Regan's inquiries have been shaped by the need to establish that nonhuman animals have any moral standing at all. This was a genuine problem both in academic philosophy, where canonical figures such as Descartes and Kant had staked out positions affording no moral standing to nonhumans, and in scientific research, where the view that animals have no feelings had become deeply entrenched (Rollin, *Unheeded Cry;* Rudacille). Given this problem, there is every reason to challenge those who pretend to see a difference between human and animal interests to justify their view, as Singer and Regan have done. However, a pragmatist would not expect that philosophy developed singularly in response to one particular problem will be adequate to the task of solving all problems in animal ethics.

In particular, a pragmatist would question whether the diagnosis of problems in the use of animals in laboratory research would apply to all relations between humans and animals. Yet this is largely what foundational animal ethicists have assumed when they have turned to livestock production. The style of thought in Singer and Regan (and Frey) is to presume that once claims about the moral standing of animals have been established, they can serve as foundations on which further inferences can be based. Thus, having arrived at moral conclusions regarding the use of animals in research, these philosophers expect to use these conclusions as a starting point for evaluating livestock production. It is this tendency, this approach to philosophy, which keeps them from being pragmatic. While both DeGrazia, who claims to be a pragmatist, and Varner, who claims otherwise, develop philosophical insights derived from the work of Singer and Regan, they are both working on quite different problems, and the philosophy they produce differs accordingly.

Certainly any philosopher will be troubled if these distinct occasions for philosophical thinking produce overtly contradictory results. That would be a problem, indeed. But the above discussion really indicates not so much any clear contradiction as a gradual shift in emphasis. Someone like Varner, who is working toward determining a minimal set of foundational premises, immediately sets out on a reductive quest for a universally applicable specification of the normative status of animal interests. A pragmatist, in contrast, might suspect that peculiarities of context that distinguish biomedical research, on the one hand, from livestock production, on the other, will turn out to be critical to the norms specified in either case. This suspicion makes the pragmatist less hopeful about the project of deriving a minimal set of logically consistent normative premises, but such suspicions do not refute the foundational project. Rather, they provide a rationale for putting one's energy elsewhere.

Getting Pragmatic in Application: Understanding Livestock Production

Authors such as Singer, Regan, Frey, and DeGrazia have discussed livestock production within the same philosophic and practical context as their discussion of animal research. Generally speaking, the latter has enjoyed an expository priority that has bestowed a de facto logical and ontological priority on the positions in animal ethics developed in response to it. The suffering of animals used in research is documented, as is the animal researchers' belief that animals have no moral standing given the important scientific and medical goals that their research is intended to advance. This characterization of the problem supports a philosophical argument that rebuts the "no moral standing" claim; in the case of Singer, Frey, and DeGrazia, at least, it leads to discussion about the relative value of human and animal suffering, and about whether the use of animals is truly necessary to achieve the researchers' putative scientific and medical goals. When these authors get around to agriculture, they typically discuss animal suffering and abuse associated with CAFOs (which they refer to as "factory farming") and do not examine in much detail agriculture's goals and philosophy.

Pragmatism is, in one sense, born as a riposte to the de facto prioritization of those philosophical doctrines developed in response to problems that philosophers happened to get around to first. The problem orientation of Peirce is absorbed into Dewey's critique of academic philosophy in *Reconstruction in Philosophy.* Dewey argues that the philosophy of Descartes and other early modern figures must be seen as a response to a deep and systematic epistemological and social problem faced by those who were attempting to establish a secular basis for scientific inquiry. But by Dewey's time, the kind of opposition experienced by Galileo no longer faced those who would undertake scientific research. The early moderns' development of philosophical lines of inquiry that continue to interest and occupy academic philosophers notwithstanding, responsible philosophical inquiry should be as attentive to the problems of our own day as Descartes was to those of his. This is particularly true in virtue of the way that philosophy functions within higher education as an institution that produces and reproduces criteria and methods of inquiry for the arts and sciences. To educate a young scientist who will face the kind of problems confronted by David Fraser exclusively in the philosophy of the modern period is to produce an intellectual whose brain is out of sync with the twenty-first century.

Foundational theories of animal ethics that have been developed as a critique of animal research create a similar (if less thoroughgoing or systematic) kind of disjunction. Singer, for example, claims in *Animal Liberation* that the abuses of factory farming are "the logical extension of the attitudes and prejudices that are discussed elsewhere" in that work (94). That is to say, livestock producers (like most people, according to Singer) see animals as lacking any moral standing and as mere objects available for human exploitation. Others describe livestock production as an industry seeking to provide those who consume food the relatively trivial aesthetic pleasure of eating tasty meat (see Gruzalski; Comstock). This characterization would suggest that the livestock industry sees itself in roughly the same light as the producers of Hollywood movies or television sit-coms: servicing an economically lucrative but otherwise rather insignificant form of consumer demand. The upshot is a moral portrait of the stock producer that appears much worse than that of the medical researcher. Animal producers, like the researcher, are characterized as insensitive to animal suffering because they believe that animals are unworthy of moral consideration; but unlike the scientist trying to relieve human suffering, they are portrayed as wholly venal, driven solely by the profit motive.

In more than twenty years of research and writing on agricultural ethics, I have met two animal producers who fit this stereotype. Both were owners of very large animal production operations, and it is doubtful that either more than twice a year saw an animal from a distance of less than 100 feet. The countless others in animal husbandry that I have encountered are not at all like this. In fact, animal producers do, as Fraser suggests, acknowledge a moral responsibility toward their livestock, and this responsibility of good husbandry entails, beyond not inflicting unnecessary pain or suffering, offering the animals proper care. However, as Bernard Rollin argues in *Farm Animal Welfare,* the traditional ethic of husbandry has gone sour of late. And of course, even foundational animal ethicists are aware that not *all* livestock producers are venal and insensitive, as is evidenced by their distinction between family and factory farms. DeGrazia, for example, notes, "Family farms cause much less suffering to animals than do factory farms due to their far less intensive rearing systems," though he goes on to find even family farms unacceptable because they, too, inflict on livestock the harm of death (288).

Singer's *Animal Liberation* also locates the source of the problem in factory farming, which he contrasts to the idyllic vision most people associate with farming: "a house, a barn, a flock of hens, overseen by a strutting rooster, scratching around the farmyard, a herd of cows being brought in from the fields for milking, and perhaps a sow rooting around in the orchard with a litter of squealing piglets running excitedly behind her" (93). And though Regan's primary discussion of livestock production occurs in the course of raising a problem for Singer's utilitarianism, he, too, describes it as "big business" (221), leaving to the reader the inference that the commercialization and industrialization of the livestock industry has created a class of animal producers wholly insensitive to animal needs.

Yet we may question whether drawing a distinction between family and factory farming is sufficient for analyzing contemporary animal agriculture. For one thing, the distinction itself leaves an unanalyzed gap in foundational animal ethics. Factory farmers farm for profit, according to the foundational analysis, but why do family farmers farm? This question is never answered. And why should family farmers think that animals have moral standing when factory farmers do not? Is it all the Descartes and Kant that is being taught in our agricultural colleges? our business schools? It is far from clear why the foundational analysis provides any basis at all for distinguishing between factory and family farming, even though this is a distinction that the foundational theorists all seem to make.

Furthermore, it is much more difficult to tell the difference between family and factory farming than the foundational analysis suggests. Relatively few CAFOs worldwide are corporately owned (with the exception of small family businesses that are incorporated largely for tax reasons). In many cases, owner-operators of CAFOs farm under contract to firms that integrate the various links of the food chain, from hatching chicks to purchasing feed to growing out to slaughtering to processing and finally to delivery at the supermarket or fast-food outlet. These "integrators" contract with family-owned and -operated firms at each stage, from independent truckers to the owner of the CAFO itself. Integrators generally own a fairly small component of the total chain, and it tends to be the slaughtering and processing facility, not the "factory farm" (Kunkel). If CAFOs are family-owned, and if families (as opposed to corporations) are the good guys, why is there a problem here? The foundationalists' diagnosis of problems in animal agriculture has no coherent view of why animal interests are neglected in intensive production systems (family-owned or not), nor of why traditional diversified family farms should be found morally acceptable. Lacking such an explanation, it is far from clear why a new appreciation of the moral status of animals would make any difference.

In fact, animal producers are in a bind that is partly the result of policy, partly the result of technology, and partly the result of a pervasive mentality. The policy component relates both to the general organization of agricultural production throughout the industrialized world and to the specific subsidies paid to grain farmers. Generally, farmers must recover their production costs and then some, or they will not be able to pay their taxes, not to mention repay the loans that they may have taken out to cover operating expenses. The economic story is especially complex in animal agriculture. Many producers make profits only one year in four, and even in good years raising livestock will not make the average person rich. Moreover, in some important components of the industry producers actually lose money on their farming year in and year out, yet continue to support it with off-farm employment. But the root meaning of the "farming is a business" mantra (which anyone who talks to farmers hears over and over again) is that even family farmers—whose primary goals may have to do with lifestyle, permanence, and loyalty to place—who do not recover most of their costs do not continue in farming for very long. Except for the dairy industry, American animal producers do not receive any kind of direct government payments that subsidize their cost of production. Corn and soybeans *are* heavily subsidized in almost every industrialized country, however, and the cheapness of delivered animal feeds is part of the reason that CAFOs have become formidable economic competitors to extensive production systems.

The technology component of the equation relates in part to the buildings, to the feed delivery systems, to the computers for managing large numbers of animals, and to the drugs that enable large numbers of animals to be kept close together without risk of epidemic disease. CAFOs would not exist without this technological base, which was largely developed through publicly financed agricultural research. But this is only part of the technology story. Companies with an economic interest in selling their buildings, machines, and medicines promoted this technology to farmers. Company representatives took pains to show farmers how to use it, providing figures to convince them that incorporating technology would be profitable. There may be alternative ways to farm that rely on good management skills, but unless someone is out there promoting them as aggressively as the technology is advocated, we should not be surprised when farmers choose the system that someone has taken pains to explain to them. The researchers, machines, investors, and company representatives make up a network of actors that engage animal producers, hoping to draw them in. Over time, the network grows and a particular technologically based set of practices (e.g., CAFOs) becomes pervasive.

What has just been described is an example of the actor-network sociology developed by Bruno Latour. Latour himself has used it to explain the success of pasteurization in France (*Pasteurization of France*) and has put it forward as a general theory for what drives scientific and technological change (*Science in Action*). Latour presents actor-network theory as a philosophical alternative to the idea that science is inherently progressive, that science always has the most rational approach (*We Have Never Been Modern*). Actor-network theory suggests that science and technology can take routes that simply reflect the interests of successful (or powerful) networks. For this reason, Latour has sometimes been characterized as a postmodernist. But pragmatism also emphasizes social networks, and the point on which Dewey's view of inquiry most sharply differs from that of the great defender of scientific rationality Karl Popper concerns the way that institutions and social context can divert science from piecemeal and evolutionary improvements. It therefore seems reasonable for pragmatists to view Latour as a philosophical ally who has provided a means of understanding how technological endeavors can go wrong, and also right.

Philosophy plays a key role in framing and reinforcing the mentality or general mind-set that facilitates the formation of social networks and that enables them to make their way through society with comparative ease. Part of the mentality that paved the way for CAFOs is modernism, not in the sense of a well-worked-out empiricist or rationalist epistemology but as an uncritical faith that science and technology are inherently progressive. Again, Dewey is one of the first philosophers to provide a basis for questioning this faith (see Hickman). But within agriculture, the modernist faith takes on a form tied to a normative vision of the potential for industrial society. The normative foundations of this vision are utilitarian, and they are articulated in the aphorism that has guided agricultural science since the mid–nineteenth century: make two blades of grass grow where one grew before (Thompson, "Animals in the Agrarian Ideal" and *Spirit of the Soil*).

In summary, the argument for industrialization ran thus: traditional agriculture was tied to inefficient and often politically reactionary forms of land tenure, and it was supported by dubious claims about agriculture's links to moral virtue. It is far better to think of agriculture as just another sector of the industrial society. Agricultural production should be organized to serve the greatest good for the greatest number, by producing key commodities in the most efficient way possible, all things considered. "All things considered" means that government regulation should ensure that there are no excessive external or social costs, such as pollution, rapid depletion of soil or water resources, or unsafe production practices. Once the proper regulatory structure is in place, "the greatest good" will be achieved by allowing producers—not only farmers but also farm suppliers and equipment manufacturers—to compete.

Animal welfare can be understood as an external cost. That is, the suffering of farm animals is something that should be considered among "all things"; but what to include in the regulatory structure is a decision made *socially,* not by the individual producer, who must simply seek to maximize profit (Coase). On this view, farmers should not be blamed for animal suffering, nor should an individual producer alone be expected to bear the costs of securing welfare. It is a social failure that allows this suffering to occur. One can see the kinds of social action promoted by Singer in *Animal Liberation* as an attempt to muster the social will for requiring that the costs of animal well-being be internalized. Such efforts have borne little fruit over the past quarter century, however, and there are multiple reasons for their lack of effectiveness.

For one thing, the message of this social movement is badly mixed. The loudest animal activists, including Singer and Regan, have promoted vegetarianism far more aggressively than they have promoted better living conditions for farm animals. As a result, what most animal producers have heard is a campaign designed to put them out of business altogether. They saw precedents for this loss of an entire sector. Far from creating a market structure that internalizes cost, some environmental regulations have simply driven industries such as steel and chemical production offshore, where the costs are now borne by people in poor countries. Aggressive animal welfare regulation could have a similar effect, making it too costly for American farmers to compete with foreign producers who can mistreat their animals without penalty.

But lingering elements of the traditional agrarian mind-set have also been at work. According to this view, the farm or ranch is an island unto itself. Government regulation is simply interference in personal property rights. Besides, farmers are, as Thomas Jefferson famously wrote, "the most virtuous citizens," and they can be relied on to do the right thing. Unfortunately, this has played out in such a way that animal producers are Jeffersonian yeomen when it comes to regulation and profit-motivated industrialists when it comes to making a production decision. In the end, animals have lost out; but it is misleading to think that this is because animal producers are in thrall to Cartesian metaphysics or Kantian moral theory and it is mistaken to draw a sharp distinction between family and factory farming.

Yet livestock producers do care about their animals, and increasing numbers of them have been disturbed about the production systems that they felt compelled to adopt. I do not want to overstate this point. They also felt with some justification that while CAFOs may be detrimental to some aspects of animal welfare, they are beneficial to others (see Stricklin and Swanson). Animal scientists have also mounted challenges to unreflective modernism and the industrial paradigm within (see Kunkel and Hagevoort; Schillo; Cheeke). There is thus growing opportunity for a counternetwork to form. I have argued that it is important to resist the idea that this is a contest between family and factory farming. It is equally critical that people interested in animal welfare realize that animal producers face challenges on other fronts, including food safety and the environment, which compete both for resources and for regulatory attention. It is therefore important to be inclusive as new, alternative networks emerge (Thompson, "Animal Welfare").

In short, the philosophy that will enable one to apply animal ethics within the livestock production sector is *not* one that attributes the problem to a "logical extension" of the view that animals do not deserve moral consideration. It is instead a philosophy that combines a Latourian-pragmatic conception of technical change with a sophisticated understanding of how philosophy influences the mentality of people involved in agriculture. Such an understanding will lay the groundwork for an alternative mind-set that facilitates the building of a counternetwork. Obviously, people like David Fraser will play a pivotal role in this counternetwork, for which he sees a different, more pragmatic kind of animal ethics as potentially more helpful. But consumers will also play a role, a point that brings us to the final way in which we must get pragmatic.

Getting Pragmatic in Practice: Ethical Meat Consumption

Many of the philosophers who have worked in the field of animal ethics (including some key contributors to this volume) have become vegetarians after an earlier life of meat consumption more typical of Americans. It is not surprising that the reasoning that led to their conversion appears frequently in their writings. This "ethical vegetarianism" component is also one of the most popular subjects for students and others who read about animal ethics. Yet arguments for ethical vegetarianism represent a form of philosophy that distinguishes them from other topics in the literature. For one thing, they are the most concrete and practical part of the analysis typically offered by a foundational theorist. Everyone can at least entertain the possibility of becoming a vegetarian, and the reader can experiment with this idea within at most a few hours after reviewing the arguments. Furthermore, though academic philosophers have shown comparatively little interest in food, diet has always been one of the ways that people develop practices of self-mastery and discipline and also of freedom and expression. Diet is a natural topic within forms of ethics that take up asceticism or Epicurean aestheticism, and diet was, with sexuality, one of the topics that Michel Foucault identified as important for "the care of the self."

A central point of ascetic and aesthetic ethics is that both treat the problem of normative regulation as an exceptional rather than a universal doctrine. That is, the ethical inquiry is to find rules or standards by which one may live one's life in an exceptional manner, quite unlike what one expects of others. Such inquiries take the form of a circumstantial ad hominem argument directed at oneself: because I am this or that sort of person, I must adopt this or that dietary practice. Ethical vegetarianism can take this form, most obviously when religious doctrines are involved: because I am a Hindu, I am an ethical vegetarian. But there are many reasons why someone might come to ethical vegetarianism, and it is my strong belief that we should respect these reasons and similarly respect the wishes and sensitivities of the ethical vegetarian. I have worked out the arguments for what I take to be an analogous issue with respect to the desire not to eat genetically engineered food (Thompson, "Why Food Biotechnology").

However, there are two other forms of argument that are used with respect to ethical vegetarianism. The one that is associated with Tom Regan's version of animal rights holds that because certain moral claims are correct, everyone should be a vegetarian for ethical reasons. The one that is associated with Peter Singer holds that because certain contingent facts about animal production are true, everyone who stands in a very common relationship to the animal production industry (i.e., is among its customers) should be a vegetarian for ethical reasons. These two types of argument deserve a very different response. With respect to the Regan-style argument, we must note that one of its logical consequences is that everyone throughout human history who has eaten meat is morally wrong. In their number are African goatherds, Middle Eastern shepherds, and, for many Americans, generations of ancestors who operated diversified farms and ranches long before the first CAFO was ever conceived. Also included are many of our moral heroes—among them Jesus of Nazareth, who served up a famous meal of fishes and loaves.

We can, of course, excuse them for their wrongdoing by noting that perhaps they faced extreme want and were thus justified in eating animal flesh, or by saying simply that they could not have known better. But I believe this is a rather odd claim, and those philosophers who have been inclined to say this need to listen to themselves a bit more critically. We are, I believe, prepared to say that the generations before us who practiced human slavery were wrong in doing so. Perhaps some can be at least partially excused, and we can at least understand why they erred. But we nevertheless say that they erred. The condemnation of slavery holds up as a universal judgment against the evidence of history. But I, at least, cannot convince myself that whatever we learn about animals' mental capacities tomorrow, we will ever be in a position to conclude that everyone who ate meat throughout human history committed a moral wrong. In part this is a view rationally based on my thinking that omnivorous behavior is an element of the evolutionary history of human beings. In part this is just a considered intuition that I have found it impossible to dislodge. In either case, I have a basis for viewing any argument that claims to turn vegetarianism into a universal moral obligation as a reductio ad absurdum. There must be something wrong with it somewhere.

I can, however, follow the logic of Singer's move to ethical vegetarianism quite clearly, and I can accept many of its premises. Animals can suffer, and any suffering they bear in the course of livestock production should count in our evaluation of it. So far, I am along for the ride. Singer believes that while eating meat and other animal products is justifiable when the benefits outweigh the costs, with factory farming just the reverse is the case. We therefore must become vegetarians as a way of showing our displeasure with industrial animal production. For Singer circa 1975, contingent circumstances in the livestock industry convert a concern for animal welfare into a strong recommendation, if not strictly an obligation, for ethical vegetarianism. But it is interesting to note that Singer's view does not entail that everyone should be a vegetarian. Not only does it exclude those outside the industrial agricultural system, but it suggests that someone who can, by eating a steak and demonstrating solidarity with animal producers (something that Bernard Rollin has done a few times), have some hope of improving the lot of farm animals should probably eat the steak.

As I write this, many more of us are in a position to improve the quality of life for farm animals by eating particular animal products. The key is to build and bolster the alternative network that will include animal welfare among the parameters considered in livestock production. The consumer's role in this is to demand (and when we use the word *demand* next to *consumer* it means "pay for") animal products that are produced under conditions that meet the criteria for animal welfare derived from the work of people like David Fraser. It will be useless to call for such products with placards and signs and then either eat cheaply or not eat meat at all. The greatest single barrier to improvements in animal welfare is the belief that people will not pay for it. The empirical support for this belief resides in several decades of market research indicating that food consumers respond to two things: price and appearance, with price being the more important of the two. Thus anything that consumers can do to shake this belief will open up opportunities for an alternative network to get established.

The obvious thing to do is to purchase products labeled "welfare-friendly" or "free-range." Equally, we should frequent restaurants such as Philadelphia's White Dog Cafe that claim to use welfare-sensitive suppliers of animal products. The next best thing is to seek out labels such as "organic" that *may* reflect these concerns, though they may not. Many consumers are justifiably skeptical about such labels, but it is important to remember that even buying a product that is falsely or ambiguously labeled actually helps the cause of animal welfare, because establishing the market structure that communicates demand for animal welfare is the first priority. It is important to create and enforce standards, but those steps come later. The immediate and overriding need is to establish a demand for them. Lobbying legislative representatives won't hurt, but it is reasonable to think that quicker progress will be made through the marketplace. But pipe down about vegetarianism. Such calls only force livestock producers into a bunker mentality.

What are we to say to someone like DeGrazia, who claims to be a pragmatist, yet argues for vegetarianism because even when animals are well-treated, their death is, for him, an unacceptable harm? Here we must reiterate two points. First, it is not unreasonable for someone to want no part of meat eating. The proto-pragmatist Henry David Thoreau offers a sensitive portrait of a tension many feel in the "Higher Laws" chapter of *Walden* when he writes, "I have found repeatedly of late years, that I cannot fish without falling a little in self-respect" (263). So becoming a vegetarian is certainly entirely acceptable. But second, we must recall that extending such feelings into a universal moral law produces untenable results. The point here is thus not to overcome some individual's empathetic vegetarian preferences but simply to indicate why someone who is both comfortable with eating meat and willing to structure his or her consumption habits according to a politico-economic rationale of promoting animal welfare should feel fully justified in doing so. In this regard we might note that while being slaughtered is certainly contrary to the interests of any individual animal, it is difficult to deny that enduring slaughter has proved to be an enormously successful evolutionary strategy for domesticated livestock species.

Stephen Budiansky has suggested that these species "chose" domestication, and that in eating them we are in some sense doing what they want. His argument has not gotten much serious attention from philosophers, and this is not the place to launch into a full-scale discussion of it. Yet it is not implausible to suggest that organisms (plant *and* animal) evolve with rates of reproduction that accommodate predators typical of their respective ecological niche. They thus incorporate into their telos, to use Rollin's term, an expectation of becoming prey. In fact if wild animals do *not* fall victim to predators at the ecologically appropriate rate, they collectively destroy their own habitat, arguably imposing far more suffering on themselves than would have occurred had they been killed and eaten one by one. An evolutionary, ecological analysis of this sort provides the reason why we should not be out in the wild trying to "save" mice and voles from predation by owls or snakes. Yet humans have tended to be predators, too, and while any individual human might choose to confine his or her predation to plant species, the ecological niche created by pastoralists was filled by animals adapted to a different form of predation. Though I do not mean to imply that I have provided anything more than the suggestion of an argument, it is plausible to think that being slaughtered and eaten by human beings is indeed a component of the telos for domesticated livestock. Furthermore, this is a defense of livestock slaughter that does not translate into a defense of production abuses.

In sum, there are innumerable reasons why someone might choose to become an ethical vegetarian, and these reasons deserve respect. Nothing that has been said here provides any motive for those who accept an exceptionalist argument for vegetarianism to change their views. However, arguments that purport to establish vegetarianism as a universal moral norm face a tough hurdle. It just does not seem reasonable to claim that goat-herding peasants or pig-herding Maring of New Guinea (or, for that matter, the countless American pioneers who kept a cow, a pig, and a few chickens) are doing something to their animals that is comparable to the practice of human slavery. What is more likely is that people like ourselves, reasonably well-off and living in an advanced industrial society, may have some duties of diet that we are neglecting. But if our goal is to improve the lot of animals, the most effective way to redress this neglect is to build a network of producers and consumers who are dedicated to that end. The only way to be a part of that network as a consumer is to eat milk, meat, and eggs that appear to have been produced under welfare-friendly conditions.

In each of the above three sections, the largest part of pragmatism lies in seeing what the problem is. We become pragmatic in theory when we recognize that while failing to see animals as having any moral standing at all may have indeed been a problem among medical researchers, it is not a big problem in livestock production. In the former case, the diagnosis gives rise to a philosophy that stresses the similarities between human beings and animals as a refutation of "speciesism." But if *only* traits shared by humans can have moral significance, we wind up with an animal ethic sharply limited in its capacity to deal with the problems of livestock or of animals in the wild. It is thus not surprising that a new generation of animal ethicists have developed philosophical tools more responsive to differences among species. The claim here is not that Singer and Regan have taken positions *incapable* of attentiveness to such differences, but simply that their focus has not inclined them to develop these aspects of animal ethics. Being pragmatic in theory requires being responsive to the first two of David Fraser's observations about Type II animal ethics: recognizing that species differences matter, and noting that no one in livestock production is denying that animals deserve moral consideration.

Applying the tools that the new generation of animal ethicists has produced also requires an understanding of the problem, and few animal ethicists have given much thought to the socioeconomic forces that have given rise to industrialization in animal agriculture. Foundational approaches in ethics and epistemology are geared to problems caused by faulty beliefs, and in foundational animal ethics the arguments have been focused on refuting beliefs that favor human interests. But no matter what one believes about human *or* animal interests, one cannot raise livestock without attending to the imperatives of commodity and credit markets. CAFOs have become dominant because market structure and public policy make alternative systems difficult to maintain. A response to this problem demands a change in market structure or public policy (or both), not a change in animal producers' belief system. In this case, Fraser's third observation—that the first generation of animal ethics philosophers doesn't know much about agriculture—has resulted in philosophical prescriptions inadequate to the task of reform.

In fact, the practices on which animal ethicists have been focused are not agricultural but dietary. Many philosophers writing on animals have become vegetarians, and have advocated vegetarianism for their readers. While I do not try to convince any committed ethical vegetarians to change their views, I submit that an equally pragmatic response is to reform not our dietary practice but our purchasing habits. By integrating ourselves into a network of consumers willing to pay for humane farming practices, we can send an economic signal that is far more potent than that of vegetarian protest. Producers will respond positively to effective demand, but they will regard the advocacy of vegetarianism as a threat to their way of life. Of course, ethical animal consumption should go along with appropriate political activism, and here there may be some opportunity to link arms with vegetarian animal protectionists. But note that such alliances will be a tricky business, for even livestock producers committed to humane farming may feel threatened by animal activists dedicated to political action that will put them out of business. Getting pragmatic in practice requires some sophistication about *which* practices we want to affect.

Problem diagnosis makes a huge difference that too few appreciate. The works of Peirce, James, and Dewey help to explain and articulate why this is the case. Familiarity with them will benefit anyone who wants to get pragmatic with respect to animal ethics. But pragmatic animal ethics is by no means simply a matter of extending some doctrine from Peirce, James, or Dewey into the domain of human-animal relations. Philosophers who do not think of themselves as pragmatists, such as Gary Varner, may be contributing as much or more to a pragmatist animal ethics as any follower of the classical figures. Moreover, it is difficult to see how any amount of reading in classical American pragmatism could prepare someone to appreciate the mentality of contemporary animal agriculture. Getting pragmatic means getting the facts, and on this point, even a foundational ethicist such as Peter Singer would surely agree. Are Fraser's new generation animal ethicists also pragmatists? Not necessarily. Yet those who do think of themselves as pragmatists have every reason to be attentive to the points Fraser raises, and to develop philosophical tools that will assist in the amelioration of problems in contemporary livestock production.

Bibliography

Budiansky, Stephen. *The Covenant of the Wild: Why Animals Chose Domestication.* New Haven: Yale University Press, 1999.

Callicott, J. Baird. "Animal Liberation: A Triangular Affair." *Environmental Ethics* 2 (1980): 311–38.

Cheeke, Peter R. *Contemporary Issues in Animal Agriculture.* 2nd ed. Danville, Ill.: Interstate Publishers, 1999.

Coase, Ronald J. "The Problem of Social Costs." *Journal of Law and Economics* 3 (1960): 1–44.

Comstock, Gary. *Vexing Nature? On the Ethical Case against Agricultural Biotechnology.* Dordrecht: Kluwer Academic Publishers, 2000.

DeGrazia, David. *Taking Animals Seriously: Mental Life and Moral Status.* Cambridge: Cambridge University Press, 1996.

Dewey, John. *The Quest for Certainty. The Later Works, 1925–1953,* edited by Jo Ann Boydston, vol. 4, *1929.* Carbondale: Southern Illinois University Press, 1984.

———. *Reconstruction in Philosophy.* In *The Middle Works, 1899–1924,* edited by Jo Ann Boydston, vol. 12, *1920, 77–201.* Carbondale: Southern Illinois University Press, 1982.

Foucault, Michel. *The Care of the Self.* Translated by Robert Hurley. 1986. Reprint, New York: Vintage Books, 1988.

Fraser, David. "Animal Ethics and Animal Welfare Science: Bridging the Two Cultures." *Applied Animal Behavior Science* 65 (1999): 171–89.

Frey, Raymond G. *Interests and Rights: The Case against Animals.* Oxford: Clarendon Press; New York: Oxford University Press, 1980.

Gruzalski, Bart. "The Case against Raising and Killing Animals for Food." In *Ethics and Animals,* edited by Harlan B. Miller and William H. Williams, 251–63. Clifton, N.J.: Humana Press, 1983.

Hickman, Larry A. *Philosophical Tools for Technological Culture: Putting Pragmatism to Work.* Bloomington: Indiana University Press, 2001.

Kunkel, H. O. *Human Issues in Animal Agriculture.* College Station: Texas A&M University Press, 2000.

Kunkel, H. O., and G. R. Hagevoort. "Construction of Science for Animal Agriculture." *Journal of Animal Science* 72 (1994): 2849–54.

Latour, Bruno. *The Pasteurization of France.* Translated by Alan Sheridan and John Law. Cambridge, Mass.: Harvard University Press, 1988.

———. *Science in Action: How to Follow Scientists and Engineers through Society.* Cambridge, Mass.: Harvard University Press, 1987.

———. *We Have Never Been Modern.* Translated by Catherine Porter. Cambridge, Mass.: Harvard University Press, 1993.

Peirce, Charles Sanders. "The Fixation of Belief." In *Philosophical Writings of Peirce,* edited by Justus Buchler, 5–22. 1940. Reprint, New York: Dover Publications, 1955.

Regan, Tom. *The Case for Animal Rights.* Berkeley: University of California Press, 1983.

Rollin, Bernard E. *Farm Animal Welfare: Social, Bioethical, and Research Issues.* Ames: Iowa State University Press, 1995.

———. *The Frankenstein Syndrome.* Cambridge: Cambridge University Press, 1995.

———. *The Unheeded Cry: Animal Consciousness, Animal Pain, and Science.* Oxford: Oxford University Press, 1989.

Rudacille, Deborah. *The Scalpel and the Butterfly: The War between Animal Research and Animal Protection.* New York: Farrar, Straus and Giroux, 2000.

Sagoff, Mark. "Animal Liberation and Environmental Ethics: Bad Marriage, Quick Divorce." *Osgoode Hall Law Journal* 22 (1984): 297–307.

Schillo, Keith K. "Toward a Pluralistic Animal Science: Postliberal Feminist Perspectives." *Journal of Animal Science* 76 (1998): 2763–70.

Singer, Peter. *Animal Liberation: A New Ethic for Our Treatment of Animals.* New York: Avon Books, 1975.

———. *Practical Ethics.* 2nd ed. Cambridge: Cambridge University Press, 1993.

Stricklin, W. Ray, and Janice C. Swanson. "Technology and Animal Agriculture." *Journal of Agricultural and Environmental Ethics* 12 (1993): 207–14.

Thompson, Paul B. "Animal Welfare and Livestock Production in a Postindustrial Milieu." *Journal of Applied Animal Welfare Science* 4 (2001): 191–205.

———. "Animals in the Agrarian Ideal." *Journal of Agricultural and Environmental Ethics* 6, special suppl. 1 (1993): 36–49.

———. *The Spirit of the Soil: Agriculture and Environmental Ethics.* New York: Routledge, 1995.

———. "Why Food Biotechnology Needs an Opt Out." In *Engineering the Farm: Ethical and Social Aspects of Agricultural Biotechnology,* edited by Britt Bailey and Marc Lappé, 27–43. Washington, D.C.: Island Press, 2002.

Thoreau, Henry David. *Walden and Other Writings by Henry David Thoreau.* Edited by J. Wood Krutch. New York: Bantam Books, 1981.

Varner, Gary E. *In Nature's Interests? Interests, Animal Rights, and Environmental Ethics.* Oxford: Oxford University Press, 1998.

White Dog Cafe. Home page, July 11, 2003. http://www.whitedog.com (accessed August 2003).

8 Pragmatism and the Production of Livestock

Erin McKenna

Do nonhuman animals have moral standing? Do nonhuman animals have interests that we must consider when making decisions about how to act in the world? Do we have moral obligations to, or responsibilities for, nonhuman animals?

These are some of the more abstract philosophical questions that stand behind such questions as, Are we justified in liquefying the eyes of rabbits so we can feel safe using toxic chemicals to clean our homes and beautify our bodies? Should we use our closest living relative, chimpanzees, who share 98.76 percent of our genetic structure, to test nasal sprays and hepatitis vaccines, or to do research on HIV? Is it OK to raise animals in intensive factory farm conditions so that humans can have a ready and inexpensive supply of meat?

Humanity has been debating questions about its use of nonhumans throughout the ages. For example, vegetarianism is nothing new. Ancient scholars argued for various forms of vegetarianism on religious and philosophical grounds. The Bible gives humans plants and fruits to eat first and then animals only after the Fall; religions whose doctrines include belief in the transmigration of souls forbade the consumption of meat because it might lead to eating a friend or relative. Health reasons have been cited from the beginning as well—eating meat was seen to slow the body and the mind. Eating that caused the suffering of another was also seen to harm character; further, the slaughtering of nonhuman animals was thought to harden us to pain and suffering, thereby leading to bad character and bad habits with regard to our treatment of all other living things, including humans. Injuring character is an argument that has been used against using animals (human and nonhuman) in experimentation and testing as well. In addition, many have questioned how productive or helpful such testing is. While we share a great deal in common with our animal cousins, toxic reactions and medical protocols often differ between, and even within, species. Nonetheless, experimentation continues and the mass production of animal flesh is a huge industry.

I believe that practices of use and consumption are the result of humans' sense of place in the world. Humans have a history of separating ourselves into groups and believing that one group is better than another. Racism, classism, nationalism, and sexism are all examples of this tendency, of which, as others have argued, speciesism is another and often overlooked manifestation. There is a high cost to speciesism, however, and we cannot continue to ignore it.

Speciesism endangers our health and well-being in many ways. We believe we are justified in raising and slaughtering billions of animals to eat them as food. This diet contributes to heart disease and cancer, and it depletes water and topsoil while making the land toxic. We believe we are justified in running toxicity tests on millions of animals, but find that human reactions do not always match the reaction of our nonhuman counterparts. We believe we are justified in using countless animals, from rats to chimpanzees, in medical experiments, though many of these experiments provide misleading—and even fatally misleading—results. We need to realize that our disregard for the well-being of others puts ourselves at risk.

Such inattentiveness directly affects our health and our outlook on and treatment of the environment on which nonhuman and human animals alike depend. It also endangers us indirectly, leading to habits of objectifying and using other living beings as disposable objects.[1] By ignoring our own connectedness to other living beings, and thus failing to understand our interdependence, we risk destroying ourselves and other life. Yet when we do acknowledge this connectedness we usually combine it with objectification and subjugation, and so fall back into the same habits that endanger all life on this planet. We must expand our understanding of community to include nonhuman animals in our social and moral universe. I will use the philosophy of William James and of John Dewey to argue for just such an expansion.

Some Philosophical Perspectives on Nonhuman Animals

I will briefly present some basic information about human animals' use of nonhuman animals for food, examining these practices primarily from a pragmatist point of view. A quick overview of some more standard approaches to such issues will help to explain what makes a pragmatist approach different and perhaps useful.

The first two standard positions—deontological and utilitarian theories—are well-studied philosophical schools of thought, and each has a well-known spokesperson on topics of our use of other animals: Tom Regan and Peter Singer, respectively. While they differ in their specific conclusions, both agree that our current practices must radically change. Basically Regan argues that any being that has an interest in life should have those interests considered. Nonhuman animals are not just resources for us to use; they have an equal right to be treated with respect. His deontological approach demands that we end all use of animals as food and as subjects of experimentation. Singer, drawing on utilitarianism, measures right and wrong in terms of the suffering caused by the action and suggests it is speciesist to consider the suffering of humans as automatically more important than the suffering of nonhumans. This approach requires that we critically examine our practices with regard to raising and slaughtering livestock and using animals in experiments. It demands not necessarily that such practices stop but that we consider and mitigate the suffering involved. If taken seriously, it does demand that we greatly reduce our use of nonhuman animals and alter our treatment of them, perhaps at the cost of inconvenience to humans.

A third perspective is that of ecofeminism. While no one approach or person can be seen as representing the ecofeminist perspective on our treatment of nonhuman animals, all ecofeminist views ask us to radically alter our worldview. Karen Warren and Carol Adams both present positions that suggest we must change not only our practices but also our understanding of our connectedness to all other living things. They push us to see how women, nature, and nonhuman animals have been similarly oppressed and harmed by the dominant systems of thought. Systems of thought that arrange things in dichotomies and hierarchically have historically lumped women, nature, and animals on the side that is viewed as not fully rational. They are to be ruled and manipulated by the more active, more valued side of the dichotomy—the side identified with men. Warren and Adams suggest we see fluid connections instead of rigid dichotomies; in so doing, they hope, we will lose our propensity to see land, trees, animals, and women as objects to be dominated and used as we please. Ecofeminists not only challenge our ethics but suggest a different metaphysics, pushing us at the same time to see traditional epistemology differently. They reject the reason/emotion dichotomy and challenge the traditional focus on reason. This challenge also works to dismantle the metaphysics of dichotomies.

Older than ecofeminism is a school of thought which has been absent from these debates, that of American pragmatism. It is not as well known or as widely studied as the other views and has no established spokesperson on the issue of animals. I want to add this perspective because I think it can embrace the strengths of the other positions, while providing a strength of its own as an approach that is pluralistic, fallibilistic, and flexible. This means pragmatism can more readily adapt to changing circumstances and practices without becoming stuck in absolutistic principles that are divorced from people's experience. It starts with where we are and continually checks in with experience. At the same time, pragmatism challenges received experience and inherited wisdom and pushes people to be critical of their habits. Rather than just laying out principles to guide practice, it focuses on developing a critical approach to life that all people can use to arrive at guiding principles and to analyze their practices.

Like the utilitarian and deontological views, pragmatism challenges speciesism and the automatic privileging of human interests and suffering. But it goes further, challenging the split between metaphysics and ethics that can be found in utilitarian and deontological approaches. Despite asking us to abandon speciesism, both are grounded in a philosophical view that privileges reason and reinforces the dichotomous and hierarchical approach that supports speciesism in the first place. Like ecofeminism, pragmatism rejects the dichotomies of traditional metaphysics and epistemology and thereby makes a more consistent challenge to speciesism possible. Furthermore, pragmatism and ecofeminism can reinforce and enhance each other. Pragmatism can offer a compatible tradition, helping to prevent ecofeminism from being seen as lacking in philosophical support and history. Ecofeminism, in turn, can push pragmatism on issues of gender and power. Thus, I believe a pragmatist perspective on our treatment of nonhuman animals must be articulated. It is a voice, hitherto missing, that more deeply challenges our views of our place in the world and so can also more effectively serve to alter current practice.

As I have argued elsewhere ("Pragmatism and Primates"), both James and Dewey present philosophies that should lead us to see human and nonhuman life on a continuum and not as a hierarchy. However, in specific passages each also contradicts his own view. For example, James's declaration that dogs are enslaved to routine and cats cannot reason or that "the lowest savages reason incomparably better than the highest brutes" (*Principles of Psychology* 2:345) contradicts his wider philosophical perspective that calls for tolerance and openness. In "On a Certain Blindness in Human Beings" he criticizes

> the blindness with which we all are afflicted in regard to the feelings of creatures and people different from ourselves. . . . Hence the stupidity and injustice of our opinions, so far as they deal with the significance of alien lives. . . .
>
> Take our dogs and ourselves, connected as we are by a tie more intimate than most ties in this world; and yet, outside of that tie of friendly fondness, how insensible, each of us, to all that makes life significant for the other!—we to the rapture of bones under hedges, or smells of trees and lamp-posts, they to the delights of literature and art. As you sit reading the most moving romance you ever fell upon, what sort of a judge is your fox-terrier of your behavior? With all his good will toward you, the nature of your conduct is absolutely excluded from his comprehension. To sit there like a senseless statue when you might be taking him to walk and throwing sticks for him to catch! What queer disease is this that comes over you every day, of holding things and staring at them like that for hours together, paralyzed of motion and vacant of all conscious life? (629–30)

This blindness "absolutely forbids us to be forward in pronouncing on the meaninglessness of forms of existence other than our own; and it commands us to tolerate, respect, and indulge those whom we see harmlessly interested and happy in their own ways, however unintelligible these may be to us" (645). Here James shows a deep understanding of, and sympathy for, a being of a different kind and recognizes the need to respect this difference. He assumes not that the dog has no interests, plans, or purposes, but just that the dog's interests, plans, and purposes often differ from our own. This difference does not render the dog's existence meaningless, and James exhorts us to respect the meaning of that existence on its own terms and not to unduly interfere with it.

Similarly, Dewey's remarks that there is nothing wrong with nonhuman animal experimentation if physical pain is mitigated, that nonhumans lack the capacity to use signs or to have a sense of time, that they lack the social capacity possessed by humans, and that they merely imitate rather than reason contradict the science of today as well as his own philosophical perspective. In *Human Nature and Conduct*, Dewey observes that "[t]he intelligent acknowledgment of the continuity of nature, man and society will alone secure a growth of morals which will be serious without being fanatical, aspiring without sentimentality, adapted to reality without conventionality, sensible without taking the form of calculation of profits, idealistic without being romantic" (11). Pragmatism is based on the idea of human beings as live creatures in a transactional relationship with their physical and social environments. That is, they continually and mutually transform one another. Dewey (like the ecofeminists) is adamant that we should not make the mistake of buying into dualisms such as mind/body, reason/emotion, or culture/nature. Instead, we need to see these as transactive relationships (see my "Feminism and Vegetarianism," with response by Singer).

He also attributes the development of intelligence in human beings to their social complexity. Our physical dependence and the increasing complexity of social arrangements evolved together. Our increased brain capacity comes at the cost of lengthened developmental time. During that long period we are vulnerable and must be cared for and protected by a social group of our kind, from which we must learn. For Dewey it is important that as human beings we are born to and dependent on other human beings. In *The Public and Its Problems* he notes,

> We are, from the beginning, associated. There is no sense in asking how individuals come to be associated. They exist and operate in association. . . . There is, however, an intelligible question about human association:—Not the question how individuals or singular beings come to be connected, but how they come to be connected in just those ways which give human communities traits so different from those which mark assemblies of electrons, unions of trees in forest, swarms of insects. . . . When we consider the difference we at once come upon the fact that the consequences of conjoint action take on a new value when they are observed. . . . *Individuals still do the thinking, desiring and purposing, but what they think of is the consequences of their behavior upon that of others and that of others upon themselves.* (250; emphasis added)

No person, or any other being in nature (except perhaps the protozoa), can claim to be an isolated individual. Even the choice to "leave society" is influenced by one's social experience and nurturing. Reproduction, at least for the large-brained mammals, requires association and survival requires extended nurturing. But extended nurturing and caring for other beings is what Dewey uses to distinguish human associations from the association of electrons and other animals and is what he sees as giving human life its moral element.

With the recognition of our interdependence, we begin to take others into account when making decisions about what to do, how to act, and what to believe. The anticipation of the responses of others affects the behavior of at least all social mammals. It is our awareness of our connectedness that enables us to direct our behavior to certain goals; it is this ability to give intentional direction to our actions that, Dewey believes, makes us different from many other beings

in our environment. Furthermore, social complexity is thought to be the foundation for intelligence and the ability to communicate and plan. But humans
are not unique in this regard. For example, the great apes, among other nonhumans, display a similar lengthened period of physical and social dependence
and life span (forty to sixty years). This life span and social dependence require
that these nonhuman animals be aware of "the consequences of their behavior
upon that of others and that of others upon themselves." Frans de Waal writes
of the bonobos' great social capacity, "Understanding the intentions and feelings of others may help bonobos smooth relationships, provide assistance where
needed, and intensify sexual experiences. Conflict resolution, for example, depends on taking early notice when something bothers a companion, and on
knowing what to do so as to prevent frustration. In the sexual domain, we have
seen suggestions that bonobos regulate their performance based on what they
read in their partner's eyes" (154).

Many argue that the great apes display a highly developed ability to understand and communicate with their social peers. They are able to form alliances,
plan for the future, and deceive others. If social complexity is seen as the root
of intelligence and language, and if the great apes display a social complexity
similar to that of humans, then a consistent pragmatist view should push us to
include "them" with "us" in a community of beings whose interests must be
taken seriously. Such a shift sets us on a path that requires us to drastically alter
our attitudes, habits, and behavior toward all animals.

A Brief Sketch of Pragmatism

In this section I rely on the work of John Dewey to provide a brief sketch
of a pragmatist perspective that can be fruitfully applied to our current treatment of nonhuman animals as a source of food. Altering habits is the key to this
pragmatist perspective. As Dewey argues when describing his method of critical
intelligence, habit is both what makes a satisfying life possible and what can get
us stuck in unsatisfying practices. For Dewey, investigative practice begins with
a problem. Because something in our lives is not working satisfactorily, we seek
alternatives. A solution may be hit on by chance or may be reached after more
rigorous scientific investigation. This is then adopted as a habit—something that
requires little or no reflection—until it begins to fail to be satisfactory. A habit
can become unsatisfactory through some alteration, whether in desired ends-
in-view or in circumstances or environment. Since life is dynamic, most if not
all habits eventually need to be changed. This necessity explains why Dewey
focuses so much of his attention on the need to educate people to embrace the
method of critical intelligence and to become flexible regarding their habits
rather than remain unreflective and stuck. It is when we get stuck that problems
can start to escalate.

A great portion of our lives is lived at a habitual level. Since we cannot afford
to apply critical investigation to everything we do, much of our life is lived as
what Dewey calls "received experience." However, as I have argued in *The Task*

of Utopia: A Pragmatist and Feminist Perspective, we cannot live life this way continuously. The path to the future is an ongoing process aimed at a variety of ends-in-view. The quality of the present and the future is in large part determined by the quality of our chosen ends-in-view. We must give intelligent direction to the future if we want to live well. Michael Eldridge emphasizes the role of intelligence:

> The point is to live well. Dewey thought we can do this best by developing the intelligent elements within our personal and collective experience in such a way that our practices and institutions become more fulfilling. We can modify who we are and what we do in such a way that we increase our satisfactions and create the conditions for future satisfactions. Being intelligent is not an end in itself; living well is the point. But intelligence is the best way to enhance our practices and institutions so that we might live well. (41)

As Dewey puts it, "what is needed is intelligent examination of the consequences that are actually effected by inherited institutions and customs, in order that there may be intelligent consideration of the ways in which they are to be intentionally modified in behalf of generation of different consequences" (*Quest for Certainty* 218).

When one lives with this kind of critical intelligence, one is at the level of what Dewey calls lived experience. Giving the future intentional and intelligent direction makes it possible to turn obstacles into opportunities and problems into possibilities. We must therefore select our ends-in-view intelligently and subject them to continual examination. What might happen if we subjected the current end-in-view of producing meat, dairy, and egg products through the practice of factory farming to Dewey's method of critical intelligence? What if we look at the old and familiar habits of raising and eating animals and their by-products in a new light? What if we subject these habits to critical examination and make them part of our lived, rather than our received, experience?

Animals' Situatedness

In this section I focus discussion on U.S. factory farming—the condition in which most U.S. livestock live. Specific numbers vary from source to source, but a general sense of U.S. agribusiness can be summed up in an account by Karen Davis, which focuses on poultry:

> Of the eight billion animals slaughtered in U.S. federally-inspected plants in 1995, 7.8 billion were birds. Of these, 7.5 billion were chickens. Every week, between 125 and 140 million "broiler" chickens are killed in the United States—more than 25 million birds every working day. . . .
> To illustrate the comparative number of broiler chickens, a poultry scientist noted that during a certain week in 1993, U.S. hog producers slaughtered 1.7 million pigs, an average of 10,000 pigs an hour that, standing in single file, would stretch 1,200 miles, from New York City to Kansas City, Missouri. During the same week, U.S. broiler producers slaughtered 135 million chickens, an average of

800,000 chickens an hour that, standing in single file, would stretch 25,000 miles, or completely around the middle of the earth.

In 1995 the U.S. egg industry slaughtered over one hundred million "spent" laying hens, and killed 247 million unwanted male chicks at the hatchery. (105)

Meat and dairy products come from living animals. We refer to these animals as livestock—living inventory. Dairy products come from the milk of females. The female must give birth to start lactation, though the production of milk can be extended with hormones. The life span of a dairy cow is about six years, rather than the fifteen to twenty years of a cow allowed to live more naturally. By the end she is used up, her udder often torn. The modern dairy cow produces ten times as much milk as she would to feed her calf (Coats 51). "Thirty years ago, the average cow produced 2.5 tons of milk a year; today, after many generations of selective breeding and programs of intensive nutrition, she produces nearly 7 tons a year; and still the industry searches for new means of raising her productivity" (Coats 53). Feeding the animals bovine growth hormone is one way that milk production is increased. While a shrinking number of dairies do allow the cows time out to graze, many of the cows cannot easily walk to the field because of their unnaturally large udders. Most are confined to barns and dry lots where they lie in the mud and their own manure. The life of most dairy cows is not a pleasant one.

> By the time the regular modern milking cow is six to seven years old, she has been worn out. She has been artificially inseminated four to five times, has had four to five calves taken away from her in the first few days after birth, and has produced about twenty-five to thirty tons of milk. When her milk production slows down, this no longer efficient unit of agricultural production is sent off to slaughter. Her body, not yet old but already too tough for prime cuts of beef, is usually ground into hamburger—and ends up on a sesame bun with ketchup, relish, and, ironically, cheese. (Coats 55–56)

Besides producing dairy products, the dairy industry produces calves. Some calves are raised as replacements, but most are raised as veal calves. The unhappy life of a veal calf has received a good deal of publicity in recent years. It will live about four months in a 22″ by 54″ stall in which it cannot even turn around. These crates have slatted floors and no bedding is provided. The calf is tied so that it will not lick its own urine in an attempt to supplement its completely liquid and iron-deficient diet of "a mix of growth stimulators, powdered skim milk, starch, fats, sugar, vitamins, mold inhibitors, and antibiotics" (Coats 64). The calf is made anemic and prevented from developing muscle tone so that its meat will be white and extra tender. Because they are ruminants, the calves crave roughage, but this is denied them. Its lack leads to digestive diseases and diarrhea. Antibiotics are used to prevent disease in these filthy and cramped conditions and also to promote faster growth. The life of a veal calf is one of complete deprivation:

> Like most young animals, a calf is playful, active, and naturally curious about its surroundings. It likes to run and frolic, and enjoy the social activities so important

to a herd animal. But by the time it is slaughtered at sixteen weeks—barely adolescent and years before its natural life span is over—it will never have stretched its legs, run in green fields, or played with other calves. It will only escape its tiny prison when it is shipped off to be killed, the final episode of trauma, terror, and pain. (Coats 67)

While public awareness about the production of veal is fairly high, the focus on these calves seems to lead many to think that the conditions under which other sources of meat are raised are cleaner, kinder, more natural, and more morally acceptable. This is not the case.

Around 85 million pigs are slaughtered each year in the United States. More than 90 percent of these pigs are raised in the confinement of a factory farm. Each sow has an average of two and a half litters a year, with around eleven piglets per litter, for four or five years. Then she is used up and so is slaughtered. Once impregnated the sow is confined, for about four months, in a concrete-and-steel cage that measures two by six feet; she is given no bedding with which to nest. She cannot turn around or move forward or backward. She cannot socialize with the other sows who are packed row upon row in similar cages. Then she is moved to a farrowing cage, again with no bedding to build a nest. After she gives birth she is strapped to the floor or held in a nursing position by wire bars, so she cannot get away from her young, even for a moment. This constant access to her milk helps them grow faster, and they are removed at a very young age—about three weeks (rather than the usual eight to twelve weeks needed for weaning). The piglets are then confined in cages, measuring 3' 9" by 3' 9", or in large pens with seventy-five or more other piglets. Either way, each has less than two square feet of space. The cages have wire floors which cause foot deformities and lameness. They are stacked row upon row, and the confined and polluted conditions make disease a constant threat. As a result, they are fed a diet which includes antibiotics. Today these drugs, originally meant to thwart the spread of disease in pens of such unnatural high density, are used because they promote faster and greater growth. Pigs are intelligent, clean, social animals with a highly developed sense of smell and a desire to root in the dirt. In these confined conditions the pigs never get to satisfy their natural tendencies and they develop pathologic repetitive behaviors such as weaving, sucking, gnawing the cage, and biting each other.

The poultry industry is no better. While such practices as force-feeding geese to produce fois gras and breeding turkeys who have unnaturally large breasts might be examined, my comments here are limited to chickens. Indeed, chickens —broilers and layers, as they are called in the business—may suffer the most and in the greatest numbers. The egg industry is a $4.2 million industry and the broiler chicken industry is a $25 million industry (Davis 83). Layers are crammed into cages and kept under artificial light to stimulate their hormones and keep them continuously laying. While a wild chicken will lay 12 to 24 eggs in a year, the average domestic hen will lay between 25 and 100 eggs in a year, and a factory-farmed hen will lay 240 to 250 eggs a year. This overuse leads to a short life (one year versus fifteen years) that ends in slaughter. "In the United States, a 3 to 4 pound hen with a wing span of 30–32 inches may be legally confined with four to eight other hens in a cage that is 14–16 inches high and 18–20 inches across. Each hen has an average living space of 48 square inches" (Davis 54). To keep them in such cramped conditions and minimize wounds from pecking, the hens are debeaked as young chicks—that is, the end of their beak is cut off with a hot blade. Despite the debeaking, they still confront and injure one another. The small, densely packed cages also lead to many diseases, foot deformities, loss of bone tissue, and infections. Again, the antibiotics introduced to contain disease were found to have the bonus effect of promoting growth:

> For sheer overprescription, no doctor can touch the American farmer. Farm animals receive 30 times more antibiotics (mostly penicillins and tetracylines) than people do. The drugs treat and prevent infections. But the main reason farmers like them is that they also make cows, hogs and chickens grow faster from each pound of feed. Resistant strains emerge just as they do in humans taking antibiotics—and remain in the animal's flesh even after it winds up in the meat case. (Sharon Begley, qtd. in Davis 61)

These intensive growing conditions also harm the environment. A one-million-bird farm facility produces 125 tons of manure a day and about 1,500 dead birds each week (Davis 63). Human workers wear gas masks because of the high levels of ammonia. The ground becomes toxic as well.

The industry of broiler chickens is even bigger and more damaging. Tens of thousands of birds are cramped into a single poorly ventilated shed in which the air becomes highly contaminated, causing problems for both the chickens and the human workers. It again fouls the soil; not much can be done with land that has been used for many years as a poultry farm. Disposal of manure and corpses leads to air and groundwater pollution. While most broiler chickens are kept on the shed floor (though some producers are beginning to use cages here as well), they still do not have enough living space. Those attempting to maximize "product" have found that "[b]y reducing the birds' living space from a square foot to a half square foot per bird, twice as many birds die. However, almost twice as many birds survive long enough to go to slaughter. As a result, the producer gets seven and a half pounds of meat per square foot instead of four—almost twice as much flesh per square foot of floor space" (Davis 100). The only good news is how short their life is. Rather than living fifteen years, the broiler goes off to slaughter at about sixty days.

As just mentioned, factory farming leads to concentrations of manure and of corpses that pollute land and water. It creates many other environmental concerns as well. Some of these have to do with the amount of water used to run such facilities, and to grow the large amounts of grain fed to confined animals. According to David Coats, "The water used to grow the animal's grain, combined with their drinking needs and the water used in processing their carcasses, amount to some 2,500 gallons per day for each person in the U.S. who eats meat. . . . In contrast, one who eats no meat accounts for no more than 300 gallons per day for [their] food" (133). Topsoil erosion is connected both to the large amounts of grains that must be produced to support this industry and to the overgrazing of range land. (Beef cattle and sheep are the two main animals that still get to spend time grazing before being confined to be "finished" with a high-grain diet.) In South America, grazing cattle also contribute to the destruction of the rain forest which is cleared for this purpose. Factory farming of grain and animals is a highly mechanized process that consumes large quantities of petroleum products—another limited energy resource. This is clearly a costly diet, and I have not even addressed how many more people could be fed if we ate the grain products directly rather than through the intermediary of meat, or the health risks and costs related to a diet high in meat.[2]

A Pragmatist Perspective on Factory Farming

So where does a pragmatist begin? In my view, while utilitarianism, deontological theories, and ecofeminism all have strengths, they tend to fail to have a sense of the problems and needs that lead to how we are currently situated. They propose solutions based on reason or feeling, but pay little or no attention to how to change habits. Reason alone will rarely lead one to alter an ingrained habit, nor will sympathy. As Dewey argues, we must reach a point of crisis and practice critical intelligence. For this process to succeed, we need a fuller understanding of context and purpose. Pragmatism provides this kind of perspective. It also, unlike the other theories mentioned, begins with the realization that humans are animals. Humans, among other mammals, are live creatures (organisms) that transact with their environment. The level and complexity of our transactions often exceed those of other animals, but we are not different in kind. Thus, rather than searching for some commonality that can support their position, as proponents of the other theories do, pragmatists take the commonality as a given. Taking evolution seriously, however, we find that change is also a given for the pragmatist. Instead of absolute principles and final ends, with pragmatism we get guidelines and flexible ends-in-view. For many this appears to be an unsatisfactory slip into absolute relativism, where no judgments can be made. But I believe to the contrary that we are given enough by pragmatism to make judgments and act on them, all the while knowing we could be mistaken or face changing circumstances in which different ends-in-view will emerge.

The pragmatic method requires that we look into the nature and situatedness of the beings and environments involved in any transaction if we want to find productive and satisfactory ways to act. Dewey's method of intelligence demands a hands-on investigative approach to the questions raised; what follows is the start of one possible investigative path. The method of intelligence begins with a problem or need: in this case, with a need to consume calories to survive and thrive. According to most anthropological accounts, the early human diet was largely composed of gathered fruits and plants, and at some point meat was added as well. Anthropologists do not yet agree on whether these early humans were mainly hunters or scavengers, and some suggest the two strategies coexisted.[3] But whether they waited for meat to become available to scavenge or more purposefully waited for or followed a herd and put a great deal of effort into the hunt, early humans did not have ready access to animals they could kill for food.[4] In some climates it is not possible to support domesticated herds, and there hunting is still a common method of providing food.[5] In more hospitable climates, however, where people could grow food for themselves and for other animals, they were able to domesticate and breed herds, flocks, and clutches (Smith). Already, we see that a problem and its solution involve elements of both the live creatures and the environment. And we see that such transactions alter both the creatures and the environment. Human domestication of nonhuman animals eventually led to a more settled life for both. At first (and in some places still), herds grazed over natural range and moved in regular seasonal patterns. Under these conditions, while humans control and manipulate the animals, the environment still dictates aspects of their care. This wandering life takes a great deal of work, and the herds are at risk of becoming a meal for another predator (human or nonhuman). Efforts to protect herds from predation and theft may well have encouraged the creation of more confined spaces to house livestock. This change was made possible by advances in agriculture which enabled humans to bring food to animals instead of taking the animals to the food.

However, as with every solution to a problem, a host of new problems arose. Pragmatists see this cycle as part of the ongoing nature of inquiry. With a greater ready supply of nonhuman animals at hand, more uses are found for them, and more regular use and demand emerge. A desire to increase herd size results, and care of the growing numbers of confined animals—feeding, watering, and cleaning up after them—becomes a bigger and bigger task that takes ever greater amounts of land (to grow hay and grain), water, and labor. Issues of disease and pollution also emerge. Animal husbandry is at this point less about protecting herds or flocks from predation than about keeping them healthy in conditions that are not natural. The severity and extent of many diseases are heightened by the close living conditions and by the transportation that this method of raising animals requires, and many "problems" result directly from their confinement.

For example, animals whose digestive system is designed for a low level of constant movement and intake of food—grazing—develop digestive problems when they are fed large quantities only twice a day and are not able to move around to keep the food going through their gut. The introduction of grains to their diet creates more problems. Thus the "solution" of confinement has created a host of new "problems" with which we must deal. Similarly, the accumulation of manure leads to more insects, leading to more disease, leading to the use of pesticides, leading to the contamination of animals (human and nonhuman), and so on. Manure and pesticides also pollute the soil and water, creating problems for the humans and nonhumans who rely on the land and water supply. Another line of intertwined problems and solutions involves the ability to transport and refrigerate—even can—meat. This moves us from local production and small slaughterhouses to centralized and large slaughterhouses that process meat at such a pace as to cause pain and suffering to human and nonhuman alike (for further discussion, see Eisnitz; Schlosser). I could go on.

It is important both to see how the method of intelligence has operated in our culture with regard to the issue of food production and to note that not all cultures have followed the same path. Meat, for early humans, was an intense source of fat, energy, and protein,[6] and this probably led to a habit of a small amount of meat consumption (as meat constitutes about 5 percent of the diet of chimpanzees, our closest living relative; see Foley 307). Perhaps starting by chance, the method of intelligence was applied to make it easier to obtain meat; the domestication of animals probably also led to a habit of consuming dairy products. As animal products (and by-products) became easier to obtain, they figured more prominently in our diet and became a more deeply ingrained habit. As Dewey says, we are not moved to change habits unless they stop working for us; and we can absorb many problems and challenges before we admit that old habits have failed. Thus despite the problems that emerged with the confinement of animals, we have chosen to address the problems of disease, labor, insects, and manure by increasing, respectively, our use of antibiotics, intensive farming, insecticides, and processing plants.

While systems to use manure to produce electricity may be an example of a creative and productive solution to one issue, it is important to note that we have another option that most people continue to overlook. We can change our habits of consumption. When habits fail to be productive and satisfactory, then those immersed in the method of critical intelligence apply critical thought and experimentation to alter or replace them. We need to seek ends-in-view that promote growth and open up possibilities. Those who refuse to examine habits are fixed and rigid. Dewey speaks of the ossification of the brain. Our culture seems ossified with regard to our habits of consuming animals and animal by-products. Today plenty of alternatives are available that require less reliance on animals. We need to start exploring these possibilities.

In short, we must begin as a society to examine ways of replacing, refining, and reducing our use of nonhuman animals, because these uses are very costly habits. While such changes would involve big-money industries, we must start considering the less obvious and the long-term costs of continuing down the road we are on. We can replace the meat at one or more of our daily meals with the convenient and tasty alternatives that are now readily available. This kind of replacement would reduce demand for meat, a reduction would enable producers to meet demand while refining (improving) the conditions in which the animals live and die. Thus, more free-range, small-scale farming is a feasible end-in-view, reducing the consumption of such resources as water, topsoil, and energy; reducing the intense pollution associated with factory farms; and reducing the demand for grain to feed livestock.[7]

Some pragmatists (e.g., Paul Thompson in this volume) argue that if one is concerned about animal welfare, changing to a diet that includes free-range meat, dairy, and eggs is more effective than becoming a vegetarian because it supports producers who adopt more humane and sustainable practices. That is one option. It is also the case, however, that once consumption of meat is reduced the habit loosens its hold. The added health and environmental benefits of eating lower on the food chain may lead some to prefer the vegetarian option. Pragmatists recognize the impossibility of living as we do in complex ecosystems without using other beings, but we must remember James's call to understand other beings on their own terms and take their interests into account. Thoughtfully designed experiments exploring animal welfare can help us here. We may never know the mind of another—human or nonhuman—but we can learn some preferences. We can get better information on what various animals prefer regarding food, footing, and bedding, timing and method of weaning, and so on. Some argue that we should "leave nature alone" and end all domestication. Pragmatists realize, however, that we can never pull back and separate ourselves from nonhumans. There is no sharp divide between humans and the rest of nature. We will always interact in complex ways, but we must be more thoughtful about how we interact. Pragmatists must examine their past, present, and future situatedness carefully and seek ends-in-view which diminish harm and promote growth in a sustainable way. So, while pragmatism does not *require* that we move to vegetarianism, it may well require the end of factory farming practices. It does, at the very least, demand that we be more reflective about our habits and more flexible in responding to emerging problems.

Because of our interconnectedness, the problems associated with the production and consumption of meat must concern us all. The end-in-view of factory farming is a costly form of efficiency that is likely to limit or foreclose future possibilities. The future is ours to make—but given that new habits emerge from the old, a completely vegetarian society is an unlikely end-in-view any time soon. Nevertheless, issues of health, environment, and suffering all call us to consider other possibilities if we want a satisfactory future—if we want to live well or live compassionately. I am not saying that relying on animal products is the only unreflective habit we have that causes suffering and harm. The current methods of producing fruits and vegetables use high amounts of pesticides and exploit human labor; the consumption of material goods in developed nations depends largely on the poverty of others; and of course the current cycle of violence in which the humans of the world are engaged is quite costly. However, what we eat is a very basic habit whose ripple effects stretch in many directions. As Plato noted in *The Republic,* the truly ideal society would be vegetarian because adding the need to raise livestock increases the need for resources, leading to war and thus the need to sustain a warrior class. A more sustainable diet could go a long way toward ameliorating the ills of our current global economic and political situatedness. Our individual and collective choices do make a difference as we seek to create the future we desire.

Notes

1. For further discussion of this issue, see McKenna, "Women, Power, and Meat."

2. The health costs include obesity, heart disease, food poisoning from *E. coli* and other sources, and increased exposure to hormones and antibiotics.

3. For more discussion, see Bunn and Kroll; Shipman; Stinson; Stiner.

4. As Foley points out, "The other characteristics of meat (which are frequent correlates of high quality foods in general) that would impinge on evolutionary processes are that, by and large, animals are patchily distributed in an environment, certainly through space and frequently over time as well (e.g. seasonal variation in biomass), and they are often unpredictable within the environment (Schoener 1971; Krebs and Davies 1984). . . . Thus, in shaping evolutionary responses, meat will be considered here as a patchy, unpredictable and high-quality resource" (306). He also notes that "meat-eating would be seasonally variable, depending upon resource abundance (Foley 1987, 1993; Stanford et al. 1994), and, hence, would be part of a flexible foraging strategy with high levels of dietary variability" (310).

5. "[A]mong contemporary human populations meat-eating may vary from zero (e.g., some religious sects) to almost 100% (among high latitude hunter-gatherers) (Lee and DeVore 1968b; Kelly 1995). Among ethnographically observed hunter-gatherers, the level of meat-eating varies with latitude and environment (Lee and DeVore 1968b). For tropical populations living in an environment not dissimilar to those of the African Pliocene, estimates may be as low as 20% (Lee and DeVore 1968a), or more than 50% (Hawkes et al. 1991). Furthermore, there may be seasonal variations and periods when meat may not be eaten at all or may be the primary source of food" (Foley 307).

6. Foley's calculation (306) gives a sense of the nutritional value of meat to early hominids: "a small antelope . . . would yield approximately 52,000 kilojoules (kJ), 200 g of fat, and 2,600 g of protein (Leung 1968; Kingdon 1997). A very rough estimate indicates that this is the equivalent of eating nearly 300 figs (a favored food among chimpanzees) for energy, 2,000 figs for protein, and 666 figs for fat (Wrangham et al. 1993; Conklin and Wrangham 1994)."

7. Among the host of issues and problems that surround our transition to the industrial farming of grain and hay are the increased use of pesticides; the increased reliance on petroleum products in planting, harvesting, and transport; the increased concentration of land in the hands of a few large companies; a reliance on monoculture crops; and the development and use of genetically modified (and patented) seeds.

Bibliography

Adams, Carol. *Neither Man nor Beast: Feminism and the Defense of Animals.* New York: Continuum Press, 1994.

Bunn, Henry T., and Ellen M. Kroll. "Systematic Butchery of Plio/Pleistocene Hominids at Olduvai Gorge, Tanzania." *Current Anthropology* 27, no. 5 (December 1986): 431–52.

Coats, C. David. *Old MacDonald's Factory Farm.* New York: Continuum, 1991.

Davis, Karen. *Prisoned Chickens, Poisoned Eggs: An Inside Look at the Modern Poultry Industry.* Summertown, Tenn.: Book Publishing, 1996.

de Waal, Frans. *Bonobo: The Forgotten Ape.* Berkeley: University of California Press, 1997.

Dewey, John. *Democracy and Education. The Middle Works,* vol. 9, *1916.*

———. "The Ethics of Animal Experimentation." In *The Later Works,* vol. 2, *1925–1927,* 98–103.

———. *Human Nature and Conduct. The Middle Works,* vol. 14, *1922.*

———. *The Later Works, 1925–1953.* Edited by Jo Ann Boydston. 17 vols. Carbondale: Southern Illinois University Press, 1981–90.

———. *The Middle Works, 1899–1924.* Edited by Jo Ann Boydston. 15 vols. Carbondale: Southern Illinois University Press, 1976–83.

———. *The Public and Its Problems.* In *The Later Works,* vol. 2, *1925–1927,* 235–72.

———. *The Quest for Certainty. The Later Works,* vol. 4, *1929.*

———. *Reconstruction in Philosophy.* In *The Middle Works,* vol. 12, *1920,* 77–201.

Eisnitz, Gail. *Slaughterhouse: The Shocking Story of Greed, Neglect, and Inhumane Treatment inside the U.S. Meat Industry.* Amherst, N.Y.: Prometheus Press, 1997.

Eldridge, Michael. *Transforming Experience: John Dewey's Cultural Instrumentalism.* Nashville, Tenn.: Vanderbilt University Press, 1998.

Foley, Robert. "The Evolutionary Consequences of Increased Carnivory in Hominids." In *Meat-Eating and Human Evolution,* edited by Craig B. Stanford and Henry T. Bunn, 305–31. Oxford: Oxford University Press, 2001.

James, William. "On a Certain Blindness in Human Beings." In *The Writings of William James: A Comprehensive Edition, Including an Annotated Bibliography Updated through 1977,* edited by John J. McDermott, 629–45. Chicago: University of Chicago Press, 1977.

———. *Principles of Psychology.* 2 vols. 1890. Reprint, New York: Dover Publications, 1918.

McKenna, Erin. "Feminism and Vegetarianism: A Critique of Peter Singer." *Journal of Philosophy in the Contemporary World* 1, no. 3 (Fall 1994): 28–35.

———. "Pragmatism and Primates." *American Journal of Theology and Philosophy* 22, no. 3 (2001): 183–205.

———. *The Task of Utopia: A Pragmatist and Feminist Perspective.* Lanham, Md.: Rowman and Littlefield, 2001.

———. "Women, Power, and Meat: Comparing *The Sexual Contract* and *The Sexual Politics of Meat.*" *Journal of Social Philosophy* 27, no. 1 (Spring 1996): 47–80.

Schlosser, Eric. *Fast Food Nation: The Dark Side of the All-American Meal.* Boston: Houghton Mifflin, 2001.

Shipman, Pat. "Scavenging or Hunting in Early Hominids: Theoretical Framework and Tests." *American Anthropologist* 88 (1986): 27–43.

Singer, Peter. "Feminism and Vegetarianism: A Response." *Philosophy in the Contemporary World* 1, no. 3 (Fall 1994): 36–38.

Smith, Andrew B. "Origins and Spread of Pastoralism in Africa." *Annual Review of Anthropology* 21 (1992): 125–41.

Stanford, Craig B., and Henry T. Bunn, eds. *Meat-Eating and Human Evolution.* Oxford: Oxford University Press, 2001.

Stiner, Mary C. "Modern Human Origins—Faunal Perspectives." *Annual Review of Anthropology* 22 (1993): 55–82.

Stinson, Sara. "Nutritional Adaptation." *Annual Review of Anthropology* 21 (1992): 143–70.

Warren, Karen. *Ecofeminist Philosophy: A Western Perspective on What It Is and Why It Matters.* Lanham, Md.: Rowman and Littlefield, 2000.

5

Part Three: *Pragmatism on*
Animals as Cures,
Companions, and Calories

9 Is Pragmatism Chauvinistic? Dewey on Animal Experimentation

Jennifer Welchman

In 1926, John Dewey, one of the founders of American pragmatism, wrote an opinion piece for the *Atlantic Monthly*, "The Ethics of Animal Experimentation," in which he decries attempts to regulate animal experimentation, categorically dismissing the suggestion that it is ethically problematic. Dewey does not deny that animals suffer pain nor that cruelty to animals is wrong (98). Yet he insists that "there is no ethical justification for the assumption that experimentation upon animals, even when it involves some pain[,] . . . is a species of cruelty" (98). He continues: "No one who has faced this issue can be in doubt as to where the moral right and wrong lie. To prefer the claims of the physical suffering of animals to the prevention of death and the cure of disease—probably the greatest sources of poverty, distress, and inefficiency, and certainly the greatest sources of moral suffering—does not rise even to the level of sentimentalism" (100). As a pragmatist, Dewey could not justify this position by an appeal to a hierarchy of inherent values in animals and humankind. One cannot help asking, Is this pure speciesism, the arbitrary preference for the interests of one's own species over the interests of others? Is Dewey a species chauvinist? More important, is Dewey's *pragmatism* chauvinistic?

Sympathizers might dismiss Dewey's editorializing as irrelevant to a fair assessment of pragmatic moral and social theory. Critics would beg to differ. Pragmatism's opponents have long argued that the pragmatic account of facts and moral values as social constructs licenses majority rule on ethical and scientific issues. In one of the earliest responses, Bertrand Russell deplores pragmatism's rejection of independent universal standards of truth, justice, or good, arguing that minority values and minority opinion could not be protected unless communities agree to "a standard of justice which is a cause, and not an effect, of the wishes of the community; and such a standard seems incompatible with the pragmatist philosophy." He warns, "This philosophy, therefore, although it begins with liberty and toleration, develops, by inherent necessity, into the appeal to force and the arbitrament of the big battalions" (110).[1] The minorities Russell had in mind were human minorities, but environmental ethicists have made parallel claims about pragmatism's implications for our dealings with nonhuman nature. Eric Katz has argued that recognition of inherent values in nature independent of human interests is essential for the preservation of nature:

> The key point is that human desires, interests, or experiences cannot be the source of moral obligations to protect the environment. . . . If environmental policy is based on an "articulation" of human desires and experiences related to a plurality of human values, then it becomes extremely important *who* is articulating the values: *whose* desires and experiences are being used as the source of moral obligations? Environmental policy will depend on the "feelings" of the decision makers at the particular time the policy is established, the ever changing flux of human feelings concerning the natural environment does not appear to me to be a secure or reliable "common ground." (315–16)

Thus it is a matter of some importance to determine whether Dewey's little 1926 paper advocates species chauvinism—and if it does, whether the source is Dewey's character or the character of his pragmatic moral and social philosophy.

Dewey on Animal Experimentation: Issues and Concerns

Dewey argues that (1) "scientific men are under definite obligation to experiment upon animals so far as that is the alternative to random and possibly harmful experimentation upon human beings, and so far as such experimentation is a means of saving human life and of increasing human vigor and efficiency," and (2) "the community at large is under definite obligation to see to it that physicians and scientific men are not needlessly hampered" in these tasks ("Animal Experimentation" 98). Dewey's insistence that animal experimentation for human benefit is not merely excusable but actually obligatory appears to align his position with that of a self-proclaimed "speciesist," Carl Cohen. In his (in)famous defense of animal experimentation, Cohen seems to echo Dewey, declaring that "the wide and imaginative use of live animal subjects should be encouraged rather than discouraged. This enlargement in the use of animals is our obligation" (112).

Cohen's defense is intended as a rebuttal of Peter Singer's argument that speciesism violates the ideal of moral equality in essentially the same way that racism and sexism do. In *Animal Liberation,* Singer suggests that

> Racists violate the principle of equality by giving greater weight to the interests of members of their own race when there is a clash between their interests and the interests of those of another race. Sexists violate the principle of equality by favoring the interests of their own sex. Similarly, speciesists allow the interests of their own species to override the greater interests of members of other species. The pattern is identical in each case. (9)

Cohen replies that for the experimental use of animals to be analogous to racism or sexism, it would have to be the case that "it wrongly violates the rights of animals, and second, . . . it wrongly imposes on sentient creatures much avoidable suffering" (103). He claims that neither of these two necessary conditions are met. The ideal of moral equality between individuals, he argues, extends only to members of the moral community—to beings capable of understanding what equality means and of enshrining that ideal in systems of mutual rights and obligations. Racists and sexists violate the ideal by irrationally treating members of other races and sexes as if they lacked the necessary understanding of equality. Nonhuman animals, however, genuinely do fail in this respect; thus they cannot be members of the moral community nor can they share in its special benefits. Having established to his own satisfaction that animal experimentation is not a violation of moral equality, Cohen then argues that cost-benefit accounting suggests that the harm done to animals is outweighed by the good produced.

We are meant to conclude that in calling himself a speciesist, Cohen is being ironic. He thinks he is not a speciesist in Singer's sense, because his preference for his own species' interests is not arbitrary. But when he turns to the problems of "marginal cases"—that is, human beings who lack normal human capacities to understand and exercise rights—Cohen undercuts his own argument. Rather than accept the repugnant conclusion that cognitively impaired human beings would have no right to be protected from involuntary experimental use, he insists that "humans are of such a kind that they may be the subject of experiments only with their voluntary consent" (106), while animals are not. But if possession of rights depends not on one's abilities but simply on one's "kind" or species, then animals' inability to understand or exercise rights is not after all what makes Cohen feel justified in exploiting them. So it turns out that Cohen is what he jokingly calls himself, a speciesist.

Cohen's attempt to rebut Singer's argument for species equality founders on the problem of marginal cases, as will any and every attempt that starts from Singer's premise that satisfying the impartial ideal of moral equality is the overriding moral issue for proponents of animal experimentation. No matter which traits one fixes on—rationality, linguistic ability, self-consciousness, sentience— there will always be human beings who lack them. Thus it seems impossible to defend a non-species-based distinction between the moral claims of humans and animals.

By contrast, for Dewey the problem of marginal cases does not arise, because in Dewey's philosophy there are no independent impartial moral obligations to trump the experimentalist's obligations to other members of his or her community. The rights and duties of experimentalists grow out of and are constrained by their positions in human societies. Thus Dewey does not see the problem of animal experimentation as one of deciding what scientists are *free* as individuals to do with animal or human subjects in isolation from other considerations. It is instead one of determining what scientists are *obliged* to do as members of a cooperative social community. As he puts it, "Instead of being the question of animal physical pain against human physical pain, it is the question of a certain amount of physical suffering to animals—rendered in extent to a minimum . . . —against the bonds and relations which hold people together in society, against the conditions of social vigor and vitality, against the deepest shocks and interferences to human love and service" ("Animal Experimentation" 100).

What Dewey means is that a scientific researcher's primary obligation is to make decisions based on their impact on social welfare. Dewey writes: "The person who is ill not merely suffers pain but is rendered unfit to meet his ordinary social responsibilities: he is incapable for service to those about him" ("Animal Experimentation" 99). Biomedical research is socially supported to reduce the impact of disease and suffering not merely on the unfortunate invalid but also on the society of which he or she is a part. Thus a scientist has a positive duty to his or her community to maintain and enhance the health and welfare of all its members. Because animals are not members of the social community supporting the researchers' efforts, there is no comparable duty to promote their health and well-being. Dewey concludes, "It is accordingly the duty of scientific men to use animal experimentation as an instrument in the promotion of social well-being; and it is the duty of the general public to protect these men from attacks that hamper their work" (100).

Innocuous as these remarks may have seemed in 1926, they are positively chilling to readers who recall the atrocities committed by biomedical researchers in totalitarian regimes against minority groups in the name of social welfare. In Nazi Germany, Jewish internees and prisoners of war were used in experiments to which no able-bodied German would have been subjected, on the grounds that social welfare required it. Cognitively impaired German citizens were euthanized for the reason that their impairments rendered them incapable of service to others. Anticipating success in conquering Europe, German researchers sought economical ways to perform mass sterilizations of "inferior" peoples (Poles, Slavs, etc.) in order to make way for future generations of "superior" German citizens. The allied Japanese government made similar use of prisoners of war for medical research (see Annas and Grodin; Lifton). Even in demonstrably more democratic countries such as the United States, unpopular minority groups were selected for experimentation that would never have been tried on members of more socially valued groups. The infamous Tuskegee Institute study in which African American men were denied treatment for syphilis in order to study the long-term course of the disease is too well-known to need discussion (Jones). Less well-known is that in the United States, convicts were used for experiments almost as appalling: for example, a study in which prisoners were fed a diet deficient in Vitamin C in order to observe the severely debilitating effects of scurvy, although this was already a well-understood and treatable condition (Hodges et al. 1971; see the discussion in Mitford 151–361). If the primary moral consideration is the researchers' obligation to the community that pays the bills, does it not follow that if a society does not allow an individual or group to contribute to its institutions, researchers may subordinate their welfare to the welfare of the contributing community? Could any conclusion be more repugnant?

Welfare, Pragmatism, and Democracy

Dewey characterizes biomedical researchers as "in this matter acting as ministers and ambassadors of the public good" ("Animal Experimentation" 100), a view reiterated in other texts.[2] But he does not say here what he takes the public good to be, so we must flesh it out in light of the broader social theory expressed in *Democracy and Education* and elsewhere. When we do, it is immediately evident that Dewey's ideas about personal and social welfare are strikingly different from those of Singer or other subjective consequentialists. Dewey does not define welfare in terms of an individual's or group's internal states (e.g., pleasure, satisfaction of desire, absence of pain). Instead, he views welfare as a process: welfare, personal and social, is *faring well over time* in the ongoing process of adjusting changing interests, abilities, and needs to changes in the social and physical environment. To evaluate individuals' welfare it is not enough to know whether they feel pleased or happy. One needs to look at how they are faring in adapting their existing interests, plans, and resources to changes in their environments and personal capacities. Because welfare means faring well in the face of continual and novel challenges, there is no particular set of material goods or technical skills whose possession is a sufficient condition to ensure it. We must constantly make use of reason, imagination, and social cooperation to fare well. But because the future holds unpredictable and novel developments in store for all of us, we must all perpetually fine-tune our intellectual skills, resources, and social networks to cope. Or in more Deweyan language, we must engage in continual self-education. Education, he argues, is the chief determinant of welfare within our own control: "Our net conclusion is that life is development and that developing, growing, is life. Translated into its educational equivalents, that means (i) that the educational process has no end beyond itself, it is its own end; and that (ii) the educational process is one of continual reorganizing, reconstructing, transforming" (*Democracy and Education* 54).

Since educational opportunities rather than specific talents, resources, or offices are the chief determinants of personal and social welfare, pragmatic social theorists must be as much or more concerned about how societies arrange access to educational experiences, resources, and networks as they are about how societies arrange access to material wealth or political office. The greater the access to educational opportunity, the better for social and personal welfare over time. Thus, Dewey argues, pragmatism provides a new and important justification for establishing egalitarian democracy. The more democratic a society, the freer the individuals within it are to interact with whoever has knowledge or skills they need and to work cooperatively with whoever is willing and able to help to develop new forms of expertise where none exists.

Nondemocratic societies create internal class divisions that divide people against one another, inhibiting cooperation and the free flow of information within the society. Similarly, they tend to divide the human community into races or classes, "people like us" and "people like them," a division that interferes with the free flow of communication across their borders. As contacts decrease, so does the stimulus to take seriously any new ideas or theories proposed by outsiders. And in reducing their educational opportunities, such societies reduce the odds that they will be able to adapt efficiently to change caused by internal and external pressures. By contrast, democracy—the shaping of social institutions and projects through discussion and consensus—enhances educational opportunities by removing barriers to interaction and cooperation along class and ethnic lines. There is, after all, no "race" of human beings without intellectual traditions, knowledge, technologies, and arts that could prove invaluable resources for other societies. Thus a democratic community will tend to have open borders and open inquiring attitudes toward other societies. Exclusion of individuals or groups would never be in its interest. As Dewey remarks,

> A democracy is more than a form of government; it is primarily a mode of associated living, of conjoint communicated experience. The extension in space of the number of individuals who participate . . . so that each has to refer his own action to that of others, and to consider the action of others to give point and direction to his own, is equivalent to the breaking down of those barriers of class, race, and national territory which kept men from perceiving the full import of their activity. . . . [Such contacts] secure a liberation of powers which remain suppressed . . . [in] a group which in its exclusiveness shuts out many interests. (*Democracy and Education* 93)

Since egalitarian democracy promotes ongoing education, and since education is essential to personal and social welfare, to promote personal and social welfare we should promote egalitarian democratic principles, domestically and internationally.

For egalitarian democracies to succeed in practice, these communities must ensure that their members recognize both *negative* and *positive* duties to one another. First, interference with free movements of persons and ideas must be kept to a minimum. Thus pragmatic communities will recognize *negative duties of mutual noninterference* with one another. Second, material obstacles (poverty, distance, and both physical and mental barriers) must be reduced as far as possible. Pragmatic communities will therefore recognize *positive duties to help* one another to lessen their impact. Ill health is one such obstacle. Thus, Dewey argues, we must acknowledge a general duty to support the development of new technologies, skills, and ideas for reducing the obstacle ill-health presents. This positive duty is mutual, but we cannot all contribute to biomedical research ourselves. We meet it by supporting scientists as our communities' trustees, who develop the information, technical skills, and investigative methodologies by which we are collectively enabled to educate ourselves to cope with new and existing obstacles to health by whatever means egalitarian democratic principles allow. But health is only one of the constituents of social welfare for which continual education is required. Thus the methods by which biomedical researchers pursue it must be consistent with the larger social project. Researchers may neither demand sacrifices from any group (however small or despised) not demanded of others, nor make discoveries available to any group (however large) not made available to others. Thus pragmatic constructivism does not justify discrimination of the sort that tarnished the history of human subject research in the twentieth century.

Animals and Marginal Cases

From a Deweyan perspective, biomedical scientists and the public for whom they act have a *positive duty* to use and improve their health-related knowledge, skills, and resources for the benefit of every member of the community. Animals live inside and outside human communities. But they are not members, and thus the positive duty to promote health and welfare does not encompass animal health and welfare. Animals are excluded not because they lack the capacities to understand or exercise civil rights, but because they lack the capacities to understand and participate in human communities' social and educational projects.

Some animals live among us and perform socially important services, such as transportation, agricultural labor, and protection of people and property. Animals and people can become emotionally attached to one another, Dewey thought, but never actually share common projects. He notes:

> Human beings control animals by controlling the natural stimuli which influence them; by creating a certain environment in other words. Food, bits and bridles, noises, vehicles, are used to direct the ways in which the natural or instinctive responses of horses occur[,] . . . [but] the horse does not really share the social use to which his action is put. Some one else uses the horse to secure a result which is advantageous by making it advantageous to the horse to perform the act—he gets food, etc. But the horse, presumably, does not get any new interest. He remains interested in food, not in the service he is rendering. He is not a partner in a shared activity. (*Democracy and Education* 16–17)

Drug-sniffing dogs do not *intend* to protect people from illegal drugs. Horses do not want to *win* show-jumping contests. Oxen neither know nor care why fields are plowed. Dogs, horses, and oxen can (and indeed should) get satisfaction from performing the activities for which they are trained. But their satisfaction comes from performing the activities themselves (sniffing, jumping, moving), together with rewards of food or affection from their handlers, not from the furtherance of human projects that are beyond animals' comprehension.[3]

Animal welfare differs from human welfare in that voluntary cooperative self-education plays no role in its success or failure. Individual welfare is a matter of success or failure of the animal's species-specific responses to environmental contingencies, responses that are determined by its particular evolutionary history. Inclusion in the human community and its practices is no help to animals in coping with the challenges that their natural environments pose to their welfare. All we can really do to promote most animals' welfare is to avoid interfering with their environments or their behavioral repertoires as much as possible.[4] That the best way to serve animals is by avoiding interference seems to hold true even when the animals in question are domesticated species. The best one can do for a cow's or a chicken's or a pig's subjective welfare is to arrange matters so that it is left to conduct itself in as nearly normal a manner for its species as is possible. Thus from a Deweyan perspective, the only duties we owe animals are negative duties of noninterference.

With so-called marginal cases, however, the conclusion goes the other way. Biomedical researchers and the general public are obliged to promote their welfare as far as possible. At first glance this may seem sheer speciesism, on par with Cohen's. How can we have a duty to promote the welfare of an adult in a persistent vegetative state or an infant whose congenital defects will prevent it rising above the intellectual level of a three-month-old and yet have *no* positive duty to promote the welfare of healthy dogs, oxen, or horses, when each is far better suited to "render service" to the human beings around them?

Many severely cognitively impaired individuals have not been impaired from birth and so have had opportunities to make contributions to their social groups; in such cases, loyalty and gratitude for their past conduct could ground positive duties to them. Some of those impaired from childhood were victims of others' negligence or malfeasance, and thus promotion of their welfare is a duty of rectificatory justice. But there are humans severely impaired from birth through no one's fault who are unlikely ever to render anyone any kind of social service. What grounds can a Deweyan pragmatist offer for saying we have *positive* duties to them?

The answer is none at all. They cannot participate in our social projects and shared inquiries into social welfare; thus we cannot have *positive* duties to help them participate more fully in these projects. Our duties to these unfortunate people are the same *negative* duties we owe to animals—duties of noninterference. But what noninterference means for infant human beings and for healthy adult animals is very different. A defective infant is still a member of the human species, however defective it may be. Human beings are a species that maintains its dependent young until they become independent or perish through accident or misfortune. It is often pointed out that premature separation of dependent social animals from their parents or social group is distressing to both the young and their natural caregivers and thus constitutes a form of (harmful) interference. The same is true for the human species. Premature separation of a human being, even a defective human being, from its parents or social group is harmful both to the sufferer and to the group denied the opportunity to provide care. Denying such human beings assistance would be a kind of interference in the life and activities of their kind and thus a violation of our duty of noninterference. On a Deweyan approach, therefore, marginal cases do not entail the repugnant conclusion that defective human beings are no more entitled to our care than healthy adult members of other species.

Tragic Choice and Animal Experimentation

The biomedical community and the public whom it serves have no positive obligation to promote the health or welfare of animals.[5] But we all have negative duties to avoid interference with animals' species-typical lives and behavior. Cruelty, negligent unconcern for the effects of one's acts on others' welfare, and insensitivity to suffering are as vicious in pragmatic moral theory as in any other. Thus we must seek to avoid cruelty, negligence, and insensitivity to animals. But does it follow from this that we may not interfere with animals by performing experiments intended to fulfill our duty to promote health and social welfare?

Usually it is cruel and immoral to deliberately cause pain to third parties who will gain nothing in compensation. But sometimes the choice is a tragic necessity. When an important value is threatened and causing pain to a third party is our "least-worst" option for protecting that value, it is tragic rather than cruel to exercise that option. Again, depending on circumstances, making a tragic choice is sometimes merely excusable but sometimes actually obligatory. And this is the case even when the third parties to be harmed are human beings.

Consider the following examples:

- It was the duty of Canadian army snipers in Afghanistan to fire on Taliban soldiers to protect other troops, even though the targets would be injured or killed.[6]
- Prison guards are obliged to confine convicted criminals even when such confinement is manifestly not for the criminal's good—for example, when the individuals have been sentenced to death or when they are likely to be targeted by other inmates.
- In earlier times, ships carrying highly contagious diseases among the passengers and crew would be "quarantined," that is, kept from docking to prevent the passengers and crew spreading the disease on land. Uninfected passengers and crew were thus put at risk of illness and death. Nonetheless, harbormasters and ship captains were thought to be doing their duty by imposing quarantines.
- Parents of children attending public schools are obliged to vaccinate their children for a number of childhood diseases that pose their children little or no risk at all, in order to prevent the spread of these diseases to others (e.g., adults without immunity, fetuses). This is required although a small but significant number of the children vaccinated will not only be pained or distressed by the shot, but will experience serious and even life-threatening reactions.[7]
- Biomedical researchers are obliged to perform Phase I drug trials in healthy volunteers in order to discover what side effects patients might experience. As the side effects are unknown, serious adverse reactions are always possible.

These are just a few examples involving threats to life and physical well-being. There are many more involving psychological distress:

- Professors are obliged to fail students whose work is incomplete or inadequate, even when doing so will cause a student terrible distress. The purpose of assigning failing grades is not to benefit the students failed (although they may benefit in the long run).
- David Hume notes that the executor of a will is obliged to follow the maker's directions even when the provisions harm the interests and expectations of worthy heirs for the sake of others too rich or self-satisfied to experience any benefit (94).
- We may be obliged to tell a painful truth to someone who we know will not benefit in any way.

In many of these instances, the individuals we harm in order to meet obligations to others will experience some benefit indirectly. In some cases, when the good we are upholding is a public good, such as health, veracity, security, or justice, the tragic dimension of these acts is diminished. But clearly this is not always so. The victims of Canadian sniper fire, convicts legally executed or killed by fellow inmates despite efforts to protect them, passengers on plague-stricken ships who would have survived if released from quarantine, and vaccinated children and Phase I experimental subjects who die from reactions to medications do not benefit even indirectly from the harm done their interests. Nevertheless, if the value at stake is sufficiently important (as public goods may be), if the alternatives are few and their outcomes as bad or worse, we do not condemn agents who take "least-worst" options that involve harm to third parties. In situations such as the ones I have listed above, we condemn them when they fail to do so.

Thus it appears that in supporting the use of animals as subjects to improve the health and welfare of human beings, Dewey would not necessarily be guilty of chauvinism toward animals. He would be guilty only if he used different standards for deciding which situations warranted tragic choices when the subjects were human and when they were not. For example, if he were to hold that it took an urgent threat to a public good such as health or justice to justify causing pain to humans, but only an urgent threat to the satisfaction of a private interest to justify causing pain to animals, then Dewey could reasonably be charged with chauvinism.[8] Dewey himself may or may not have operated with a double standard—the evidence of the 1926 essay is not decisive either way. But if he did, the failing lay in his own personal character and not the character of the pragmatic constructivism he espoused.

If we take a pragmatic approach to contemporary forms of animal exploitation for food, clothing, shelter, entertainment, and scientific research, it turns out that many are already immoral or are likely to become immoral in the near future, owing to advances in human technology. Traditional agricultural practices—especially the less invasive forms of the "harvesting" of animal protein, such as keeping poultry for their eggs or goats for their milk—may once have been morally justifiable, from a pragmatic perspective, given the lack of alternative protein sources available to some peoples and the relatively "normal" activities these creatures were often able to pursue. Similarly, both rearing animals for their wool or hair and hunting animals for their pelts could have been justifiable responses to urgent threats to the social welfare of members of some traditional societies living in environments that provided few other sources of material to make clothing or shelters. Today modern industrialized farming provides a stable and affordable supply of plant-based sources of protein while simultaneously interfering drastically in the most basic activities of the unfortunate animals involved.[9] We also have stable sources of cheap fibers for textile production (supplemented by other synthetic materials), making the captive rearing or hunting of animals solely for their wool or pelts unnecessary for human welfare. Thus a pragmatist should consider a failure to replace painful animal exploitation for these purposes with nonexploitive alternatives to be a failure to acknowledge our negative duties to animals.

Animal experimentation may be a different matter, however. It is unlikely that we will ever learn all we could benefit substantially from knowing about how animals cope physically and psychologically with internal and external challenges to their health and functioning. So it seems unlikely we will ever be able to fully replace animals with computer modeling or other forms of nonanimal substitutes for medical or other socially important research. Still, in the not too distant future, biomedical research could well be the *only* practice for which infliction of pain and suffering on animals could still be justified from a pragmatic perspective. That pragmatic constructivism can lead to such a radical conclusion suggests that it is not inherently and offensively chauvinistic toward nonhuman nature.

With the benefit of hindsight, I think we can say that Dewey was guilty of complacency about the justifiability of much of the animal experimentation in his day. Dewey thought that laboratory animals were not treated cruelly because he apparently believed that most animal experiments involved little or no prolonged pain and that most experiments performed were carefully crafted scientific investigations intended to improve human health and welfare. If he had been right about the facts of animal experimentation in his day, his conclusion might have been justified. But he was wrong on both counts.

In 1926, scientific and popular wisdom held that animals did not experience pain or psychological distress as intensely as human beings and thus did not require the same degree of relief for invasive procedures as would human beings. It was, moreover, widely believed in the medical community that pain relief retarded healing even in human beings. So by our standards, human patients were often undertreated for the pain of injuries and surgical procedures. Since animals were supposed to require even less relief than humans for comparable injuries, undertreatment of their pain and distress would have been all the greater. When we consider further that no minimum standards for the species-appropriate forms of diet, housing, exercise, and social contact as yet existed and that separate housing of predator and prey species was not yet routine, let alone required, for publicly funded experimentation in North America, we can only conclude that enormous numbers of animals experienced much avoidable suffering. By our standards, the conditions of laboratory animals were often lamentable.

Dewey's second presumption is as dubious as the first. In 1926, experiments on live subjects (human or animal) were not generally reviewed by outside agencies or review boards to ensure that experiments were neither redundant nor so ill-designed as to undercut the value of their results. Live animal dissection and other forms of experimentation were routinely conducted in secondary and undergraduate classes purely as demonstrations, by individuals untrained in proper techniques for anesthetizing their victims. Few of these demonstrations would have advanced scientific knowledge or even significantly increased the students' familiarity with scientific methodology.

No doubt many of the failings of the treatment of animal subjects in 1926 were the result of simple ignorance or misunderstanding of animal consciousness and the differing needs of different species, especially of rare and exotic species that were little known or understood by laboratory scientists. Even so, we would have to conclude that very many experimental animals were cruelly used. With the passage of time, conditions have improved for laboratory animals in North America. Laws now exist that set minimum standards of diet, housing, and exercise for many (though not all) of the species most commonly used in publicly funded research. External oversight of animal facilities is now required. Reviews of experimental protocols prior to their approval help to prevent repetitive or poorly designed investigations from going ahead. Anesthesia is more frequently and more appropriately used. Although critics argue that existing safeguards are still inadequate and often poorly enforced, we may nevertheless conclude that many animals fare better in scientific laboratories today than they would have done in 1926.

But Dewey's error should serve as an object lesson for pragmatists and others. We should not presume that avoidable and unjustifiable suffering is not still routine. And we should take more care than Dewey did to stay abreast of what actually goes on in research facilities. Public regulations covering animal experimentation still do not protect all the species used. Birds, rats, and mice do not receive the protections other species do (for an overview, see Orlans). Researchers still know less than is desirable about the diet, shelter, activities, or social interactions necessary to prevent the frustration of the instinctual drives of many animal species. Regulations and practice still lag behind the advances in understanding that have been made (see, e.g., Gluck).

To meet their negative duties to prevent cruelty and minimize interference with animal welfare, pragmatists cannot be complacent about the laboratory practices permitted. Pragmatists should insist on the development of ethics review guidelines that extend the same protection to every species of animals considered for laboratory use and should support research into and the development of alternate techniques. But beyond these obvious points, pragmatists should do their best to retain the sense that the decision to use animals is *tragic*: always to be regretted and whenever possible avoided. One cannot maintain a proper sense of the genuinely tragic dimension of what biomedical researchers do on one's behalf if one makes no effort to appreciate the extent of the animal suffering involved. Pragmatists should neither turn their faces away from research laboratories nor permit them to be closed off from public inspection and review. To lose one's sense of the genuine tragedy of animal experimentation is a sure first step toward a negligent and inexcusable complacency.

Notes

I should like to thank Leanne Kent for her helpful comments on an earlier draft of this paper.

1. The article was a review of William James's *Pragmatism*, but Russell's concerns were not allayed by the later contributions of Dewey or other pragmatists.

2. In *Freedom and Culture*, Dewey takes a similar line about scientists generally, remarking: "A former president of the United States once made a political stir by saying that 'public office is a public trust.' The saying is a truism although one that needed emphasis. That possession of knowledge and special skill in intellectual methods is a public trust has not become a truism even in words" (170).

3. Social animals such as horses and dogs undoubtedly pick up on the emotions of their human handlers in various settings, becoming excited along with their handlers at competitions, anxious in search-and-rescue settings, and so forth. But it is one thing to share in another's *emotional state* and another to share in another's *projects*. Animals can often do the former but rarely if ever the latter. (Any that could—primates, perhaps— would constitute a special case for which special moral protections would be in order.)

4. As national park rangers keep reminding us, when it comes to wildlife, even the most seemingly innocuous efforts to "help" often cause harm. A fed bear, they tell us, usually ends up a dead bear, and the same is true for many other wild animals, large and small. Animals attracted to human settlements, roads, and structures by intended acts of kindness such as feeding (and not by their innate ability to make use of structures for nesting sites, etc.) often die prematurely from ingesting unsuitable foods; contracting diseases; being hit by cars, trains, boats, planes, etc.; or being trapped or killed as "nuisance" animals.

5. The possible exception to having no positive obligation to promote animals' health or welfare may be by way of rectifying harm caused by human interference. Injustice and ingratitude are undesirable traits, whenever or wherever they show themselves. Thus if an animal has been injured through human interference—knocked down with a car, forced to jump fences at show-jumping competitions, used to locate disaster victims in the unstable rubble of damaged buildings, etc.—the persons responsible would surely be obligated to the injured animal to try to return it to normal functioning.

6. This example presumes, of course, that the shots were fired in a "just war." Those who do not agree that this particular military action was just or who do not agree that war can ever be justified should feel free to ignore it.

7. This is not to say that parents who object to certain vaccinations are never justified in doing so—if the risks to the children vaccinated outweigh the good done to others, as some argue is the case for certain childhood vaccinations (e.g., pertussis), then the obligation would be defeated.

8. An example of satisfying a relatively trivial interest would be subjecting animals to tests to determine the toxicity of cosmetics or other products not essential to human health or efficient action.

9. On the conditions of animals in "factory farms," see Singer 95–157.

Bibliography

Annas, George J., and Michael A. Grodin, eds. *The Nazi Doctors and the Nuremberg Code: Human Rights in Human Experiments*. New York: Oxford University Press, 1992.

Cohen, Carl. "The Case for the Use of Animals in Biomedical Research." In *Animal Experimentation: The Moral Issues,* edited by Robert M. Baird and Stuart E. Rosenbaum, 103–27. Buffalo: Prometheus Books, 1991. (Originally published in *New England Journal of Medicine* 315 [1986]: 856–69.)

Dewey, John. *Democracy and Education. The Middle Works, 1899–1924,* edited by Jo Ann Boydston, vol. 9, *1916.* Carbondale: Southern Illinois University Press, 1980.

———. "The Ethics of Animal Experimentation." In *The Later Works, 1925–1953,* edited by Jo Ann Boydston, vol. 2, *1925–1927,* 98–103. Carbondale: Southern Illinois University Press, 1984.

———. *Freedom and Culture.* In *The Later Works, 1925–1953,* edited by Jo Ann Boydston, vol. 13, *1938–1939,* 63–188. Carbondale: Southern Illinois University Press, 1988.

Gluck, John P., Tony DiPasquale, and F. Barbara Orlans, eds. *Applied Ethics in Animal Research: Philosophy, Regulation, and Laboratory Applications.* West Lafayette, Ind.: Purdue University Press, 2002.

Hodges, R. E., J. Hood, J. E. Canham, H. E. Sauberlich, and E. M. Baker. "Clinical Manifestations of Ascorbic Acid Deficiency in Man." *American Journal of Clinical Nutrition* 24, no. 4 (1971): 432–43.

Hume, David. *An Enquiry Concerning the Principles of Morals.* Edited by J. B. Schneewind. Indianapolis: Hackett Press, 1983.

Jones, James H. *Bad Blood: The Tuskegee Syphilis Experiment.* New York: Free Press, 1981.

Katz, Eric. "Searching for Intrinsic Value: Pragmatism and Despair in Environmental Ethics." In *Environmental Pragmatism,* edited by Andrew Light and Eric Katz, 307–18. London: Routledge, 1996.

Lifton, Robert Jay. *The Nazi Doctors: Medical Killing and the Psychology of Genocide.* New York: Basic Books, 1986.

Mitford, Jessica. *Kind and Unusual Punishment: The Prison Business.* New York: Alfred A. Knopf, 1971.

Orlans, F. Barbara. "Ethical Themes Governing Animal Experiments: An International Perspective." In Gluck, DiPasquale, and Orlans 131–47.

Rollin, Bernard E. "Ethics, Animal Welfare, and ACUCs." In Gluck, DiPasquale, and Orlans 113–30.

Russell, Bertrand. "Pragmatism." In *Philosophical Essays,* 79–132. 1910. Reprint, New York: Simon and Schuster, 1966.

Singer, Peter. *Animal Liberation.* Rev. ed. New York: Avon Books, 1990.

10 A Pragmatist Case for Animal Advocates on Institutional Animal Care and Use Committees

Todd M. Lekan

In our times, scientists who use animals for research and advocates who work for animal welfare organizations seem to live in separate moral worlds. Scientists might think that things should remain this way, but over the long run such a strategy will probably only exacerbate extremist elements on both sides of the debate over whether, and when, animals ought to be used in experiments. I believe it is time to consider the good reasons for creating more opportunity for regular dialogue between animal advocates and researchers by including advocates on the committees that review animal experiments at institutions. At this time, in the United States, no legal requirement exists for animal advocates to sit on institutional animal care and use committees (IACUCs)—the committees charged with evaluating research proposals involving animals.[1] Inclusion of animal advocates on IACUCs does occur, but relatively rarely. By drawing on some conceptual resources from the pragmatist tradition,[2] I think we can flesh out a framework for justifying the claim that their inclusion ought to be a matter of course. Pragmatists have long argued that thriving democratic societies require robust communication between experts and the interested lay public for the purpose of resolving common problems. Pragmatists have also developed a nuanced account of inquiry as a social practice with emotional, political, and cultural dimensions that are as important to take account of as more narrowly "cognitive" matters. Such an approach promises rich insights into questions regarding proper oversight of morally problematic scientific research.

My argument presupposes a middle-ground position between absolute permissibility of animal use and complete abolition. Seeking such a middle ground reflects another feature of pragmatist philosophy: the use of philosophical conceptual resources to help resolve what Dewey calls the "problems of men" (what we might call the "problems of sentient beings"). I believe that many research scientists hold some kind of middle-ground view. Therefore, my argument that inclusion of animal advocates follows from some such middle-ground view is offered in part because this conclusion is a doable improvement of our current protocol evaluation practices, which, ultimately, should benefit research animals. I do not, in this essay, specify the precise qualifications of an IACUC animal advocate, let alone what it takes to be an "advocate." I assume that advocates will be dedicated to animal welfare and will usually be members of animal welfare organizations. I certainly do not claim that anyone who calls him- or herself an advocate will be a suitable member of an IACUC, nor do I claim that people who do not consider themselves advocates, including research scientists, are incapable of strong moral concern for the well-being of animals used in experiments. My primary goal is to explore the philosophical rationale for a strong commitment to robust moral deliberation on IACUCs that entails the inclusion of an animal advocate on such committees. Setting out that philosophical context is a necessary first step, but much more needs to be done. Thus, my proposal is only a moral minimum—offered as a modest first step in improving our research practices involving animals. I concede that my proposal may well be *too* modest. We do not always have the luxury of easily separating a solution that is a realistic temporary compromise from one that is a betrayal of a moral ideal.

Since philosophic pragmatism views moral ideals as deliberative aims that regulate our judgments about how to improve our practices, it may not be surprising that my proposal is tentative and in need of further work. What is a bit surprising is that John Dewey, one of the most prominent of all pragmatists, takes a fairly strident position against more oversight of scientific research using animals. Since my contradiction of a founding pragmatist in the name of pragmatism might seem odd, it will be useful to pause for a brief consideration of Dewey's views. These views, I think, turn out to be a function less of Dewey's pragmatist commitments than of a somewhat narrow view of the potential moral conflict in animal research.

Dewey's Dismissal of Animal Advocates: Anti-Pragmatist Dogmatism?

In *The Public and Its Problems*, Dewey wrote: "Knowledge cooped up in a private consciousness is a myth, and knowledge of social phenomena is peculiarly dependent upon dissemination, for only by distribution can such knowledge be either obtained or tested. A fact of community life which is not spread abroad so as to be a common possession is a contradiction in terms" (345). Knowledge about our common social problems and their acceptable long-term solutions requires deep communication between those who work in technical fields and the lay public. Communication between experts and the public is one part of Dewey's account of ideal democracy understood as communities that promote the development of individuals through shared activities. Dewey is not naive. His ideal of optimal communication between public and scientists is something we need to continually work to achieve in domains such as education, government, and civic organizations. Viewed in this light, Dewey's remarks regarding public oversight of scientific experiments that cause pain and death to animals become more striking. In 1926—the very same year that he delivered the lectures that would later become *The Public and Its Problems*—Dewey writes about new laws regulating scientific experiments using animals: "Agitation for new laws is not so much intended to prevent specific instances of cruelty to animals as to subject scientific inquiry to hampering restrictions. The moral issue changes to this question: What ought to be the moral attitude of the public toward the proposal to put scientific inquiry under restrictive conditions?" ("Ethics of Animal Experimentation" 101). Dewey's answer is that the (then) current anti-cruelty laws are adequate. His main concern is with the potential dangers arising from those who would challenge the status quo by advocating more oversight of scientists. Dewey complains, "But opponents of animal experimentation are not content with such general legislation; they demand what is in effect, if not legally, class legislation, putting scientific men under peculiar surveillance and limitation" (100).

Dewey claims that animal advocates—not content to allow standard cruelty laws to govern the treatment of animals in scientific research—seek to put "scientific men under peculiar surveillance and limitation." One wants to ask Dewey what counts as *peculiar* surveillance and limitation. Is *any* public oversight or participation in the moral evaluation of animal experiments "peculiar" or "hampering"? Dewey seems to think so, assuming that any oversight would be tantamount to "anti-science." His rhetorical pitch rises when he compares animal advocates to the unenlightened who have blocked scientific progress throughout human history (presumably the superstitious and religious). Dewey assumes that all human progress has come through science, that "science is the single greatest instrumentality in bringing humans from 'barbarism to civilization'" ("Animal Experimentation" 101). He predicts that laws regulating animal experiments would foster anti-scientific attitudes contributing to behaviors and attitudes that would hamper the very enterprise of science. Setting aside the crude generalization about science being the single greatest instrument in human progress, one wonders how Dewey could offer an argument that smacks of absolutist certitude that oversight of animal experiments is always a bad thing. The substance of his moral argument seems to be that painful animal experiments are justified because of the particular kind of "moral suffering" experienced by diseased humans. It has no counterpart in "the life of animals, whose joys and sufferings remain upon a physical plane" (99). By "moral suffering" Dewey seems to have in mind the psychosocial suffering that occurs when a person can no longer fully function in social relations and that affects others as much as it does the sick person. How is Dewey so sure that all animal suffering remains merely physical? At the very least, such a claim requires evidence. Even granting this dubious claim, how could Dewey be so sure that such physical pain, although perhaps needing amelioration when possible, never becomes a consideration more important than the potential benefits to the human?

There is a tension if not downright contradiction here, given that Dewey believes fallibilism to be one of the most important epistemic improvements introduced by the "scientific method." Knowledge claims are tested by reference to their future consequences, and any knowledge claim may be shown wrong in future inquiry (more on this shortly). Furthermore, Dewey certainly believes that moral claims should be tested through a method of inquiry that is virtually the same, in its basic pattern, as that employed by science (this seems to be his argument in "Logical Conditions"). Thus, one would expect Dewey to be a fallibilist about his moral claims regarding animal experiments. Dewey's admission that cruelty to animals is wrong indicates that he does not hold a strongly anthropocentrist view that dismisses animal interests altogether. However, his declaration that oversight of experiments beyond such laws is an illegitimate intrusion on science suggests that Dewey does maintain that the value of scientific research *in general* outweighs animal interests (though he admits that we must address animal pain as best we can). If we interpret his view charitably, Dewey is not claiming that new laws regulating animal experiments could *never* be justified. Nor would he be claiming that we could know a priori that every scientific experiment using animals is always justified. Rather, the claim might be that at the time of writing the essay, Dewey believes that there are no serious moral issues regarding the use of animals in experiments. Any problems can be handled by the extant cruelty laws; however, there might come a time when we could provide a pragmatist justification for a more robust oversight of animal experiments.

We have already seen Dewey's view that the knowledge produced by experts should be communicated to the lay public. In a later work, Dewey emphasizes that the very "logic" of social inquiry requires public participation. Although "experts" may develop hypotheses or proposals for treating public problems relating to matters such as health and safety, the *full test* of these hypotheses must include the larger public whose problems these hypothetical solutions are supposed to address. Consider this passage from *Logic: The Theory of Inquiry*:

> An inquirer in a given special field appeals to the experiences of the community of his fellow workers for confirmation and correction of his results. Until agreement upon consequences is reached by those who reinstate the conditions set forth, the conclusions that are announced by an individual inquirer have the status of a hypothesis, especially if the findings fail to agree with the general trend of already accepted results. While agreement among the activities and their consequences that are brought about in the wider (technically non-scientific) public stands upon a different plane, nevertheless such agreement is an integral part of a complete test of physical conclusions wherever their public bearings are relevant. (484)

If someone objects that animals don't constitute any sort of public, we may reply that even if this were true, those citizens who advocate on their behalf do constitute part of the "public" who are affected by animal experiments. Nevertheless, it is not clear that Dewey's own view rules out the notion that animals are publics to whom proxy representation is due. After all, Dewey does agree that anti-cruelty laws are appropriate, so he might well concede that animals have important interests that ought to be represented by advocates.[3] Whatever turns out to be the best account of Dewey's views, we can see that his pragmatist commitments to communication between experts and lay public make committee oversight of animal experiments a viable option. If Dewey did not see this clearly because of a blind trust in "scientific progress," which he understood to serve unshakable anthropocentric values favoring human knowledge and well-being, then we pragmatists must be willing to question that absolutist judgment in ways appropriate to our own circumstances. Nothing less than such a critical attitude demonstrates commitment to Deweyan pragmatism. Therefore, let's take a fresh look, with *our* pragmatist eyes, at the moral issues involved in public oversight of animal experiments.

Starting in the Middle

I begin by defining more precisely a "middle ground" that ought to be acceptable to many of the interested parties. Consider the *important benefits principle* (IB): scientific experiments that thwart basic needs and interests of animals are justified only if they yield great benefits to humans or to animals.[4] Even though the IB seems fairly noncontroversial, we should note that nothing like it is explicitly codified in U.S. law pertaining to committee review of animal experiments. Acceptance of the IB requires that we accept the general moral view that the use of animals in experiments involves a moral conflict between possible benefits of scientific knowledge and the costs to the basic interests of animals. In short, the very practice of animal experimentation entails a value conflict, which invites continual moral inquiry.

We might wonder whether the IB is simply a "cost-benefit" principle, and therefore, whether the pragmatist position defended here really amounts to utilitarian or consequentialist moral philosophy. Animal rights defenders may complain that this approach begs the central issue at hand, namely, whether we have obligations to not harm individual animals irrespective of whether such harm would produce a greater aggregate gain for others.

Two points need to be made. First, nothing about the IB per se commits us to the utilitarian view that the correct moral response is to do whatever maximizes the most benefit for the most concerned. For example, we might argue that some experiments that may have a high probability of producing very important benefits are morally unacceptable because they cross a "moral threshold," perhaps because they inflict particularly harsh suffering on the animal.

Second, as I have already mentioned, the IB stakes out a moral middle ground. The IB and any conclusions that may follow from it are moral minimums. More robust moral claims advocated by animal rights theorists may well have merit. However, the pragmatist approach that I adopt here seeks gradual reform of social practices based on a real social consensus won through shared inquiry. We must not forget that the IB is proposed in the context of a specific problematic situation where the immediate concern is improving our protocol evaluation.[5] My argument is directed at scientists who may accept the IB but be reluctant to require animal advocates on IACUCs. Pragmatist accounts of inquiry center on basic properties of good inquiry, such as fallibilism and publicity. A brief reflection on features of good inquiry should help unseat skepticism about opening IACUCs to the input of animal advocates. Once we grant the IB and view the work of IACUCs as moral inquiry into whether experiments satisfy this principle, inclusion of animal advocates is an irresistible conclusion.

Fallibilism

Fallibilism is roughly the idea that any outcome of inquiry may be wrong. Thus, no outcome should be immune from criticism. That we might be wrong is nothing to lament. In fact, as C. S. Peirce pointed out long ago, doubts are productive: they are the impetus to engage in further inquiry, since they drive the production of new knowledge by goading us to search for new hypotheses.

Fallibilism appears innocuous enough. Most philosophers and laypeople endorse the idea that they are not always right, and that they learn from their mistakes. In practice, the real controversies seem to be over which *kinds* of claims are fallible. Most people would agree that they could be wrong about claims pertaining to medicine, plumbing, biology, and astronomy. However, there seems to be less agreement that claims pertaining to morality, religion, and art are fallible. Some might wonder how we could be wrong about claims that do not even have cognitive content. Thus, when pragmatists say that any outcome of inquiry may be wrong, many would agree while denying that moral claims could be an object of inquiry at all. What could a pragmatist say to scientists who would reject the very idea of "moral inquiry"?

Certainly we don't need to embrace every detail of a worked-out pragmatist theory of moral inquiry to make the point that many moral claims are fallible objects of deliberation. For example, consider an IB-type judgment: "This Draize eye test of a new baby shampoo product that will cause severe eye damage to 45 rabbits is morally permissible because of great benefits such as the prevention of harm to children." Perhaps some would say that the moral content expressed in the judgment "is morally permissible" is not the sort of thing that could be tested in inquiry. (Maybe this denial is based on some kind of non-cognitivist meta-ethical view about the nature of moral language.) Pragmatists would challenge this doubt, but let's concede it for the sake of argument. It would hardly follow that the entire moral judgment about the policy that states "this Draize test yields important benefits that justify the costs in the suffering of these rabbits" cannot be the object of inquiry. At the very least, this judgment defends a policy by citing reasons that could be challenged.

Consider related practical judgments, such as "I should buy picture A instead of picture B." Reasons might include various facts: "A will perform the function of decorating my living room better than B," "no other available picture will perform this function better than A," and "the costs of A are an acceptable use of my resources." I could be wrong about any of these facts cited in support of my judgment: I might find that the picture clashes with my living room in ways that I could not have anticipated, I might learn later of another cheaper picture that would work just as well, and so forth. Thus nothing more exotic need be implied by the idea that our moral claims about animal experiments are fallible outcomes of moral inquiry than the idea that we could be wrong about whether this experiment was worth the costs. The so-called three-Rs of reduction, refinement, and replacement (first set out in 1959 by Russell and Burch) carve out three types of errors that IACUCs might commit. They might overestimate the number of animals needed (reduction). They might overlook noninvasive alternatives (replacement). They might not do the best possible job in refining the procedures to reduce pain (refinement).

It should be clear that scientists who reject the idea that judgments about animal experiments are fallible outcomes of moral inquiry must be those who would not endorse the IB in the first place. After all, the IB just encapsulates the idea that there is a generalized moral conflict involved in the use of animals in research. Thus one practical test of a person's commitment to the IB is whether he or she is willing to accept its direct implications, which include the view that moral judgments about animal experiments are fallible outcomes of moral inquiry.

Publicity

A second property of good inquiry is publicity, the idea that we gain epistemic confidence in claims through the process of public testing. To say that I might be wrong about some hypothesis H is, in part, to say that others could detect an error in H. Likewise, to say that H is probably true is, in part, to say that others could arrive at H through the same procedures that I used.

As fallibilists committed to norms of good inquiry, we should acknowledge that any claim about an experiment satisfying the IB should be able to survive public scrutiny.[6] But who is the relevant public? Most obviously, those directly involved in the research and those knowledgeable about animal physiology are included. Yet also among the relevant public would seem to be those with direct interest in the welfare of the animals themselves, because the IB concerns whether animal pain and suffering is worth possible benefits.

Some might wish to argue that the current situation is basically adequate, since interested citizens can generally get access to information about experiments —especially those that use public moneys. As this view maintains that the current status quo is adequate to satisfy the need for proper input by nonscientists in the evaluation of research protocols, we need to look more closely at the current laws and at their moral and legal grounding. And since my argument is an effort to address the current situation in the United States, a look at the relevant laws is pragmatically required.

The Current Laws

Currently, U.S. law requires that animal research facilities be evaluated by an institutional animal care and use committee. IACUCs must oversee basic provisions of the federal Animal Welfare Act passed in 1966, including provisions about proper housing, food, cage size, transportation, handling, and the like. A 1985 revision to the law requires that the IACUC review any research practices that involve pain to animals. The Public Health Service developed a policy in 1986 with similar but more specific provisions. These include sections in PHS grant applications that deal with such questions as whether less painful alternative techniques have been considered, whether appropriate anesthesia is used, whether appropriate euthanasia methods are implemented for those animals killed after experiments, and whether lab personnel are trained and qualified (see Orlans 83–84). Significantly, the Animal Welfare Act leaves mice, rats, and birds out of its purview, whereas the PHS includes these animals.

The law mandates that the committee include at least one scientist from the facility, one veterinarian, and one "community member." The community member must not be affiliated with the institution or a relative of someone affiliated with the institution. The community member is supposed to represent general community interests in the proper care and treatment of animals (see Orlans 100). Currently, there are no legal standards governing the selection of the community member, nor does the law specify that the community member must come from an animal advocacy group. There is also no current uniform legal requirement that IACUC meetings be open to the public.

The law reflects the view that scientists at publicly funded institutions are accountable to the public. Scientists need to justify their claim that a particular line of scientific research is worth its costs in public or private financial and institutional resources, let alone in animal suffering. In light of these facts, we can offer an anti-elitist, democratic argument for public oversight of animal experimentation. Scientists are not necessarily moral experts about whether the possible benefits of research involving painful experiments are worth the costs (the IB). Scientists may be experts about technical matters, but we should not assume that they are experts on the question of whether their research goals have morally justified benefits. In fact, as I will argue shortly, there is some reason to doubt that scientists are well-positioned to morally evaluate experiments. The claim that scientists are not necessarily moral experts is linked to the belief that in democratic societies, people ought to have some say about the importance of their own needs. Citizens ought to have chances to comment on whether they have a need, whether the need is serious enough to warrant using costly means, and whether other needs might be more pressing. Thus, the denial to scientists of moral expertise is, in part, a critique of the social elitist view that says some favored group has special access to knowing the real needs of the rest of society.[7]

A similar moral justification applies to sunshine laws. In democratic societies, members of the public should have access to information about the activities of government institutions because such information is necessary for them to make rational choices about social policies and elected officials. Since research using animals frequently takes place in government agencies or public universities funded by tax dollars, interested citizens ought to have access to information about how their tax dollars are being spent.

The federal Freedom of Information Act can be used by animal advocates to obtain information about laboratory inspections and violations, the breakdown of funding from the National Institutes of Health, and details about research proposals. The state sunshine laws vary greatly, but some provide for public access to IACUC meetings. Animal advocates have used such laws to argue for the right to attend IACUC meetings at universities.[8] State sunshine laws tend to allow for more access to a greater variety of institutions. As Barbara Orlans notes, "under the state laws, information can be obtained from state-funded institutions at an earlier time, and from a wider range of funding-sources. In contrast, federal law applies only after funding has been approved and excludes commercial funding" (173).

One problem with a reliance on freedom of information laws is that researchers opposed to community participation might assert their rights to academic freedom, which may sometimes override assertions of a public right to know. For one thing, if the research is conducted without public funding, right-to-know laws do not directly justify public access to experiments. The right of privacy of the researcher, or of the private institution by which he or she is employed, might trump any public right even to know of the existence of animal experiments, let alone to participate in their development.

A second problem with relying on legal arguments based on state sunshine laws is that the actual case law is mixed. Some courts have ruled that IACUCs are not bodies that make public policy and thus are not required to have open attendance; other state courts have upheld open attendance at IACUC meetings. One might argue that although IACUCs are not making public policy per se, they are regulatory bodies charged with ensuring that certain legal and moral requirements are met in the use of laboratory animals. Even so, the fact remains that sunshine laws will vary from state to state; and if we accept the claim that access is justified because of the serious moral concern for the interests of animals, we are then faced with the uncomfortable result that animals used in research in a state with liberal sunshine laws and more active animal welfare organizations will probably get better advocacy (and perhaps better treatment). Therefore animals receive different treatment on morally irrelevant grounds. Furthermore, many private institutions that use animals in experiments are exempt from public scrutiny under sunshine laws because the Animal Welfare Act does not define rats, mice, and birds as "animals" for the purposes of the statute. Therefore, the U.S. Department of Agriculture does not inspect or monitor facilities using these species, even though they are used in about 85 percent of animal research.[9] This exclusion is morally arbitrary, reflecting the USDA's limited resources. Nevertheless, if we were to mount an argument for public access to information about this group of excluded animals, it could not be based on the use of public moneys to support the research.

Even if sunshine laws changed to favor greater public access and the Animal

Welfare Act were revised to cover all animals, the result would still restrict citizen input. Open meetings in effect grant concerned citizens "observer status" in the review process. As important as public access to information may be, such information will rarely tell the complete story about the nature of the experiments. Citizens can scrutinize records, to determine whether there are violations of legal or moral standards, but researchers are not obliged to enter into any meaningful dialogue with animal advocates who are not scientists. Even at open meetings of IACUCs, where the attendance of nonvoting members of the public may generate discussion that actually affects the deliberations of the voting members, the power of animal advocates is quite limited because they lack a vote on the committee.

No doubt many researchers currently view the participation of community members on IACUCs not as a necessary part of open moral deliberation but, more cynically, as part of their own public relations efforts. In a more positive light, citizen participation may be taken as a fail-safe device to prevent egregious abuses that might tarnish public support for research. Orlans, after conducting an informal survey of researchers who chaired IACUC committees, notes that "a commonly stated opinion among the survey respondents was that the value of being a community member lies not so much in the specific reforms effected but in being a constant reminder to the institution of the outside world" (112). The researchers see community members' primary function as reminding scientists about approved social values that may be at odds with particular experiments. This view verges on an outright denial of the IB, because the reason given for community oversight of IACUCs is that the "the public cares what scientists do" and not that the "animal's important interests might be thwarted." This last point is critical to understanding the overall limitations of the reasoning presented thus far: the "democratic argument" is concerned with a citizen's right to determine whether benefits—particularly those affecting the health of the general community—were worth the costs to animals. This approach focuses more on the democratic rights of citizens than on the interests of animals themselves.

We have just seen that much current U.S. law goes some way toward respecting the norm of publicity. A "community member" must sit on IACUCs, and right-to-know laws provide concerned animal advocates some avenue for evaluating the morality of animal experiments. Nevertheless, reliance on current laws is of limited effectiveness because these laws do not take seriously enough the moral significance of the interests of the animals themselves, and they do not ensure a robust process of deliberation with advocates before the experiments are implemented.

Selective Emphasis

It seems clear that the current status quo does not provide the conditions for a vigorous committee review. Although the inclusion of an animal advocate is only a small step in the right direction, I think we have some reason to think that he or she would provide a valuable perspective in the deliberations of IACUCs. Think of advocates as proxies for the animals who cannot represent their own interests. The role of the advocate is not simply to remind scientists of what some people in society think about the morality of using animals in research, or to have their fair say, qua citizens, in whether benefits are worth the costs. Rather, the advocate should be a *deliberative partner in a process of moral inquiry*. The function of the advocate is to emphasize one important dimension of the moral problem. If we are serious about adhering to the norm of publicity in moral inquiry, then we should require animal advocates to sit on IACUCs.

It might be claimed that a neutral community member could provide some focus or perspective on the values at stake. However, it is unlikely that he or she will bring the *sympathy* for the animal's perspective necessary for determining whether an experiment adheres to the IB. To see why sympathy matters here, consider first the straightforward idea that all intelligent thought requires "selective emphasis" (in Dewey's phrase). Moral inquiry, like other kinds of inquiry, requires that an individual focus on some relevant facts while ignoring others. Information processing involves information filtering. In order to think about some bit of information, I have to select some item for attention and disregard much else. This selection process is guided by a variety of interests: practical, cognitive, aesthetic, political, and moral. Moreover, pragmatists remind us that interests motivating inquiry have *emotional dimensions*. Scientists, doctors, bricklayers, lawyers, and parents engage in a variety of inquiries guided by emotions such as pride, curiosity, love, and fear.

Dewey makes the point that selective emphasis is "inevitable whenever reflection occurs." Selective emphasis is therefore a necessary feature of thought or inquiry, neither good nor bad. However, Dewey notes that trouble comes from failure to acknowledge selective this choice. He writes, "Deception comes only when the presence and operation of choice is concealed, disguised, denied" (*Experience and Nature* 34).[10] Scientists understandably select animals for the purpose of accomplishing research goals, ignoring or setting aside moral questions in favor of solving a problem or answering a question within some research domain. That focus is not itself a flaw. But it does suggest that scientists may conceal the full moral import of their use of animals by not paying sufficient attention to animal interests. Such concealment does not imply that scientists conspire deliberately to shield their research from moral judgments; rather, it indicates that scientists have beliefs and attitudes—an ideology—shaped by institutions and practices that have, historically, functioned to marginalize this kind of moral reflection from scientific concern. Their largely unarticulated background assumptions form the self-understanding of scientific practitioners. The "common sense" of science, as Bernard Rollin dubs it, is a subject too complex to adequately treat here, but it involves the belief that "value" questions are not amenable to rational resolution and that science deals with "facts" alone. This belief leads to the notion that scientific inquiry pursued for its own sake, though it may have a kind of cognitive value, is morally neutral. As Rollin puts it, "if values have anything whatever to do with science, it is with the *applica-*

tions of the results of science decided on by politicians, and in the use of atomic theory for weaponry, but such decisions are not the concern of the scientist *qua* scientist, only *qua* citizen" (8).

The problem with the claim that questions about moral values only apply to the results of scientific inquiry is that it ignores the unavoidable necessity of making many value judgments during the initial stages of particular inquiries. Scientists do not, in practice, pursue "knowledge in general" but a particular bit of knowledge judged to be important enough for their investment of time, means, resources, and energy. A valued end like "knowledge" is always pursued in specific contexts, with specific means and resources. The IB is a general principle that directs our attention to the fact that any animal research involves morally significant trade-offs. How is it possible to wait until the inquiry is over to test the moral judgment that a particular bit of medical knowledge was worth the pain and suffering of the animals? If we always suspend moral judgment until the knowledge is "applied" to the real world, then all animals used in experiments that turn out to be unjustified suffer unnecessary and unjustified harms. If scientists want to claim that animals are indispensable tools or models for a line of research, then they can scarcely deny that a morally significant conflict is intrinsic to their research (unless they dismiss animal interests altogether).

Once we take seriously the point that scientists pursue inquiries in specific institutional contexts, competing for scarce resources and striving for specific ends, then legitimate concerns about conflict of interest emerge. Professional success, status, and advancement frequently depend on successfully conducting experiments—especially if these experiments help to secure funding for the home institution of the researcher. The existence of such potential conflicts of interest need not point to character flaws in scientists. They occur whenever individuals pursue professional goals that may be at odds with moral considerations, and here they make it difficult for scientists to be impartial about whether a particular experiment satisfies the IB.

Moreover, there is evidence that scientists are unlikely to be reliable in carefully attending to animals' pain and suffering. Historically scientists have been reluctant to admit that animal experiments involve serious moral concerns precisely because they have denied the legitimacy of attributing states of consciousness and pain to animals.[11] The conceptual grounds for this denial are complex, tied to a certain positivistic interpretation of scientific objectivity which demotes as "subjective" all statements not directly verifiable in sensory experience.

These particular facts about scientific practice—the way that scientists selectively ignore certain value implications of their practice—make a case for the inclusion of animal advocates on IACUCs as a reasonable legal requirement. The objection might be made that the best candidates for sympathizing proxies are not animal advocates but neutral veterinarians who have the qualifications necessary to judge how well or poorly the basic needs of various species are met. On this view, opening the door to animal activists is a recipe for pointless debates based on uninformed evaluations of the impact of the experiments on an animal's well-being. The activist, lacking the best scientific knowledge of the species and its needs, will simply tend to take emotional stands. So, although some kind of sympathy with animals' suffering may be appropriate, it should be a sympathetic response informed by scientific knowledge of animal health, presumably including facts about animal physiology and psychology.

We might reply to this complaint by making sure that the animal advocates are trained veterinarians. Alternatively, we might simply hold that IACUCs contain at least one qualified veterinarian, preferably someone who is neutral about the moral status of animals and who is not affiliated with the institution in question. Right now, current PHS policy mandates the presence of a veterinarian, and I certainly think this is sound policy. Having laypeople sit on IACUCs has the added benefit of forcing scientists to translate technical language into an understandable form. The hope would be that over time this translation would actually increase understanding not just among the members of particular committees but even among those in the broader public who might take an interest in animal research.

Moreover, the worry about "emotional advocates" downplays the significance of sympathetic emotions in moral evaluation. The issue is not so much how to maximize or minimize blind emotional heat but rather how to skillfully use emotions in order to perceive, understand, and interpret the experiences of animal subjects. Research scientists who use animals, and those charged with evaluating the merits of their proposals, are motivated by a host of emotions, including curiosity, pride, love of fame, anxiety, boredom, fear, and the like. These emotions may get out of hand from time to time, but most would agree that emotions such as curiosity are a fitting and reasonable part of scientific life. We have good reason for believing that certain cultivated emotions are similarly fitting to and important for moral evaluation. Sympathetic emotional identification is required in a range of moral judgments.[12] Consider the moral judgment "I should help someone in pain." In order to know when an individual needs help, I need to know how much pain is being felt, what sorts of things might be causing the pain, and what sorts of things might best alleviate it. I do not need to feel the same sensations as the distressed being, but I must have enough information about its feelings to form an evaluative judgment about the phenomenal character of the pain, its sources, and the possible ways to address it. Surely the same sort of sympathetic identification with animal suffering is needed when experiments are being evaluated.

Although we need "objective" information, such information is not sufficient for adequate moral evaluation; it may even function to create psychological distance from the subjective reality of animal consciousness and animal pain—a point already mentioned. Fair evaluation of these costs requires proper sympathy for the animal's perspective because sympathy provides moral information vital for an adequate understanding of the moral conflict in a particular case. Animal advocates will most likely tend to sympathize with animal interests in ways that will provide a favorable balance to IACUCs. Scientists may be experts about how to minimize pain, but they frequently have vested interests in sacrificing pain control for the sake of the experiments' efficiency. I certainly am not claiming that scientists are incapable of such sympathetic identification, nor do I claim that sympathy *alone* will provide the animal advocate with the knowledge necessary to adequately judge animal suffering. I am only saying that because of the habits of selective emphasis mentioned above, scientists are understandably less likely to take up that sympathetic perspective.[13]

The inclusion of animal advocates on IACUCs is a first step in acknowledging the general importance of the sympathetic perspective of a proxy. To be sure, more work needs to be done to explicitly spell out the sorts of epistemological and affective "competencies" that we should expect from members of IACUCs.[14] No doubt some familiarity with basic ethical issues as well as some understanding of scientific methodology as it pertains to the use of animals in research would be an important part of the training of all involved in evaluating protocols. I do think sympathetic identification with animals is probably the most important competency an advocate ought to have, though I'm not sure how that could be measured—perhaps the best approach would be to assume that those committed enough to be members of animal welfare groups meet the mark. Clearly, more remains to be said on this topic.

Finally, even if someone wishes to reject the idea that emotions play an important cognitive role in moral judgments, we could still argue that animals would be more fairly represented on IACUCs by animal advocates than by those who are neutral about their interests. Even if emotions play no *cognitive* role, they have a *motivational* function instrumental to fairness. Animals have a right to an advocate or proxy whose concern for their well-being is strong enough to sustain a vigorous defense of their interests.

Scientists are understandably reluctant to allow lay animal advocates to participate in committees that decide the fate of their research. Research scientists are also worried about breaches of confidentiality, perhaps the passing of information to another scientist or, even worse, to radical animal rights groups who might respond with break-ins, harassment, and other intrusions. Thus scientists tend simply to deny animal advocates access to the processes of protocol evaluation. While this response might preserve a level of security in the short term, it nevertheless generates suspicion over the long run. If animal advocates are included on IACUCs, a new level of trust and understanding might develop among researchers, animal welfare groups, and the general lay public. I certainly make no claims that the presence of animal advocates will make the deliberations of such committees easier, nor do I believe that animal advocates will *always* be best able to represent animal interests. But I do think that including animal advocates on IACUCs with a self-conscious understanding that all are participants in a moral inquiry based on the IB will ultimately improve moral discussion and debate about animal experimentation. Empirical study of the function of committees that include animal advocates will no doubt be required to ensure that this hypothesis is correct.[15] As fallibilists, moreover, we should not expect that the IB itself will remain a fixed principle, as moral inquiry progresses over time. Perhaps the joint deliberations between animal advocates and scientific researchers will help to further the evolution of a social consensus about the moral status of research animals that will lead to the rejection of the IB. We can only hope that the evolution of this consensus ethic will be guided in some measure by shared inquiry. It is this kind of social hope in democratically organized inquiry that is the lasting legacy of the pragmatist tradition. The first step in establishing the trust for such shared inquiry is the will to believe in its possibility.

Notes

I wish to thank Erin McKenna for helpful comments and criticisms. Earlier versions of this paper were presented to a meeting of the Ohio Philosophical Association at Wooster College in April 2002 and to the annual meeting of the Midwest Pragmatist Study Group in September 2002. I thank participants of both meetings for valuable comments, especially the helpful criticisms from Peter Horn.

1. In this regard, U.S. law differs from that of some other countries, like Germany, that requires research review committees to have members affiliated with animal welfare organizations. A government agency selects names from lists provided by prominent animal welfare groups. In this essay, I do not recommend policies for selecting animal advocates, confining myself to the philosophical rationale for the claim that they ought to be selected.

2. The theory of inquiry is best expressed in Dewey, *Logic*. Dewey's view of moral theory can be found in his *Ethics* (Dewey and Tufts).

3. Dewey's position could be instead that our obligation to refrain from cruelty to animals is based on a more fundamental obligation to human beings, on the assumption that cruelty to animals is causally linked to cruelty to humans.

4. My approach is somewhat at odds with the stated purpose of the Animal Welfare Act, which claims to be concerned not with evaluation of the scientific merit of experiments but with the care and use of animals. However, as Rollin points out, once we concede that scientists need to consider alternatives to the use of animals or reduce the numbers of animals used, it is practically impossible not to take up evaluation of the scientific merits of experiments (181).

5. To fully address all of the matters relevant to improving protocol evaluation, we would need to look into the specific guidelines contained in National Institutes of Health policy and the revised Animal Welfare Act. I will not evaluate the adequacy of these per se. No doubt they will need to evolve in response to evolving scientific knowledge, as well as changing moral views about animals. Furthermore, the pragmatist approach that I take in this essay rejects the idea that the best way to handle conflicts in practice is for all parties to agree to an overarching set of moral principles; rather, we ought to begin with a focus on the particulars of the moral problem, engaging actual participants who have a serious stake in its satisfactory resolution. For a good account of a bottom-up approach to moral problem solving, see Jonsen and Toulmin; see also Wallace.

6. This is perhaps the single greatest insight in Jürgen Habermas's discourse ethics.

7. The rejection of social elitism need not entail the notion that individuals have no

false beliefs about their own needs. It is simply the rejection of the idea that individuals are usually completely in error about their own needs.

8. For example, the Progressive Animal Welfare Society (PAWS) sought the rights to vote and attend meetings of the University of Washington IACUC. PAWS won the right to attend meetings in 1987. See the discussion of this case in Orlans et al. 103–17.

9. If federal moneys are involved, the NIH does require the monitoring of facilities using birds, rats, and mice.

10. We should distinguish between two kinds of concealment: concealment of choice *as such* in inquiry or reflection, and concealment of some relevant conditions and consequences affected by a particular inquiry. In the case of animal experimentation, it is unlikely that scientists would disavow the need for selective emphasis as such, a move that appears to be more of a problem in the history of philosophical reflection than in other kinds of intellectual or practical pursuits. Philosophers sometimes tend to view their theories simply as responses to timeless problems that are "given" rather than selected during the course of historically evolving problem-solving events. Or philosophers take the view that their theories are simply reflections of the voice of "being itself."

11. See Rollin, who shows how scientists internalize an ideology that denies animals' pain in the face of common sense as well as Darwinian evolutionary theory.

12. Because emotions are not absent from scientific inquiry and research, the issue is not their presence but rather which kinds of emotions might or might not be appropriate for the purpose of determining whether experiments satisfy the IB. Intrascientific conflicts over theories and research projects can be deeply emotional as well as cognitive disagreements. Science is not simply a search for knowledge but a career, so the intense emotional connections a scientist has to his or her favorite theory are perfectly understandable. Nevertheless, there does seem to be an asymmetry between moral and scientific inquiry in the role played by emotional response in evaluating particular judgments or claims. We may say that a scientist acts inappropriately when he or she is not proud, happy, or overjoyed at the success of some just-created extraordinary hypothesis (what counts as an appropriate emotional response to personal success to some extent varies with factors such as culture and personal temperament). But our judgment pertains to a personal response to success, and not to the content of the scientific claim.

13. For the view that sympathy is a prerequisite to even understand what it means to treat another fairly, see Mercer, chap. 7. Also, an overall account of the relationship between moral regard for animals and sympathy and care can be found in Donovan.

14. I am indebted to Peter Horn for bringing the issues of competency to my attention.

15. Such empirical study is needed because fallibilism applies to the general arguments I am offering about the very nature of moral inquiry and what moral inquiry implies in the case of IACUCs.

Bibliography

Dewey, John. "The Ethics of Animal Experimentation." In *The Later Works*, vol. 2, *1925–1927*, 98–103.
———. *Experience and Nature. The Later Works*, vol. 1, *1925*.
———. *The Later Works, 1925–1953*. Edited by Jo Ann Boydston. 17 vols. Carbondale: Southern Illinois University Press, 1981–90.
———. *Logic: The Theory of Inquiry. The Later Works*, vol. 12, *1938*.

——. "Logical Conditions of a Scientific Treatment of Morality." In *The Middle Works,* edited by Jo Ann Boydston, vol. 3, *1903–1906,* 3–39. Carbondale: Southern Illinois University Press, 1977.

——. *The Public and Its Problems.* In *The Later Works,* vol. 2, *1925–1927,* 235–372.

Dewey, John, and James Hayden Tufts. *Ethics. The Later Works,* vol. 7, *1932.*

Donovan, Josephine. "Attention to Suffering: Sympathy as a Basis for Ethical Treatment of Animals." In *Beyond Animal Rights: A Feminist Caring Ethic for the Treatment of Animals,* edited by Josephine Donovan and Carol J. Adams, 147–69. New York: Continuum Publishing, 1996.

Jonsen, Albert R., and Stephen Toulmin. *The Abuse of Casuistry: A History of Moral Reasoning.* Berkeley: University of California Press, 1988.

Mercer, Philip. *Sympathy and Ethics: A Study of the Relationship between Sympathy and Morality with Special Reference to Hume's "Treatise."* Oxford: Clarendon Press, 1972.

Orlans, F. Barbara. *In the Name of Science: Issues in Responsible Animal Experimentation.* Oxford: Oxford University Press, 1993.

Orlans, F. Barbara, et al. *The Human Use of Animals: Case Studies in Ethical Choice.* Oxford: Oxford University Press, 1998.

Rollin, Bernard E. *The Unheeded Cry: Animal Consciousness, Animal Pain, and Science.* Expanded ed. Ames: Iowa State University Press, 1998.

Russell, W. M. S., and R. L. Burch. *The Principles of Humane Experimental Technique.* 1959. Reprint, Potters Bar, Eng.: Universities Federation for Animal Welfare, 1992.

Wallace, James D. *Ethical Norms, Particular Cases.* Ithaca, N.Y.: Cornell University Press, 1998.

11 Pragmatism and Pets: Best Friends Animal Sanctuary, Maddie's Fund℠, and No More Homeless Pets in Utah

Matthew Pamental

Deweyan pragmatism is what one might call an "engaged" philosophical approach. For John Dewey it would be better "for philosophy to err in active participation in the living struggles and issues of its own age and time than to maintain an immune monastic impeccability, without relevance or bearing in the generating ideas of its contemporary present" ("Does Reality Possess Practical Character?" 142). Thus, philosophy should begin with the problems of the day—or, as he called them, the "problems of men"—rather than with the problems of philosophers. In his view, the process of reflection ought to be governed by the notion of intelligent, democratic inquiry.[1] Intelligent inquiry, as Dewey saw it, is a matter of carefully delineating a problem, hypothesizing various possible courses of action, choosing the ideal combination of ends and means—Dewey's "end-in-view"—and testing that choice in activity (*Logic* 105–22). Thus, Dewey saw pragmatism as an approach for solving problems in the real world, not for solving abstract philosophical conundrums.

There is, however, an immediate difficulty if one attempts to apply a Deweyan approach to problems involving nonhuman animals, first because Dewey did not actually say much explicitly about animal welfare, rights, or experimentation, and second because what he does say seems to automatically relegate the interests of nonhuman animals to an inferior status.[2] However, my aim in this essay is not to enter into a discussion of such matters as Dewey's approach to animals' "inherent value" or "rights," or animal psychology, as revealing as those investigations might be. Rather, I am interested in taking Dewey's exhortation seriously, and examining how the pragmatic method of democratic intelligence might be applied to a real problem: the problem of the overpopulation of domestic pets, or companion animals, in the United States. Since recent approaches to dealing with that problem have gone on against the backdrop of the animal rights movement, and since the move away from discussions of animal rights to the solution of the problem of pet overpopulation is itself a pragmatic move, I begin by providing some background on the animal rights movement.

In the years since the publication in 1975 of Peter Singer's *Animal Liberation,* the animal rights movement in the United States has transformed itself from a scattered group of mostly small to medium-sized groups working largely in isolation into a coalition of grassroots and national organizations whose local state and federal activism has resulted in remarkable numbers of felony anti-cruelty statutes (in thirty-one states), laws against dog and cock fighting (in forty-three and thirteen states, respectively; see Ascione and Lockwood 47), and a 50 percent reduction in the number of animals used in research (see Rowan and Loew 113). However, Gary Francione argues that the overall "measurable progress of the animal movement has been minimal," and that even though the animal rights movement has increased awareness significantly, "increased awareness has not yet translated into significant decreases in animal exploitation" (113).

That the debate has, at least on one level, gone on in terms of rights is not a surprise. After all, Singer explicitly—and provocatively—couched his discussion in terms of the *liberation* of animals (iv–v), a clear and deliberate reference to other liberation movements. In addition, he explicitly compared what he calls *speciesism*—the arbitrary exclusion or dismissal of the interests of nonhumans in favor of human interests—to racism and sexism. Hence, many groups organized around the idea of making progress *toward* rights for animals (Unti and Rowan 24). However, Francione argues even further that the debate *must* proceed in terms of the introduction of significant rights for animals, specifically claiming that they ought to be removed from the category of property. As long as animals are still considered property under the law, he declares, their interests will lose out to human interests (126–39).

In this essay I will argue that Francione's argument goes too far. Grassroots, welfarist approaches can and do have significant effects on the conditions and treatment of nonhuman animals. In particular, by focusing solely on animal rights legislation Francione overlooks two crucial components in any reconstruction of social conditions: community support and education. He therefore ignores the successes of local, grassroots, volunteer activities in improving the treatment of animals. These programs focus pragmatically on community activism and an experimental approach to solving problems—a method, I argue, that exemplifies the notion of democratic, intelligent inquiry expressed in the work of Dewey.

To prove this last contention, I describe the efforts of Maddie's Fund[SM], Best Friends Animal Sanctuary, and the No More Homeless Pets in Utah program, showing that these efforts constitute a Deweyan approach to the problem of the overpopulation of domestic dogs and cats in the United States. Specifically, their approach can be seen to follow the five steps of a Deweyan democratic inquiry. Its astonishing success over the past decade and a half in reducing the number of healthy, adoptable dogs and cats euthanized each year itself constitutes a warrant for my conclusion. These results indicate both the kind of progress that can be made and the role that education and communal activism need to play if that progress is to be realized. The five sections of this essay correspond to Dewey's understanding of the stages of successful inquiry, beginning with the felt tension, or problematic situation. The following sections discuss the way the problem was defined, various possible ideal solutions, and some ways in which the solution might have been worked out. I conclude with the final stage of a Deweyan inquiry, that of testing the solution in practice, and examine what beliefs are warranted on the basis of the inquiry as a whole.

The Felt Tension

Enter one of the more than 5,000 animal shelters in the United States and you will likely be inundated with sensory stimuli: the institutional feeling of the concrete-and-steel construction, the sometimes overwhelming cacophony of human and animal voices, and the ever-present smells of animal waste and disinfectant. What you will almost certainly *not* see or hear (or even hear about) are the euthanizations. According to the Humane Society of the United States (HSUS), although the number of "no-kill" shelters has risen dramatically over the past twenty years, the vast majority of animal shelters in the United States still euthanize nearly ten animals per week. But most euthanasia policies—for example, that euthanasia not be discussed with the general population—reflect the problems inherent in killing healthy, friendly animals; and most shelter staff and veterinarians will agree that euthanasia is at best a necessary evil, and at worst a callous, indifferent response to the problem of pet overpopulation.

The HSUS estimates that somewhere between 6 and 8 million cats and dogs will enter animal shelters in 2003. Of those animals, between 600,000 and 750,000 are reclaimed by their human companions, and new families adopt another 3 to 4 million animals. The remainder, roughly 3 to 4 million cats and dogs, will be euthanized. Even the conservative figure of 3 million animals averages to more than 8,000 cats and dogs killed every day in the United States. To be sure, some of these animals may not be optimal candidates for family pets—some dogs don't do well with small children, others have issues with dominant men, and some cats and dogs are just too sick or aggressive to live safely with humans—but a large proportion are healthy and quite capable of living rich, full lives as companions to humans.

The overpopulation of domestic cats and dogs is due largely to human ignorance, greed, and apathy—intact dogs and cats left to roam free, kitten and puppy mills producing more animals than can reasonably be expected to sell, and the conscious choice to breed animals are just three obvious ways that human choices have led to pet overpopulation. A single, intact female cat can have up to three litters of kittens per year, with an average of three to six kittens per litter. This means that in seven years, one female cat and her offspring can theoretically produce up to 420,000 cats. For dogs, the number of potential offspring is nearly 70,000. Of course, these theoretical numbers rarely come close to being reached; the point is that left alone an animal is likely to breed prolifically, and so far Americans have been slow to reduce those chances. This inaction has led to a rapidly growing number of stray animals, animals that frequently end up in animal control shelters. Once there, overwhelmed and underpaid shelter staff have the unenviable task of determining which animals are adoptable and which not. The latter, of course, are the animals destined for a lethal injection.

The numbers given above represent only the latest figures, which reflect a marked improvement over what the status of domestic pets had been from the late 1970s to around 1987. At that time, nearly 17 million healthy, adoptable cats and dogs were being euthanized each year in shelters. It was then that the initial members of what would become Best Friends Animal Sanctuary felt the need to respond to the growing pet overpopulation crisis and offer an alternative to the standard responses. Animals that were "unadoptable"—those with serious illness, such as feline leukemia or (more recently) feline immunodeficiency virus, those who had bitten a human (even once), or those who simply were not adopted during a shelter's set time limit—were euthanized.[3] Policies included (and still includes, in some municipalities) killing any animal that the shelter could not afford to take care of, such as unweaned kittens or puppies, which were automatically put down. Euthanasia, in other words, was a nearly universally accepted "necessary evil" simply because people were not willing to deal with the causes of pet overpopulation: deliberate overbreeding, an unwillingness to spay or neuter, and a lack of compassion for animals with special needs (Finsen and Finsen 149–52; see Armstrong, Tomasello, and Hunter 75).

The founders of Best Friends were repulsed by what they saw as a complete lack of compassion for these animals.[4] At first they worked individually, saving discarded animals where and when they could. Later, they decided to have a shelter dedicated to homeless pets—rehabilitating and adopting out those they could, but with space for a haven for those that were for any reason no longer adoptable. They purchased property, first in Arizona and later in Angel Canyon, near Kanab in southern Utah, in order to have a permanent home for the animals. Best Friends was founded, then, on a no-kill philosophy: no unwanted animal would be euthanized, save to keep it from unnecessary, unavoidable suffering at the end of its natural life (see Glen). That the founders understood that the no-kill philosophy was limited by the suffering of the animals is the first of their pragmatic attitudes: they viewed their principle not as an absolute but rather as a general rule to guide their efforts, tempered and ultimately outweighed by their compassion for the animals and by another principle, that of avoiding unnecessary suffering.[5]

So the first part of the felt tension is simply their recognition of a number of facts. First, the population of domestic cats and dogs had grown far beyond the human demand for animal companionship. Second, diseases, bad training, and failed attempts at socialization were producing animals—mostly cats in the first category, mostly dogs in the latter two—who had become unwanted or "unfit" to be the companions of humans. Third, humans were dumping these animals at an increasingly alarming rate. And finally, the accepted response to this development was simply to kill the animals "for their own good." The founders believed this situation to be simply unacceptable, and Best Friends was their initial response to it.

It turns out that there was (and is) more to the problem than just the facts of overpopulation and euthanasia, but the complexities did not become apparent until a few years into the Best Friends project. Starting from a few dozen animals, Best Friends grew to more than 1,000 animals by 1995, including 600 dogs and more than 100 *special needs* cats (i.e., distinct from their population of healthy and adoptable cats and kittens; rough estimates from Glen 168, 251). In addition, by 1990 the organization was nearly broke. The founders' willingness to take in nearly any animal, coupled with their unwillingness to kill an animal unless absolutely necessary, created logistical, fiscal, and organizational problems that even such a dedicated group of individuals could not overcome. The incomes of those members not living at the sanctuary, together with the residents' savings and the monthly payments for a property they sold before moving to Kanab, simply did not provide enough—particularly after the developer who had bought the Arizona property went bankrupt and filed for Chapter 11 protection, effectively cutting Best Friends off from a significant source of funding (Glen 151). Thus the organization was faced with an increasing number of needy animals, along with a shrinking budget.

Initial Responses, or Discovering the Real Problem

Obviously, Best Friends had a problem. However, the true nature of that problem was not yet clear. The failure of those in Best Friends to recognize its true nature is evident from the piecemeal and small-scale approach they initially took to solving it. Their first forays took one of three forms. In the nonprofit world of animal rescue organizations, the standard method used by groups to gain funding was to build up a database of willing supporters: they would sit in front of supermarkets with a money box, brochures, and a sign-up sheet for a mailing list. This was the course the founders chose for overcoming their budget crisis. By building up their database the group could gain a large number of persons on whom they might rely in emergencies as well as for steady contributions (Glen 157–58). In addition, the group began to develop new policies aimed at the other side of the problem—pet overpopulation. Finally, members continued the practice of adopting out individual animals from the sanctuary to homes they felt would give those animals a good life. All of these courses of action were motivated by the same overall goal that had initially galvanized them to build an animal sanctuary—to save animals from a premature death, one animal at a time (Glen 11). In this section I briefly examine each of these initial attempts at a solution, and the successes (or lack thereof) of each.

Organizing and "tabling," as the group called it, though difficult, did in fact bring in enough money to keep the group going in the short term, and keep it growing in the long term. Because it took in animals from all over the country, the group had already begun to make a name for itself; thus, once the founders began to solicit passersby at supermarkets in cities all over the West, it did not take long for donations arriving by mail to be added to those being dropped in the collection boxes (Glen 168–79). Through a monthly newsletter, they kept their members apprised of happenings at the sanctuary. In this way, the group brought in enough cash to sustain them on a daily basis as well as to support special projects. However, in addition to this traditional method of bringing in money, the founders added a new twist. They felt a connection with all these people—sometimes from clear across the country—who were willing to give up $5, $10, or even $100 for animals. Implicitly the individuals at Best Friends recognized that their effort would require more than just a list of names on a membership directory: they needed a *community* of members who all shared a strong interest in the welfare of their animals and a commitment to their ideal of no-kill shelters. Therefore, in their mailings they did not threaten the reader with the death of innocent animals, as other organizations regularly do. And the group responded to the donations that began to come in so regularly with thank-you letters that were not themselves calls for more money (Glen 169–71). This approach, which brought a tremendously favorable response, enabled the organization to develop deeper ties with its membership. Through tabling, mailing lists, and, eventually, electronic mail and the World Wide Web, the membership of Best Friends has grown to more than 180,000 from countries all over the world (Glen 239–43).

While membership was seen as an extremely important source of ongoing funding, the founders of the sanctuary also realized that unless something was done to stop the rampant breeding of feral animals and loose pets, as well as the operations of kitten and puppy mills, the numbers of homeless pets would continue to grow. Therefore, as they began to take in more and more cats—and especially kittens—they decided on a new policy: no litters would be accepted unless the mother was brought in to be spayed. In addition, the group would not adopt out any animal that had not been or would not be spayed or neutered. The procedure was not cheap, however, and the group had to rely on the kindness of volunteer veterinarians, who frequently halved their normal fees to enable the sanctuary to afford to practice these new policies (Glen 109). Eventually, the costs of such procedures would be covered by a combination of membership donations, fee reductions from the veterinarians, and adoption fees, but by 1992 it had become clear that reliance solely on the sanctuary's veterinary facilities would not bring about sufficient changes in the number of homeless pets to satisfy the group (Glen 192).

The third method the group used to resolve the problem was adoption. In 2002, there were never fewer than 1,800 animals at the sanctuary, but almost 75 percent of the animals that came to the shelter were adopted out to good homes after a period of rehabilitation (Glen 239–43). Yet their earliest approach to adoption involved no more than simply making individuals aware of the animals at the sanctuary and inviting them to come to Angel Canyon as they wished. Many successful adoptions resulted, but as the numbers of animals coming into the sanctuary grew, direct adoptions from Best Friends could not keep pace and strains on the sanctuary's resources increased. Moreover, the group felt a deepening frustration at the number of people who still saw pets as disposable or didn't understand the need to control pet overpopulation.

All in all, these methods were fairly successful, as far as they went. Money began to flow into the sanctuary's accounts, buildings and grounds were improved, and the numbers of adoptions and of spayings and neuterings were up. But in 1987 there were still 17 million animals being put down in shelters across the country, and those statistics—though they were beginning to improve—were discouraging to the people of Best Friends. Then, in 1992, a revelation occurred. In the process of rescuing a litter of kittens—from the Grand Canyon, of all places—a young German couple brought to Best Friends not only several additions to their feline population but also the astonishing news that in Germany, it is *illegal* to kill homeless pets. This piece of information stunned the founders, and crystallized in their minds the problem with their methods: "The concept of simply housing and finding homes for the unwanted wasn't enough. One day there must be no more homeless pets. . . . And that would require a radically different approach" (Glen 192). The *real* problem was the *culture itself*, which allows animals to be treated as if they are as disposable as one's favorite toy. Thus, the initial problematic situation had not been fully understood—a realization that became clear only after they had spent nearly ten years working through their first solutions.

New Approaches and an End-in-View

The third stage of a Deweyan inquiry is the investigation into various ends-in-view. For Dewey, an end-in-view is a hypothesized combination of means and end(s) that represents a possible solution to a problematic situation, or what I have been calling a felt tension. An end-in-view is thus a plan of action formulated by the imagination as the means by which a hypothesized ideal state of affairs will be brought about (*Human Nature* 155).[6] In reflective deliberation, various ends in view should be considered—we should imagine both various courses of action and different ideal end-states (*Human Nature* 132–33). Such deliberations must take into consideration more than the interests of the individual who is reflecting (Dewey and Tufts 257). They must encompass the interests not just of those directly affected by a proposed action but also of those in the community who are concerned about the success of the individual or group considering the action. In this section, I describe the efforts of the Best Friends organization to develop the "radically different approach" that would yield a satisfactory solution.[7]

Once the group decided that the problem was broader than the lives of individual animals, they began to develop strategies that went beyond local rescue, spay and neuter, and adoption programs. To devise a means of ending the phenomenon of homeless pets across the United States they had to think in far more sweeping terms than they had previously, and none of them had done anything on such a large scale before. In addition, such an endeavor would require them to raise far more money than the already considerable amount needed to cover the day-to-day expenses of running the sanctuary. In order to reach their goal, they would need to (1) demonstrate to the country that even the most physically challenged of the animals could live a good life given the right conditions, (2) educate the population on the need for population control and for halting the practices that lead to pet overpopulation, (3) develop an adoption outreach program to significantly raise the number of animals that they could take in and then place in good homes, and (4) massively increase the number of spay and neuter procedures performed. These four objectives eventually became the mainstays of the Best Friends' approach to their ultimate goal of no more homeless pets. Each bears an aspect of Dewey's pragmatism, but even more Deweyan is the pragmatic and democratic approach they took to the entire process of developing programs to further them. Not only was each objective approached experimentally, as they tested various methods, sorted successful methods from failures, and so on, but the goals themselves shifted as some aspects were realized, other aspects were given up as impediments to more important outcomes, and new goals appeared as the process took shape. Although the ultimate goal has never been abandoned—something I will have more to say about in my conclusion—the path they have taken toward that goal has been thoroughly pragmatic.

Because deliberation, the construction of an end-in-view, and a satisfactory resolution to a problematic situation depend on its felt tension being recognized, it is even more important to get the attention of the public for social problems that are as yet unrecognized. One of the first radically new approaches Best Friends undertook was an effort to place some of the special needs cats—those blind, lame, or chronically ill felines who, with care, could still lead relatively normal lives. At first, the group had tried simply to rescue such animals and keep them at the sanctuary; but as their number grew to 100, it became clear that in many cases these cats were just as adoptable as the "normal" ones. The group decided to build a home for these animals and to publicize it. As word began to spread about the lives these cats were living, it wasn't long before requests for adoption started coming in. According to the group, thousands have offered to take special needs cats into their homes (Glen 251–52). Best Friends had demonstrated decisively that contrary to popular wisdom, cats with special needs could live good lives, and in the process they brought the need for doing something about the euthanization of *healthy* animals into sharper focus. In this way, they began to make the public aware of the problem of homeless pets, helping to define the problem for citizens both in Utah and in the United States more generally.

Another aspect of social problem solving for the pragmatist is collective participation in resolving problematic situations. For Dewey, democracy "is primarily a mode of associated living, of conjoint communicated experience" (*Democracy and Education* 80–81). Since all members of the community have an interest in resolving problems, only collective inquiry is likely to lead to outcomes that satisfy everyone.[8] A Deweyan approach to transforming the cultural response to the problem of homeless pets required that Best Friends gather all of the small shelters and rescue organizations who followed the no-kill philosophy into a community coalition that could effect change on a large scale (see "What Do Liberals Want?").[9] To publicize the plight of homeless pets and to galvanize such a coalition, the group also staged Utah's first "Week for the Animals." It was the group's commitment to this event that forced them to tackle head on the problem of getting the smaller animal welfare and rescue groups to come together and work out a successful plan. This week would also spark the beginnings of the idea for the No More Homeless Pets in Utah program (discussed in greater detail in the next section).

A final element in generating the end-in-view was the participation of veterinarians in ensuring that more animals were spayed and neutered. Controlling the population of companion animals required more than just finding homes for those animals already in the community. If the problem of excessive breeding was not addressed, then it would simply remain chronic, as each new generation of intact animals bore another generation of homeless pets. Thus, Best Friends worked continually to increase the reach of its spay and neuter programs, enlisting veterinarians to donate time or to discount services and educating the public on the value of the procedure. Putting all of these elements together, Best Friends had generated an end-in-view: the organization would work to problematize the plight of homeless animals for the population at large, using its newsletter, website, and other means of communication. By publicizing the problem, the group could involve the general public in lowering the number of homeless pets through greater numbers of adoptions, as well as reducing the excessive breeding that was causing the problem. And once the public was educated, the problem could be solved by individuals in their own communities rather than by Best Friends alone.

Working the Ideas Out in Practice:
No More Homeless Pets in Utah

The idea behind the "Week for the Animals" was to focus attention on the plight of homeless pets through a series of events, including adoption fairs, contests, spay and neuter opportunities, and so on (Glen 236). Relying on the media and on cooperation from city and county officials in the Salt Lake City area, the local animal welfare and rescue groups would present the people of Utah with a chance to learn about the problem of homeless pets, to adopt new pets or get their current pets "fixed," and to find out about all of the grassroots organizations that exist in and around the state. In this way, Best Friends could further its goal of problematizing the status of homeless pets for the general population. In addition, the event made it possible to undertake large numbers of adoptions and spay and neuter procedures—an important goal in every year for the sanctuary.

One of the most pragmatic functions of the "Week for the Animals" was more fundamental: it united the animal welfare groups. As an agent of social change, Best Friends was at a disadvantage because of its relative isolation. Although a burgeoning membership from all over the world was contributing to the sanctuary coffers, bringing in more animals as well as generating growing numbers of adoptions, the group was unlikely to change people's behavior toward homeless pets unless members created a common interest with communities around Utah. Conversely, if they could form alliances with groups already operating in those communities, those volunteers and staff would provide Best Friends with a base of support that could help to reach out to the general population *from within*. And that is the idea behind the No More Homeless Pets (NMHP) in Utah program.

In July 2000, Best Friends was given a grant by Maddie's Fund to launch No More Homeless Pets in Utah. Maddie's Fund is a philanthropic organization whose goal "is to help build a no-kill nation where all adoptable . . . and treatable . . . shelter dogs and cats find loving new homes" (Maddie's Fund). Maddie's Fund and Best Friends thus have identical goals, though the former works through funding other organizations and the latter, in effect, works in the trenches. In addition, the two have nearly identical, pragmatic approaches to solving their common problem. Both recognize that external agencies can have only limited success without the full participation of the communities in which they are acting. An editorial on the Maddie's Fund website argues that "it takes a village" to succeed in meeting their goals: when "no-kill organizations, traditional shelters and animal control agencies[,] . . . breed rescue groups and feral cat caregivers, . . . [and] private practice veterinarians" collaborate together, "*community* goals can be established, *community* strategies created and *community* successes achieved and celebrated" (Maddie's Fund). The grant to Best Friends was made with this strategy in mind. So the first pragmatic aspect of the Maddie's Fund–Best Friends alliance is a dedication to community collaboration and inquiry into prospective solutions to the problem of homeless pets.

The second pragmatic aspect of the programs is their experimental, inquiring approach to the creation of ends-in-view. Dewey argued that ends, such as putting a stop to the euthanization of homeless pets, are "those foreseen consequences which influence present deliberation and which finally bring it to rest by furnishing an adequate stimulus to overt action" (*Human Nature* 154). While the goal of the program has not changed, NMHP's focus is not on that end itself. Rather, that goal has been used as a tool of deliberation to enable the NMHP staff and volunteers to develop ends-in-view to help them to deal with specific problematic situations that they encounter.

NMHP operates as a sort of shell organization, conducting fund-raisers, adoption fairs, spay and neuter clinics, and educational programs in the state of Utah. It now has seven elements: adoption programs; events and promotions; animal control, rescue partners, and veterinarians; spay/neuter programs; marketing and public relations; corporate sponsorship; and a volunteer program. Each of these elements has emerged as a response to specific situations, and each functions as a focal point for deliberations regarding specific aspects of the overall plan for attaining the NMHP's goal. Rather than describing each aspect of the program, in what follows I focus on three specific examples of how the NMHP and Best Friends staffs have approached problematic situations as opportunities for intelligent inquiry, understood in a Deweyan fashion.

The first examples of experimental responses to a problematic situation come from NMHP's adoption program. In fact, this program has led to two separate experimental projects designed to increase the number of no-kill adoptions (i.e., adoptions from no-kill rather than traditional shelters). The first is the biannual "Super Adoption," a three-day adoption fair held in the parking lot of a local Petsmart (Schnepel, Castle, and Castle 3, 15). At the Super Adoption, as many rescue organizations and shelters as have animals and can attend bring their animals to a large, enclosed space containing enclosed tents for the cats and large open tents for the dogs. Each partner organization is responsible for bringing the animals and doing all of the paperwork for their adoptions; NMHP is responsible for providing the tents, caring for the animals—giving them water, walking the dogs, and scooping cat litter—and covering all financial aspects of the adoptions. Generally, organizations have their own procedures for doing adoptions, but NMHP felt that standardizing the method and the costs would make the process easier and thus help families to choose the animal that suited them best. In addition, the staff of NMHP has worked on finding the most strategic location and time of year, increasing the scope and efficiency of their marketing and public relations campaigns, training the rescue and shelter partners in advance of the events, and (in a particularly pragmatic move) devising exit surveys in order to gain feedback on how the event was perceived by the public. Finally, the staff has tried and rejected a number of procedures that failed or did not go as planned (Schnepel, Castle, and Castle 16–18). The first Super Adoption attracted more than 9,000 visitors and resulted in 397 adoptions; as a result of continual changes and better publicity, the fourth Super Adoption (in May 2002) saw more than 13,000 visitors and more than 500 adoptions (3).

NMHP's second innovative adoption program is Furburbia, a permanent pet adoption center in a donated space in one of Salt Lake City's malls. Best Friends' goal of no more homeless pets includes the elimination of puppy mills, and mall pet stores are a large source of the demand that makes those factory farms for pets profitable. Thus, Furburbia was created to compete with the area mall pet stores and to further multiple goals: to increase adoptions, reduce the consumer base for puppy mills, and so on. Soon after the store opened, the staff decided to expand its operation from four to seven days a week. In the end, the change resulted in a 40 percent increase in the number of adoptions, but the immediate result was a drop in the number of animals on hand at any given time. Initially, partner shelters rotated in and out, to give each an opportunity to place more animals and increase its name recognition. However, the need to keep the store at full capacity led the staff at Furburbia and NMHP to choose an anchor group—a shelter large enough to provide staff and a sufficient supply of animals. In the process of eliminating the kinks in the procedures, NMHP has worked on making the store a better neighbor in the mall (keeping noise and odors down, moving animals in and out through the back instead of the front, etc.), involving the mall management in decisions, and creating and following a cleaning protocol in order to maximize animal and human safety and welfare. Furthermore, the staff has been willing to shelve problematic procedures in the interests of maximizing the benefits of the store for NMHP's goal (Schnepel, Castle, and Castle 5–7). By July 2002 Furburbia was overseeing nearly 35 adoptions a week, making it even more successful than the Super Adoptions project.

Finally, NMHP has created partnerships with animal control, rescue partners, and veterinarians. In Utah, there are no fewer than fifty-six animal control agencies, each with its own staff, policies and procedures, and jurisdiction; all have begun to cooperate with NMHP. In addition, so far NMHP has recruited twenty-two area rescue partners who participate in the program. Finally, NMHP works with veterinarians around the state to increase the number of spay and neuter procedures (Schnepel, Castle, and Castle 19–28). The emphasis in each of these partnerships is on collaboration—and as Kate Schnepel, Julie Castle, and Gregory Castle point out (27), that is one of the guiding principles of Maddie's Fund (see also Maddie's Fund). But again, the NMHP strategy has been experimental as well as collaborative, as evidenced by biannual "Idea Exchange" meetings, which are designed "to build the skills of our participating rescue partners and shelters" as "participants are actively engaged in the learning process" (Schnepel, Castle, and Castle 24).

Relations with each partner group—animal control agencies, partner rescue groups, and veterinarians—has forced the staff at NMHP to try out various methods or approaches to interactions, and to continually assess and reassess the success or failure of those interactions in light of their ultimate goal. For example, in working with animal control officers, many of whom are overwhelmed with animals, underfunded, and often burned out, skeptical, and less than willing to change, members of NMHP have had to give up the assumption that all individuals and agencies are as interested in the goals of the program as they are. But they found that adding a staff member whose sole responsibility is to foster better relationships with animal control—going on ride-alongs with animal control officers, offering nonmonetary assistance, and designing events or inviting animal control to events—has had beneficial results, allowing for more, deeper, and richer collaborations with animal control agencies (Schnepel, Castle, and Castle 19).

Working with rescue partners entails less friction caused by burnout or skepticism, but it too has involved some trial and error. For example, NMHP has had to act as negotiator among these groups, preventing them from antagonizing one another, encouraging networking between rescue groups and animal shelters, winning agreements on standardized procedures, and so on. However, the groups themselves are seeing benefits from the experiment with collaborating with NMHP. Increased adoptions, increased name recognition, and advertising are some of the more obvious advantages, but even more important, perhaps, are the "camaraderie, networking ideas, and strength in numbers" gained by aligning themselves with a broader coalition (Schnepel, Castle, and Castle 21).

Though collaborating with veterinarians has been perhaps the bumpiest road for NMHP staff, they have still managed to exhibit the spirit of experimental intelligence. When it became apparent that winning over the president of the Utah Veterinary Medical Association (UVMA) was not enough to foster good relations with local practitioners, they formed a liaison committee in order to communicate better with veterinarians. When NMHP began its mobile spay and neuter clinic—a large mobile home called "The Big Fix"—local vets expressed resentment that it was taking business away from their practices. In response, NMHP simply involved those local vets' practices in the spay and neuter promotions, subsidizing their procedures with voucher coupons and sending them business (Schnepel, Castle, and Castle 28). Over the first two years of NMHP's existence, the Big Fix performed more than 8,600 surgeries, and in addition almost 21,000 NMHP spay/neuter vouchers were used (2).

The above examples demonstrate quite clearly that the staff of Best Friends and NMHP have an experimental, pragmatic attitude toward their endeavors— an attitude that they themselves express explicitly in their second-year progress report: "While we recognize that [the] results are remarkable, we nevertheless find ourselves questioning and re-questioning our progress: Are we doing enough? Are we doing it right? Are we doing it as efficiently as possible?" (Schnepel, Castle, and Castle 2). The results of their experimental attitude truly are extraordinary: as of April 2003, the number of animals euthanized in shelters every day in Utah is nineteen, down more than 50 percent from forty-five in 1999. The number of adoptions in the state has risen more than 30 percent, and the number of no-kill adoptions has nearly doubled. Nearly 30,000 spay and neuter procedures have been performed in connection with NMHP (NMHP).

The Pragmatism of Best Friends and NMHP

The final stage of inquiry, according to Dewey, is the evaluation of the end-in-view as a means to solve a problematic situation. As the euthanasia of healthy pets is still taking place, Best Friends and NMHP are technically still in the process of working toward their ultimate goal of its elimination, and are not yet in a position to fully evaluate their ends-in-view. I therefore use this concluding section to bring together the pragmatic themes involved in the Best Friends project as it has been realized so far. Those themes can be placed under two general headings: democratic community and experimental inquiry.

Dewey has been referred to as "America's philosopher of democracy," a title that, however overused, is nevertheless apt.[10] For Dewey argued repeatedly that democracy as he understood it is the *ideal* of associated living. His theories of human nature, reflective thought, and community all point to democracy as the best way to organize a community. And his work on ethics and education makes it clear that ideal human development can take place only *in* such a community. Thus any argument that some organization or institution is "Deweyan" must show how that organization or institution is democratic, as Dewey understood that term. In particular, Dewey saw democracy not as a set of political institutions—universal suffrage, for example—but as an ideal of associated living governed by certain criteria. In *Democracy and Education,* he asks, "How numerous and varied are the interests which are consciously shared? How full and free is the interplay with other forms of association?" (76–77). By these standards, Best Friends is clearly democratic, for its members have demonstrated throughout its existence that they are willing to take on the interests of any other group with which they associate *as their own,* and adjust their ends-in-view to accommodate those interests. Furthermore, they are committed to associating with a broad range of groups and institutions whose interests they share. Finally, they make extraordinary efforts to ensure full and free communication between themselves and their associates and partners, not just conveying their intent or interests to that audience, but also soliciting from others *their* ideas, needs, and interests.

This is not to say that Best Friends is the perfect Deweyan institution. Its unwavering focus on the goal of ending the phenomenon of homeless pets, with its accompanying insistence on working solely at the level of grassroots activism and education, has been un-Deweyan in two senses. First, it has kept the members of Best Friends from exploring other avenues—for example, political alliances and legislative solutions. Second, their fixed adherence to the ultimate goal may ultimately prove too idealistic and, as Dewey would have predicted, shortsighted. As I noted, for Dewey an end-in-view is simply a means-ends hypothesis for resolving a current problematic situation. Enactment of that end-in-view will lead to a new situation, in which new problems will invariably arise. For example, if the goal of zero euthanizations is reached, then the question of how to maintain that status will arise. That Best Friends and NMHP appear not to have considered this eventuality shows a certain lack of foresight in their deliberations. Furthermore, their adherence to this goal is, as Gregory Castle told me, based in part on a "somewhat deontological" value—the value of the lives of healthy adoptable animals. If they choose to continue to ignore these un-Deweyan aspects of their pursuit, they may create new problems. First, they may leave themselves without resources to deal with the problem of maintaining the zero level of euthanizations of healthy pets once it has been reached. And second, if they allow the deontological value to come to the fore, they may begin to harm their excellent relations with other groups. To date, however, they have clearly and steadfastly committed themselves to the ideals of collective, democratic community rather than to unilateralism or dogmatism.

The foundation for Dewey's commitment to democracy is his commitment to intelligent inquiry, for democracy as an ideal of associated living is arguably simply the extension of his theory of intelligent inquiry from individuals or small groups to the level of whole communities.[11] As the account above demonstrates, Best Friends' approach to the problem of homeless pets and euthanasia has been especially Deweyan. From their recognition of a problematic situation, to their realization that the problem is far greater than the "one animal at a time" focus they initially took on, through the experiments with the Big Fix, Furburbia, Super Adoptions, and the like, the members of Best Friends have deliberated; considering the relations among their competing interests; kept an even temperament throughout their interactions with varied, often fractious animal control and rescue partners; and pursued their goals in Deweyan fashion: with an open mind, a whole heart, and a deep sense of responsibility ("How We Think" 136–39). Where they don't live up to those ideals is, as I have noted, in not considering "what happens after."[12]

If Best Friends and No More Homeless Pets are truly Deweyan, then I am finally in a position to conclude that Francione has overstated his case in claiming that new "welfarist" approaches to the problem of the treatment and conditions of animals in this country have simply failed to have any significant effect (113). We can clearly see that this is simply not true of domestic pets, a case that Francione overlooks. As I mentioned in the introduction, the number of states with laws prohibiting cruelty to animals, animal fighting, and so on is climbing, with legislatures increasingly taking these issues to heart; and where legislatures are unconcerned, activist citizen groups are mobilizing to put initiatives on the ballot. However, that point is ancillary to my main argument, which is rather that Best Friends, by eschewing the usual protests, demonstrations, and attempts to influence policy by ballot or legislation, took a much more pragmatic approach, working in collaboration with local communities; with city, county, and statewide agencies; and with hordes of volunteers from within those communities.[13] This approach has more than halved the number of euthanizations in shelters across the state of Utah; and the no-kill philosophy, embraced by shelters and rescue organizations across the country, has resulted in a 75 percent reduction in euthanasia nationwide (HSUS; Irwin 1). I therefore conclude that while Francione may be correct in arguing that legislative approaches to the problem of animal welfare may not be moving very fast, he is wrong about the ability of welfarist approaches to make significant gains. What has to happen is that those approaches need to be followed in a Deweyan, pragmatic fashion—in other words, democratically and intelligently.

Notes

1. See, e.g., *Human Nature and Conduct,* part III, "The Place of Intelligence in Conduct" (121–89), and "Why Reflective Thinking Must Be an Educational Aim" (*Later Works [LW]* 8:125–39), to name just two such arguments by Dewey.

2. The term *vivisection,* for example, comes up exactly twice in Jo Ann Boydston's thirty-seven-volume critical edition of Dewey. For what he did say, see, e.g., "The Ethics of Animal Experimentation" (*LW* 2:98–103), where he claims that animals may be experimented on if there is a "real" human need and if the experiment does not cause "wanton and needless suffering" (103). Or see "The Unity of the Human Being" (*LW*

13:323–37), where he claims that the difference between a physical pain such as the one "suffered by a dog undergoing an act of vivisection" is *different from* "distinctively human pain—a pain that is what it is because the processes of the human organism have been profoundly affected by relations with another human being" (333).

3. At the time, it was also possible for healthy animals to be seized for animal research. However, by 2000 only three states still mandated that unclaimed animals be given up for research, a practice called "pound seizure"; fourteen states had banned it outright.

4. Throughout this essay, I am offering an *interpretation* of the Best Friends' approach to the issue of homeless pets. While I have spoken with Gregory Castle, one of the organization's founders, and he largely agrees with my interpretation, I in no way mean to speak for the group as a whole. My understanding of Best Friends relies on public sources: Samantha Glen's book *Best Friends;* the Best Friends website (Best Friends); and the second-year report on No More Homeless Pets in Utah (Schnepel, Castle, and Castle).

5. "Principles are methods of inquiry. . . . But the experimental character of moral judgments does not mean complete uncertainty and fluidity. . . . [They] exist as hypotheses with which to experiment" (Dewey, *Human Nature* 164–65).

6. Such "ideal states of affairs" are, for Dewey, not end points but rather temporary resolutions, for they will inevitably lead to other difficulties. Dewey describes the enactment of an end-in-view as a "consummatory experience," an evaluatively neutral phrase—consummatory experiences can be good or bad, depending on the quality of the deliberations and the presence or absence of unforeseen interference from environmental factors. In this essay I call a resolution "satisfactory" when a consummatory experience does in fact harmonize the interests at stake in a problematic situation and is evaluated positively by all concerned; it does *not* indicate a complete and final solution.

7. While No More Homeless Pets in Utah has the stated goal of eliminating the euthanization of healthy adoptable pets in Utah by 2005, it is by no means clear that they have thought about what will happen when they reach that goal. I will discuss this point further in my conclusion.

8. For a full exposition of this aspect of Dewey's work, see, e.g., Campbell, *Community Reconstructs,* esp. chaps. 4 and 6, and "Democracy as Cooperative Inquiry." See also Eldridge, chaps. 2–4.

9. The essay of Dewey cited actually discusses the organization of the liberal party in the late 1920s. However, I believe that Dewey understood these remarks to apply not to political parties alone but generally to making changes in a large-scale democracy. See Campbell, "Democracy as Cooperative Inquiry" 18.

10. Two of the recent spate of biographies of Dewey have the word "democracy" in their titles, and a third work, more political philosophy than biography, uses the exact phrase "America's philosopher of democracy." See Westbrook, *John Dewey and American Democracy;* Rockefeller, *John Dewey: Religious Faith and Democratic Humanism;* and Fott, *John Dewey: America's Philosopher of Democracy.*

11. See, e.g., "The Existential Matrix of Inquiry: Cultural," chap. 3 of *Logic* (48–65), and "The Democratic Conception in Education," chap. 7 of *Democracy and Education* (81–99). The former places inquiry into a cultural context, and the latter makes democracy the ideal cultural context for inquiry.

12. I make this claim cautiously, for the Best Friends educational programs are, in part, an effort to make NMHP obsolete. After the euthanization of healthy adoptable

animals is eliminated the educational programs would continue, helping people to avoid re-creating the homeless pet problem. So NMHP may have a rebuttal to this criticism after all.

13. It is worth noting that by changing public opinion through their educational projects, Best Friends and NMHP may be setting the stage for legislative change as well. At an NMHP event in May 2003, a petition was circulated to reclassify the crimes covered by the state animal cruelty laws from misdemeanors to felonies. The petition was sponsored, in part, by Best Friends.

Bibliography

Armstrong, Martha C., Susan Tomasello, and Christyna Hunter. "From Pets to Companion Animals." In Salem and Rowan 71–85.

Ascione, Frank R., and Randall Lockwood. "Cruelty to Animals: Changing Psychological and Legislative Perspectives." In Salem and Rowan 39–55.

Best Friends. Best Friends home page. http://www.bestfriends.org (accessed August 2003).

Campbell, James. *The Community Reconstructs: The Meaning of Pragmatic Social Thought.* Urbana: University of Illinois Press, 1992.

——. "Democracy as Cooperative Inquiry." In *Philosophy and the Reconstruction of Culture: Pragmatic Essays after Dewey,* edited by John J. Stuhr, 17–36. Albany: State University of New York Press, 1993.

Dewey, John. *Democracy and Education. The Middle Works,* vol. 9, *1916.*

——. "Does Reality Possess Practical Character?" In *The Middle Works,* vol. 4, *1907–1909,* 125–42.

——. "How We Think." In *The Later Works,* vol. 8, *1933,* 105–352.

——. *Human Nature and Conduct. The Middle Works,* vol. 14, *1922.*

——. "Intelligence and Morals." In *The Middle Works,* vol. 4, *1907–1909,* 31–49.

——. *The Later Works, 1925–1953.* Edited by Jo Ann Boydston. 17 vols. Carbondale: Southern Illinois University Press, 1981–90.

——. *Logic: The Theory of Inquiry. The Later Works,* vol. 12, *1938.*

——. *The Middle Works, 1899–1924.* Edited by Jo Ann Boydston. 15 vols. Carbondale: Southern Illinois University Press, 1976–83.

——. "What Do Liberals Want?" In *The Later Works,* vol. 5, *1929–1930,* 346–48.

Dewey, John, and James Hayden Tufts. *Ethics. The Later Works,* vol. 7, *1932.*

Eldridge, Michael. *Transforming Experience: John Dewey's Cultural Instrumentalism.* Nashville, Tenn.: Vanderbilt University Press, 1998.

Finsen, Lawrence, and Susan Finsen. *The Animal Rights Movement in America: From Compassion to Respect.* New York: Twayne, 1994.

Fott, David. *John Dewey: America's Philosopher of Democracy.* Lanham, Md.: Rowman and Littlefield, 1998.

Francione, Gary L. *Rain without Thunder: The Ideology of the Animal Rights Movement.* Philadelphia: Temple University Press, 1996.

Glen, Samantha. *Best Friends: The True Story of the World's Most Beloved Animal Sanctuary.* New York: Kensington Books, 2001.

Humane Society of the United States. "HSUS Pet Overpopulation Estimates." http://www.hsus.org/ace/11830 (accessed August 2003).

Irwin, Paul G. "Overview." In Salem and Rowan 1–19.

Maddie's Fund. "Maddie's Funding Strategy for a No-Kill Nation." http://www.maddiesfund.org/aboutus/about_pdfs/fund_strat.pdf (accessed August 2003).

No More Homeless Pets in Utah. Home page. http://utahpets.org (accessed April 2003).

Rockefeller, Steven C. *John Dewey: Religious Faith and Democratic Humanism.* New York: Columbia University Press, 1991.

Rowan, Andrew N., and Franklin M. Loew. "Animal Research: A Review of Developments." In Salem and Rowan 111–20.

Salem, Deborah J., and Andrew N. Rowan, eds. *The State of the Animals, 2001.* Washington, D.C.: Humane Society Press, 2001.

Schnepel, Kate, Julie Castle, and Gregory Castle. "What Worked, What Didn't, What's Next: A Review of Year Two of the No More Homeless Pets in Utah Campaign." http://www.maddies.org/projects/project_pdfs/what_worked_y2.pdf (accessed August 2003).

Singer, Peter. *Animal Liberation.* Rev. ed. New York: Avon Books, 1990.

Unti, Bernard, and Andrew N. Rowan. "A Social History of Postwar Animal Protection." In Salem and Rowan 21–38.

Westbrook, Robert B. *John Dewey and American Democracy.* Ithaca, N.Y.: Cornell University Press, 1991.

12 Dining on Fido: Death, Identity, and the Aesthetic Dilemma of Eating Animals

Glenn Kuehn

My goal in this chapter is to present an old dilemma in a new context. While concerns about eating animals are not new by any means, the traditional concerns are overwhelmingly ethical in nature. I have very few strictly ethical concerns about eating animals, but I do have strong aesthetic concerns. Two of the categories in which they lie are identity and death. Identity in art is also nothing new. From the cave of Lascaux to Plato and Aristotle to contemporary mimetic arts, accuracy in resemblance is integral to many art genres. Likewise, death is a topic richly treated through a long history of still-life artistic representations.[1] However, when we get to the topic of aesthetic pleasure and combine it with the daily question of eating, these two traditional aesthetically important issues make it hard for us to simply sit down and eat without discomfort. We do not appreciate identifying with what we eat and we do not want to think about death when we eat it.

Dining on Fido is unimaginable for many people. However, this "horrifying" act is most commonly placed solely in an ethical context. That is, it is wrong, morally wrong, to eat a dog or cat or anything that can be seen as a pet. I do not deny that the ethical concerns are relevant, but I intend to show that the ethical is here driven by the aesthetic. Clearly, in the work of John Dewey, ethical and aesthetic issues are not strictly separable; and by examining the topic of eating I show that it is primarily our aesthetic and artistic impulses that keep us from putting Fido on a rotisserie—that is, such an act is distasteful before it is immoral.

The Glory of the Supermarket

The glory of going to Kroger, Schnucks, Winn-Dixie, the Wal-Mart Superstore, Whole Foods, or any other grocer to buy our food is that it is all laid out for us in a very organized, consistent, and (despite its deliberate organization) disengaged manner. We pick out our foods at the supermarket as we pick out virtually any other consumer item, and we're even given opportunities to taste them as samples, trying them on to see if they suit us.

There is an interesting irony, however, in the manner in which food items are presented to us, and this manner is an aesthetic relationship to our potential diet. Vegetables are supposed to look like what they are when we buy them. Bell peppers, though varying in color (green, red, orange, yellow, or purple), should look like a bell pepper—shiny, roundish, not wrinkly. Potatoes need to look like potatoes; kiwis need to look like kiwis; avocados should be dark green (like an emerald); cantaloupes should be round and possess a surface that looks as if an artist has carved a million tiny grooves in it—and like a snowflake no two are alike—and it should smell like the musty earth which gave it life. We hold it in our hands, tap it to hear the dense resonance, and say, "This is a good canta-loupe."

We do not do this with the items in those areas of the grocery store where animal flesh is procured. We go to the butcher's section and pick up "ground chuck," which is wrapped in a 5-pound log and has a "Kroger" label on it. There is nothing to suggest that this was once a cow. We do the same with lamb, veal, and pork. We go to the butcher's section and choose a pack of chicken pieces, but their presentation (and the fact that the parts perhaps came from eight dif-ferent chickens) suggests no connection to an actual chicken (there is no head; it has no feathers or feet; the smell has been removed); its identity as an assem-blage of poultry parts is lost in the presentation, and we easily put it in our cart. Nearby we also see a display of seafood—salmon, mackerel, catfish, and the shrimp that have been deveined, deheaded, and often presteamed—"cleaned" and laid out as food for the taking. Unlike the vegetables, the meats are pre-sented in a manner that is as far removed from their original states as possible: the meat does not look like what it was when it was living.

There is another option in the seafood section: the 1½-pound lobsters in that square tank that just sit there and move their antennae. We look at them, smile, and tap the glass. Some of us think they're cute, and others feel pity at such a tragic life, spent in a small tank waiting to die in someone's kitchen when they could be happily swimming along the northern Atlantic coast. We leave them there. We leave them there because they are alive and kinda cute.

The lobsters are alive; they are presented as what they are and as baldly as an onion or cucumber, as though they are supposed to say, "Here I am. . . . Eat me." But so many of us can't do it. How can we eat such a lovely creature? They are so cute and identifiable as living beings that we want to take the rubber bands off their claws and set them free. How can we enjoy an oyster on the half shell when we know that in order for it to be good and tasty (and not deadly) it must be alive when it slides down our throats? It's an interesting demonstration of the distance that has evolved in our eating that people used to go to the butcher's and see the animals hanging from hooks and ask for a particular portion to be cut off. Of course, this practice is still common in many countries, but not in the United States.

We detach ourselves from two things: we dismantle the connection between our identity with the food as something that is (or was) living much as we live, and we avoid the idea that in order to continue living we feast on the dead and dying. At the heart of ethical concerns regarding the carnivores, omnivores, and herbivores among us is an underlying aesthetic concern regarding the ways in which we identify with the animals we eat or don't eat.

An argument for aesthetics getting in the way of eating animals is necessarily intertwined with our traditional understanding and manner of approaching art as such. First, in terms of art and aesthetic experience, understanding food as art is greatly hampered by the traditional methods of experiencing "art": that is, historically we have a limited range of ways to access and experience art, and they are not naturally suited to our experience of food. Specifically, we were not taught to take art, put it in our mouths, and swallow it. Further, the commonality and functionality of food have also precluded consideration of it as art.

But our sensations are our connectors to the world, and our ability to sense our environments enables the experiential continuum to exist. Engaging in the act of tasting enacts an experience of our environment in several key ways: taste is the most physically interactive of the senses. Tasting reinforces the contextual nature of our experiences; tasting affords no distance between self and other, and that ontological continuum between the self and its environment reveals an identification with the things that are eaten. This enhances the unnerving connection between food and death, which works on two levels: bodily and symbolic. With very few exceptions, virtually everything we eat was at some point alive, and we therefore nourish our corporeality by feeding off the dead and dying bodies in our environment. Symbolically, as we live off the dead and dying, we are reminded that we also are perishing and will some day become food for something else.

This is a connection and continuity that has been created and accepted. Overcoming disconnection is part of Dewey's charge to the person who would take on the challenge of writing about art.

> This task is to restore continuity between the refined and intensified forms of experience that are works of art and the everyday events, doings, and sufferings that are universally recognized to constitute experience. Mountain peaks do not float unsupported; they do not even just rest upon the earth. They *are* the earth in one of its manifest operations. It is the business of those who are concerned with the theory of the earth, geographers and geologists, to make this fact evident in its various implications. The theorist who would deal philosophically with fine art has a like task to accomplish. (*Art as Experience* 9–10)

We Do Not Put Art in Our Mouths: Art Is Unique and Separate

As Westerners, we were never taught to take "art," put it in our mouths, and swallow it. The distance we have from art is a reinforcement of the separation of the self from its environment. Art has traditionally been something special, out of the ordinary; and, as an object, it is kept in a place where we cannot come into direct, physical contact with it. Art exists at a distance; it hangs on a wall or sits on an end table or is up on a stage or is framed inside glass. Art is outside of the precariousness of our changing environments and therefore cannot be experienced in a way that involves physical interaction and transformation.

The separation of the self from the environment is manifest in the separation of art from everyday life. As Richard Shusterman declares, this "historical separation of art from life has issued in the impoverishing evisceration of aesthetic experience by repudiating its connection to bodily energies and appetites, by defining its delight in contrast to the sensual pleasures of living" (*Pragmatist Aesthetics* 52). Shusterman has done much to promote the importance of popular art and to show how day-to-day pleasures are erroneously debased to promote the exaltation of contemplating fine art. He argues that disparaging the day-to-day pleasures we undergo and viewing popular art as trivial are connected to a disparagement of the body and its desires. The pleasures of day-to-day living may be entertaining (and tasty), but they are not *art* precisely because they are common, unrefined, and involve the physical. Overcoming this view requires seeing importance in the ordinary and everyday.

Over and over we eat, and the frequency of this act has dissuaded investigations of its deeper meanings. If we conservatively estimate the number of times we will eat in a lifetime, the severe ordinariness of eating becomes more apparent. Assume an average of two meals a day (ignore the first ten years, during which our ability to choose what we ate was highly restricted, as well as between-meal snacks) and a life span of 85 years: our 75 years of volitional gustatory experiences would yield roughly 54,750 acts of voluntary eating.[2] This is a staggering number to consider. For an artist to create 54,750 paintings, she would have to be superhuman. If a person visited an art museum (or a variety of art museums) 54,750 times, we would call him an obsessive-compulsive. To go to 54,750 plays, concerts, operas, or poetry readings is unimaginable (and probably impossible for both physical and financial reasons). Yet engaging in 54,750 acts of eating elicits no special label or judgment—it simply happens, largely without serious attention or flourish. The evanescent nature of food and eating in part explains why it has not been given serious consideration in the history of Western philosophy.

This level of common repetition inherent in the act of eating makes the project of claiming that food is of any special significance seem futile precisely because it is not special. Food is not unique or out of the ordinary. Just as Dewey charged us to see that fine art derives its nature from the day-to-day experiences of our lives and that the "specialness" of fine art is due not to its greatness but to its simply coming to be understood as "classical," so seeing food as art requires overcoming an emphasis on the idea that art must be classical and special and out of the ordinary.

The apparent futility is compounded when we compare food and art in terms of necessity. While we need food to live, there simply is no essential, life-threatening reason to experience art. That is, our common detachment from art, our ability to seclude and segregate it from everyday life, allows us to accept its existence as tangential to our own; by and large we can take it or leave it. We can deny ourselves food, but not for very long without causing serious damage to our bodies; and if the denial lasts long enough, we will die. Shusterman points out an interesting paradox in this realization: "More dangerously, the fetishism of disinterested neutrality obscures the fact that philosophy's ultimate aim is to benefit human life, rather than serving pure truth for its own sake. Since art is a crucial instance and cherished resource of human flourishing, philosophy betrays its mission if it merely looks on with abandoning neutrality at art's evolving history without joining the struggle to improve its future" (*Pragmatist Aesthetics* 45). If, as Shusterman states, the goal of philosophy is to improve life, and if art in fact forms an essential part of the quality of our lives, then it is perplexing that we collectively see art as separate from our day-to-day lives. We do not need art to survive, yet the quality of our survival is dependent on aesthetic experiences. Thus we need to resituate art in the everyday and see the "fine" arts not as separate but as a refined edge of a range of aesthetic experience, with meaning found over the entire range.

Again, this resituation was Dewey's overall project in *Art as Experience*. When we see art only as a luxury, something to be engaged in during leisure time, then it is separate from the potential meanings in our daily life. When we see art only as a luxury, then something we engage in 54,000 times cannot be more than routine and even the best meals are still just meals; even the finest dining experiences become submerged in that stream of eating. Food is functional, and this characteristic has also disqualified it from the company of fine arts. Because food is to be eaten, because it fuels the body, even a meal prepared for the delectation of an expert, with wines so complex they can be described only with the help of a vintner's thesaurus, cannot escape the practical, functional dimension of continuing our existence (Korsmeyer 108).

This situation can be addressed by continuing to show that the project of distinguishing art from non-art is flawed from the start because it presumes that art is a thing and not an experience. If art is a thing, then it can be demarcated and judged collectively: its existence is necessarily separate from my existence, and that distance makes possible my personal reflection on and contemplation of the art. However, if we continue to promote the view that the real art lies within a transformative aesthetic experience, then the distance between the art and the self falls away.

The idea that art is really located within aesthetic experience leads us to a new presumption: all five senses have equal involvement in art. When art is an object or event at a distance, then sight and hearing are the senses valued in experiencing it. But when art exists within an environmental interaction, then smell, touch, and taste become just as important in the reception of aesthetic qualities. Thus the senses that allow us the greatest distance from what is being perceived (sight and hearing) have been overshadowing the senses that require greater levels of physical involvement. Identifying this hierarchy of the senses is essential to understanding the project of rejecting art as a thing and embracing art as aesthetic experience. This restructuring will reveal that our sense of taste is the most essential of our five senses for bringing us to the conclusion that food is art.

The Problem of Taste and the Hierarchy of the Senses

Since we were never taught to put art into our mouths, it is difficult to understand how the sense of taste can lead to an understanding of food as art. Art has traditionally been experienced through the eyes and ears, and our level of interaction with it is a very distanced pondering. Carolyn Korsmeyer shows that when art is understood primarily through acts of contemplation and reflection, we can label food "art" on some level; but since contemplation and reflection are associated with the senses of sight and hearing, this method will ignore the artistic qualities inherent in eating. She explains, "the concept of art, dominated as it is today by the idea of *fine* art, is a poor category to capture the nature of foods and their consumption. While one earns a bit of stature for food by advancing it as an art form, the endeavor is apt to divert attention from the interesting ways in which the aesthetic importance of foods diverges from parallel values in art" (Korsmeyer 141). Because interaction with the physical aspects of our existence has traditionally been seen as less important, as distracting, and as detrimental to our contemplative abilities, it has been marginalized. Tasting, an act that necessarily requires us to take a bit of the physical world and put it into our bodies, has not been seen as worthy of artistic contemplation precisely because of its physicality. "Exercise of gustatory taste does not qualify as a 'judgment of Taste' partly because eating is quite evidently a practical activity bound up with intimate interests. . . . Gustatory pleasures were habitually conceived as clearly bodily and animal and thus were not taken seriously as candidates for higher aesthetic pleasure" (50).

The language we use when discussing art, and when discussing our experience of tasting, reveals a difference among the senses. Comments about art are contemplative and reflective, and rely on a distance from the art object or event. Comments about eating demonstrate subjectivity and physical interaction. For example, we do not talk about something tasting beautiful or gorgeous. Nor do we refer to paintings and sculpture as delicious or yucky. Beauty is usually a contemplative, reflective judgment. Deliciousness is usually an immediate, visceral, tactile judgment.

Someone might here object that the type of aesthetic experience is being confused: the vocabulary surrounding eating simply is inappropriate for judging paintings. Of course a Picasso is not literally delicious. Of course a cheesecake does not literally taste gorgeous. The differences revealed through the senses are in the degree to which those senses involve us in the experience. One thinks about a sculpture or painting, and one muses over a sonata. The sensations of sight and hearing are intellectual and speculative. Tasting, on the other hand, is physically interactive. To taste we must become physically involved with the object. So involved are we with the object of taste that we must destroy the object as we experience it.

Korsmeyer notes that while much of her work in *Making Sense of Taste* is devoted to defending the theoretical significance of food, nevertheless the "discontinuities between meals and art should not be gainsaid" (141). While she wishes to preserve important similarities between food and art, it is in the experience of each that the dissimilarities are most apparent; and it is in the dissimilarities that a hierarchy of the five senses is revealed.

This hierarchy is based on how we experience through each given sense, and what the sense affords us. The assumption underlying the hierarchy is that the senses that operate at a greater distance (sight and hearing) are more refined, objective, and reliable, in accordance with the Western tradition of valuing a separation of mind/body, self/other, theory/practice, and so on. The senses that rely on greater levels of physical interaction (smell, touch, and taste) are vague, subjective, and unreliable, and engaging in them breaks down the traditional dichotomies. The hierarchy, ordered from greatest value to least, is sight, hearing, smell, touch, and taste; it prevents us from simply claiming that all the senses are philosophically equal and therefore taste is no better or worse than sight. As Korsmeyer observes,

> One cannot simply add taste and the other bodily senses to philosophy as it has evolved and correct theories accordingly to be more comprehensive in their treatment of sensory worlds. [Hans] Jonas's reasons for why sight is the noble sense make this clear: philosophy is (or at least used to be) built upon attention to the eternal over the temporal, to the universal over the particular, to theory over practice. Taste is a sense that is not suited to advance the first term of any of these pairs. (36)

The traditional views regarding the priority of the senses are strong and cannot be dismissed as no longer relevant. The project, therefore, must be one of identifying and explaining the senses and their philosophical implications.

The more physical senses force us to connect more directly with the world and remind us of our embodiment. They also hinder our ability to think clearly and reasonably, for the pursuit of their pleasures can lead to self-indulgence, gluttony, laziness, incapacitation, and overall moral degeneration. For example, it is unwise to shop for groceries when one is very hungry because the physical hunger is misinterpreted as a need for a great amount and variety of food, making it too easy to buy far more food than one needs or can reasonably afford. Moreover, overindulgence in eating inhibits one's ability to think clearly because an engorged stomach sets in motion many physical processes to which the body must attend, thereby detracting from our intellectual energy and ability. Thus both hunger and eating are disruptive.

In exploring the more physical senses we find varying degrees of interaction with the environment. Smell is a rather murky sense and is the most distanced of the more predominantly physical senses. It involves us in the world because we must inhale some part of it into our nasal passages, and in that strange and dark area we get a sense of our environment's atmosphere. Yet the precise things that we are smelling (the particles in our nasal passages) are typically invisible, and the source of the smell is normally at a distance. Often we have to make an effort to get close to that which we are smelling. We bring the flower to our nose, or waft the steam from the soup toward our faces, or (as I did in grade school) glide the freshly duplicated piece of paper across our faces to experience the sweet methanol smell of the purplish ink. Yet even in the effort of bringing the smell closer, we still operate at a distance because the source of the odor is almost always kept separate from the self.

More intimate than smell is touch. While that which we smell is largely invisible and has no real texture or shape, we cannot experience touch without a direct physical encounter. Through touch we go out to meet the world and learn what it and the others in it feel like. The sense of touch is also essential in many aspects of food experiences—we knead bread dough and through the texture know when it is ready to be set to rise; we squeeze, ever so slightly, the tomato, peach, and plum to see if they are ripe; we feel the texture in chewing the chicken and sense if it is tough or tender. Touch is a connecting sense, and through it we shake hands, hug, engage in intercourse, hit, and caress. Through touch we physically engage our environment; yet as physically involved as it is, that which we touch remains primarily separate from us.

Taste is the most physically intimate of the five senses. Taste cannot be experienced without our taking a bit of the world and putting it into our body. Like the sense of touch, taste involves a direct physical contact with an object; and like the sense of smell, taste involves something entering the body. But unlike the operations of those senses, in tasting we incorporate objects into the body. The objects we taste are assimilated, processed, and transformed through the body. Further, while the senses of sight, hearing, smell, and touch can act individually, tasting relies on the combination of the other two physical senses (touch and smell) for it to operate fully. On its own, taste yields only salty, sweet, bitter, and sour; but when it is united with smell and touch, we get an almost infinite array of flavor and texture combinations. Thus, taste not only is the most physically interactive of the senses, it also relies on the other physical senses. Taste grounds us in the physical and the interactive.

To taste is to take in, and *sapere* (the Latin infinitive meaning "to taste") forms the etymological root of *sapiens*. So *Homo sapiens,* our vaunted, likable self-label, means "man the taster" before it means "man the wise." Humans are beings with taste, and taste not only grounds us in our environment, it defines who and what we are. This point is essential for reframing an understanding of art as a type of experience that can include eating. Aesthetic experience based on the qualities of the body and on interaction can embrace food through the ability to taste. When we eat, we are ingesting (willingly taking in) a bit of our environment and are reinforcing our physical interconnection with it.

In the context of food and eating, this is not always a happy realization. Many people cannot bring themselves to eat certain foods because of an identification with them. That is, since there is very little distance between eater and eaten, the more one identifies with the food to be eaten, the less one is able to eat it. The problem of identifying with one's food manifests in several ways.

First, there is the realization (regarding red meat, for example) that what is on one's plate was once walking around. One becomes aware that, like oneself, this food was once alive. The problem caused by identifying with one's food in this manner is demonstrated in the conflict surrounding the decor in a McDonald's in Black River Falls, Wisconsin, where many customers lodged complaints about the paintings and portraits of cows throughout the restaurant.[3] They found it very distasteful to look at pictures of cows while eating their Big Macs because of the obvious identification.

Second, the more one identifies with something edible on a personal level, the more difficult it will be to eat it. Thus on farms family members may grow emotionally attached to a particular animal and find it very difficult to kill and eat it. Household pets demonstrate this point even more strongly, for while dogs and cats are edible, most people would cringe at the thought of eating their pets. The strongest example of a reluctance to eat something with which one identifies is the case of other humans. People are also edible, but by and large we do not see each other as food.

Such reflections make us aware that there is a sizable distinction between what is edible and what is food. A large proportion of our environment is edible. Things such as paper, cotton, grass, and cashmere may not be all that tasty or nutritious, but eating them will not cause any great harm if it is not done in great quantities.[4] Dogs, hamsters, ants, people, and even this essay are all edible, yet I assume most of us would not consider them to be food. The category of objects that we call "food" are those that we accept as existing within that ontological continuum between the self and the edible other. Food is not just what will become me, it is that which I *accept* as becoming me.

Eating is a profound act because what I am willing to put in my mouth defines a large part of what I am: I know that what I eat will be incorporated into my being. The mouth is a heavily guarded area of the body because it is the primary entrance into the body; its job is to receive. Consequently, we are very picky about what we allow into it, aware that whatever goes in is in some way going to affect what we are.

Therefore, because so much of our environment is edible, a philosophy of food does much more than reveal that we are connected to our environment through the act of eating. It concludes that through eating, we demonstrate on a daily basis that we exist with our environment in an ontological continuum defined by and given meaning through our choice of which objects we are going to ingest. In other words, Jean-Anthelme Brillat-Savarin was right when he said (in the slogan presented at the beginning of each episode of the *Iron Chef*), "Tell me what you eat, and I shall tell you what you are" (Brillat-Savarin 16–17). Aesthetically, what you like to eat tells you what you want to be.

Food and Death

As Elizabeth Telfer so clearly points out in *Food for Thought,* food is highly temporal and it is in a constant state of perishing: bread goes stale, milk spoils, cheese gets moldy, old meat breeds maggots, and wine turns to vinegar—food's ontology is rotten and rotting. Thus, the connection between food and death is very strong, and I will address it on two levels. First, we only eat things that are, or at one time were, alive, so eating is always either a direct or indirect act of killing. Second, eating is a symbolic reminder of our own impending death, because as we live off the perishing, we perish. It thus also leads to a reinforcement of the ontological cyclical continuum between self and environment, as we realize that while today we are eaters, there will come a time when we will be that which is eaten.

First, aside from condiments such as salt, everything we eat was in some way alive before we ate it. Of course, not all of our foods have sentient life, and salads are certainly not instances of murdered masses of lettuce and tomatoes. Yet these items came into existence, grew, and were nourished; and at the appropriate time, their lives were ended so that another life could continue. Even a loaf of bread (not to mention the grain that went into making the flour) is alive until the baker puts it into the oven to kill the yeast.[5] Some form of life must die for my life to persist.

Reactions to this fact vary depending on the intensity of the diner's awareness of this connection between food and death. Much as some people cannot eat a food because they identify with it, others cannot eat a food because it had to die for them to consume it. Many vegetarians cite the death of animals as the reason for their choice of diet. We can live just fine without beef, pork, lamb, veal, chicken, and duck, they argue, and thus we should not kill them merely so we can have the experience of a particular flavor and texture.

Individuals can have great difficulty eating certain foods because they feel a strong connection to the necessary death of what is being eaten. In his diary, Richard Gordon Smith recounts the revulsion he experienced during a particular meal because its presentation so starkly underscored issues of life and death. While he was living in Japan, he asked the cook at an inn to prepare a carp in a way that was reserved for the nobility. The cook prepared a live fish, still gasping on the plate and surrounded by symbolic decorations that mimicked the look of the bottom of a sandy ocean, and served it to Gordon Smith. At first it did not occur to him that the fish had been made ready for eating; he describes the dish as "really pretty in spite of the gasping fish which, however, showed no pain, and there was not a sign of blood or a cut." But the skill (artistry?) of the chef was revealed when he dribbled a little soy sauce into the fish's eye:

> The effect was not instantaneous: it took a full two minutes as the cook sat over him, chopsticks in hand. All of a sudden and to my unutterable astonishment, the fish gave a convulsive gasp, flicked its tail and flung the whole of its skin on one

side of its body over, exposing the underneath of the stomach parts, skinned; the back was cut into pieces about an inch square and a quarter of an inch thick, ready for pulling out and eating. Never in my life have I seen a more barbarous or cruel thing—not even in the scenes of Spanish bull fights. Egawa [Gordon Smith's Japanese companion] is a delicate-stomached person and as he could eat none, neither could I. It would be simply like taking bites out of a large live fish. I took the knife from my belt and immediately separated the fish's neck vertebrae, much to the cook's astonishment and perhaps disgust. (Gordon Smith 205)

I experienced a similar meal in Japan, when, at a "Jumping Sushi" bar I was invited to choose a fish from the large tank that spanned the length of the bar. After my choice was made the chef captured the fish and prepared the sashimi presentation so quickly that when I bit into the flesh the still-active nerves caused it to quiver in my mouth. These are extreme examples, to be sure, and Gordon Smith's disgust is perhaps mostly a matter of timing, for he was presented with food that was still very much in the process of dying (and my meal was on the edge of being completely dead). Nevertheless, the experience of eating something that is dying or still quite alive and well is often cultivated by gourmets, and these experiences force us to confront the actuality that something must die for us to live. M. F. K. Fisher gives an excellent account of the life of an oyster and of all of the dangers it faces, and how, if it survives, its life ends quickly in a simple swallow:

> Men have enjoyed eating oysters since they were not much more than monkeys, according to the kitchen middens they have left behind them. And thus, in their own one-minded way, they have spent time and thought and money on the problems of how to protect oysters from the suckers and the borers and the starvers. . . . Its chilly, delicate gray body slips into a stew-pan or under a broiler or alive down a red throat, and it is done. Its life has been thoughtless but no less full of danger, and now that it is over we are perhaps the better for it. ("Love and Death" 128)

Second, there is a strong symbolic connection to death in the act of eating, which Korsmeyer addresses in terms of what we learn from the inevitable transience of food:

> The inescapable cycle of hunger and eating is in a sense commemorated by the fragility of food itself, which melts, collapses, is eaten and digested, rots, molds, and decays. Because eating is a repetitive and transient experience, because food does not last but spoils, because it not only nourishes but poisons, eating is a small exercise in mortality. Rather than transcend time, as romantic ideas of art suggest is the goal of masterworks, food succumbs to time—as do we ourselves. This is perhaps the final reflection that tasting prompts: not just that it is pleasurable but that it fades so quickly. (145)

The connection between food and death should not be overdone, but there is an implicit act of faith in the eating and conservatism in taste. We must trust not only that what we put into our body is going to taste good and be nourishing, but also that it will not cause any great discomfort or harm—or death.[6] The symbolic confrontation of death in the act of eating can be disturbing.

As we ingest the other, we effectively eliminate the self/other dichotomy. As a consequence, we realize that we may become the other that is in turn eaten by something else. A well-known exposition of this cycle occurs in act 4 of Shakespeare's *Hamlet*, as Claudius questions Hamlet on the whereabouts of the body of Polonius, whom Hamlet has recently killed.

> King: Now, Hamlet, where's Polonius?
> Hamlet: At supper.
> King: At supper! where?
> Hamlet: Not where he eats, but where he is eaten: a certain convocation of politic worms are e'en at him. Your worm is your only emperor for diet: we fat all creatures else to fat us, and we fat ourselves for maggots: your fat king and your lean beggar is but variable service, two dishes, but to one table: that's the end.
> King: Alas, alas!
> Hamlet: A man may fish with the worm that hath eat of a king, and eat of the fish that hath fed of that worm. (4.3.18–30)

Through eating, we feed off that which is dead; yet when we are dead, the very thing that we ate may in turn feed off us. Neither of these realizations concerning the connections between food and death fits well into a traditional scenario of artistic appreciation. Although death is certainly a theme in the history of art, it has rarely been an artistic medium.

The connection between food and death does fit well into a Deweyan aesthetic which embraces the changing, temporal nature of experience. Experience, especially aesthetic experience, is perishing even as it grows. This pitfall can easily be overcome if we see cooking and eating as profound symbolic expressions of our inherent state of living. That food is perishable makes it a symbol of life and a paradigm for aesthetic involvement and enjoyment.

Food and Assimilation

Food stands in an ontological relationship to the self in terms of potential assimilation, and therefore it cannot be seen as a radical other. Food is the possible-self, and because of this we are very careful about what we put in our mouths. Philosophers who take food seriously will respond to the admonition "Know thyself" differently than those who do not.

Although Dewey did not write much about food, two strong conclusions concerning ontology may be drawn from a Deweyan consideration of food and philosophy.[7] First, food is a primary mode of connection to our world. Eating is an act that eliminates the illusion of the self/other dichotomy and demonstrates that our physical ontology is determined by which bits and pieces of our environment we are willing to ingest. Eating is a meaningful incorporation of the physical *other* that determines and transforms *our* physicality and health.

Food is an integral part of the growth made possible for us through our environment, for it is a part of the environment that allows our lives to continue.

Thus it is in the continuity of the growth of the organism-in-its-environment that we find meaning in eating. Dewey relies on this biological explanation of the "organism" and its "environment" to explain the intense connection between the self and its surroundings. As Thomas Alexander puts it, "The organism and its environment are mutually implicated at each moment; they are aspects of one situation fundamentally related through the act. The organism is just this ability to draw on a range of material in the world and transform the energy in that material into an organized pattern of activity. An environment is in turn that range of energy which is available to the organism and necessary for its survival" (135). In terms of interactive experience, our situatedness as existing through an environment is the basic fact that must be acknowledged in order to cultivate meaning out of experience. Ordinary experience is the starting point from which we begin to become aware of the "felt" and "had" senses of the meaningfulness of living through an environment. Thus "Aesthetic meaning is but the capitalization of the fact that the sense of the world is directly encountered or had in ordinary experience" (169).

The way in which this sense of the world is had depends on seeing the organism not merely as existing but in an environment that already has a degree of organization and potential meaning. "Order arises from the possible conjunctions of the organism and its environment realized through interaction. There must be a world with a certain order to it and an organism with a certain order to it prior to any activity which may be undertaken. A body is an implicit range of interpretation and the structured range of objects to which it can respond marks its environment" (Alexander 169). We have an inherent organizing capacity through the temporal dynamism of living moment to moment. We are therefore naturally suited to construct meaning from this dynamism, and change and growth are essential to the environmental self. The self acts as a complete organism, changing, anticipating, and adapting through its environment. Alexander explains,

> Dewey is indicating that the organizing quality is nothing other than the temporality of the developing event as a whole. It is present throughout the phases either tacitly or explicitly as the guiding sense or context, the horizon of the event. An organism is not something distinct from all its parts; it is the integrating of those parts which allows them to function *as* members of an organized whole. Nor does an organism exist as one changeless instant but throughout a temporally extended period during which change and transformations constitute its activity. (252)

Change and transformation are highlighted by Dewey as entailing growth. Growth through adaptation and anticipation yields an awareness of the qualitative tensions of experiential living. Yet change and transformation also can entail decay, as a progression forward through ongoing experience does not last forever. Both of these senses of change are indicated by the concerns of a stomach-oriented philosopher: in both choosing to eat and, in that act, choosing something specific to eat, an individual is engaging the aspects of change that will lead either to growth or decay.

Growth is an essential part of any aesthetic experience. As the qualities of the experience are transformed and our involvement in the experience takes the form of change and development, aesthetic richness develops and is cultivated. Engaging in eating entails both physical and intellectual growth, for food nourishes the body and our sense of meaning in eating develops through taste. As our sense of taste changes and grows, the aesthetic experience of eating is of great concern to the stomach-oriented philosopher, because as the sense of taste is the gatekeeper of the body, it is important that taste is functioning properly so that something harmful is not ingested inadvertently.

Thus, philosophical stomach-orientation comes directly from a depiction of the self as an embodied, interactive organism-in-an-environment. From this perspective, our concerns are specific, contextual, temporal, and concrete. That is, stomach-orientation locates meaning in the ordinary events of our lives through which we may cultivate greater meaning, yet it keeps us grounded in the everyday.

Dewey also clearly shows that as the organism exists through its environment, its epistemic problems exist in a concrete continuum within contextual experience: our day-to-day lives are filled with many specific, concrete issues and generally not with overarching, abstract generalizations. The stomach-oriented Dewey explains that the organism exists in a "continuous stretch of existence," and the illusion of epistemological separation must fall away in order for us to be able to address the epistemological issues at hand. We can no more create a great distance between our stomach and the food we eat than between the manner in which we acquire knowledge and the experiential sources of that knowledge in a specific environment.

Dewey himself used a stomach-oriented illustration to point out a flaw in traditional epistemology caused by a transcendent view of knowledge. In "The Need for a Recovery of Philosophy," he addresses the "problem of knowledge," which was how the problem of knowledge "in general" was customarily framed. The difficulty with this project, according to Dewey, was that although we can certainly make general statements about knowledge or methods of attaining knowledge, the phrase "knowledge in general" does not refer to anything in day-to-day life—it is far too abstract, ignoring the specific instances and pluralities of knowledge-in-situations. The real problem Dewey highlights is a presumed distance between knower and known, and he addresses it by providing a bodily example that draws on the act of eating:

> The problem of knowledge "ueberhaupt" exists because it is assumed that there is a knower in general, who is outside of the world to be known, and who is defined in terms antithetical to the traits of the world. With analogous assumptions, we could invent and discuss a problem of digestion in general. All that would be required would be to conceive the stomach and food-material as inhabiting different worlds. Such an assumption would leave on our hands the question of the possibility, extent, nature, and genuineness of any transaction between stomach and

food. But because the stomach and food inhabit a continuous stretch of existence, because digestion is but a correlation of diverse activities in one world, the problems of digestion are specific and plural: What are the particular correlations which constitute it? How does it proceed in different situations? What is favorable and what unfavorable to its best performance?—and so on. (23–24)[8]

Thus, in the context of epistemology, stomach-orientation demonstrates that concerns about knowledge must exist within a continuum of contextual experience. Our concerns about knowledge are located in specific circumstances and operate through an interactive relationship within an environment.

Incorporation

When attention is directed toward incorporating or assimilating the other as a necessary means of survival, someone who is stomach-oriented naturally becomes aware of being very careful about what he or she eats. Within her discussion of taste, Carolyn Korsmeyer continues the project of pointing to the body, and to the stomach in particular, as the place where a philosophy of food could be situated as the perspective that overcomes dichotomies: "In short, the fact that food is taken into the body contributes a certain conservatism to taste. (Perhaps the stomach should be considered that site philosophers have long sought for the interaction between mind and body)" (93).

As noted above, in eating we must trust that whatever we put into our mouth will be good, not bad. This concern goes beyond taste, because as we learn the short- and long-term consequences of ingesting certain things we become more concerned about what they will do to us. Thus, stomach-oriented philosophers consider carefully the sources of various food items and how that food is grown, because such issues pertain directly to their ontology through the food they are eating. As attention to these concerns sharpens, greater numbers of grocery stores and farmers' markets stress that their produce is grown organically, locally, or both. Restaurants, even those selling fast food, advertise meals made from the freshest ingredients—even the producers of prepackaged airline meals are quick to proclaim that although they may turn out over 10,000 meals a day, they use only the freshest ingredients. Advertisers for stores such as the Whole Foods chain boast that all the food sold is local and grown organically, thereby easing the worries of the stomach-oriented customer who becomes confident that no matter what he or she buys, it will not have any added chemicals that may harm those eating it.

The implications of these concerns are clear. In emphasizing where and how food is grown, stomach-oriented shopping and dining display an attention to the continuum between the food source and the person who eats that food. That is, the stomach-oriented eater is aware of and concerned about the specific means of transmission, because he or she does not believe there is a separation between the source of the food and how it finally arrived on the plate. Such concern also reveals an awareness that there is no ontological separation between the food and the eater, heightening the importance of judgments about food. In asking where some food item "came from," we do not assume that it grew in some "other" place that is completely separate from us, from which it traversed unknowable territory and then magically appeared as food to be consumed. The stomach-oriented person sees the question of where the food came from as crucial to understanding the range of experiences surrounding the food from its point of origination to its eventual consumption.

The stomach-oriented person is also concerned with how food is prepared and the degree to which that preparation affects its natural state. Underlying this concern is the assumption that food that is closer to its natural state when eaten is more healthy and a more appropriate element to introduce into the body. Here we often find a conflict between the desires of taste and genuine ontological concerns about health. That is, sometimes the taste of the food is indicative of how nutritious and beneficial it is to us, and sometimes it is not. Our senses, including that of taste, can deceive us. As stated before, taste offers us the last moment of judgment before food is swallowed. Therefore, we would expect the sense of taste to be naturally calibrated to allow only the best and most beneficial foods to enter the body, while rejecting those that will do harm. Though this assumption tends to be true, it is not always valid.

Thus, a stomach-oriented philosophy demonstrates how we begin in a state of inherent interaction with our environment. This involves a concern about the source of our nourishment, attention to its taste, and knowledge of what effect it will have once ingested. Dewey's conclusion that we live not *in* an environment, but *through* and *with* it, provides a valuable perspective because we literally live off an environment. A stomach-oriented philosopher is therefore going to be very careful about what he or she eats, knowing that what a person eats is going to determine what a person is.

Eating as a Symbolic Engagement with the World

According to Dewey, artistic expression comes out of everyday bodily existence, and art is an articulation of the dynamic elements of embodiment. By keeping the symbolic projection within concrete experience, we can see food as performing a doubly symbolic duty: while we are aesthetically encountering the symbolic forms of tension among the senses within taste, in eating we are also engaging life itself. This conclusion points toward future projects developing an aesthetics of food and cooking in the context of aesthetics and ontology. We can have a profound aesthetic experience triggered by eating a fresh raspberry or sweet bell pepper, but the food prepared by a chef is a medium that can express the symbolic form of an intentional arrangement of flavors, textures, and temperatures. There is a continuity between the two types of event, for both rely on the awareness that aesthetic potential underlies all experiences.

As outlined above, taste involves more than the salty, sweet, bitter, and sour; when it is combined with smell and touch, seemingly endless flavors and textures can be created. Further, the addition of the element of heat (both in spiciness and temperature) enables even more variations in taste to exist. As tasters, we are prepared for all these potential aesthetic tensions in eating because, as Dewey would say, in any aesthetic experience there must exist first the capacity or potential for a meaningful organization of the qualities available to that experience.

We can encounter symbolic forms in eating because the chef-artist is presenting flavors so arranged that they symbolize formal elements encountered in the act of tasting. The formal elements are the tensions involved in taste, manifest in our reactions to what we are tasting. Among such manifestations are cringing, savoring, the patterns in which the tongue moves about the mouth when we chew, the natural movement of some foods to the side or front of the mouth, and the effects of different tastes on different parts of the mouth. These physical manifestations result from the symbolic form of tasting, as we encounter the projection of a dynamic harmony among the flavorful tensions. The chef-artist creates an experience within the mouth that highlights tensions that arise from forms of feeling expressed symbolically in the arrangement of flavors: when we taste the food, we are made conscious of the physical reactions involved in savoring food and accepting it into the body. Tasting, then, is a fulfilling engagement of life.

However, food goes beyond these elements because it is the only art which involves all the senses interacting together while simultaneously taking parts of the world that are incorporated into the eater. Beyond involving the projection of forms of human feeling and the tensions of biological and sentient life, eating food is an active, volitional engagement with the world in which both virtual and physical distinction between self and other vanishes.

Our experience of food begins in the context of environmental interaction and ends in the act of environmental assimilation. Therefore, food offers the only aesthetic encounter that, from beginning to end, remains in a most physically profound continuum of environmental experience. As foods are picked, cleaned, prepared, arranged, and presented, at no time is any great distance created between the self and the object. Then, as we eat, we engage in the aesthetic culmination of this ontologically concrete continuum of experience by assimilating the art into ourselves. No other aesthetic experience involves such an intense level of connection between the self and its environment. Baldly stated, there are instrumental and functionally appropriate distinctions between our selves and the objects we ingest—but those functional and instrumental distances become problematic in the context of ethics and aesthetics.

An aesthetics of eating should be embraced as existing within the range of what is edible. And since, by and large, so much of our world, our environment, is edible, the desire to taste and take bits of it and swallow them is an extremely important aesthetic concern. Since eating is the incorporation of one body into another, to engage food is to engage the environment; and beyond providing sustenance for life, food affords us a chance to engage our environment in a unique manner. To choose (or to choose not) to dine on Fido then is not just an ethical concern. It is also not just a matter of "taste." It is a personal and environmental concern. We are faced with the dilemma of what we *like* to eat—and what we consider to be food.

The commonness of eating need not deter us from this approach, because art and the aesthetic must arise from ordinary experience. Since eating is so common (so "everyday"), more highly articulated instances of it can certainly be seen as moments of aesthetic greatness. Further, the hierarchy of the senses, based on levels of environmental and physical interaction, also need not work against this view of food. As eating is an everyday activity, and as Dewey shows that our interactive experiences are the ones out of which aesthetic experience grows, then the most interactive of senses *should* be at the forefront of art. With this degree of interaction, we gain a high level of connection and identification with the elements of our environment. Identifying what is and is not food (as distinct from everything that is edible) demonstrates how we define ourselves through what we are willing to eat. In this context, food is indicative of what we think we are and what we wish to be. So why, then, is it so hard to dine on Fido? And what are you willing to eat?

Notes

1. For example, see Pieter Aertsen, *Cook in Front of the Stove* (1559); Alexander Adriaenssen, *Still-Life with Fish* (17th c.); and Frans Snyders, *Still Life with Dead Game, Fruits, and Vegetables in a Market* (1614).

2. This rough figure also leaves out other acts of ingestion, such as drinking or taking medicine.

3. McDonald's seems not to have intended any such connection; instead, the portraits were clever parodies of famous works of art by artists including Dali and Warhol, with cows substituted as their subject. For example, a cow's head replaced that of Marilyn Monroe in Warhol's four-color series.

4. The point of the edibility of our environment was pushed to great lengths by a television show in the early 1980s, *That's Incredible,* on which a guest ate a bicycle.

5. Yeast, often thought to be some sort of buggish microorganism, is actually a type of fungus that can long reproduce and maintain colonies. Sourdough starters—yeast-laden flour and water mixtures that are kept refrigerated—have been known to live for more than 100 years.

6. Certain foods test the precarious connection between eating and the possibility of dying. For example, those eating fugu, a poisonous blowfish, often desire that it be prepared in such a way that a tiny bit of the poison is present, allowing them to experience a slight numbing of the lips and tongue without suffering illness or death (which might nevertheless result if the cook miscalculates).

7. Besides a couple of references to "that meal" in explaining a consummatory experience (i.e., the experience of enacting an end-in-view), in a letter to his wife Dewey suggests that there is much to be learned from cuisine: "Speaking of civilized places, the nearest dip into civilization I have made was at the Lorings' Thursday evening. . . . Mrs. Loring's dinner was a work of art, just as individualized as everything else. I suppose life in a boarding house makes me unduly aware of this petty side of things, but after all the innate barbarism of America seems to me indicated by the lack of sense

for what constitutes a meal" (John Dewey, letter to Alice Chipman Dewey and children, July 28 and 29, 1894, in *The Correspondence*).

8. I wish to thank Dr. Lewis Hahn for directing me to this passage.

Bibliography

Alexander, Thomas. *John Dewey's Theory of Art, Experience, and Nature: The Horizons of Feeling*. Albany: State University of New York Press, 1987.

Bosivert, Raymond D. *John Dewey: Rethinking Our Time*. Albany: State University of New York Press, 1998.

Brillat-Savarin, Jean Anthelme. *The Physiology of Taste, or, Meditations on Transcendental Gastronomy*. Translated by M. F. K. Fisher. 1949. Reprint, Washington, D.C.: Counterpoint, 1986.

Curtin, Deane, and Lisa Heldke, eds. *Cooking, Eating, Thinking: Transformative Philosophies of Food*. Bloomington: Indiana University Press, 1992.

Dewey, John. *Art as Experience. The Later Works*, vol. 10, *1934*.

———. *A Common Faith*. In *The Later Works*, vol. 9, *1933–1934*, 1–58.

———. *The Correspondence of John Dewey* [computer file]. Vol. 1, *1871–1918*. General editor, Larry A. Hickman. Edited by Barbara Levine, Anne Sharpe, and Harriet Furst Simon. Charlottesville, Va.: InteLex Corp., 1999.

———. *Democracy and Education. The Middle Works, 1889–1924*, edited by Jo Ann Boydston, vol. 9, *1916*. Carbondale: Southern Illinois University Press, 1985.

———. *Experience and Nature. The Later Works*, vol. 1, *1925*.

———. *The Later Works, 1925–1953*. Edited by Jo Ann Boydston. 17 vols. Carbondale: Southern Illinois University Press, 1981–90.

———. "The Need for a Recovery of Philosophy." In *The Middle Works, 1889–1924*, edited by Jo Ann Boydston, vol. 10, *1916–1917*, 3–48. Carbondale: Southern Illinois University Press, 1985.

Fisher, M. F. K. *An Alphabet for Gourmets*. In *The Art of Eating*, 575–744.

———. *The Art of Eating*. New York: Macmillan, 1990.

———. *The Gastronomical Me*. In *The Art of Eating*, 353–572.

———. "Love and Death among the Molluscs." In *The Art of Eating*, 125–28.

———. *With Bold Knife and Fork*. New York: Barnes and Noble Books, 1969.

Gordon Smith, Richard. *Travels in the Land of the Gods, 1898–1907: The Japan Diaries of Richard Gordon Smith*. Edited by Victoria Manthorpe. New York: Prentice-Hall, 1986.

Hickman, Larry. *John Dewey's Pragmatic Technology*. Bloomington: Indiana University Press, 1990.

Hickman, Larry A., and Thomas M. Alexander, eds. *The Essential Dewey*. Vol. 1, *Pragmatism, Education, Democracy*. Bloomington: Indiana University Press, 1998.

Korsmeyer, Carolyn. *Making Sense of Taste: Food and Philosophy*. Ithaca, N.Y.: Cornell University Press, 1999.

Labensky, Sarah R., and Alan M. Hause. *On Cooking: Techniques from Expert Chefs*. Upper Saddle River, N.J.: Prentice Hall, 1995.

Langer, Susanne. *Feeling and Form: A Theory of Art*. New York: Scribner, 1953.

———. *Philosophy in a New Key*. Cambridge, Mass.: Harvard University Press, 1942.

McGee, Harold. *The Curious Cook: More Kitchen Science and Lore*. New York: Macmillan, 1990.

———. *On Food and Cooking: The Science and Lore of the Kitchen.* New York: Collier Books, Macmillan, 1984.

Polushkin Robbins, Maria, ed. *A Cook's Alphabet of Quotations.* 1991. Reprint, Hopewell, N.J.: Ecco Press, 1997.

Revel, Jean-François. *Culture and Cuisine: A Journey through the History of Food.* Translated by Helen R. Lane. New York: Doubleday, 1982.

Shakespeare, William. *Hamlet.* In *The Unabridged William Shakespeare,* edited by William George Clark and William Aldis Wright, 1007–52. Philadelphia: Running Press, 1989.

Shusterman, Richard. *Practicing Philosophy: Pragmatism and the Philosophical Life.* New York: Routledge, 1997.

———. *Pragmatist Aesthetics: Living Beauty, Rethinking Art.* Oxford: Blackwell, 1992.

Tannahill, Reay. *Food in History.* Rev. ed. New York: Crown Publishers, 1988.

Telfer, Elizabeth. *Food for Thought: Philosophy and Food.* London: Routledge, 1996.

Waters, Alice. *The Chez Panisse Menu Cookbook.* New York: Random House, 1982.

Contributors

James M. Albrecht is associate professor of English at Pacific Lutheran University. His work on Emerson has appeared in *MLA; ESQ: A Journal of the American Renaissance;* and *19th-Century Prose*. He is working on a book manuscript tentatively titled *Ethical Individualism: A Pragmatic Tradition from Emerson to Ellison*.

Douglas R. Anderson teaches in the Philosophy Department at the Pennsylvania State University. He is author of *Creativity and the Philosophy of C. S. Peirce* and *Strands of System: The Philosophy of Charles Peirce,* and has written numerous articles on American philosophy and culture.

Steven Fesmire teaches philosophy and is chair of Environmental Studies at Green Mountain College, Vermont. He is author of *John Dewey and Moral Imagination: Pragmatism in Ethics* (Indiana University Press).

Glenn Kuehn, Ph.D., is a philosopher and noted teacher. Kuehn is a former caterer and a founding member (along with Lisa Heldke and Ray Boisvert) of "Convivium: The Philosophy and Food Roundtable." He has addressed many conferences and colloquia on various topics within the "philosophy of food," and is famous for his cheesecakes and sauces.

Todd M. Lekan is associate professor of philosophy and chair of the Religion and Philosophy Department at Muskingum College. He is author of *Making Morality: Pragmatist Reconstruction in Moral Theory*. He is working on the role of sympathetic understanding in moral deliberation, especially in connection to the treatment of nonhuman animals.

Andrew Light is assistant professor of environmental philosophy and director of the Environmental Conservation Education Program at New York University, as well as research fellow at the Institute for Environment, Philosophy, and Public Policy at Lancaster University in the United Kingdom. He is author of *Reel Arguments: Film, Philosophy, and Social Criticism* and has edited or co-edited fourteen books on environmental ethics, philosophy of technology, and aesthetics, including *Environmental Pragmatism, Technology and the Good Life?,* and *Moral and Political Reasoning in Environmental Practice*.

Erin McKenna is associate professor and chair of the Department of Philosophy at Pacific Lutheran University. She is author of *The Task of Utopia: A Prag-*

matist and Feminist Perspective. She has written numerous articles on feminism, vegetarianism, and pragmatism.

Phillip McReynolds is assistant professor of philosophy at Gonzaga University. He has written on the philosophy of John Dewey, phenomenology, ethics, and the philosophy of science and technology.

Ben A. Minteer is assistant research professor in the Human Dimensions of Biology Faculty at Arizona State University. He is co-editor (with Bob Pepperman Taylor) of *Democracy and the Claims of Nature* and (with Robert E. Manning) *Reconstructing Conservation: Finding Common Ground*. He is currently working on a new book that explores the moral and democratic roots of American landscape conservation.

Matthew Pamental is adjunct assistant professor of philosophy at the University of Utah. His main areas of interest include Dewey's moral psychology and ethics, environmental ethics, and ethical issues with regard to animals.

Paul B. Thompson holds the W. K. Kellogg Chair in Agriculture, Food, and Community Ethics at Michigan State University. He is author of *The Spirit of the Soil: Agriculture and Environmental Ethics* and *Food Biotechnology in Ethical Perspective*.

Jennifer Welchman is an associate professor of philosophy at the University of Alberta. She is author of *Dewey's Ethical Thought* and articles on ethics, applied ethics, and the history of philosophy.

Index

225n5; *Knowing and the Known,* 69; *Logic,* 65, 69–70, 106, 196, 207n2, 210, 225n11; "The Logic of Judgments and Practice," 80n10, 82n18; "Logical Conditions," 196; "Moral Theory and Practice," 82n16; "The Need for the Recovery of Philosophy," 241; "Outlines of a Critical Theory of Ethics," 80n10; "Periods of Growth," 57; *The Public and Its Problems,* 58, 164, 194–195; *The Quest for Certainty,* 143, 166; *Reconstruction in Philosophy,* 33, 40–41n17, 82n18, 106–107, 109, 143, 147; "The Social Self," 56; "The Theory of Emotion," 56; *Theory of Valuation,* 57–58; "Three Independent Factors in Morals," 45, 108; "The Unity of the Human Being," 57, 224–225n2
Dichotomies, 7, 10, 27, 73, 162, 164, 239
Dizard, Jan, 113
Dombrowski, Dan, 16n2
Dominion, 24, 48, 129
Donavan, Josephine, 7, 208n13

Ecofeminism, 7, 162–163, 170
Eldridge, Michael, 60n10, 166, 225n8
Embodiment, 230, 234, 240–243
Emerson, Ralph Waldo, xii, 12, 19–26, 30, 37, 39, 39nn1,2,3,4,5, 40n7; "Circles," 22, 39n3; "Fate," 21, 39nn2,5; "History," 22–26, 39n4; "Nature," 21–26, 39n1; "Rule of Life," 23; "Self-Reliance," 22, 37
Emotion, xi, 7, 10, 20, 26, 36–39, 43, 54, 56, 88, 93, 191n3, 193, 203, 205–206, 208n12
Environmental ethics, 13, 34–35, 43, 45, 48, 55, 97–98, 100–105, 114–115, 119–122, 126, 132–133, 136–137, 144
Equal consideration, 3
Equality, 2–3, 181
Ethic of care, 7, 46
Ethics. *See* Deontological ethics; Ethic of care; Pragmatism; Utilitarian ethics; Virtue ethics

Factory farm, 14, 34, 38–39, 51, 100, 127, 133, 137, 147–148, 152, 160, 166–170, 172–173, 174n7, 189, 192n9. *See also* Confined Animal Feeding Operation
Fallibilism, 9, 113, 162, 198–199, 206, 208n15
Feminism, 7, 9–10, 38, 46, 80n5
Fesmire, Stephen, 59n1, 60n9
Fisher, M. F. K., 238
Food, 3, 15, 31, 53, 77, 153, 160–161, 170–173, 174nn2,3,4,5,6, 188–189, 228–245, 245n6
Foucault, Michel, 79n2, 153
Fouts, Roger, 56, 92, 93n4

Francione, Gary, 5, 7–8, 11, 16n3, 131, 211, 224
Fraser, David, 140–152, 154, 156–157
Free range, 154, 172
Frey, Raymond, 142, 146–147

George, Kathryn, 49
Goodall, Jane, 90–92
Griffen, Donald, 56
Growth, 21–22, 89, 91–92, 164, 173, 183, 239–241

Habermas, Jorgen, 207n6
Haraway, Donna, 81nn11,12,15, 91
Hickman, Larry, 48, 121, 151
Hierarchies, ix–x, 6–7, 10, 13, 23–24, 27, 48, 52–53, 72, 80n4, 90, 162–163, 179, 181, 184, 188, 216, 233–236
Holism, 99, 101–104, 114, 116n5, 122, 125, 127–128, 133, 144
Human exceptionalism, 3
Hume, David, 188
Hunting, 13, 43, 46–47, 77, 92, 100, 103–105, 113, 121, 131–138, 171, 189

Imagination, 49, 53, 57, 90, 107
Inquiry, 10–15, 20, 28–33, 38, 44, 49, 57, 68, 80n10, 81n14, 91–93, 97–98, 105–115, 142–143, 150, 162, 165–166, 170–173, 193–199, 203–204, 207, 207n2, 208nn10,12,15, 210–224
Institutional Animal Care and Use Committees, 14, 193–194, 197–203, 205–206, 208nn8,15
Interdependence, xii, 24, 34–36, 39, 48, 63, 74, 77, 161–162, 164–173, 237

James, William, xi, 9, 12, 19, 25–30, 37–39, 39n2, 40nn7,8,9,10,16, 47–48, 78–79, 86, 120, 143, 157, 161, 163; "The Moral Philosopher," 25, 28–29, 40n9; "On a Certain Blindness," 25, 27, 163; *Principles of Psychology,* 26–27, 40n16; "The Sentiment of Rationality," 30, 47; "The Stream of Thought," 26–27, 40n16; "What Makes a Life Significant," 27–28; "The Will to Believe," 30, 78–79
Jamieson, Dale, 2, 103–104, 126, 128

Kant, Immanuel, 2, 30–34, 36, 43–48, 55, 63, 79nn1,2, 100, 140, 146, 149, 152. *See also* Deontological ethics
Kateb, George, 23
Katz, Eric, 98, 115n1, 116n7, 119, 179–180